SOCRATES
& THE FAT RABBIS

Daniel Boyarin

The University of Chicago Press | Chicago and London

DANIEL BOYARIN is professor of Talmudic culture and holds the Herman P. and Sophia Taubman Chair in the Departments of Near Eastern Studies and Rhetoric at the University of California, Berkeley. He is the author of more than a dozen books, most recently of *Border Lines: The Partition of Judaeo-Christianity* (2004).

The University of Chicago Press, Chicago 60637
The University of Chicago Press, Ltd., London
© 2009 by The University of Chicago
All rights reserved. Published 2009
Printed in the United States of America

Frontispiece: Yigael Tumarkin, *Ahava Doheket et Habbasar* (by permission of the artist).

18 17 16 15 14 13 12 11 10 09   1 2 3 4 5

ISBN-13: 978-0-226-06916-6 (cloth)
ISBN-10: 0-226-06916-8 (cloth)

Library of Congress Cataloging-in-Publication Data

Boyarin, Daniel.
    Socrates and the fat rabbis / Daniel Boyarin.
        p.   cm.
    Summary: An innovative attempt to read Plato with the Talmud, and the Talmud with Plato, this book examines Platonic and Talmudic dialogues to show that in a sense they are not dialogic at all, but a monological discursive form yoked incongruously with a comic mode.
    Includes bibliographical references and index.
    ISBN-13: 978-0-226-06916-6 (cloth : alk. paper)
    ISBN-10: 0-226-06916-8 (cloth : alk. paper)   1. Plato. Dialogues.
2. Talmud—Criticism and interpretation.   3. Comic, The.   I. Title.
    B398.C63B69 2009
    184—dc22

                                                           2009013814

For Carlin Barton,
from whom I have learned so much

As to jests. These are supposed to be of some service in controversy. Gorgias said—speaking correctly—that you should confute your opponents' seriousness with jesting and their jesting with seriousness.

Aristotle, Rhetoric *1419b*

Most excellent of Strangers, we ourselves, to the best of our ability, are the authors of a tragedy at once superlatively fair and good; at least, all our polity is framed as a representation of the fairest and best life, which is in reality, as we assert, the truest tragedy. Thus we are composers of the same things as yourselves, rivals of yours as artists and actors of the fairest drama, which, as our hope is, true law, and it alone is by nature competent to complete.

Plato, Laws *7.817a–b*

Read Lucian! Lucian holds the keys to the Talmud.

Prof. Saul Lieberman, OBM

Rabba before he commenced [his lesson] to the scholars used to say a joking word [מילתא דבדיחותא], and the scholars were amused. After that he sat in dread [אימתא] and began the lesson.

Shabbat 30b

How well Plato knows to satirize [ἰαμβίζειν]!

Attributed to Gorgias in Athenaeus, Deipnosophistae *11.505d*

CONTENTS

The Cheese and the Sermons:
Toward a Microhistory of Ideas

"The rabbis think nothing of making their most profound comments on the nature of God in the midst of discussing the uses of cheese."[1] For quite a long time (and through the introductions of several books), I have been worrying, what, precisely, am I as a scholar. Whatever it is that I do has not seemed to fit into any of our usual disciplinary divisions or rubrics. I am not quite a historian, at least not in any clearly recognizable sense; I tend to make too much of individual texts, which precludes the kinds of sweeping coverage of an entire field of evidence that most historians claim is necessary. I'm also not quite a literary critic, as I am much too interested in the social practices in which my texts are embedded, of which they are part (perhaps, sometimes, of which they are evidence—metonymic, not metaphoric). I'm much too literary critical to be quite a traditional Talmudist either, so my work seems not to fit any of the formal disciplines in which the Talmud is studied. I've tried on for size intellectual historian, practitioner of cultural studies,

---

1. Rosemary Radford Ruether, "Judaism and Christianity: Two Fourth-Century Religions," *Sciences Religieuses/Studies in Religion* 2 (1972): 8.

practitioner of cultural poetics, and (new) historicist literary scholar of the Talmud; none of them seem quite to work for me, so like a bumblebee, I just keep on flying, bumbling, and buzzing around the disciplines.

Thinking, however, of the work that I most admire, learn from, and even enjoy, I seem always to gravitate toward scholars such as Robert Darnton, Natalie Zemon Davis, or Carlo Ginzburg. Hence I have, for the moment, decided to be a microhistorian. Like them, I like to take a single case and study it to death, torturing the text, interpreting every detail that I can think of, and contextualizing it in as many ways that I know of. I like to suggest, at least, that this particular case is at least possibly a window into much larger phenomena, even if I can't show that (this is where I come a cropper with most historians). The difference between my work and that of Darnton and company is that they usually work in some particular area of social history, whereas I am still, most often, thinking about texts and ideas. Hence, I am a microhistorian of ideas, actually perhaps more of a microintellectual historian, in that, for me, the ideas are always fully planted in the soil of human social and political life. Hence my joking (I hope better than half-witty) caption for this confession: The cheese and the sermons (apologies to Professor Ginzburg are in order).

John Herman Randall has written, "Plato is for us moderns the consummate expression of Greece. But what is Greece? For us, it is a group of literary monuments suspended in time, together with the archeological remains discovered during the last century. The documents are all we really know."[2] There are various ways in which this summary statement by a pre-eminent historian of ideas could be pressured. One, of course, would be with the methods and tools developed since that writing in 1970 to unearth the voices hidden in texts, the voices hidden from history, whether those of women and slaves or just ordinary Athenian citizens, the methods of social history and critical cultural archaeology. That is not the route that I will take here. Remaining essentially within the realm of intellectual (micro)history, I wish to contribute to a revision of our notion of the consummate expression of Greece and thus a reconsideration of the

---

2. John Herman Randall, *Plato: Dramatist of the Life of Reason* (New York: Columbia University Press, 1970), 36.

impact of "Greece" on Hellenism, especially in late antiquity, and within that rubric, especially on the Judaism of late antiquity. For this book too, the documents are all we really know, but I hope that we can look differently at those documents and the ways that they intersect with each other.[3] My friend and colleague Carlin Barton—to whom this book is dedicated—for years protested with passion contra my earlier work that I too had read Plato as the consummate expression of Greek culture (to the detriment of the latter), and that Plato was an atypical and even idiosyncratic figure in his own cultural and intellectual context and perhaps for centuries afterward.[4] She finally persuaded me, and set me off on one of the trajectories that resulted in this book; I hope that the results of this persuasion will have been worth her effort.

Mikhail Bakhtin (and his great American translators and commentators, especially Michael Holquist), has been my constant companions on the journey that produced this book. To quote here only one of the many passages of Bakhtin with which this book is studded:

> The means for formulating and framing internally persuasive discourse may be supple and dynamic to such an extent that this discourse may literally be *omnipresent* in the context, imparting to everything its own specific tones and from time to time breaking through to become a completely materialized thing, as another's word fully set off and demarcated. . . . Such variants on the theme of another's discourse are widespread in all areas of creative ideological activity, and even in the narrowly scientific disciplines. Of such a sort is any gifted, creative exposition defining alien world views: such an exposition is always a free stylistic variation on another's discourse; it expounds another's thought in the style of that thought even while applying it to new material, to another way of posing the problem; it conducts experiments and gets solutions in the language of another's discourse.[5]

3. See, too, Judith Lieu, *Christian Identity in the Jewish and Graeco-Roman World* (New York: Oxford University Press, 2004), 24–25, with her characteristic sense and sensibility.

4. For the marginality of Plato, as perceived by two outstanding Platonists, see Plutarch, *Mor* 328a; and Origen, *Contra Celsum* 6.2.

5. Mikhail Bakhtin, "Discourse in the Novel," in *The Dialogic Imagination: Four Essays by Mikhail Bakhtin,* ed. Michael Holquist, trans. Michael Holquist and Caryl Emerson, University of Texas Press Slavic Series (Austin: University of Texas Press, 1981), 347.

While hardly willing to claim the name "gifted," and perhaps creative to a fault (as I have been accused of being), I find this description by Bakhtin an apt description of my own practice with respect to his discourse (and to a lesser extent that of others, mostly working broadly speaking out of his texts). His language permeates mine whether cited directly or not. I have found his analyses key to my own experiments with both Plato and the Talmud. In general, and following his distinction between "authoritative" and "internally persuasive" languages, I do not put long citations into block indents, preferring not to set them off "as another's word fully set off and demarcated." When I do use block indents, it is precisely "authoritative" discourse that I am citing, that is, the so-called primary texts which I am seeking to understand. Bakhtin's work is precisely not "authoritative discourse" in t/his sense but a constant dialogical and dialogized partner in my conversation.

One final idiosyncrasy: I do not use BCE and CE to mark the years before and after Christ, respectively, as these are usually glossed with reference to a "common era," to which I wish not to submit myself. I write BC and AC for before and after Christ, in accordance with continental usage, adapted for English (of course, AD would be an even more uncomfortable submission).

In Praise of Indecorous Acts of Discourse:

An Essay by Way of Introduction

C. S. Lewis in an oft-quoted remark opined that, "this universe, which has produced the bee-orchid and the giraffe, has produced nothing stranger than Martianus Capella."[1] I would like to claim that the dialogues of Plato and, even more, the Babylonian Talmud are as strange as Martianus Capella, bee-orchids, or giraffes. The interpretative traditions, both premodern and modern, have done everything in their power to reduce the embarrassment of such strangeness. I am delighted rather than embarrassed by the "monstrosity" of my "holy" books and find in them the key to a significantly different approach to the question of truth than what we are used to.[2] Literary criticism

1. C. S. Lewis, *The Allegory of Love: A Study in Medieval Tradition* (1936; repr., New York: Oxford University Press, 1958), 78.

2. Note that I am not claiming "right of discovery" on this different approach at all, one that is, after all, deeply related to and dependent on extant philosophical traditions, notably, but not exclusively, pragmatism (e.g., Henry S. Levinson, *Santayana, Pragmatism, and the Spiritual Life* [Chapel Hill: University of North Carolina Press, 1992]: I am grateful to Sheila Delaney for this reference and other important comments at this juncture). What I am claiming is, rather, an ancient pedigree for these approaches and a particular variation on them that may contribute to their further development. For explicit connection between the revaluation of the Sophists and of American pragmatism, see Edward Schiappa, *The Beginnings of Rhetorical Theory in Classical Greece* (New Haven [Conn.]: Yale University Press, 1999),

with its near ubiquitous insistence on "decorum" provides—even in my dispute with that very term—the grounds of my engagement and production of the different way of reading that I propose.

The literary term, *decorum,* used slightly differently than in common parlance, will be a very helpful one for the analysis throughout:

> Decorum [dikorŭm], a standard of appropriateness by which certain styles, characters, forms, and actions in literary works are deemed suitable to one another within a hierarchical model of culture bound by class distinctions. Derived from Horace's Ars Poetica (c.20 BCE) and other works of classical criticism, decorum was a major principle of late Renaissance taste and of neoclassicism. It ranked and fixed the various literary genres in high, middle, and low stations, and expected the style, characters, and actions in each to conform to its assigned level: thus a tragedy or epic should be written in a high or grand style about highranking characters performing grand deeds, whereas a comedy should treat humble characters and events in a low or colloquial style. The mixture of high and low levels, as in Shakespeare, was seen as indecorous, although it could be exploited for humorous effect in burlesques and mockheroic works.[3]

Horace's definition of the opposite of decorum is very helpful here too: "The poetic body must avoid the monstrous conjugation of foreign parts."[4] As we will see further on, human obesity is frequently figured in antiquity as a sign of the opposite of decorum and the nonserious. This is not owing, I think, to any inherent humor in fat or mocking of fat people, so much as to the alleged incongruity of the body engendered by certain parts of it being out of proportion with

---

162. Indeed, the whole point of part 4 of Schiappa's chapter is to "locate Isocrates vis-à-vis the concerns and interests of contemporary pragmatism." I probably would have done the same with respect to the texts I approach here, had I the *Sitzfleisch.*

3. Chris Baldick, *The Concise Oxford Dictionary of Literary Terms,* Oxford Paperback Reference (Oxford: Oxford University Press, 2004).

4. This analysis makes problematic Bakhtin's earlier assumption in the Rabelais book that what seems incongruous to modern eyes was not so in antiquity; Mikhail Bakhtin, *Rabelais and His World,* trans. Hélène Iswolsky (Bloomington: Indiana University Press, 1984), 108–9. Lucian, at any rate, seems exquisitely aware of the chimera he creates.

others, as well as the sheer fleshliness that it forces us to pay attention to. As we will see, this is a figure, as well, for malformed and disproportionate, indecorous discourses, condemned by most authors, but praised—highly—in this book of mine. When the high, the middle, and the low, the serious and the comic, the realistic and the fantastic, the "classical" and the grotesque, are all conjoined in a single text, we have a monstrous conjugation.

One of the very emblems of the concatenation of the serious and the comic in Plato's work is the incident of Aristophanes' hiccups in the *Symposium:*

> Pausanias came to a pause—this is the balanced way in which I have been taught by the wise to speak; and Aristodemus said that the turn of Aristophanes was next, but either he had eaten too much, or from some other cause he had the hiccough, and was obliged to change turns with Eryximachus the physician, who was reclining on the couch below him. Eryximachus, he said, you ought either to stop my hiccough, or to speak in my turn until I have left off.

> I will do both, said Eryximachus: I will speak in your turn, and do you speak in mine; and while I am speaking let me recommend you to hold your breath, and if after you have done so for some time the hiccough is no better, then gargle with a little water; and if it still continues, tickle your nose with something and sneeze; and if you sneeze once or twice, even the most violent hiccough is sure to go. I will do as you prescribe, said Aristophanes, and now get on.

This incident involves a double "lapse in tone." First of all, a text in which a serious investigation of the place of Eros in human endeavor is being discussed is hardly the occasion, it would seem, for such low bodily burlesque. As adumbrated just above, Plato himself insisted on a criterion of seriousness as being of ultimate import. Furthermore, the *spoudaios* is precisely that at which it is wrong to laugh, as we learn from the *Euthydemus* (300e): So I remarked: "Why are you laughing, Cleinias, at such serious and beautiful things? [κἀγὼ εἶπον: τί γελᾷς, ὦ Κλεινία, ἐπὶ σπουδαίοις οὕτω πράγμασιν καὶ καλοῖς]." Secondly, the implication of this hiccups passage is that the text itself (or at least its order), which one would have thought is carefully planned to make its points, has, in fact, been partly generated out of the out-of-control antics of the lower body. This all hardly conforms to Plato's claim to composing the fairest of all, the truest of all, the most *spoudaios* of all texts. Why are you laughing, Plato, at such serious and beautiful things?

The Serious, the Comic, and the Seriocomic

Five quotations on page vii—four from ancient sources and one from a modern writer—announce the theme of this book as its epigraphs or mottos. Since these quotations track the overall structure of the argument of the book, I have chosen to gloss them each briefly as a way into the essay presented here. The first epigraph: "As for jests, since they may sometimes be useful in debates, the advice of Gorgias was good—to confound the opponents' seriousness with jest and their jest with seriousness. Περὶ δὲ τῶν γελοίων, ἐπειδή τινα δοκεῖ χρῆσιν ἔχειν ἐν τοῖς ἀγῶσι, καὶ δεῖν ἔφη Γοργίας τὴν μὲν σπουδὴν διαφθείρειν τῶν ἐναντίων γέλωτι, τὸν δὲ γέλωτα σπουδῇ ὀρθῶς λέγων" (Aristotle, *Rhetoric* 1419b).[5] It is clear from this quotation that at least as far back as Aristotle's time, and if we trust him in his report, as far back as Gorgias himself, the categories of *spoudaios* and *geloios*—"serious" and "humorous"—were already active in Greek culture and recognized modes of discourse. An oblique witness can be found, perhaps, at the *Gorgias* 473e, where Socrates upbraids Polus: "What's this, Polus? You're laughing? Is this still another kind of refutation, to laugh someone down whenever he says something, but not to refute him?" According to Gorgias, moreover, they stand somehow in opposition to each other, such that one can "confound" the other; *either one* can demolish the other (this is a key point). Aristotle, perhaps surprisingly, entirely endorses Gorgias's view on this issue.

We don't quite know what Gorgias meant by *spoudaios,* and we can only guess at the cultural import of this opposition. One clue, however, is provided by the following passage from Herodotus (1.8.1):

---

5. For a slightly different reconstruction of Gorgias's "original" saying, see Edward M. Cope, *The Rhetoric of Aristotle with a Commentary* (Cambridge: Cambridge University Press, 1877), 3:215–16.

VIII. This Candaules, then, fell in love with his own wife, so much so that he believed her to be by far the most beautiful woman in the world; and believing this, he praised her beauty beyond measure to Gyges son of Dascylus, who was his favorite among his bodyguard; for it was to Gyges that he entrusted all his most important (*spoudaiestera*) matters.

VIII. Οὗτος δὴ ὤν ὁ Κανδαύλης ἠράσθη τῆς ἑωυτοῦ γυναικός, ἐρασθεὶς δὲ ἐνόμιζέ οἱ εἶναι γυναῖκα πολλὸν πασέων καλλίστην. ὥστε δὲ ταῦτα νομίζων, ἦν γάρ οἱ τῶν αἰχμοφόρων Γύγης ὁ Δασκύλου ἀρεσκόμενος μάλιστα, τούτῳ τῷ Γύγῃ καὶ τὰ σπουδαιέστερα τῶν πρηγμάτων ὑπερετίθετο.

From this eloquent passage, we can learn something of the meaning of *spoudaios*. The most *spoudaios* is that with which one entrusts the most trusted of one's retainers (indeed the story goes on to inform us that he wished to share the beauty of his wife's nakedness with said Gyges).[6]

Derived originally from meaning "haste," *spoudaios* came to mean "energetic," and thus, perhaps paradoxically to our ears, "in earnest"; hence *spoudaios* as the earnest, the important, the serious, as opposed to the joking, the laughable, as the next citation from Aristophanes' *Frogs* (391), makes clear:

Chorus:
and that I may say much that is funny and much that is serious

Χορός
καὶ πολλὰ μὲν γέλοιά μ' εἰ-
πεῖν, πολλὰ δὲ σπουδαῖα

One wonders how serious the Chorus of the Frogs is in stating that it will say much that is *spoudaia* in the course of that play, but in any case, we see here the contrast between *spoudaios* and *geloios,* as used by (Pseudo?)Gorgias.

6. Chava Boyarin, who called this story to my attention initially, compares it with the story of Ahasuerosh and Vashti in the book of Esther.

One final quotation, from Demosthenes (*Speeches* 24.4), will help further specify the meaning of *spoudaios* among Plato's contemporaries:

> Now it is the common practice of those who take up any piece of public business to inform you that the matter on which they happen to be making their speeches is most momentous, and worthy of your best attention.

> εἰώθασιν μὲν οὖν οἱ πολλοὶ τῶν πράττειν τι προαιρουμένων τῶν κοινῶν λέγειν ὡς ταῦθ' ὑμῖν σπουδαιότατ' ἐστὶ καὶ μάλιστ' ἄξιον προσέχειν τούτοις, ὑπὲρ ὧν ἂν αὐτοὶ τυγχάνωσι ποιούμενοι τοὺς λόγους.

This quotation adds further specification to the meaning of *spoudaios* by defining it precisely as "that which is most worthy of attention," the implication being further that the *geloios* as the opposite of the *spoudaios* is not worthy of attention, or at any rate less worthy of attention. (Note that I am not claiming that the only antonym of *spoudaios* in Greek is *geloios*.) This meaning will be crucial for understanding Plato's usage of these terms, which is what is central, of course, for this book.

Plato, in any case, expounds what he means by "serious," and he shows it to be consistent with all of the above citations when he writes, "for we have come to see that we must not take such poetry seriously as a serious thing that lays hold on truth" [ᾀσόμεθα δ' οὖν ὡς οὐ σπουδαστέον ἐπὶ τῇ τοιαύτῃ ποιήσει ὡς ἀληθείας τε ἁπτομένη καὶ σπουδαίᾳ] (*Republic* 10.608a). Plato has given us here, indirectly at any rate, quite a precise definition of the *spoudaios* as he sees it, namely that which seeks to seize on Truth. Any other kind of discourse, from tragedy to rhetoric, any discourse that resists the notion of Truth, will be by definition not serious, but *geloios*. The Truth, the whole Truth, and nothing but the Truth is that which according to Plato is worthy of attention (which is not to claim that Plato thinks it accessible).

Andrea Nightingale has discussed this issue with respect to Plato's attitude toward tragedy. She shows that Socrates repeatedly uses the term "serious thing" (*spoudaios*) and grammatical variants to discredit tragedy as not being *spoudaios*: "Socrates claims at [Republic] 602b that tragedy is a 'mimesis' that is παιδιάν τινα καὶ οὐ σπουδὴν [a child's play and not serious]."[7] Most important for my semantic purposes, however, are her following remarks:

> In that text [the *Laws* 7], after distinguishing comedy and tragedy as genres concerned with (respectively) γελοῖα (816d9, e5; cf. γέλωτα, e10) and σπουδαῖα (817a2), the Athenian proceeds to contrast the "so-called serious" creations of the tragedians (τῶν δὲ σπουδαίων, ὥς φασι, τῶν περὶ τραγῳδίαν ἡμῖν ποιητῶν, 817a2–3) with the "most beautiful and finest tragedy" that he and his interlocutors are themselves producing in their construction of a good code of laws (ἡμεῖς ἐσμὲν τραγῳδίας αὐτοὶ ποιηταὶ κατὰ δύναμιν ὅτι καλλίστης ἅμα καὶ ἀρίστης, 817b2–3). Here, Plato not only denies that tragedy is truly "serious," but confers upon his own creations the title of serious tragedy.[8]

In contrast to and defiance of general Athenian usage (as so frequently in Plato), that which they call *spoudaios,* namely tragedy, is declared by Plato to be only "so-called." What we learn very well and clearly from this passage is that, for Plato, "seriousness" is the mark of an important, significant discourse, that which deserves the name "tragedy," while the playful and mimetic—even on tragic themes—is not serious, not beautiful, and without virtue. The comic, it would seem, is even more contemptible than the tragic in poetry, as Nightingale elegantly argues.[9] In contrast to Aristophanes, who seems to allow for both the *spoudaios* and the *geloios* in a comedy such as the *Frogs,* for Plato neither the comic nor the tragic is *spoudaios.*

Perhaps the richest, most explicit reflection by Plato on "seriousness" is given in the *Laws* 7.803.

ATHENIAN: [803b] And notwithstanding that human affairs are unworthy of serious effort [*spoudes*], necessity counsels us to be serious

---

7. Andrea Wilson Nightingale, *Genres in Dialogue: Plato and the Construct of Philosophy* (Cambridge: Cambridge University Press, 1995), 88. This book would not have danced had not Nightingale sung first. For a useful discussion of παιδιά, see Stephen Halliwell, "The Uses of Laughter in Greek Culture," *Classical Quarterly,* n.s. 41, no. 2 (1991): 283.

8. Nightingale, *Genres in Dialogue,* 88. On this passage, see too at length Richard Patterson, "The Platonic Art of Comedy and Tragedy," *Philosophy and Literature* 6 (1982): 78–82.

9. Nightingale, *Genres in Dialogue,* 88–89.

[*spoudazein*]; and that is our misfortune. Yet, since we are where we are, it is no doubt becoming that we should show this earnestness in a suitable direction. But no doubt [803c] I may be faced—and rightly faced—with the question, "What do I mean by this?"

CLINIAS: Certainly.

ATHENIAN: What I assert is this—that a man ought to be in serious earnest about serious things [*spoudaion spoudazein*], and not about trifles [*me spoudaion*]; and that the object really worthy of all serious and blessed effort is God, while man is contrived, as we said above, to be a plaything of God, and the best part of him is really just that; and thus I say that every man and woman ought to pass through life in accordance with this character, playing at the noblest of pastimes, being otherwise minded than they now are.

[803d] CLINIAS: How so?

ATHENIAN: Now they imagine that serious work should be done for the sake of play; for they think that it is for the sake of peace that the serious work of war needs to be well conducted. But as a matter of fact we, it would seem, do not find in war, either as existing or likely to exist, either real play or education worthy of the name, which is what we assert to be in our eyes the most serious thing. It is the life of peace that everyone should live as much and as well as he can.[10]

This text is worthy of a longer analysis than I shall give it here for my present purposes. The subject of this text is no less than educa-

---

10. [803b] ἔστι δὴ τοίνυν τὰ τῶν ἀνθρώπων πράγματα μεγάλης μὲν σπουδῆς οὐκ ἄξια, ἀναγκαῖόν γε μὴν σπουδάζειν· τοῦτο δὲ οὐκ εὐτυχές. ἐπειδὴ δὲ ἐνταῦθά ἐσμεν, εἴ πως διὰ προσήκοντός τινος αὐτὸ πράττοιμεν, ἴσως ἂν ἡμῖν σύμμετρον ἂν εἴη. λέγω δὲ δὴ τί ποτε; ἴσως μεντἂν τίς μοι τοῦτ' αὐτὸ ὑπολαβὼν ὀρθῶς ὑπολάβοι.

[803c] Κλεινίας· πάνυ μὲν οὖν.

Ἀθηναῖος· φημὶ χρῆναι τὸ μὲν σπουδαῖον σπουδάζειν, τὸ δὲ μὴ σπουδαῖον μή, φύσει δὲ εἶναι θεὸν μὲν πάσης μακαρίου σπουδῆς ἄξιον, ἄνθρωπον δέ, ὅπερ εἴπομεν ἔμπροσθεν, θεοῦ τι παίγνιον εἶναι μεμηχανημένον, καὶ ὄντως τοῦτο αὐτοῦ τὸ βέλτιστον γεγονέναι· τούτῳ δὴ δεῖν τῷ τρόπῳ ξυνεπόμενον καὶ παίζοντα ὅτι καλλίστας παιδιὰς πάντ' ἄνδρα καὶ γυναῖκα οὕτω διαβιῶναι, τοὐναντίον ἢ νῦν διανοηθέντας. [803d]

Κλεινίας· πῶς;

Ἀθηναῖος· νῦν μέν που τὰς σπουδὰς οἴονται δεῖν ἕνεκα τῶν παιδιῶν γίγνεσθαι· τὰ γὰρ περὶ τὸν πόλεμον ἡγοῦνται σπουδαῖα ὄντα τῆς εἰρήνης ἕνεκα δεῖν εὖ τίθεσθαι. τὸ δ' ἦν ἐν πολέμῳ μὲν ἄρα οὔτ' οὖν παιδιὰ πεφυκυῖα οὔτ' αὖ παιδεία ποτὲ ἡμῖν ἀξιόλογος, οὔτε οὖσα οὔτ' ἐσομένη, ὃ δὴ φαμεν ἡμῖν γε εἶναι σπουδαιότατον· δεῖ δὴ τὸν κατ' εἰρήνην βίον ἕκαστον πλεῖστόν τε καὶ ἄριστον διεξελθεῖν.

tion, the education of the young. The speaker, if not Plato's "mouth-piece," certainly one of his approved voices, asserts that human affairs in general are hardly worthy of serious attention (*spoudaia*). But given that we are constrained to deal with them, it becomes necessary to distinguish the serious (*spoudaios*) from the nonserious (*me spoudaios*).[11] Much more, of course, could be said about this passage, but here it is sufficient to cite it for my philological purpose of articulating what the "serious" is for Attic writers.

Like Plato, albeit with nothing like the same fulsomeness, the Babylonian Talmud (or the Bavli; both terms will be used below) knows explicitly, it seems, of a distinction between the serious and the comic in discourse. In a famous passage we are informed that

> Rabba before he commenced [his lesson] to the scholars used to say a joking word [מילתא דבדיחותא], and the scholars were amused. After that he sat in dread [אימתא] and began the lesson. (Shabbat 30b)

The Bavli thus invokes the same structural opposition between comic (*milta debdiḥuta*) and solemn ('*ēmta* = literally "fear") with which Plato is working (although we are never told in the Bavli of what these "joking words" consisted). It is clear from the context that the "solemn" words and not the joking ones are the real matter at hand. Further consideration of the larger context of this passage will repay us. After observing that Kohellet (Ecclesiastes) contradicts itself several times on the question of the goodness (or evil) of laughing, the Talmud sorts out the contradiction between two of these verses in the following fashion:

> "And I praised happiness" [8:15]—the joy of performing a commandment. "And happiness what [good] is it" [2:2]—this is joy that is not caused by performing a commandment. This comes to teach you that the Indwelling of God (*Shekhina*) rests [on a person], neither out of sadness, nor out of laziness, nor out of laughing, nor from lighthead-

---

11. See Jacques Derrida, *Dissemination,* trans. Barbara Johnson (Chicago: University of Chicago Press, 1981), 157–58; Elliot R. Wolfson, "Structure, Innovation, and Diremptive Temporality: The Use of Models to Study Continuity and Discontinuity in Kabbalistic Tradition," *Journal for the Study of Religions and Ideologies,* special issue, *Reading Idel's Works Today* 6, no. 18 (2007): 151.

edness, nor out of [idle] conversation, nor out of useless words, but from the joy of performing commandments. . . . Rav Yehuda said, "And the same is true for a matter of halakha."

It is certainly to the point that these contradictions are drawn from Kohellet, certainly one of the most palpably seriocomic texts in the biblical canon, explicitly thematizing, as it does, *dissoi logoi.* The way the contradiction of the verses is resolved, then, is to contrast two kinds of happiness, one that is praiseworthy, namely the happiness of performing a commandment, and one that is not praiseworthy, any happiness that is not produced from performing commandments. An inference is then drawn to the effect that God rests on a person only when he or she is in a state of happiness occasioned by the performance of commandments. A further statement is then cited, to the effect that one should enter into the study of a matter of halakha (Torah law) only in such a lighthearted mood. But the Talmud immediately objects to this last position:

Is that indeed so?! But didn't R. Giddal say in Rab's name: "If any scholar sits before his teacher and his lips do not drip bitterness [from *dread*, Rashi], they shall be burnt, for it is said, 'his lips are as lilies [*shoshanim*], dropping liquid myrrh [*mor ʿober*]' [Canticles 8:13]: Read not *mor ʿober* [dropping myrrh], but *mar ʿober* [dropping bitterness]; read not *shoshanim* but *sheshonin* [that study]?" There is no difficulty: The former applies to the teacher; the latter to the disciple. Alternatively, both refer to the teacher, yet there is no difficulty: the one means before he commences; the other, after he commences. Like the case of Rabba, who before he commenced [his lesson] to the scholars used to say a joking word [מילתא דבדיחותא], and the scholars were amused. After that he sat in dread [אימתא] and began the lesson.[12]

12. ושבחתי אני את השמחה שמחה של מצוה ולשמחה מה זה עושה זו שמחה שאינה של מצוה ללמדך שאין שכינה שורה לא מתוך עצבות ולא מתוך עצלות ולא מתוך שחוק ולא מתוך קלות ראש ולא מתוך שיחה ולא מתוך דברים בטלים אלא מתוך דבר שמחה של מצוה שנאמר (מלכים ב ג) ועתה קחו לי מנגן והיה כנגן המנגן ותהי עליו יד ה' אמר רב יהודה וכן לדבר הלכה אמר רבא וכן לחלום טוב איני והאמר רב גידל אמר רב כל תלמיד חכם שיושב לפני רבו ואין שפתותיו נוטפות מר תכוינה שנאמר (שיר השירים ה) שפתותיו שושנים נוטפות מור עובר אל תקרי מור עובר אלא מר עובר אל תקרי שושים אלא ששונים לא קשיא הא בתלמיד ואיבעית אימא הא והא ברבה ולא קשיא הא מקמי דלפתח הא לבתר דפתח כי הא דרבה מקמי דפתח להו לרבנן אמר מילתא דבדיחותא ובדחי רבנן לסוף יתיב באימתא ופתח בשמעתא

Rav Gidal's statement implies that only the most severe gravity must attend the study of halakhic matters and asks how would it be possible to say that one should enter into this pursuit in any form of levity. The resolution is offered that one begins with levity and passes quickly into a state of awe and dread. According to the Talmud's resolution, then, although there is a place for lightheartedness and even joking before the study of halakha, at the time of the study itself the student and the teacher must feel a bitterness, a dread occasioned by the overwhelming graveness of the enterprise. The dialectical study of halakha is, for the Bavli, the activity that is most "serious" of all.

For both the Babylonian Talmud and Plato, therefore, it is the "seriousness" of the business at hand that defines its importance, its worthiness as an enterprise to which to devote time. Both the Platonic corpus and the Bavli, however, "confound" their own avowed seriousness by embedding their dialogues in a narrative context entirely different in tone from the dialogues in the texts themselves,[13] frequently enough, offering us hiccups, moments of grotesquerie, in the text, although to be sure the two corpora should not be conflated with each other in their literary means or politics. Some scholars have positivistically gone so far as to argue that these comic narratives in the Bavli are precisely a record of the jokes that Rava told in the beginning of his lessons. Who knows? They may be right, but we will never know. What we do know is that the Bavli seems to incorporate much material that is antithetical to its own declared solemn purpose of investigating the halakha in dread and dour "bitterness," and that this needs to be accounted for, for the result is a peculiar kind of hybrid text.[14] It is a major argument of this book that this particular form of literary hybridity or incongruity is not at all sui generis in the Babylonian Talmud, but, indeed, rather marks that text as part and parcel of its own literary and cultural world. I argue that it is this

---

13. To be sure, there are important differences in the formal role of narrative in Plato's dialogues and in the Bavli. In the former, the narrative is literally the framing within which the dialogue takes place, while in the latter the stories are more like interspersed interventions into the discourse. However in a larger sense, in that the stories which concern me here are biographical narratives about the heroes of the halakha of the Bavli, they can be read too as a kind of narrative framing if only for heuristic purposes.

14. For the association of fear and the serious, see Bakhtin, *Rabelais,* 47.

recognition that enables us to ask, and perhaps at least tentatively answer, the question: What is the Babylonian Talmud? Not what is this
piece or that piece, this element or that element; not what can I learn
about something else from this or that in the Talmud, but What is the
Talmud? I find, moreover, the beginnings of the literary and cultural
movements that produced this kind of strange literature as far back
as Plato's dialogues. Hence the dual textual study that comprises this
book, Plato on the one hand, the Babylonian Talmud on the other.

Philosophy as True Tragedy

The second epigraph to the book:

> Most excellent of Strangers, we ourselves, to the best of our ability, are
> the authors of a tragedy at once superlatively fair and good; at least,
> all our polity is framed as a representation of the fairest and best life,
> which is in reality, as we assert, the truest tragedy. Thus we are com-
> posers of the same things as yourselves, rivals of yours as artists and
> actors of the fairest drama, which, as our hope is, true law, and it alone
> is by nature competent to complete. (Plato, *Laws* 7.817a–b)

It is clear from this that Plato is appropriating the term "tragedy"
as that which Greeks themselves understand as the fairest and truest
of uses of language, the representation on the stage of the noblest
of men and women, the noblest of actions, and the truest of fates.
Plato negates this (as he does much of Athenian high culture), arguing
that drama cannot, by definition as poetry or fiction, represent the
true and noble. Only the discourse of philosophy—with lawmaking
as its executive branch—produces the truly tragic, that is, the truly
true and fair, the truly serious and worthy of attention. Presumably,
at least on the face of it, and more than just the face, Plato's own texts
are intended to show us that truly serious, genuinely "tragic," form
of discourse, and laughing—on Socrates' own account—ought to be
banished from its presence. What shall we do, then, with Aristophanes' hiccups?

There are nearly as many strategies for reading Plato's dialogues
as there are readers of Plato. All of them have to be partly right and
none of them can be all right. Richard McKeon has described what

I take to be almost the exact nature of the argument that I wish to make here:

> The statement of a theory or of a history of dialectic is involved in the same dialectical problems as any other statement or argument; it is an opinion contradicted by other well-established positions, and it is an argument about argument dependent for its facts on assumptions about arguments. . . . More than one account is possible. . . . Each account, theoretical or historical, is self-instantiating and self-justifying, and therefore demonstrably establishable, and each is contradicted by other accounts, and therefore demonstrably refutable. . . . The highly divergent accounts of later philosophers and historians of the essence and influence of, say, Plato's dialectic bring to attention aspects of Plato's description and use of argument which might be overlooked in a single "true" account of Plato's dialectic.[15]

Likewise for the Bavli, of course. The account in this book of both Plato and the Talmud is certainly an opinion contradicted by well-established opinions which cannot simply be refuted or disregarded. I hope here to be contributing another turn of a kaleidoscope, each turn of which reveals (and conceals) aspects of both Plato and the Talmud.

What is characteristic of my reading of Plato's texts (and the Bavli too, mutatis mutandis) in this book is a strenuous refusal to ignore the hiccups. I stand, of course, on the shoulders of others who have long paid attention to these puzzling moments in Plato. Indeed, Aristophanes' hiccups have been a classic locus for discussion of method in the reading of Plato. Thus A. E. Taylor observes: "The tone of this part of the dialogue is wholly playful and . . . it would be a mistake to regard it as anything more than a delightful specimen of 'pantagruelism.' The numerous persons . . . unhappily without anything of the pantagruelist in their own composition will continue, no doubt, to look for hidden meanings in this section of the *Symposium* as they looked for them in Rabelais, and with much the same kind of success."[16] The term "Pan-

---

15. Richard McKeon, "Greek Dialectics: Dialectic and Dialogue, Dialectic and Rhetoric," in *Dialectics,* ed. Chaïm Perelman (The Hague: Nijhoff, 1975), 2.

16. A. E. Taylor, *Plato: The Man and His Work* (London: Methuen, 1960), 216, as quoted in Kevin Corrigan and Elena Glazov-Corrigan, *Plato's Dialectic at Play: Argument, Structure,*

tagruelism" as used by Taylor here is problematic. He himself seems to be referring to the moment in Rabelais in which we are told: "For in every soldier I detect that specific trait and individual quality that our ancestors used to call Pantagruelism; which assures me that they will never take in bad part anything that they know to spring from a good, honest, and loyal heart. I have so often seen them take the will for the payment, and be content with it, when that was all the debtor had."[17] The context in Rabelais is hardly sanguine, however, given as it is in the context of fear that readers will read him uncharitably, taking his good-natured humor negatively, and seek to kill him. But, of course, Rabelais's text is anything but merely good-natured. This Pantagruelism ends up being more Panglossian than Rabelaisian, that is, as itself, an optimism that Rabelais, as much as Voltaire, mocks. I find Taylor's a somewhat pallid way to read Plato's hiccups, apparently ascribing to him no more intent than to amuse. In his use of the term "Pantagruelism," he seems to miss a major part of the term's definition (as given in the *OED*): "extravagant and coarse humor with a satirical or serious purpose," denying, as he does, any serious purpose to the hiccups. This certainly does not, paradoxically, answer to Rabelais's own textual practice. I would read Rabelais too as deeply satiric in his very definition of Pantagruelism, and thus applying this Rabelaisian term to Plato would, for me, issue in rather a different direction of interpretation. Putting my thesis as concisely as possible, I want to argue for the notion of the seriocomical, that is, the *spoudogeloion,* as developed by the great theorist of the last century, Mikhail Bakhtin, as the key to open this strait gate. The genre name itself implies rather a yoking together of the seemingly incompatible, even antithetical, and that is precisely the circumstance that confronts us in both Plato and the Bavli, so this seems, a priori, a promising line of thought and research. But what is the *spoudogeloion?*

For Taylor, it seems to be simply a matter of delight and the entirely playful. He thus splits completely the "serious" business of the dialogues from his understanding of the "Pantagruelism." This is

---

and Myth in the Symposium (University Park: Pennsylvania State University Press, 2004), 68. For the searchers for hidden meanings and allegorical interpretations of Rabelais, see Bakhtin, *Rabelais,* 111–16.

17. Rabelais, *The Histories of Gargantua and Pantagruel,* ed. and trans. J. M. Cohen, Penguin Classics, vol. 147 (Harmondsworth, Middlesex: Penguin Books, 1955), 286.

the case for other scholars as well. For the most systematic writer, so far, on the *spoudogeloion,* Lawrence Giangrande, matters are similarly sweet and quite genial: "It was only later, with the *spoudaiogeloioi,* that good-natured laughter asserted a moral purpose. Now the *dulce* and the *utile* were combined formally, and the *utile* was reinforced by means of the *dulce.* Exciting laughter and giving wise advice to the reader or listener were, after the formulation of a definite theory, subsumed under one term: *spoudaiogeloion.*"[18] Giangrande completely evacuates any sense of tension, conflict, or even incongruity between the *spoudaios* and the *geloios.* For Stephen Halliwell, even Gorgias's talk of confounding one's opponent with the *geloios* does not comprehend the deep contradiction between the *spoudaios* and the *geloios,* the latter being, for him, purely "rhetorically induced laughter not so much for a direct expression of animosity, as in order to win one's audience's amused approval and thus to manipulate the mood of a public gathering in one's favor."[19] Halliwell, like Giangrande and Taylor, ignores the double confounding of the serious by the comic and the comic by the serious. Further consideration of both *spoudogeloion* and "pantagruelism" itself will suggest a much less "good-natured" and "delightful" reading of the Platonic text. Whatever else it is or is not, I hope to have shown by the end of this book that the "seriocomic" is *not* a "kindly philosophy of the comic art wherein good-natured laughter asserts a moral purpose,"[20] but rather the name of a form in which Gorgias's edict that the serious and the comic must constantly and forever undercut each other comes into its own in literature.

In a remarkable and celebrated reading of Rabelais, Bakhtin wrote that "Rabelais' basic goal was to destroy the official picture of events. He strove to take a new look at them, to interpret the tragedy or comedy they represented from the point of view of the laughing chorus of the marketplace." On this account, Pantagruelism is hardly so innocent and delightful a force as Taylor has made it out to be. The remarkable thing about both subjects of this book, Plato and the Talmud, is that in both, "the resources of sober popular imagery" are summoned "in order to break up the narrow seriousness dictated

18. Lawrence Giangrande, *The Use of Spoudaiogeloion in Greek and Roman Literature* (The Hague: Mouton, 1972), 10.

19. Halliwell, "The Uses of Laughter," 293.

20. Giangrande, *The Use of Spoudaiogeloion,* 19.

by the ruling classes,"[21] by and in the very texts in which that narrow seriousness is itself being promulgated.

This book, to be sure, represents a certain ripening and mellowing of my own take on Plato in the wake of some forty years of intermittent Platonic reading. From the first Platonic dialogue that I read in my first year of college (1964), the *Meno* as it happens, I have felt that (Plato's) Socrates' ways of dealing with his interlocutors involve a great deal of bad faith, of manipulation and exercise of intellectual power, to mislead those who were not as clever or as quick on their feet as he is.[22] I have found many allies in this charge, from Nietzsche to Popper, from Havelock to Beversluis.[23] It is important to note that this set of critical responses to Plato (including my own) is based essentially on the same reading strategies with respect to the Platonic text as the classical "philosophical" approach, namely treating "Socrates" in the text as in some powerful sense as the "mouthpiece" for Plato,[24] with the interlocutors as Plato's opponents. The texts are then read, classically, as dialogical representations of philosophical doctrine (including the doctrine of unknowing) and as advertisements for the academy as the path to true knowledge (including the knowledge that knowledge is impossible). The critical readings are pitted against the classical readings only with respect to the success or failure, the ethicality or unethicality of Socrates/Plato as operator in the dialogues. The terms of the reading are not shifted dramatically; the hiccups are still unread. My reading of Plato in this book is generated in part still out of that deeply suspicious response to the dialogues. In the course of the years of concerted reading that produced this book, however, the bars to such a simplistic reading of Plato have increasingly impinged upon my single-mindedness. Identifying Socrates *as* Plato, or even as Plato's so-called "mouthpiece," has proved a highly unsatis-

---

21. Bakhtin, *Rabelais,* 439.

22. I would like to remember my wonderful teacher for that course, entitled "Dialogue and the Self," Prof. Thomas Whitaker ("Tom to you, son"!) who had such a profound impact (without either of us being quite aware of it at the time) on my intellectual development.

23. Karl Raimund Popper, *The Open Society and Its Enemies* (London: Routledge & K. Paul, 1962); Eric Alfred Havelock, *Preface to Plato* (Cambridge, Mass.: Harvard University Press, 1963); John Beversluis, *Cross-Examining Socrates: A Defense of the Interlocutors in Plato's Early Dialogues* (Cambridge: Cambridge University Press, 2000).

24. Debra Nails, "Mouthpiece Schmouthpiece," in *Who Speaks for Plato: Studies in Platonic Anonymity,* ed. Gerald A. Press (Lanham, Md.: Rowman & Littlefield, 2000), 15–26.

factory intellectual procedure, not least owing to the fact that everything I know about "Socrates," I know, of course, from Plato—it's
Plato's Socrates of whom I speak after all—engendering an enormous
question about Plato's intent (let the problematic of this construct
be for the moment). The argument has seemed increasingly circular
to me, as well. To put it simply, how can I criticize Plato for seeming
to turn a blind eye to the ethical flaws of his hero Socrates himself
if my own clear vision of those flaws is provided by Plato?[25] Any adequate reading of Plato must, in my view, incorporate insights already
hard won among certain Platonic scholars, such as Helen Bacon and
Diskin Clay. As Bacon wrote, "The dramatic parts of the dialogues
then cannot be set aside as mere interruptions of the real discussion,
designed to give relief from the serious business of philosophy. In
Plato's sense they are as philosophical as the more obviously theoretical sections."[26] More recently the tradition of Platonic reading most
closely associated with the name of John Sallis follows Bacon's lead
in taking these moments seriously, but fully subordinates them to a
philosophical reading of the dialogues.[27] As I will argue below in the
appendix to this book, these "continental" reading strategies, while
shifting considerably the epistemological starting point for reading
the dialogues, leave the "bad faith" discursive politics firmly in place.
My approach, therefore, is somewhat different from these. Rather
than seeing the hiccups as either "comic relief," which I take to be
the meaning, as well, of Taylor's Pantagruelism, or as support for the

---

25. My sense of the inadequacy of my relentlessly negative response to Plato's texts has
been further augmented by the critical response of Mark Jordan to the first versions of
my arguments about the *Symposium*. Jordan insisted that in my own single-minded pursuit
of Plato as monologist, my own reading was as flatly monological as could be, that it was
I, as reader, who was occluding the hiccups in the Platonic text—as well as ignoring the
entire Alcibiades episode, which he takes to be the very heart and center of the text. Mark
Jordan, "Flesh in Confession: Alcibiades Beside Augustine," in *Toward a Theology of Eros:
Transfiguring Passion at the Limits of Discipline,* ed. Virginia Burrus and Catherine Keller
(New York: Fordham University Press, 2006), 23–37. Much in this book owes, then, much
to him.

26. Helen Bacon, "Socrates Crowned," *Virginia Quarterly Review* 35 (1959): 416. Diskin
Clay, "The Tragic and Comic Poet of the *Symposium,*" *Arion* 2 (1975): 242.

27. By which I do not mean a reading that comes up with a "Platonic philosophy,"
almost the opposite of Sallis's project. See John Sallis, *Being and Logos: Reading the Platonic
Dialogues* (Bloomington: Indiana University Press, 1996), as well as the essays collected in
John Russon and John Sallis, eds., *Retracing the Platonic Text* (Evanston, Ill.: Northwestern
University Press, 2000).

"serious business" of philosophy, I read for the deeply antagonistic, dialogical relations between the *spoudaios* and the *geloios* in the Platonic writing.

I have strived in this essay for a reading strategy of Plato that would be itself dialogical.

Mark Jordan put well the choices facing readers of Plato:

> Any persistent reader of Plato has to make certain judgments on his rhetorical choices. . . . How comprehensive is his decision to write dialogues? How complete is their irony? How thorough the arrangement of dramatic details in them? How important is the absence of Plato from among the interlocutors and actors? Or do the dialogues finally betray an irrepressible dogmatism, a ferocious desire to state at last the truth about the highest things?[28]

My own choice is not quite any of the above, but rather a combination of them, a combination that ought to be impossible: I imagine on Plato's part a ferocious desire—ferocious indeed—to state the truth about the highest things, combined with a completely ironic stance, at one and the same time. Rather than abandoning my original sense of the deep bad faith of so much of Socrates' intercourse with his interlocutors and my protest against apologetic readings that implicitly or explicitly approve of this bad faith, I propose my own seriocomic reading of Plato's corpus. I do continue to believe in spite of Plato's apparent recognition and presentation of Socrates' "bad faith" that the Platonic text is a seriously meant protreptic for the academic life as the only true way for a human to live best and to search for the Truth. Thematizing my own sense of how the text works as one of the originary moments of the seriocomic, I present first with a near deadly seriousness of my own a sharply antagonistic reading of several of the dialogues, thus allowing one voice in the Platonic text to surface and be perceived (and attacked). This is exactly the voice that authorizes traditional philosophical readings of Socrates as Plato's "mouthpiece." I reserve developing the comic side of the seriocomic reading for the end of the book, miming in my reading Plato's own strategy of presenting in the *Symposium* first the "tragedy" and then

---

28. Jordan, "Flesh in Confession," 24.

the "satyr play." Both of these reading strategies have to be presented earnestly and separately for the eloquent double-voicing of the Platonic corpus to emerge clearly, or so I reckon at any rate.

While the question of how to read Plato, that is as philosophical tract or as narrative text, has been put often in scholarly and interpretive literature, for the Bavli the question has hardly even been asked. There are exceptions. David Kraemer in his *Reading the Rabbis* raises precisely the question of the genre of Talmud and suggests, "Rejecting the possibility of offering a single, limited definition of literature, we are better off positing that the Talmud *is* literature and asking what genre of literature it is. Yet, here, too, we confront immediate difficulties. Genre definition is a matter of comparison and contrast: What other literature is this literature like and in what ways is it different?"[29] Kraemer points in the right direction in two ways: on the one hand, he insists that we ask the question of what the Bavli is, as literature, and on the other, he also perceives that the question of genre and the heterogeneity of genre in the Bavli present a major classificatory dilemma.

A strict hierarchy has been established historically, that is, in the post-Talmudic period, between the halakhic discussions and the aggadic narratives in general, a hierarchy developed on notions quite similar to that of literary critical notions of decorum. Only the halakha is considered worthy of the serious attentions of Rabbis and scholars. This has been the case for as far back as we can go in a historical recovery of reading practices with respect to the Babylonian Talmud (although it must be emphasized that there is a centuries-long gap between the latest presumptive date for the production of the Bavli somewhat as we know it and the earliest commentaries on it). Beginning in the Middle Ages and continuing into the early modern period, anthologies of the aggada have been produced that take it entirely out of the context of the halakhic material. Even aside from that, traditionally, commentaries have been written that completely ignore, skip over, the aggadic portions and especially the grotesque aggada.[30] Some giants of scholarship wrote separate commentaries on the hal-

29. David Kraemer, *Reading the Rabbis: The Talmud as Literature* (New York: Oxford University Press, 1996), 7.

30. For such strategies with respect to Rabelais, see discussion in Bakhtin, *Rabelais,* 134–36.

akha and the aggada. When these were joined in modern prints into a continuous text, the halakhic commentary was printed in large type, the aggadic in small type. In a kind of deconstructive mode, in recent times, in many quarters the aggada has been privileged for its "literariness" and the hierarchy has been reversed. The net effect of the traditional practices has been to cordon off the halakha as both serious and "sacred," leaving the aggada as either edifying or embarrassing by turns. Indeed, as the very distinction between these two "genres" is not marked in the text of the Talmud at all, of late it has been argued that the entire construction of this binary is for the purpose of such cordoning off and should be abandoned in scholarly usage.[31] The older modes of reading are thus analogous to the practices of those readers of Plato who read him for philosophy and philosophy alone. In neither case can these readings be dismissed or even marginalized without doing violence to the text, but they aren't the whole story either. In recent scholarship on the Bavli, most studies are either thematic or philological in nature. Studies which nevertheless engage questions of structure and composition do so mainly in the context of "higher" (source) criticism, attempting to distinguish between different layers in the Babylonian Talmud (for example, Shamma Friedman and his students),[32] thus allowing for historical reconstructions

31. Barry Wimpfheimer, *Telling Tales Out of Court: Literary Ambivalence in Talmudic Legal Narratives,* Divinations: Rereading Late Ancient Religions (Philadelphia: University of Pennsylvania Press, 2009). This is not to say, of course, that there is absolutely no basis for this distinction at all. The Talmud in Baba Qamma 60b relates a charming story about a teacher with two students: one student desired halakhic traditions [*shema 'tata*] and the other aggada. Neither would let the teacher teach the other genre. The teacher told them of a man who had two wives, one young and one old. The young one would pull out all of his grey hairs and the older one all of his black hairs, until he remained "bald from this side and that." And these boys would have remained without Torah. The teacher cleverly found something to teach them that incorporated both halakha and aggada. A distinction was therefore clearly recognized. Nevertheless, Wimfpheimer is correct that there is no distinction between what we call halakha and what we call aggada in the body of the talmudic text. There is every reason to believe, moreover, that what is called aggada in the Talmud itself, as in this passage from Babba Qamma, means homiletical interpretations of the Torah and not biographical narratives, which, to the best of my knowledge, are never designed aggada within the classical rabbinic literature.

32. Shamma Friedman, "A Critical Study of Yevamot X with a Methodological Introduction," in *Texts and Studies: Analecta Judaica I,* ed. H. Z. Dimitrovsky (New York: Jewish Theological Seminary Press, 1977), 227–441; Shamma Friedman, *Talmud Arukh Perek Ha-Sokher et Ha-Umanin: Bavli Bava Metsi'a Perek Shishi: Mahadurah al Derekh Ha-Mehkar Im Perush Ha-Sugyot* (Jerusalem: Bet ha-midrash le-rabanim ba-Amerikah, 1990).

of these layers.[33] The composition as a whole is rarely discussed, and it seems that most scholars believe (without ever having spelled it out) that the Babylonian Talmud is indeed sui generis. This book seeks to highlight the scandal of a text in which sublime discussion of prayer and Bakhtinian "slum naturalism" are apprehended in the same sheets and between the same covers in flagrante.

Readers of the dialogues of Plato and the Babylonian Talmud are shocked, if they let themselves experience the shock, if they don't censor out or marginalize the incongruity. Why is the great and almost holy Socrates acting the buffoon? Why is this passage about God and proper behavior in synagogue next to what appears to be a dirty joke? Both of these textual corpora present the same (or near enough to be worth thinking the same) conundrum. On the one hand, both are highly serious texts. As Whitehead has famously put it, for the community of Western thinkers, all philosophy is footnotes to Plato. Plato represents for them no less than an exhaustive investigation (even instigation) of the basic agenda of all philosophy, ontology, epistemology, aesthetics, and ethics. For traditional Jews, the Bavli constitutes the basis for Jewish religious life, both in terms of thought and spirit and in terms of practice. It is easy (and has been for millennia) to read Plato's dialogues as philosophy and the Babylonian Talmud as a Jewish legal text or a religiously uplifting text. The formal consistency of such readings is comforting and also offers these communities of readers a sense of their own intellectual/moral/religious purity. What shall we do, however, with a text in which the most sublime of spiritual matters is discussed alongside the matter of a certain rabbi's sexual prowess (his ability, in one saying, to have intercourse with several virgins without drawing blood)?

I have to be careful here. Especially with the Bavli, further away from us culturally than even Plato in many ways, it is important not to impose anachronistic or otherwise culturally inappropriate categories. Much in that text that would seem to us somehow quintessentially "low" in theme seems not to have been taken as such by the Babylonian rabbis. In this sense, there is something of the Rabelaisian

33. For example Jeffrey L. Rubenstein, *The Culture of the Babylonian Talmud* (Baltimore: Johns Hopkins University Press, 2003); Richard Kalmin, *Jewish Babylonia between Persia and Roman Palestine* (Oxford: Oxford University Press, 2006).

already in the ordinary, the "serious" discussions of the halakha, the *sugya*. I shall be using this term often in this book to mean the halakhic dialectic for which the Talmud is famous, that which is named most frequently in Jewish sources the *šaqla wetarya*, the "give-and-take" of the Talmud. It will not do, then, to make sharp distinctions between the high and low on our (Greek) cultural terms, nor between halakha as the enterprise of the higher parts of the human person and aggada as that of the lower parts. This simply will not work for multiple reasons that anyone with any familiarity with the Talmud at all can immediately identify.

I wish, however, to go beyond that insight, developed in some of my earlier work.[34] My concern here is with a different—if surely not unrelated—phenomenon, one that is particularly textual or literary in nature and deals with the meanings of that phenomenon. This phenomenon, as I am calling it, is double-faced: one face is simply the presence of narratives that not only celebrate the lower body but actively portray the rabbis, the very heroes of the Talmud, in grotesque, compromising, or ethically problematic light. The second face, which is even more important than the first, is the literary choice to produce and have only one book in rabbinic Babylonia, the book that we know of as the Babylonian Talmud, in which precisely cheek by jowl we find the *same* rabbis as the producers of all that is ethical, religious, and fine in the tradition and as being involved in wild aggadic narratives that so sharply disturb and disrupt the picture of the rabbis as objects to be imitated and indeed the picture of the Torah as eternal and holy. This is nearly unique within the rabbinic corpus, as in Palestine genres are kept much more clearly (even if not entirely) distinct from each other. The heterogeneity of the Bavli is well known: "Much more so than Palestinian rabbinic compilations, the *Bavli* is encyclopedic in character, meaning that it contains more varieties of rabbinic literature than do roughly contemporary Palestinian compilations."[35]

---

34. Daniel Boyarin, "The Great Fat Massacre: Sex, Death and the Grotesque Body in the Talmud," in *People of the Body: Jews and Judaism from an Embodied Perspective,* ed. Howard Eilberg-Schwartz (Albany: SUNY Press, 1992), 69–102.

35. Richard Kalmin, "The Formation and Character of the Babylonian Talmud," in *The Cambridge History of Judaism,* vol. 4, *The Late Roman-Rabbinic Period,* ed. Steven T. Katz (Cambridge: Cambridge University Press, 2006), 841.

What has not been noted before, I think, is how close this multi-generic character of the Babylonian Talmud brings it to major strands of broadly contemporaneous literature in which such mixtures of genre are explicitly thematized.

Some medieval talmudic commentators grasped the profoundly heterogeneous nature of the Bavli (and even thus explained its name): "We, who busy ourselves with the Babylonian Talmud, it is sufficient for us, because it is mixed up with Bible, with Mishna, and with Talmud" (Tosafot A.Z. 19b).

With this statement, the great Rabbenu Tam, the leading talmudic commentator (northern France) of the late eleventh century, evinces the common sentiment that the Bavli is a very strange book indeed, a unicum even on the rabbinic scene, a fortiori in world literature, one composed of many and disparate elements, all "mixed up" with each other. Hence the pun "mixed up" = *balul,* Babylonian = *bavli.* The pun itself goes back to the Bible itself, of course, where the Tower of Babylon is interpreted as the Tower of the mixing up of languages (the Tower of Heteroglossia), best translated perhaps as the Tower of Babble. The Bavli is a heteroglossic Tower of Babel. In the original talmudic text to which Rabbenu Tam is referring, the meaning is quite different. In that version a Palestinian rabbi condemns Babylonians (not the Talmud, but the Jewry there in general) for being mixed up in their Bible, their Mishna, and their Talmud. Rabbenu Tam turns this around into a positive statement (accurately descriptive) to the effect that all these genres are mixed in the Babylonian Talmud and one can fulfill the command to learn all three of these parts of the Torah by studying that text alone! It is this cacophony of languages, likened to the situation at Babel after the mixing up of languages, that is the analogue of the grotesque sublime emblematized by Aristophanes' hiccups. The question, then, has been set: how are we to account for what appear to be gross violations of decorum in Plato, on the one hand, and in the Babylonian Talmud on the other? An answer has been hinted at as well: these two corpora are related in some way, shape, or fashion to the explicitly designed genres of the *spoudogeloion.* One of the most important of ancient practitioners of this genre was the second century (AC) Syrian Greek satirist, Lucian of Samosata.

"Read Lucian! Lucian Has the Keys"

The command of my teacher, the great Talmudist Prof. Saul Lieberman z"l, quoted in the third epigraph to this book, was that I must
read Lucian, for Lucian holds the keys to the Talmud. Lieberman's
admonition has, indeed, proven (to me) its deep and abiding wisdom.
Thirty years or more after hearing that command but not quite remembering it, I was reading Lucian for the sheer pleasure of it, when
a synapse fired and a light went on. I began to understand in what way
he is the key and why we should read him to understand the Talmud
(and Plato). Lucian, in a way that neither Plato nor the Bavli does,
explicitly reflects on the incongruity of his textual monsters, calling
them fish-horses and goat-stags:

> Dialogue and comedy [that is, Plato and Aristophanes] were not en-
> tirely friendly and compatible from the beginning. Dialogue used to
> sit at home by himself and indeed spend his time in the public walks
> with a few companions; Comedy gave herself to Dionysus and joined
> him in the theatre, had fun with him, jested and joked, sometimes
> stepping in time to the pipe and generally riding on anapaests. Dia-
> logue's companions she mocked. . . . She [comedy] showed them now
> walking on air and mixing with the clouds, now measuring sandals for
> fleas—her notion of heavenly subtleties, I suppose![36] Dialogue how-
> ever took his conversations very seriously, philosophizing about na-
> ture and virtue. So, in musical terms, there were two octaves between
> them from highest to lowest. Nevertheless I have dared to combine
> them as they are into a harmony, though they are not in the least doc-
> ile and do not easily tolerate partnership.[37]

Lucian's text has proven so productive for me in the conception of
this text owing to the horror that he expects to be generated by his
yoking together of disparate genres, by a total breakdown of decorum
in the production of his text: "What is most monstrous of all, I have
been turned into a surprising blend, for I am neither afoot nor ahorse-

36. Of course it is Aristophanes' *Clouds* to which Lucian alludes.
37. Lucian of Samosata, "To One Who Said 'You're a Prometheus in Words,'" in
Lucian VI, with an English translation by A. M. Harmon, 8 vols., Loeb Classics (London:
W. Heinemann, 1913–67), 427.

back, neither prose nor verse, but seem to my hearers a strange phenomenon made up of different elements, like a Centaur."[38] Dialogue and rhetoric, prose and poetry, the serious and the comic, all appear together within the covers of the same book, and this is, according to Lucian himself, a real shocker. The shock is not, I emphasize, in the presence of different elements within the literary system—a man riding a horse is not a surprising thing to see—but in their mixing into one monstrous thing, a centaur. How do we keep the text in front of us from devolving into a man riding a horse, instead of abiding in our perception and reading practice as a centaur? In his explicit thematization of these issues, not only in his production of hybrid texts, and particularly in his development (invention?) of the Menippean dialogue, Lucian, indeed, provides the keys for a deeper, richer understanding of vitally important aspects of the Babylonian Talmud.

"How Well Plato Knows to Satirize [ἰαμβίζειν]!"

If not truly Gorgian in origin, nevertheless, the above citation given in his name by Athenaeus (fl. 2nd–3rd c. AC) suggests that already in antiquity there was a deep understanding of the connections between Plato's dialogues and the genres of satire, such as the Iambic, and thus provides the fifth epigraph for my book. This book argues, following "Gorgias," for a substantially new way of reading Plato and a new way of reading the Bavli, one—in both cases, mutatis mutandis—that does not split the serious from the comic (Taylor's Pantagruelism) nor harmonize them (his anti-Pantagruelists) with each other in accord with present practices for reading both corpora. This reading seeks instead in the dialogue between these elements within the text a more intricate making of meaning than either of the above options would allow. In this reading, a set of practices, intellectual and bodily/political, are put forward in the form of a dead-serious protreptic whilst their absolute validity is put into question at the same time. Both corpora then, read in this way, provide exempla of a way be-

---

38. Lucian of Samosata, "The Double Indictment," in *Lucian III*, with an English translation by A. M. Harmon, 8 vols., Loeb Classics (London: W. Heinemann, 1913–67), 147 (emphasis mine). On this text, see too Simon Goldhill, "Becoming Greek, with Lucian," in *Who Needs Greek? Contests in the Cultural History of Hellenism* (New York: Cambridge University Press, 2002), 72–73.

yond absolutism and tolerance at the same time, precisely through, as Bakhtin puts it, "the appearance of a second accent [that] would inevitably be perceived as a crude contradiction within the author's world view."[39] But of course, in the dialogical work, or in all literature read dialogically, it is precisely this second accent for which we hunt. Bakhtin leaves tantalizingly ambiguous here the status of that "crude contradiction" itself, for if there is, anywhere, a truly dialogical text, it is in that crude contradiction that the dialogue will be found, in the textual moments, whatever they may be, in which an ideological system can (and can't) be challenged from within or without. I shall be reading my two textual bodies here as incorporating, however inorganically, such second accents and crude contradictions. For Bakhtin the kind of text that most floridly allowed for, even was comprised of, such crude contradiction of the author's worldview was the Menippean satire. What is Menippean satire?

Menippean satire, also known as *spoudogeloion,* is a peculiar type of literature produced by and for intellectuals in which their own practices are both mocked and asserted at one and the same time. According to legend, it was originated by one of the earliest of the cynics, Menippus of Gadara, in the third century BC. Menippean satire involves a kind of spoofing in which the heroes of an intellectual community are the spoofed heroes, at least in formal part via a yoking together of the serious and comical genres into single texts that observe no generic decorum, as was recognized already in antiquity. Since the force of this genre is to call into question the very seriousness and authority of the practice of the intellectuals themselves, this is also, I argue, an important avenue for understanding talmudic ideology. Significantly, however, this calling into question or putting limits on the efficacy of intellectuals' practice does not involve an abandonment of the authority of those practices.

While we generally think of satire as that which makes fun of a literary tradition or sociocultural formation, this is only true of one type of satire. We should not confuse Menippean satire with satire as we usually think of it. A scholar of the last century warned, "The applica-

---

39. Mikhail Bakhtin, *Problems of Dostoevsky's Poetics,* ed. and trans. Caryl Emerson, Theory and History of Literature (Minneapolis: University of Minnesota Press, 1984), 82.

tion of the name *satura* to two such widely different literary vehicles as Horace's work and that of Menippus and Varro has been, not a guide to the common origin of both, but a source of perennial misunderstanding."[40] Menippean satire is satire in the sense of *satura,* a mixture of things that don't belong together, of things that contradict each other, not as a censure of immorality as in the Horatian tradition.[41]

Ancient traditions give "sausage" as the etymology of *satura,* although some very learned scholars of a century ago—in their own, unintended Pantagruelistic moment—doubted whether it was in fact a sausage and not some kind of a pudding:

> This has been described as a sausage, e.g., Leo, *Hermes,* XXIV, 70, n., but a consideration of the materials used shows the absurdity of such a definition. It is due to the fact that the dictionaries give this meaning alone for *farcimen.* It is evident that this is but one of the special meanings of the word, and that it must have had a general meaning stuffing. *Satura* is not in the list of sausages mentioned by Varro L.L. v. 110 f. Fritzsche (Horace *Serm.,* p. 13) curiously takes Varro's *farcimen* to be the same as the *lanz.* He was evidently trusting his memory for Varro's recipe. There is no reason for assuming that the recipe given in the *Plautine Questions* does not apply to the *genus farciminis,* as Pease assumes in Harper's *Dict.* of *Class. Lit.,* S.U. "satura."[42]

Whether stuffing, black pudding, or sausage, the Babylonian Talmud can be better understood when it is considered part and parcel of the menippea or carnivalistic legend tradition of its world.[43] Bakhtin has already laid out the taxa of this type of literature, citing, for exam-

40. C. W. Mendell, "Satire as Popular Philosophy," *Classical Philology* 15, no. 2 (April 1920): 138.

41. Joel C. Relihan, *Ancient Menippean Satire* (Baltimore: Johns Hopkins University Press, 1993), 20. See too Bakhtin: "Medieval parody, especially before the twelfth century, was not concerned with the negative, the imperfections of specific cults, ecclesiastic order, or scholars which could be the object of derision and destruction. For the medieval parodist everything without exception was comic. Laughter was as universal as seriousness," Bakhtin, *Rabelais,* 84.

42. B. L. Ullman, "Satura and Satire," *Classical Philology* 8, no. 2 (April 1913): 176n2.

43. The term, "menippea," as opposed to Menippean satire, is, I think, Bakhtin's own coinage, referring to what is for me the most useful notion of a transgenreing or transtextual collection of Menippean elements, modified through time and place.

ple, the narrative material around Socrates (both Alcibiades' account and the legends about Xanthippe).[44] He characterizes the genre by saying that "carnivalistic legends in general are profoundly different from traditional heroicizing epic legends: carnivalistic legends debase the hero and bring him down to earth, they make him familiar, bring him close, humanize him; ambivalent carnival laughter burns away all that is stilted and stiff, but in no way destroys the heroic core of the image."[45] This could almost have been written as a description of the biographical legend that is found in rabbinic literature but most vividly in the Babylonian Talmud. We will find our rabbinic heroes in all their bodily glory and mess, all of their selfishness and meanness and not infrequently in extreme and untoward situations. Not only the aggada but, frequently enough, the halakha of the Bavli too is suffused with the grotesque in the Bakhtinian, Rabelaisian sense discussed above. There are halakhic discussions having to do with a man who penetrates his body with his own penis, or describing with what rabbis wiped their anuses after defecation, as well as imparting profound statements such as "Happy is the man whose toilet is not far from his dinner table."

Hybridity, even incongruity, is the very soil in which postclassical Hellenistic literature was nurtured. One of the most characteristic features of the literature of later Hellenism (second through sixth centuries) is its lack of decorum with respect to earlier genres and linguistic registers.[46] As educed by Bakhtin, the period is a time of literary and cultural upheaval associated with the development of such literary forms as Menippean satire, the parodic dialogues of Lucian, and the ancient novel. It is only to Menippus that antiquity refers as *spoudogeloios* (Strabo 16.2.29), hence Bakhtin's usage of the two appellations as virtual synonyms. (Although Eunapius writes of Lucian that "he was a serious man at laughing" [ἀνὴρ σπουδαῖος ἐς τὸ γελσθῆναι], suggesting that he too was considered *spoudogeloios*.)[47] To be sure, it is

44. Bakhtin, *Problems of Dostoevsky's Poetics,* 132.

45. Bakhtin, *Problems of Dostoevsky's Poetics,* 132–33.

46. For the general concept of late ancient Hellenism, see G. W. Bowersock, *Hellenism in Late Antiquity,* Jerome Lectures 18 (Ann Arbor: University of Michigan Press, 1990), not, however, focusing on these specific features in particular.

47. Wilmer Cave France Wright, ed. and trans., *Philostratus: The Lives of the Sophists; Eunapius: Lives of the Philosophers* (Cambridge, Mass.: Harvard University Press, 1998), 348 (translation modified from Loeb). C. P. Jones writes that "Eunapios may be thinking of the

not certain whether or not there truly was ever (before the Renaissance) a single "genre" called Menippean satire. Perhaps, indeed, Menippean satire is not so much a formal genre as a literary mood and a reflection of habits of thought. As Relihan has written, "A mixture of incompatible elements will hardly do as a rigorous definition of a genre, and in fact this genre has coughed up quite a few idiosyncratic works that are often taken as sui generis."[48] Whether or not the Menippean satire should be identified as a particular genre, however, Bakhtin's evocation of it provides provocative heuristic impetus to renewed ways of thinking about the Talmud. From Lucian's *Icaromenippus* on, it seems, the Menippean narrative is seen as a "proper envelope for the comic presentation of scholarly wrangling and debate."[49] It is not entirely surprising, then, to be finding affinities between the Talmud and what Bakhtin calls the menippea.

Every culture *in some way or fashion* dialogizes its own ideological productions; it is almost impossible, as Carlin Barton has remarked, to imagine a culture that does not somewhere, somehow allow for questioning, for dialogization, of its most highly charged and tightly held sancta, both theoretical and practical. In that sense, some version, for instance, of "cynics" may be found in many cultural forms, including, for instance, the paradoxical practices of Zen masters, carnival, certain practices of debate (such as those represented by Thucydides). What I wish to describe in this book is what I take to be the particular practice of a particular cultural form (Greek and then Hellenistic, including Jewish Hellenism, by which I mean *potentially all* Judaism after the coming of Alexander). What characterizes, grosso modo and inter alia, this particular cultural form is its vaunted reliance on rational inquiry as the way to truth. Consequently the dialogization of such a culture will come rather precisely from a form antithetical to the presentation of its heroes as fully rational beings. One of the ways in which this can be realized is in the form of the seriocomic in

---

term σπουδογέλοιος ('earnest-humorous'), applied by Strabo to Menippos (16.2.29)." C. P. Jones, *Culture and Society in Lucian* (Cambridge, Mass.: Harvard University Press, 1986), 22.

48. Relihan, *Ancient Menippean Satire*, ix.

49. Joel C. Relihan, "Menippus in Antiquity and the Renaissance," in *The Cynics: The Cynic Movement in Antiquity and Its Legacy*, ed. R. Bracht Branham and Marie-Odile Goulet-Cazé, Hellenistic Culture and Society 23 (Berkeley: University of California Press, 1997), 282.

literature, a literature that presents in one and the same text both the most "serious" of rational inquiries and inquirers and the most absurd or otherwise "low" aspects of their personalities and personal lives. On my hypothesis, this specific form, which we find throughout all of post-Hellenistic Western literature, appears first in the dialogues of Plato and appears also in a later form that particularly interests me in the Babylonian Talmud, so it is these that I shall investigate here.

According to Bakhtin, the Socratic dialogue (or perhaps it should be socratic dialogue) is a genre, even a subgenre, of the late ancient macrogenre of *spoudogeloion.* Socratic dialogues, of course, were written by many authors, disciples in various ways of Socrates, and most are lost except for a few fragments and the ones written by Xenophon and by Plato, of course. Bakhtin fairly sharply distinguishes between the Socratic dialogue and the Platonic dialogue. Bakhtin argues that Socrates himself had a profound sense of the "dialogic nature of truth." He did not believe that truth is in the head of a single person, nor that there is a truth that, once discovered, can be possessed and handed on from teacher to student. Socrates called himself a pander and a midwife, because he allegedly brought people together and set up a "quarrel" between them, such that truth was born: "We emphasize that Socratic notions of the dialogic nature of truth lay at the folk-carnivalistic base of the genre of Socratic dialogue, determining its *form,* but they did not by any means always find expression in the actual content of the individual dialogues."[50] Bakhtin thus draws a distinction between the Socratic dialogue per se and the Platonic instantiation of the genre, a distinction that will serve me in different ways throughout this book. I would summarize the Bakhtinian position in my own language by suggesting that an oral folk genre (this is a problematic term in itself, of course) has been formalized and rendered a written form. To put it into terms that will be better understood later on in this book, Bakhtin argues that Plato took a polyphonic speech form, dialogue, and turned it into a monological written form, dialectic. At the same time, however, once again following Bakhtin, we see that the comic narrative framework of the dialogues *incorporates dialogically* the more carnivalistic dialogism of the older form itself; the form, and Bakhtin does not make this clear enough,

50. Bakhtin, *Problems of Dostoevsky's Poetics,* 110.

constitutes a dialogization of Plato's own monological impulse (willy-nilly? I think not; Plato was too wily for that).[51]

Plato, thus (according to this hypothesis), is at the bottom of (but is not necessarily the originator of) a mode of textual production that is manifested in the Bavli much more floridly and explicitly, one in which a highly serious, even momentous practice of dialectical reasoning, presented as dialogue (or better, pseudodialogue), is embedded in a comic framework that puts into question, at least seemingly, the seriousness of the content of the dialectic itself, but does not answer the question that it puts. That is to say, it interrogates but does not constitute a rejection, by any means, of the "seriousness" of the "serious." This reading of the Bavli as a comic narrative with dead-serious dialectic embedded within it may seem to some an unwarranted exaggeration. I grant this point, but I am, nevertheless, suggesting that we read the Bavli in this fashion in order to discover things about it otherwise hidden from sight. I would compare what I am doing here to one of those Gestalt perception exercises where you can see a rabbit or a chicken but not both at the same time, both switching our perception to see the seriocomic talmudic Gestalt and also switching back to see its d(r)ead seriousness also. Without that double move much is lost.

The represented dialogue itself in both Plato and the Talmud is anything but dialogical, incorporating rather all voices into one single consciousness, that of the "author." This conundrum is generated by the apparent (more than seeming, but of course not absolute) commitment of the "author," Plato or the *stamma* (the anonymous author-redactor(s) of the Talmud), to the seriousness of that dialectic itself. That is what these texts are about, convincing the reader of the rightness of their very undialogical view of the world. Why, then, would these "authors" (a textual function in both cases) seemingly put their own serious textual practices into such an apparently facetious con-

---

51. I have arrived at these conclusions independently and by different means from those of my colleague, Leslie Kurke, who in a brilliant essay, "Plato, Aesop, and the Beginnings of Mimetic Prose," *Representations* 94 (Spring 2006): 6–52, argued for the growth of Plato's mimetic prose specifically out of a reconstructed (from later sources) Aesopic tradition, Aesop being the very figure of a "low" author. Kurke's monograph, in press as I pursue my final revisions here, will, I reckon, considerably enhance the suggestions I have made here.

text? I can't, of course, speak for the "intentions" of textual effects, but I would propose that the effects of these effects can be read as a kind of second-order reflection on the epistemological bases of those highly serious practices. It is as if the militant (philosopher, halakhist) says to herself one morning (or constantly): "But what if I'm wrong." This incessant self-critical voice, a voice of dialogue, contests with the voice of militant commitment that is the dominant "accent" of the text, enabling a look into the abyss at the same time as the practices that prevent falling into the abyss (philosophy/Torah) are being avowed so passionately. This is the thesis that I put forth; the proof of the putting, as usual, will be in the reading.

2

"Confound Laughter with Seriousness":
The *Protagoras* as Monological Dialogue

One of the most startling moves in Plato is his constant insistence that dialogue is incompatible with, is the exact opposite of, rhetoric and debate. In order to understand Plato, then, some distinctions have to be drawn between related and often conflated terms, namely, "dialogue," "dialectic," and "rhetoric/debate."[1] "Dialogue" is the most complex of the terms, referring as it does to several different conceptual and discursive entities which themselves need to be distinguished in order for this investigation to be successful.

It is always good to commence with philology.[2] As shown recently by Edward Schiappa and David Timmerman, the verb *dialegesthai* and its related forms seem only to have meant to have a conversation until some time late in the fifth century BC.[3] Marking their suggestion as "speculative," they propose that at about that time or slightly later, the term began to take on

---

1. Richard McKeon, "Greek Dialectics: Dialectic and Dialogue, Dialectic and Rhetoric," in *Dialectics*, ed. Chaïm Perelman (The Hague: Nijhoff, 1975), 1–25.

2. For all of this section I am grateful for the aid and comfort of Edward Schiappa both in his written work and especially in e-mail conversations in the summer of 2008.

3. Edward Schiappa and David M. Timmerman, "*Dialegesthai* as a Term of Art: Plato and the Disciplining of Dialectic," in *The Disciplining of Discourse: Terms of*

a more specialized meaning as a term of art among the group of intellectuals who were only later dubbed Sophists, including Protagoras,
Hippias, and Socrates. Plato is one of their major sources. As they
remark, "Eventually Protagoras is shamed into participating in 'the
dialogue' (*to dialegesthai*) and asked to have questions put to him as he
was ready to answer (348c). The passage is significant because the use
of the articular infinitive form (*to dialegesthai*) is the sort of lexical construction that can facilitate the refinement of a term of art. Though
anyone can converse, not just anyone can participate in a competitive, rule-governed Dialogue. As *to dialegesthai*, 'Dialogue' has become
a substantive capable of new sorts of conceptualization and description (cf. Snell 1953, ch. 10)."[4] Appropriately concerned that perhaps
Plato is a less-than-reliable witness for philological events that took
place before he was born, Schiappa and Timmerman support this conclusion with analysis of citations from Aristophanes, the *Dissoi logoi*
(c. 400 BC), and Xenophon as well. It is Plato himself, however, who
transforms sophistic *dialegesthai* into the full and specific *terminus
technicus, dialektikē tekhnē:*

> Plato redescribes *dialegesthai* in such a way as to claim it as a legitimate
> philosophical practice and distance it from "sophistic" practices he
> names eristic and antilogic. Second, by emphasizing the skill or art as
> sociated with dialogue, Plato is able to "locate" that skill, so to speak,
> within the properly trained person, the dialectician. Third, by disci
> plining the practice of *dialegesthai* into an increasingly rule-governed
> event (*to dialegesthai*) in which the dialectician participates, he is able
> to transform the sophistic practice of dialogue into an Art—*hē dialek
> tikē technē.*

Plato's dialogues (that is, the dialogical part of Plato's dialogues)
are not at all dialogical, if "dialogical" may be understood as conversations with different voices and languages represented by the
different speakers. They are rather examples of *hē dialektikē tekhnē,*
which Bakhtin has realized is a far cry from dialogue: "Dialogue and

---

Art in Rhetorical Theory in Classical Greece (Cambridge: Cambridge University Press,
forthcoming).

4. Schiappa and Timmerman, "*Dialegesthai.*"

dialectics. Take a dialogue and remove the voices... remove the intonations... carve out abstract concepts and judgments from living words and responses, cram everything into one abstract consciousness—and that's how you get dialectics."[5] To put it in Schiappa's terms, if Plato's *to dialegesthai* is "competitive rule-governed Dialogue," it is, I warrant, entirely nondialogical, even antidialogical.

Andrew Ford has made this point well: "There is also something ahistorical in the tendency of such analyses to contrast dialogue with allegedly more dogmatic forms of exposition dear to Sophists: treatises are doubtlessly less polyvocal than dialogues, but no one was publishing lectures at this time (Aristotle, for example, 'published' his dialogues and kept his lecture notes in his school), and the literature of 'treatises' was likely to be far more limited than philosophers imagine; as for epideixis, we will see that dialogue was hardly averse to incorporating epideictic passages."[6] I concur entirely with the main point of this sentence, namely that the notion that Plato's dialogues are non-dogmatic and somehow polyvocal is ahistorical (not to mention downright apologetic). I demur, however, from his statement that "treatises are doubtlessly less polyvocal than dialogues." Indeed, it is exactly the point of this book to challenge this view. The Platonic dialogue is all the more monological insofar as it is *to dialegesthai* or *hē dialektikē*.

"Socrates" himself alludes precisely to the depersonalization and dedialogization of dialectic in the *Symposium,* when Agathon abandons his claim:

"I cannot refute you, Socrates," said Agathon:—"Let us assume that what you say is true." "Say rather, beloved Agathon, that you cannot refute the truth; for Socrates is easily refuted."

The transmutation of dialogue into dialectic that takes place even in the most Socratic of Platonic dialogues is part of the project of Plato's displacement of what he has named *rhētorikē* by what he calls

5. Mikhail Bakhtin, *Problems of Dostoevsky's Poetics,* ed. and trans. Caryl Emerson, Theory and History of Literature (Minneapolis: University of Minnesota Press, 1984), xxxii, citing Bakhtin's Jottings of 1971.

6. Andrew Ford, "The Beginnings of Dialogue: Socratic Discourses and Fourth-Century Prose," in *The End of Ancient Dialogue,* ed. Simon Goldhill (Cambridge: Cambridge University Press, 2008), 33.

philosophia, the displacement, that is, of valid sides of a debate with absolute truth and falsity.

Andrea Nightingale has been a central figure in studying Plato's academic politics: "In order to create the specialized discipline of philosophy, Plato had to distinguish what he was doing from all other discursive practices that laid claim to wisdom. It is for this reason that, in dialogue after dialogue, Plato deliberately set out to define and defend a new and quite peculiar mode of living and of thinking. This alone, he claimed, deserved the title of 'philosophy.' It should be emphasized that gestures of opposition and exclusion play a crucial role in Plato's many attempts to mark the boundaries of 'philosophy.' Indeed, it is precisely by designating certain modes of discourse and spheres of activity as 'anti-philosophical' that Plato was able to create a separate identity for 'philosophy.'"[7] His main antecedent in this project seems to be Parmenides. Looking at Parmenides and at his encounter with his (and Plato's) bête noir, the great Sophist Gorgias, will help us articulate what was at stake for Plato in his unrelenting attack on rhetoric and debate, as opposed to dialogue/dialectic. It has to do with the very notion of knowledge (*epistēmē*) which it was Plato's work to promulgate.

For Parmenides, knowledge is defined as that for which no persuasion is needed, at all. "The truth is that which once perceived cannot be denied." Gorgias seriously (if not solemnly) opposed this epistemology; for him, as for Protagoras, truth, falsehood, wisdom are always context-bound and always bound inextricably with compulsion and discourse. Perhaps as opposed to Socrates himself, it seems that for Plato—the intellectual descendent of Parmenides—the search for this kind of Parmenidean knowledge, for that kind of truth, is the only worthy intellectual enterprise. Anything short of this he would call "sophistry." The handmaiden of sophistry is rhetoric, just as the handmaiden of philosophy is dialectic. Prior to this Platonic intervention, such thinkers as Gorgias and Protagoras did not see themselves as inhabiting a different disciplinary space than that of Heraclitus and Parmenides, although they did have very different positions on fundamental questions of epistemology and language theory from

---

7. Andrea Wilson Nightingale, *Genres in Dialogue: Plato and the Construct of Philosophy* (Cambridge: Cambridge University Press, 1995), 10–11.

the latter. Plato, in order to construct the absolute hegemony of his own philosophical program, needed to create an opposition between what he did and what they did. The name *philosophia,* obviously, is reserved for his particular doctrinal formation and practices; the names *rhētorikē* and *Sophismos* are assigned to his opponents.

Both *dialektikē* and *rhētorikē* are Platonic coinages, to mark through this newly minted binary opposition the equally newly minted opposition between his own practice, philosophy, and that of others, sophistry.[8] As Richard Robinson remarks, "The more detailed connotation of 'eristic' and 'antilogic' tends to be whatever Plato happens to think of as bad method at the moment, just as 'dialectic' is to him at every stage of his thought whatever he then considered the best method."[9] Accepting this point, Schiappa and Timmerman have, however, recently shown that Plato most often uses *dialegesthai* to refer to Socrates' special art and distinguish it from the arts—which he even denies as such—of the Sophists.[10] It is accordingly that term which is the marker of good method for Plato and thus coterminous with *philosophia* throughout antiquity. Dialectic (or even *dialegesthai*) becomes simply a nickname for philosophy in later Greek usage, as we shall see in reading Lucian presently. Richard McKeon puts it, "[Dialectic] is, finally, the only science that does away with hypotheses, in order to establish principles in eternal forms and transcendental ideas."[11] Plato's project in establishing this unique science is a twofold one: discrediting the teachers known as Sophists and rescuing his own teacher, Socrates of course, from that category.

This is not the place to actually work out even the artificial distinctions that Plato makes between good Socratic practice, *dialegesthai,* and bad sophistic practice, but the distinction between dialectic and debate is crucial for this inquiry. Erik Krabbe has introduced us to one of the most important distinctions between the two, explaining that each situation involves different forms of participation and spectatorship:

8. Edward Schiappa, "Did Plato Coin *Rhētorikē*?," *American Journal of Philology* III (1990): 457–70; Schiappa and Timmerman, "*Dialegesthai.*"
9. Richard Robinson, *Plato's Earlier Dialectic* (Oxford: Clarendon Press, 1953), 85.
10. Schiappa and Timmerman, "*Dialegesthai.*"
11. McKeon, "Greek Dialectics," 4.

In the practice of dialectic one deals with two participants, or adversaries: the Questioner and the Answerer, and perhaps with a limited company of bystanders. Typically, both participants as well as the bystanders belong to some company of discussants, where a company of discussants may be defined as a group of people who explicitly or implicitly accept a common dialogical procedure, a profile of rationality. Typically the members of a company are on equal footing in that each of them in turn could act as a Questioner or an Answerer. When bystanders from outside the company become an influence, the dialogue shifts towards a debate, and hence to a more rhetorical situation, where the bystanders constitute an audience. In the fully rhetorical situation, there is a heterogeneous crowd listening to a speech. Even though the rhetor and his audience must, of course, still share some rules of communication, the idea of belonging to one company may be lost.[12]

The difference, then, between dialogue (in the Platonic sense) and debate involves the basic speech situation: in dialogue, in this meaning, there are only two participants and any judgment of success or failure will be made only by these two, while in debate third parties are the arbiters and judges of success and failure. It will be seen from this that only the latter is appropriate for democratic discourse, while the former excludes it ipso facto. Krabbe makes a highly significant point here, one that will carry through the entire discussion in this book, including especially its talmudic parts. Dialectic and hence monologism is the very practice of a two-person question/answer structure in which the two persons are part of a closed system that effectively brooks no challenge from another "profile of rationality." It is precisely the "profile of rationality," accepted by all in the dialogical situation which constitutes its monologism, for, as we know, such profiles of rationality are themselves historically and culturally shifting regimes.

Plato's dialogues are—at least on first reading—what Bakhtin has called "monological dialogue," but not, as I will begin to show in chapter 3, only that.[13] The very relationship between speakers in the

12. Erik C. W. Krabbe, "Meeting in the House of Callias: Rhetoric and Dialectic," *Argumentation* 14, no. 3 (2000): 210.

13. As Bakhtin writes: "The idealism of Plato is not purely monologic. It becomes purely monologic only in a neo-Kantian interpretation. Nor is Platonic dialogue of the

dialogue is precisely that of an un/official monologism. My argument is not that Plato's monologism involves a particular set of truths but rather it is a monologism of Truth itself, of the nature of truth and of the procedure for discovery of that alone which Plato is willing to call Truth, whether successfully discovered or not.[14] For Plato, as for Parmenides, "Knowledge is immovable by persuasion, while true belief can be changed by persuasion" (*Ti.* 51e4).

Dialogue and Dialogicality

It is thus highly important to distinguish between dialogue as a literary form and dialogicality as the mode of a text. Various texts are presented in their literary form as dialogues, from the dialogues of Plato, through the Bavli, and into the novel (to provide a very incomplete and idiosyncratic list), but the text of represented dialogue is not necessarily (and frequently simply is not) a dialogical text. In his book on Dostoevsky, Bakhtin presents the novel, especially the Dostoevskian novel (but as Bakhtin explains at length, this has ancient predecessors as well), as the very model of a dialogical text. As we can see from the following quotation, the dialogue is *not* primarily to be found in the represented dialogues in the novel:

> The essential dialogicality of Dostoevsky is in no way exhausted by the external, compositionally expressed dialogues carried on by the characters. *The polyphonic novel is dialogic through and through.* Dialogic relationships exist among all elements of novelistic structure; that is,

---

pedagogical type, although there is a strong element of monologism in it"; Bakhtin, *Problems of Dostoevsky's Poetics,* 100n1.

14. In this my approach is quite like that of Charles H. Kahn, *Plato and the Socratic Dialogue: The Philosophical Use of a Literary Form* (Cambridge: Cambridge University Press, 1996), xiii: "For Plato is the only major philosopher who is also a supreme literary artist. There is no writer more complex, and there is no other philosopher whose work calls for so many levels of interpretation. Plato was the first author to offer a systematic definition of the goals and methods of philosophy. But he was also a social reformer and an educator, whose conception of philosophy entailed a radical transformation of the moral and intellectual culture of his own time and place. Much of his writing is designed to serve this larger cause." I too think that the major force of Plato's writing is protreptic for a new social practice, although I think our evaluation of this project is quite different. Where he sees successful pedagogy, I discern a much more tricky sort of manipulation, but more of this below.

they are juxtaposed contrapuntally. And this is so because dialogic relationships are a much broader phenomenon than mere rejoinders in a dialogue, laid out compositionally in the text; they are an almost universal phenomenon, permeating all human speech, and all relationships and manifestations of human life—in general, everything that has meaning and significance.[15]

Bakhtin goes even further: not only is dialogism not exhausted by the dialogue in the text, but frequently the represented dialogue is the least dialogical moment in the text.[16] This is owing, as Bakhtin teaches us in another place, to the fact that in represented dialogue, the dialogue is an object. Among Bakhtin's achievements is the articulation of the notion of the monologic dialogue, that is, the represented dialogue in a text that, when analyzed, can be shown to encode in any case only the point of view of the "author." Alien languages are not allowed to enter the language of the author, which remains (at least at these moments) monologically in control of the objects of representation. The dialogue "appears, in essence, as a *thing*, it does not lie on the *same* plane with the real language of the work: it is the depicted gesture of one of the characters and does not appear as an aspect of the word doing the depicting."[17] Julia Jarcho has captured this well with respect to Plato:

15. Bakhtin, *Problems of Dostoevsky's Poetics,* 40.

16. As Bakhtin points out, this point has been made *in nuce* by Viktor Shklovsky as well: "It is not only the heroes who quarrel in Dostoevsky, but separate elements in the development of the plot seem to contradict one another: facts are decoded in different ways, the psychology of the characters is self-contradictory; the form is the result of the essence." Cited Bakhtin, *Problems of Dostoevsky's Poetics,* 40.

17. Both quotations from Mikhail Bakhtin, *The Dialogic Imagination: Four Essays by Mikhail Bakhtin,* ed. Michael Holquist; trans. Michael Holquist and Caryl Emerson, University of Texas Press Slavic Series (Austin: University of Texas Press, 1981), 287. Such dialogism as will be produced by the language used by characters, and their own quarrels will be between these languages and the language of the author, not between the languages of the characters, whose explicit disagreements are all within the language of the author as a represented thing and not as language-use by the characters. "The area occupied by an important character's voice must in any event be broader than his direct and 'actual' words. This zone surrounding the important characters of the novel is stylistically profoundly idiosyncratic: the most varied hybrid constructions hold sway in it, and it is always, to one degree or another, dialogized; *inside this area a dialogue is played out between the author and his characters—not a dramatic dialogue broken up into statement-and-response, but that special type of novelistic dialogue that realizes itself within the boundaries of constructions that externally resemble monologues*" (320, emphasis added). Note again that Bakhtin hardly ever comprehends

Melancholy, as internalized intercourse with a lost object, leaves traces throughout the *Apology*. We see it in Socrates' characterization of how he will deal with the old accusers: "I cannot even have them called forward for cross-examination. My defense will have to be a kind of shadowboxing, with me cross-examining and no one responding. . . . What have my slanderers said about me? I shall read it to you as though it were a sworn indictment: 'Socrates is guilty . . .'" (18d–19b). This "shadowboxing" could be a figure for Plato's dialogical writing itself, wherein the other is only ever a manifestation of the same (this accounts for the feeling of a "fixed fight" that the dialogues often give). The dialogue is predicated on "no one responding"—from outside. Opposition to Socrates, in the form of the interlocutor, is always summoned from *within* Plato's writing. From the point of view of Plato's composition, Socrates' voicing on his enemies' behalf the claim that "Socrates is guilty" is only this same principle brought into the open. On Socrates' own "plane," however, this situation constitutes a point of crisis.[18]

Bakhtin's perception of the double plane of the language of the text enables distinctions that are unavailable without such depth of field. Bakhtin has explained eloquently the logical relation between represented dialogue and monologism, writing that "in the characters, individuality kills the signifying power of their ideas, or, if these ideas retain their power to mean, then they are detached from the individuality of the character and are merged with that of the author. Hence the *single ideational accent of the work;* the appearance of a second accent would inevitably be perceived as a crude contradiction within the author's world view."[19] A dialogue represented in an au-

---

dialogue between characters as dialogism, but insofar as they are the represented language of others, they are in dialogism in artistic prose with the language of the author. There are not separate consciousnesses produced for the different characters, but a dialogism within the consciousness of the author is. In this sense, the language of characters has the same stylistic status as the voice of a narrator or of cited genres—letters, diaries, travel notes, etc.—within the novel. At the same time, Bakhtin remarks a kind of continuum in which different novelists may use "languages introduced into a novel" either in a way that refracts intentions of the author or in a way that treats them entirely as objects, "not as a word that has been spoken, but as a word to be displayed, like a thing" (321).

18. Julia Jarcho, "The Birth of Death: A Reading of Plato's *Apology*" (typescript, Department of Rhetoric, University of California, Berkeley, 2007).

19. Bakhtin, *Problems of Dostoevsky's Poetics,* 82.

thor's work can be seen, thus, to be a monological dialogue, a dialogue in which all the speakers add up to the author's "single ideational accent."[20] Plato's dialogues (that is the dialogues within the dialogues) are in some ways, I will propose, a textbook illustration of monological dialogue.

The opposition between rhetoric and dialogue provides one of the fundamental explanatory bases of Western thought. Rhetoric, in the form of the democratic debate in the Assembly, is figured by Plato as the antithesis of dialogue. In Platonic dialogues the speaker is constrained only to answer questions or to ask them. Harold Barrett takes us further along the road to an elaboration and refinement of an explanation for this Platonic preoccupation. As Barrett argues, the difference is that in the rhetorical debate the two sides are presented with a certain equality of opportunity, and it is up to another group, the Assembly or the jury, to render a decision of what is right or wrong in the case, while the dialogue allows for the decision, as it were, to be entirely internal to the discussants: "No other agency is needed, as Plato would structure the process. . . . Fundamental to the points of difference, then, are two profoundly conflicting mentalities: democratic and authoritarian—one needing and trusting popular will and the other denying it. . . . The Platonic-Socratic way demands obedience to form and leadership."[21] Plato's "dialogue"—conflated with dialectic—is almost as far from a Bakhtinian notion of a dialogical text as can be imagined. It comes closest, within Bakhtin's typologies, to authoritative discourse, as I shall hope to show.[22]

This argument, I believe, leads defensibly to the conclusion that it is precisely the "authoritative" nature of dialogue, as opposed to the democracy of rhetoric, that renders it so appealing for Plato. These are politics that are founded on epistemology. As Cynthia Farrar puts it, "In a democracy, and indeed in response to democracy, epistemology and political ethics coincide."[23]

20. This is not, of course, always the case according to Bakhtin. See, for instance, Bakhtin, *The Dialogic Imagination,* 333, where conditions for a character's speech to introduce heteroglossia are laid out.

21. Harold Barrett, *The Sophists: Rhetoric, Democracy, and Plato's Idea of Sophistry* (Novato, Calif.: Chandler & Sharp, 1987), 60–62.

22. Bakhtin, *The Dialogic Imagination,* 344.

23. Cynthia Farrar, *The Origins of Democratic Thinking: The Invention of Politics in Classical Athens* (Cambridge: Cambridge University Press, 1987), 76.

Protagoras, Epistemology, Political Ethics

One of the most compelling of recent treatments of (the "real") Protagoras is that of Cynthia Farrar.[24] She contributes one of the clearest statements of fundamental difference between Parmenides and hence Plato, on the one hand, and Protagoras (and Gorgias) on the other: "Plato's language also suggests that there is no question of the perceiving subject becoming wiser; for Plato, becoming wise means moving from absolutely false judgments to absolutely true ones. Protagoras' vision of wisdom, by contrast, is continuous with (though not identical to) the process of becoming a measure [that is, become wiser and wiser incrementally through experience and teaching]."[25] Wisdom is, after all, for Plato the very opposite of folly (*Protag.* 332a), and the middle is forever excluded. Although I will discuss below the interpretation of a human becoming a measure, there is enough here already to perceive what different political directions a Protagoras will take from a Plato. If, as for Plato, we deal only in coin that is absolutely counterfeit or absolutely genuine and only certain special people can learn to tell the difference, then the way to a Kingdom of Philosophers is clearly paved. For Protagoras, alternately, it is surely the province of the democratic educator to help individuals to become more effective interpreters of their own experience (to become measures), in order to provide better analyses of situations and decision making. It is most relevant and important to cite Farrar's own (proleptic) conclusion: "To anticipate: what Plato seeks to represent here [in the *Protagoras*] and in the *Theaetetus* as an incoherent conflation of claims about competence and excellence [on the part of Protagoras] is in fact a coherent account of the existence and function of both levels of ability and the relationship between them."[26] The question of competence and excellence was a crucial aspect of thinking about democracy already in the fifth century, as we learn from Thucydides.[27] Both Pericles in his Funeral Oration and Diodotus in the Mytilenian Debate insist that the populace are capable of hearing persuasive ar-

24. Farrar, *Origins,* 77.
25. Farrar, *Origins,* 72.
26. Farrar, *Origins,* 81.
27. I hope to expand on this discussion of Protagoras and Thucydides in another place, *Deo volente.*

guments by men of excellence and deciding which of them is more persuasive, based on their own experience. This assumption is the very cornerstone of the democracy, and Protagoras's assertion (as read convincingly by Farrar) that experience can be educated, not to produce absolute truth but to improve judgment, becomes the very foundation of a democratic educational regime. Plato's insistence on absolute Truth or absolute falsity renders this regime mere chicanery. As we look at Plato's own work, we will find this theme of the conflict of fundamental notions of what knowledge is thematized over and over again and, more than once, where we least expect it.

Plato and Aristotle systematically—wittingly or unwittingly—distorted the thought of Protagoras by reading him through the lenses of their own epistemologies (mutatis mutandis), and, as pointed out by Farrar more than once, we need to work hard ourselves to take those lenses off our own eyes. A classic and scandalous example is Aristotle's treatment of the sophistic topos "making the weaker cause the stronger." Invented by Protagoras, "making the weaker cause the stronger" has generally been interpreted as making the worse decision or course of action seem the better for reasons of gain or other cynical motive. So fraught with the fraudulent had this term become that it is Aristophanes' charge against Socrates in *The Clouds* (and, of course, in that play Socrates is himself a Sophist par excellence). There is also more than a hint of a suggestion that this charge, derived from Aristophanes, was a major cause of the execution of Socrates some two decades after the production of the play (*Apology* 18b).[28]

According to Aristotle this topos is almost a synecdoche of the entire rhetorical/sophistic enterprise:

> The *Art* of Corax is made up of this topic; for example, if a weak man were charged with assault, he should be acquitted as not being a likely suspect for the charge; for it is not probable [that a weak man would attack another]. And if he is a likely suspect, for example, if he is strong, [he should also be acquitted]; for it is not likely [that he would start the fight] for the very reason that it was going to seem probable.

28. See comment in William Arrowsmith, "Introduction to 'The Clouds' by Aristophanes," trans. and introduction by William Arrowsmith, in *Four Plays by Aristophanes* (New York: Meridian, 1994), 17–18.

And similarly in other cases; for necessarily, a person is either a likely suspect or not a likely suspect for a charge. Both alternatives seem probable, but one really is probable, the other so not generally, only in the circumstances mentioned. And this is to "make the weaker seem the better cause." Thus, people were rightly angry at the declaration of Protagoras; for it is a lie and not true but a fallacious probability and a part of no art except rhetoric and eristic. (1402a)[29]

It is worthwhile, I think, to spend a little time glossing this passage, for through it we can arrive, against Aristotle's grain, at a more sympathetic reading of the topos. For Aristotle, at least in this passage, as for philosophical (and authoritarian) thinkers before him, rendering the weaker the stronger is only a matter of lying. Different as he is in important respects from his teacher Plato, with regard to the fundamental question of absolute truth, Aristotle's epistemology is in the same tradition as that of Parmenides and Plato, one in which truth and falsehood are absolute binary opposites. For Aristotle it seems that we can know in advance which is the "better" cause; the Sophist/rhetor himself knows that too. As he writes, "The true and the just are by nature stronger than their opposites" (*Rhetoric* 1355a15). It would follow, therefore, that the activity of rhetors (as synecdochized by Corax) consists merely of slyly overturning the truth with a lie, making the weaker cause *seem* the better.[30] It is this understanding of sophistical rhetoric that motivates philosophical disdain for sophism from Plato to the present.

There is, however, a bit of an interpretative puzzle in Aristotle's statement. In the beginning of it, he discusses a certain topos or enthymeme, allegedly invented by Corax, and names it "making the weaker cause the better." Then, however, he speaks of the people as being rightly angry at the declaration of Protagoras, an apparent reference to an incident that later (in Diogenes Laertius) is narrated as a deportation of Protagoras that resulted in his death. However, it seems highly unlikely that it is the making of the weaker cause the

---

29. George A. Kennedy, trans., *On Rhetoric: A Theory of Civic Discourse by Aristotle* (New York: Oxford University Press, 1991), 210.

30. Cf. discussion of epistemological confidence in Mark Douglas Given, *Paul's True Rhetoric: Ambiguity, Cunning, and Deception in Greece and Rome,* Emory Studies in Early Christianity (Harrisburg, Pa: Trinity Press International, 2001), 34.

better that caused the Athenian ire, for that is no declaration (τὸ Πρωταγόρου ἐπάγγελμα) but a practice, and moreover, seemingly attributed by Aristotle to Corax and not Protagoras. It seems that Aristotle refers then to another declaration of Protagoras that is associated with the practice of making the weaker cause the stronger.

As George Kennedy points out, there are two candidates for the *declaration* of Protagoras that might have aroused the ire of the Athenian demos.[31] Not choosing between them, but reading both of them together as pieces of a certain *theoretical* whole will further my investigation here. The first is the (in)famous utterance at the opening sentence of Protagoras's lost treatise, *On the Gods,* as reported by Diogenes Laertius and a host of ancient witnesses (Plato being the earliest but only affording a partial quotation or even allusion [*Theaetetus* 162d]). The fullest version of the statement as extant in Diogenes reads: "Concerning the gods I cannot know either that they exist or that they do not exist, or what form they might have, for there is much to prevent one's knowing: the obscurity of the subject[32] and the shortness of man's life."[33] According to Diogenes (and Philostratus),[34] it was owing precisely to this statement that Protagoras was exiled from Athens.[35] Edward Schiappa shows, however, that there is very little reason to credit this story, and, moreover, following Werner Jaeger, demonstrates that this fragment is not a statement of agnosticism—or worse, atheism—as it is frequently taken to be, but rather a statement of a human-centered (or anthropological) origin for order, denying only that theology provides knowledge useful for deciding philosophical and political matters.[36] To cite Farrar: "As the

31. Kennedy, *On Rhetoric,* 210n254.

32. On this phrase, Schiappa writes: "What Protagoras had in mind as 'the obscurity of the subject' is difficult to say. *Adêlotês,* translated above as 'obscurity,' can also imply uncertainty, to be in the dark about, or not evident to sense. One can imagine a number of reasons why the gods are a 'subject' too obscure to reason about confidently." Edward Schiappa, *Protagoras and Logos: A Study in Greek Philosophy and Rhetoric* (Columbia: University of South Carolina Press, 1991), 143.

33. Hermann Diels and Rosamond Kent Sprague, *The Older Sophists,* ed. Rosamond Kent Sprague (Columbia: University of South Carolina Press, 1972), 20. On this last phrase, Schiappa has compared Empedocles' claim that life is too short to acquire knowledge of 'the whole.' Schiappa, *Protagoras,* 143.

34. Diels and Sprague, *Older Sophists,* 6.

35. Diels and Sprague, *Older Sophists,* 4.

36. Schiappa, *Protagoras,* 144–48.

conception of order and autonomy shifted from acquiescence in divine determinations to active participation in an order mediated even in its divine aspect by civic institutions, tyrants and irresponsible aristocracies were replaced by the communal law-governed interaction of elite and *demos* characteristic of the developed *polis,* particularly in its democratic form. These two transformations were matched by a third, in the realm of cosmology, which gradually leached divinity from the cosmos."[37] It is not, then, that Protagoras was an atheist, far from it as far as we can know, but that he insisted on a political process that was based on what the eye could see, the hand could touch, and the ear could hear.

This brings us neatly to the next prospect for a Protagorean statement that might have been what really made the Athenians angry according to Aristotle, namely Protagoras's notorious "the human is the measure" fragment: "Of all things, the human is the measure; of that which is, that it is, and of that which is not, that it is not" (καὶ ὁ Π. δὲ βούλεται πάντων χρημάτων εἶναι μέτρον τὸν ἄνθρωπον τῶν μὲν ὄντων ὡς ἔστιν, τῶν δὲ οὐκ ὄντων ὡς οὐκ ἔστιν).[38] Although this is not the place to go into the myriad philological and philosophical issues involved in the interpretation of this passage, what is crucial for my argument here is to note the close relation between the denial of human knowledge of gods and the insistence that actual human perception and experience is the only criterion that there is. What is finally to the point (and to my point) is Jaap Mansfield's insight that "as soon as an important thinker says that the notion of 'gods' is epistemologically irrelevant as far as he is concerned, this cannot but have far-reaching consequences for his notion of 'man.'"[39] As Mansfield makes clear, the proposition is epistemological, not ontological. The "is" here is veridical and not existential: human experience is the measurer of that which is the case, that it is the case, and of that which is not the case, that it is not the case. If we take the two statements together (which they seem rarely to be), we can see an episte-

37. Farrar, *Origins,* 38.

38. Hermann Diels and Walther Kranz, *Die Fragmente der Vorsokratiker, Griechisch und Deutsch* (Zürich: Weidmann, 1966), 258, in Sextus's formulation. Once again, we have an earlier Platonic citation of the principle as well.

39. Jaap Mansfield, "Protagoras on Epistemological Obstacles and Persons," in *The Sophists and Their Legacy,* ed. G. B. Kerferd (Wiesbaden: Franz Steiner Verlag, 1981), 43.

mological theory begin to emerge at least inchoately. Since the gods
are epistemologically irrelevant (i.e., there may very well be gods, but
we don't know anything about them),[40] therefore there is no criterion
by which judgments can be made other than human experience.[41] In
other words, as Farrar emphasizes, far from making an ontological
statement (as Plato construes it), Protagoras is claiming only that the
sole basis for human knowledge is human experience and perception,
and, as a result, there may be, indeed there necessarily are, different
and even directly opposing opinions about things. It is not, then,
that there really are different universes, but rather that there is no
universe that can be known in any way other than through human
measurings. As Farrar points out, exactly what disturbs Protagoras
about Parmenides is the latter's dismissal of human beliefs and experiences, that which, according to Protagoras, it is precisely the task
of thinking and teaching to account for and ameliorate.[42] As she has
so well put it, "He [Protagoras] can argue that the beliefs of others
are defective; he appeals to what they can and do know, what they
have experienced or are capable of experiencing, and invites them to
criticize their own beliefs."[43]

In other words, not only is the major focus of each of Protagoras's
two most famous "declarations" entirely epistemological, not ontological, as Plato had misread them, but they also move in the direction
of an indeterminacy principle. It follows that in any given forensic
contest or in any given metaphysical inquiry, since we know nothing
of the gods *and* since human experience is the measure of truth, there
can be no determination of absolute truth through logic alone. Com-
bining our analyses of these two famous Protagorean utterances, we
can easily understand why "[Protagoras] was the first to say that on every issue there are two arguments opposed to each other" (Καὶ πρῶτος
ἔφη δύο λόγους εἶναι περὶ παντὸς πράγματος ἀντικειμένους ἀλλήλοις

40. When this is combined with Protagoras's evident continued practice of worship
of the gods and other observances, one might dream up an early version of Pascal's wager,
but a highly sophisticated one.

41. On perception as knowledge and its relation to the Protagorean dictum according
to Plato, see *Theaetetus* 152a–160d. Incidentally, it might be noted that, as shown by Farrar,
this account of Pythagoras's epistemology seems to reduce the force of Plato's objections
to it considerably (*Theaetetus* 160a–163a).

42. Farrar, *Origins*, 46.

43. Farrar, *Origins*, 51–52.

[DL 9.51]).[44] As a recent critical legal scholar, Michael Dzialo, has defined it, this comes startlingly close to the modern doctrine of legal indeterminacy: "Legal doctrine can never determine a legal outcome because every argument in favor of a particular outcome can be met with an equally valid counterargument."[45]

Now, however, we must return to Aristotle, for according to the passage, there is a direct entailment between these snippets of Protagoras's epistemology and the practice of the so-called Sophists of making the weaker cause the stronger. What is that entailment? Reading directly against the grain of Aristotle's text, I would answer this question in a way that credits the sophistic practices. In any given situation, one side or the other may appear stronger at the outset. Rather than glossing the weaker and stronger argument phrase as Aristotle does, then, as making the weaker cause *appear* the stronger, one could easily gloss it as making the *apparently* weaker cause the stronger.[46]

An excellent example of this practice would be, then, Gorgias's defense of Helen, which, "by introducing some reasoning into the debate" (λογισμόν τινα τῷ λόγῳ δοὺς) overturns the "single-voiced, sin-

---

44. Diels and Kranz, *Die Fragmente,* 2.266; Diels and Sprague, *Older Sophists,* 21 (for English). Schiappa discusses at length difficulties with this translation (a traditional one, to be sure) in that it reduces "all sophistic teaching to rhetoric" (Schiappa, *Protagoras,* 90), by which he means rhetoric in its least elevated acceptation (or as Kennedy would have it as sort of a founding charter for debating societies, that is, simply, it is possible to organize a debate on any topic). I cannot make short work of Schiappa's compelling discussion but suffice it to say that by the end Protagoras's statement makes a profound philosophical point (Schiappa, *Protagoras,* 91–100), in which again we find Protagoras on the side of Heraclitus against Parmenides (Schiappa, *Protagoras,* 92). This is a discussion for another venue, however, and I hope to come back to it in a forthcoming essay on Protagoras and Thucydides.

45. Michael G. Dzialo, "Legal and Philosophical Fictions: At the Line Where the Two Become One," *Argumentation* 12 (1998): 217. There is surely a certain hyperbolic element in this statement which is similar, in this respect, to Protagoras's own declaration that for every matter there are two *logoi* which contradict each other.

46. I thus directly disagree with John Poulakos, who writes, "Thus the familiar depiction of the Sophists as teachers of poeticized prose and performative skill seems warranted. Indeed, they did not claim that the weaker argument *is* the stronger argument; only that they could make the weaker argument *appear* stronger. That they should have done so is not a sign of questionable designs on unsuspecting audiences, but a mark of the well-defined motivation to deceive—a motivation tied to the pleasure of speaking," John Poulakos, *Sophistical Rhetoric in Classical Greece,* Studies in Rhetoric/Communication (Columbia: University of South Carolina Press, 1995), 45. Supporting my view, Farrar, *Origins,* 63.

gle-minded conviction that has arisen about this woman." This, then, ascribes great ethical and political force to the Protagorean practice and training, for it involves the systematic critical overturning of what appears to people to be the truth, not, however as in Platonic terms, where the real truth, the "really real," *epistēmē* (knowledge, the Truth), will be revealed, but rather in the interest of an educated *doxa,* of an educated decision regarding probability within a particular situation. As Johan Vos has shown, the practice "says nothing about the true or intrinsic values of the arguments. An argument can be weaker simply because the majority do not accept it or because the opponent has better argumentative skills."[47] Following this reasoning, there is no reason to suppose that the "weaker cause" is the ethically, theologically, or politically less worthy one; in a situation of epistemological uncertainty the weaker cause, for instance, of the liberation of the poor might very well demand rhetoric to make it the stronger one. Rhetoric, like any other practice of speech, is as good, as ethical, as the person who mobilizes it and her causes, no better or worse.[48] Clearly a case can be made for reading Protagoras's theory and his practice as an invitation to change the weaker cause and render it the stronger.[49] On this reading, the interpretation from Aristophanes forward, that sophism consists of making the ethically worse or philosophically weaker argument defeat the better one through fancy rhetoric and fallacies, is nothing but a parodic slander on the genuine practice of the Sophists.

Plato's opposition to the Sophists is also philosophical (in the expanded sense of the word, whereby that which Plato calls "philosophy" and that which he calls "rhetoric" are both comprehended). Thus George Kerferd writes that Plato takes issue with the Sophists on only one fundamental point, "their failure to understand that the flux of phenomena is not the end of the story—one must look elsewhere for the truth which is the object of the true knowledge, and

47. Johan S. Vos, "'To Make the Weaker Argument Defeat the Stronger': Sophistical Argumentation in Paul's Letter to the Romans," in *Rhetorical Argumentation in Biblical Texts,* ed. Anders Eriksson, Thomas H. Olbricht, and Walter Übelacker (Harrisburg, Pa.: Trinity Press International, 2002), 217–18.

48. As Simon Goldhill points out to me, however, for Quintillian *only* the *vir bonus* could be a truly successful orator.

49. John Poulakos, "Rhetoric, the Sophists, and the Possible," *Communications Monographs* 51 (1984): 215–25.

even for the understanding of the flux and its causes we have to go to more permanent, secure and reliable entities, the famous Platonic forms. . . . Indeed, when elsewhere Plato suggests, as he does repeatedly, that the Sophists were not concerned with the truth, we may begin to suppose that this was because they were not concerned with what *he* regarded as the truth, rather than because they were not concerned with the truth as *they* saw it. For Plato, though he does not like to say so, antilogic is the first step on the path that leads to dialectic."[50] Both Gorgias and Protagoras insist that it is precisely the human experience of change that has to be accounted for theoretically, while Parmenides/Plato insist that this experience is mere illusion. Protagoras and Gorgias can be said to be on the Heraclitean side of an older debate between that thinker and Parmenides. Since this is precisely a philosophical controversy, Plato's accusations that the Sophists are mere impostors suggests a kind of bad faith on Plato's part.[51] Knowing full well that his opponents were not charlatans, he nevertheless portrayed them thus owing to his absolute conviction that only his way of seeking truth was legitimate.[52] Rather than impugning their results, he chooses to impugn their persons.

Plato's Academic Politics

A key sequence within the eponymous *Protagoras* will provide my first point. I am speaking of Protagoras's so-called "Great Speech." As shown by Farrar, Plato's "argument" against Protagoras, or "Socrates'" elenchus of Platagoras (Farrar's delightful coinage), turns entirely on a misconstrual of a fundamental Protagorean doctrine. As she has further demonstrated, the outlines of Protagoras's own view can be descried within the thicket of Plato's obfuscations.[53] Socrates begins by asking Protagoras if he teaches excellence, and Protagoras is made to answer yes. Indeed, he suggests that a student who comes to him

50. G. B. Kerferd, *The Sophistic Movement* (Cambridge: Cambridge University Press, 1981), 67. Compare Farrar, *Origins,* 49.

51. See, however, the very interesting discussion of this point by Rosemarie Kent Sprague in her review of Kerferd, *The Sophistic Movement, Journal of Hellenic Studies* 103 (1983): 189–90.

52. This argument cannot be refuted by appealing to Plato's character and integrity, which would be, precisely, begging the question. Compare Farrar, *Origins,* 54.

53. The following paragraphs are inspired by Farrar, *Origins,* 76–87.

will become better every day, incrementally (318a6–9). Protagoras, all
the more, promises to make his pupils "good citizens" by teaching
them the "political art" (πολιτικὴν τέκνην). Socrates challenges this
claim of Protagoras on two grounds: the first one is that while in matters of carpentry or practical skills, the Athenians will accept advice
only from masters of those arts, in politics every man (*sic*) is listened
to in the Assembly. The second argument is that there are many excellent men who fail to produce excellent progeny, and if such excellence
were teachable, then certainly they would have taught their own children. Protagoras responds with a myth of the origins of humanity and
human society, which, incidentally, many scholars consider to be a
likely genuine Protagorean quotation (320d–322d).[54] The bottom line
of the myth is, for our purposes, the assertion that after producing
the polis, Zeus sent Hermes with respect and justice (*aidos* and *dikē*)
to humans, for otherwise he feared they would wipe each other out
entirely. Upon being asked to whom to give these, Zeus answered that
they should be given to all. In spite of this universal gift of respect
and justice, Protagoras is made to assert, as well, that excellence in
civic virtue is teachable and shows this by arguing that humans hold
each other accountable for their behavior, which they would do only
if there were a measure of control over it. They moreover punish each
other in order to teach them to be better. Protagoras defends against
the apparent contradiction by a brilliant analogy, arguing that if flute
playing were vital to the life of the polis, everyone would teach their
children and everyone else to play the flute and, while some would
be brilliant flute players and others middling, everyone would know
something of playing the flute. Similarly in the polis, where civic virtue is vital, all are taught by everyone. Some are first-rate and others
middling, but no one incompetent. Just as the children of great flute
players might not be brilliant, and brilliant flute players might be the
children of only fair ones, so also civic virtue in the polis. As Farrar
puts it: "The Great Speech in the *Protagoras* expresses the Sophist's
belief, reflected in the *Theaetetus,* in the beneficent socializing effect
of *polis* life and democratic political action. The man-measure doc-

---

54. Michael Gagarin and Paul Woodruff, *Early Greek Political Thought from Homer to
the Sophists,* ed. and trans. Michael Gagarin, Cambridge Texts in the History of Political
Thought (Cambridge: Cambridge University Press, 1995), 178.

trine conceives of the experience and understanding attained by ordinary men as the touchstone of social values. Protagoras' measure
is a man who notices his neighbor and who moves through life and
interacts with others as a human being, with all that implies about
basic needs, responses and capacities." The notion of the individual
human being as the measure, on the one hand, gives credence to the
experience and judgment of each individual human and, on the other,
makes possible the "collective, critical appraisal of human belief."[55]

As Farrar points out at length and compellingly, Protagoras (the
real one) does not oppose excellence to incompetence or Truth to
falsehood as Plato wants Platagoras to do, forces him to do, thus
rendering his views incoherent and self-contradictory. Nor does Protagoras produce an essential opposition between civic virtue and
other skills, as demonstrated by his own example of the flute-playing
polis.[56] For Protagoras, the opposition is between competence and
incompetence, and there is excellence as well. People are trainable to
competence in many areas, but not all can be excellent. All have some
measure of civic competence by virtue of Zeus's "gift," but there is
training that will make them better, incrementally, and perhaps, if
they have the talent, excellent in the political art as well. "Although
Platagoras defends at length both the practices of the Athenians and
the possibility of transmitting excellence, his argument is condemned
to incoherence by Plato's formulation of the issue."[57] This is so by a
determined confusion of political excellence (that which Protagoras
claims to teach) with being a good citizen (which Protagoras claims
is the province of all), such that universal competence and individual
excellence are made to contradict each other. Plato is, in part, ex-
ploiting the kind of equivocation in Greek that he so loves to exploit,
for ἀρετή connotes both excellence and also something more akin
to our virtue. Protagoras's claim that he can teach virtue and make
people better people does *not* constitute a claim that all humans can
be taught to be champions of the good life. The human's being as the

55. Farrar, *Origins,* 76 both cites.
56. Farrar, *Origins,* 82. Farrar argues throughout that we can see something of the real
Protagoras behind Platagoras, particularly in the moments of incoherence in the Platonic
text (what she calls the "crookedness of the seams"), which is precisely the way I am arguing in this book.
57. Farrar, *Origins,* 79.

only measure and Protagoras's claim to be able to teach excellence in politics, as Plato misrepresents him, are conflated in such a way that "Platagoras" does indeed end up incoherent. The real difference between Plato and Protagoras lies in their understanding of knowledge and the political implications of that understanding, for Plato (356d–357b) maintains that only absolute Truth is the key to human survival, while Protagoras insists on a gradual amelioration of human social existence through the human as measure. For the latter, the citizen teaches and is taught in the polis and by teachers such as Protagoras to examine his (*sic*) convictions and see how they contradict each other or otherwise can be criticized, which leads to a better understanding and thus better life in the city.

Protagoras does not distinguish between skill in political life and all other skills as Platagoras is made to do. For him, all learn the basic competences that make it possible for life in the polis to exist, and they learn these in the same way that children learn Greek well enough to speak and understand it. But there are different levels of talent and ability (and even industriousness) that will make it possible for some to be taught to be better and even excellent in these matters. Just as one who knows Greek can be taught to be a better or even a great rhetor, so one who knows the basics of civic virtue can be taught to be an excellent leader in the democratic polis. Plato cannot abide the notion of competence and degrees of same.

Since I have learned so much from Farrar here, let me sum up this section with a further quotation from her excellent book:

> Unlike Protagoras, Plato, repelled by the politics of democratic Athens, is anxious to show that people are not as and what they think they are (176d). The socialization characteristic of the *polis* is now seen as a destructive influence, and politics as a struggle for power rather than a realization of order. Plato's language is designed to evoke the teachings of the man who legitimized "appearances" and thereby, in Plato's view, fortified the subversive, pernicious beliefs of the masses (176d).[58]

In other words, Plato's absolute distinction between excellence and incompetence is driven by the same absolutism that drives his

58. Farrar, *Origins*, 77.

distinction between Truth and appearance with no possibilities in between in either case. This is imbricated by his politics of discourse as well, on the constructed opposition between rhetoric and philosophy or debate and dialectic.

In the conclusion to his discussion of dialogue versus debate, Barrett has put his finger on the matter:

> Thus form and substance unite. The *absolutist* position . . . finds consonance and agency in the dialogical short form of oral address. To the end of maintaining control, leadership is invested with dominant authority. Regulating all of its functions, the system rigidly restricts discussion, insists upon brief statement, denies refutation, arbitrarily acknowledges only the judgments it produces, and remains idealistically detached in seeking after the value it names as permanent.
>
> The *democratic* idea enjoys congruity with the long speech—with form more obviously rhetorical. It accommodates free expression, extended argument, choice and management of thought—subject only to *social* regulation, necessary cooperation and consensus, refutation, flexibility of behavior, popular judgment, and a practical adaptable *episteme* for particular ends.[59]

Not only, then, are different and contrasting views of authority at stake, but dialectic and debate imply different and contrasting epistemologies as well. Josiah Ober, more than any other writer that I have encountered, has clearly articulated the ways in which democracy is an epistemology. Ober makes clear that democracy is a form of knowledge, an *epistēmē,* in Foucault's terms, one that he designs precisely "democratic knowledge."[60] This is a regime remarkably "postmodern" in its assumptions that mass opinion (as opposed to scientific "knowledge") is a significant basis for the making of valid decisions, and that all claims to knowledge and truth are political, that is, power-laden.[61] Now the production of these common knowl-

59. Barrett, *Sophists,* 62.

60. Josiah Ober, *Political Dissent in Democratic Athens: Intellectual Critics of Popular Rule* (Princeton, N.J.: Princeton University Press, 1998), 34–35.

61. "In democratic Athens there was no very meaningful separation between the realms of politics, political society (citizenry), and government. In the Athenian democracy, major government decision making (by council, Assembly, lawcourts, and boards

edges upon which democracy was both theoretically and pragmatically maintained was in large part effectuated through the debating process as carried out in Assembly and law court. Although Ober does not remark it in these terms, it comes out that rhetoric is the foundation for the reproduction of democratic knowledges, as well as for their modifications.

Socratic dialectic (as given by Plato) is not only an attack on *doxa,* on that which appears to be true to the Athenian citizenry, the foundation of their legal and political decisions, but also an attack on the speech-institution, the debate, in which *doxa* is both maintained and modified for the purpose of democratic deliberation. Plato's near-obsessive disdain for rhetoric and his near-obsessive insistence on dialogue as the means of exposure of *doxa* as false, on this reading, constitute a sustained attack on democracy. Dialogue, in this Platonic sense, as often as not confounded with dialectic (both by Plato and by his interpreters), constitutes the least dialogical of speech forms. In early fourth-century Athens, not only was rhetoric an art of politics, but rhetorical theories and practices were of the very stuff of politics, and well understood by Aristotle, among others, who closely associates his *Rhetoric* with his *Politics.* Insofar as rhetoric (as in debate) was the epistemology of democracy, then Plato (in his *spoudaios* voice) argued obsessively for dialogue (as in dialectic). In the eponymous dialogues assigned to the two great Sophists, he proceeds to do just that by hook or by crook, as I shall try to show in what remains of this chapter and the next one. Plato's dialogues can be taken then as a rejoinder in an already existing debate between Parmenides, on the one hand, and Protagoras and Gorgias on the other. If Gorgias and Protagoras threw the question of truth wide open, and especially if they

---

of *nomothetai,* or 'lawgivers') was legitimate specifically because it *was* political, and thus there was no meaningful separation between supposedly objective and scientific truths of the sort used (so we are told) by modern political rulers when making 'serious' decisions, and the subjective political truths of the sort modern politicians find it expedient to present to the citizenry during elections and occasional plebiscites. In Athens, the general understanding held by the citizenry regarding the nature of society was the same understanding employed by decision-making bodies in formulating government policy for deployment in the real world. For most Athenians, the shocking 'postmodern' conclusion that 'all knowledge is political' (i.e. implicated in relations of power) was simply a truism; neither the possibility nor the normative desirability of genuinely apolitical forms of knowledge about society or its members ever entered the ordinary Athenian's head" (Ober, *Political Dissent,* 34).

denied the privileged access to Truth on the part of certain human beings; if they insisted that what you see is what you get, either by denying existents or asserting that human experience is the criterion, then they had to be challenged and discredited by any means available. This urgency was compounded by the way that such an epistemological theory that credited every human's everyday experience as the only source of knowledge about reality itself was so deeply entwined with democratic theory. And so Plato rolled up his sleeves and went to work elaborating an alternate theory of discourse in which knowledge was not to be found in experience but in something beyond experience and counter to experience, and in which the only philosophical use for speech was in dialectic. This is Plato at his most *spoudaios,* although, to be sure, something of a surprise awaits us in the *Gorgias* as well. In this chapter I wish to present Plato at perhaps his most monological and forbiddingly *spoudaios,* in the dialogue named after the great Sophist Protagoras. Some close reading of the dialogue will be necessary for my argument to have any real purchase.

The *Protagoras* as Monological Dialogue

Whatever else is going on in them, the dialogues of Plato are in essence one long protreptic discourse for the philosophical (in the Platonic sense, as opposed to the sophistic or public/political) way of speech and of life:[62] "Follow me then, as one persuaded, to where when you arrive you will be happy both in living and dying" (527c).[63] As a recent commentator has put it, "It is not even clear if the dialogue *is* a genuine dialogue in these contexts. The philosopher's interlocutor often seems just to be going along with the flow, with a very lengthy and unrelieved series of affirmatives like 'yes,' 'of course,' 'certainly.' The prominently foregrounded social and individual context, then, is presented just as prominently as external to the philosophical con-

---

62. Nightingale, *Genres in Dialogue,* 11; Debra Nails, *Agora, Academy, and the Conduct of Philosophy,* Philosophical Studies Series 63 (Dordrecht, Netherlands: Kluwer Academic Publishers, 1995), 217. Nails, however, limits this protreptic to only certain dialogues, notably the *Protagoras* and the *Gorgias,* while I hope to show in my reading of the *Symposium* that the same is true there.

63. See discussion in Plato, *Euthyphro, Apology, Crito, Meno, Gorgias, Menexenus,* vol. 1 of *The Dialogues of Plato,* trans. Reginald E. Allen (New Haven, Conn.: Yale University Press, 1984), 216.

tent."[64] That is precisely the point, to render philosophy as the realm of absolute antihistoricist truth, to show the Sophists and their rhetoric as hopelessly mired in the mud of the particular and the circumstantial. A modern Platonist, Alain Badiou, makes this perfectly clear: "The crucible in which what will become a work of art and thought burns is brimful with nameless impurities; it comprises obsessions, beliefs, infantile puzzles, various perversions, undivulgeable memories, haphazard reading, and quite a few idiosyncrasies and chimeras. Analyzing this alchemy is of little use."[65] The *Protagoras* provides one of the clearest and most blatant examples of the politics of dialogue in Plato's protreptic. As a commentator more sympathetic to Plato than I describes the dialogue, "Its primary finding, now implicit in the very name, is that the Sophist is a specious intellectual more interested in the reputation for wisdom than in wisdom itself. Protagoras is heralded as the wisest man in all of Greece, and it is fairly clear that he makes fame, and the wealth it may bring, the central focus of his endeavors."[66] Well, yes, that's what Plato would have us believe. In terms of substance, Socrates' whole point in the discussion is to convince Protagoras (or actually the hearers/readers of their dialogue) that all virtue is reducible to one, exact knowledge (*epistēmē*), for which read philosophy, arguably knowledge of the forms (357b).[67]

64. Jeremy Barris, *The Crane's Walk* (New York: Fordham University Press, forthcoming), 2.1. Barris himself glosses this as philosophy questioning itself, as it were, anticipating the thesis of this book.

65. Alain Badiou, *Saint Paul: The Foundation of Universalism*, trans. Ray Brassier, Cultural Memory in the Present (Stanford, Calif.: Stanford University Press, 2003), 2.

66. Patrick Coby, *Socrates and the Sophistic Enlightenment: A Commentary on Plato's Protagoras* (Lewisburg, Pa.: Bucknell University Press, 1987), 13. I must say that I find Coby's description of Protagoras fantastic, not allowing at all for any distance between a "real" Protagoras and Plato's representation of him, but going beyond even Plato's own vitriolic presentation (13–17). Coby's absolute assent to Plato's view of Protagoras is stunning. Thus, "What Socrates pretends has taken place is the transformation of Protagoras from an honor-loving Achilles (before the analysis) to a crafty, knowledge-loving Odysseus (after the analysis). While the hope is unfounded and will not be entertained for long, Socrates begins on the assumption that his interlocutor is a partner in a joint investigation whose object is knowledge" (131). In contrast to this, see the trenchant words on the bad faith of "Socrates" in Harry Berger, "Facing Sophists: Socrates' Charismatic Bondage in *Protagoras*," in *Situated Utterances: Texts, Bodies, and Cultural Representations* (New York: Fordham University Press, 2005), 391–93.

67. Socrates is somewhat cagey here on the last point, proposing that the precise nature of the exact knowledge can be determined on a later occasion. See also discussion in Coby, *Socrates*, 158–60.

However, it is the form of discourse itself that most embodies the Platonic idea here, and more particularly, the explicit thematization of the form of discourse.

As Harold Barrett has put it, "It is apparent that Plato's Socrates must dominate, which of course he does in all dialogues. He is never bested. In the dialogue under discussion, Protagoras, presented as a learned and self-confident teacher, holds his own in the first phases of the encounter. But when the audience cheers one of Protagoras's longer and appealing statements—when the audience finds itself in a *rhetorical* mode and behaves accordingly—Socrates feels constrained to ask for short answers. Knowing that his goal can be reached in no other way, he insists that Protagoras adopt the 'more compendious method.'"[68] As Barrett points out, when Socrates is in danger of losing the encounter, he insists that only his favorite mode of discourse may be employed. Protagoras feels group pressure and defers, and all this because "it had to be settled in Socrates' favor. Socrates' purpose and advantage depended on dialogue—not to mention his management of it."[69] Barrett goes on to insightfully point out that when, "as agreed, Protagoras takes the lead in the questioning, the power soon comes to reside with Socrates—with Plato. That, too, is inevitable. Unrestrained Platonic strategy overrides more subtle Socratic diffidence; Socrates *tells* more than he *asks*. The reader senses an insistence and force, much as in the pressing peroration of a speech that follows from more moderately styled thought."[70] By this mode, we can perceive Plato making use of the monological dialogue as the only (?) discursive mode that can produce such insistence and force reliably. Hence the repeated requirement within the Platonic text that only dialogue will do, a demand that indeed ends up in later antiquity making dialogue/dialectic the very synonym of philosophy.

In reading the *Protagoras* we can see that the question of debate versus dialogue virtually obsessed Plato. There is one moment in particular in the *Protagoras,* alluded to above by Barrett, where this issue is thematized by Plato. Protagoras has just given a nuanced and convincing speech in which he articulates his reasons for not assenting to Socrates'

68. Barrett, *Sophists,* 59.
69. Barrett, *Sophists,* 59.
70. Barrett, *Sophists,* 60.

insistence that the virtues are one by indicating the ways that certain things are beneficial to certain people in certain circumstances and distinctly harmful to them in others (I oversimplify) (334a–c). At that point, "the audience shouted their approval of his speech." Socrates with his usual ironic self-deprecation announces that he has a defective memory and cannot follow a long speech, anticipating as well his ironic and deceptive self-deprecatory reaction at a similar moment in the *Symposium*. He therefore insists that Protagoras confine himself to giving short answers to questions addressed to him by Socrates. After some byplay as to whether Protagoras or Socrates will decide what the proper length is, it becomes clear that it is Socrates who will determine this. At this point, Protagoras protests: "'Socrates,' he said, 'I've had verbal contests with a great many people, and if I had done what you tell me to do, and spoken according to the instructions of my antagonist, I should never have got the better of anyone, nor would the name of Protagoras have become known in Greece'" (335a). Plato's rhetoric here is anything but innocent. By having Protagoras formulate his preference for long speech in this fashion, he is having the Sophist "confess" that his goals are victory in speech contests and the consequent fame (and presumably wealth) that such victories portend. At the same time, Plato completely disables any conceivable thought that what is at stake for Protagoras is the possibility that one might have a better chance of explaining one's true views in an autonomous speech than as the antagonist in a conversation in which someone else entirely controls the discourse and allows one only short answers to set questions.[71] And, of course, Plato thus further occludes the point that Socrates' "purpose and advantage" are entirely served by his insistence on dialogue and the management of such dialogue.

At this point, Socrates pretends to give up: "I knew that he was dissatisfied with his previous replies, and that he wasn't willing to take the role of answerer in the dialectic [*dialegesthai*], so I felt that there was no point in my continuing the conversation [*sounousias*]" (335a–b). Socrates is about to take his football and go home, and indeed gets up with intent to do so. Predictably others intervene and insist that

---

71. It needs to be noted that in the Assembly at the *pnyx*, speakers chose their own length of time to speak, as opposed to the *dikasteria* with its water clock. Mogens Herman Hansen, *The Athenian Assembly in the Age of Demosthenes* (Oxford: Blackwell, 1987), 91–92.

he remain, upon which, after some further expressions of false modesty[72] (explicitly marked as a joke by Alcibiades just a bit further on), Socrates stipulates, "If you want to listen to Protagoras and me, ask him to answer now the way he did at first, briefly, and sticking to the question. If not, what sort of discussion [*dialogōn*] will we have? I thought that a discussion [*suneînai . . . dialegomenous*] was something quite different from a speech in the assembly [*dēmēgoreîn*]" (336a–b).[73] Of course in the two previous exchanges in which Protagoras had kept to Socrates' "rules," Socrates had managed to twist him up in thoroughly sophistical knots, which is presumably what Socrates desires to continue to be able to do.[74]

Then a further very arresting development takes place. Socrates is asked to choose a referee for the discussion, that is, someone who will determine who has successfully defeated the arguments of his opponent and defended his own point of view. Socrates, of course, refuses this option, arguing that if the referee be inferior to the speakers, then his opinion is obviously useless; if he is equal to them, he will simply "do the same as we should, so it will be a waste of time to choose him"; and, of course, it is impossible to choose one superior to Protagoras, so why bother? What has not been noticed, I think, by commentators is that what Plato is doing here is parodying and dismissing precisely the ethos of the democratic speech situation, in

72. For a brilliant account of the role of this false modesty in Socratic discourse, see Ramona Naddaff, *Exiling the Poets: The Production of Censorship in Plato's* Republic (Chicago: University of Chicago Press, 2002), 55–56. As Melissa Lane has compellingly shown, this has nothing to do, however, with the term *eirōneia*, as used in Plato's own texts. "The Evolution of *Eirōneia* in Classical Greek Texts: Why Socratic *Eirōneia* Is Not Socratic Irony," *Oxford Studies in Ancient Philosophy* 31 (2006): 49–83.

73. [336b] εἰ δὲ μή, τίς ὁ τρόπος ἔσται τῶν διαλόγων; χωρὶς γὰρ ἔγωγ᾽ ᾤμην εἶναι τὸ συνεῖναί τε ἀλλήλοις διαλεγομένους καὶ τὸ δημηγορεῖν.

74. Socrates' "generous" offer to let Protagoras be the questioner in the first round hardly changes this point: "Everyone agreed that that was what we should do. Protagoras was altogether unwilling, but none the less he was obliged to agree to put the questions, and when he had asked sufficient, to submit to questioning in his turn and give short replies" (338c–e). Protagoras may do anything, that is, but that which he wants to do: present his ideas in a reasoned and well-formed speech! It is remarkable the way in which some interpreters gloss over this compulsion of Protagoras: "It is agreed to proceed by question and answer, with Protagoras questioning first"; Plato, *Protagoras*, rev. ed., trans. with notes by C. C. W. Taylor, Clarendon Plato Series (Oxford: Oxford University Press, 1991), 135. Even more telling, in my humble opinion, is the fact that Taylor in his expansive commentary has almost nothing more to say on the topic of this clearly highly fraught contestation between speeches and dialectic.

which opposing speakers make their best arguments and others (their "inferiors") decide who was right, or more right, at any rate.

Socrates' refusal to appoint an arbiter to decide whether he or Protagoras is correct constitutes, then, an attack on the fundamental discursive structures of democratic speech, the formal debate carried out in antithetical speeches (amply exemplified at nearly every turn in Thucydides).[75] Now, since that form of discourse—the debate of antithetical speeches—was, at least arguably, invented by Protagoras, or at any rate "made familiar in Athens by him,"[76] the argument comes full circle.

Even as sympathetic a reader of Socrates as Patrick Coby here remarks that via his manipulation of "democratic nostrums," Socrates is left "free to arbitrate himself." The "natural ruler" will be the judge.[77] Coby's summation is powerful:

75. It is here that Barrett's point, as cited above, of "no other agency" being required in the antidemocratic "philosophic" speech situation, is justified. I am not unaware that my interpretation is somewhat contentious. Taylor, for instance, regards the suggestion of a referee as evidence for sophistic contests of dialectic, decided by a judge (Plato, *Protagoras* 135), remarking, moreover, that this kind of contest is deemed to have been invented by none other than Protagoras himself. This interpretation is, however, given the lie by Protagoras's extreme reluctance here to engage in any such disputation, with or without a referee. Other scholars have, however, noted the powerful analogy between epistemology and politics in Plato. See T. H. Irwin, "Coercion and Objectivity in Plato's Dialectic," *Révue Internationale de Philosophie* 40 (1986): 57 and especially n. 11 and literature cited there. See also Jonathan Cohen, "Philosophy Is Education Is Politics: A Somewhat Aggressive Reading of *Protagoras* 334d–338e," conference presentation: Twentieth World Congress of Philosophy, in Boston, Mass. (1998), Http://www.bu.edu/wcp/Papers/Anci/AnciCohe.htm. I, therefore, stick with my interpretation that the proposed "judging" of this rhetorical contest, like the similar issue in the *Symposium,* is a symbol writ small, as it were, of the kind of judging of rhetors that would take place in Athens in Assembly and courtroom. It is not insignificant that, as O'Regan points out, the viewing and judging of drama were in the same room and with the same people "seated in similar order as that which elsewhere voted the political and legal decisions of the city." Daphne Elizabeth O'Regan, *Rhetoric, Comedy, and the Violence of Language in Aristophanes' Clouds* (New York: Oxford University Press, 1992), 3. Cf. also François Jullien, "Did Philosophers Have to Become Fixated on Truth?" trans. Janet Lloyd, *Critical Inquiry* 28, no. 4 (2002): 813, who claims that what distinguishes "dialogue" from eristic is that in the former, "truth was submitted to the judgement of an interlocutor and the latter's assent to it was required." The interlocutor, however, was always the subordinated partner of the philosopher, Protagoras to Socrates, for instance. Jullien, for my taste, does not quite distinguish carefully enough between the situation of rhetoric, in which truth is recognized by winning over a third party, and the situation of philosophy ("dialogue"), in which "one's opponent's ratification is both necessary and sufficient" (814).

76. John H. Finley, *Thucydides* (Cambridge, Mass.: Harvard University Press, 1942), 15.

77. Coby, *Socrates,* 97. Cf. Josiah Ober on the "old oligarch": "Democracy is thus marked

Because the standard of dialectical brevity remains in force, Socrates can be thought to have emerged victorious. His victory and Protagoras's defeat are indicative of the relative dependence of each speaker on the audience. Socrates can endure the public's scorn; but Protagoras depends on its applause. Insofar as this procedural dispute exposes Protagoras to be a creature of public opinion, it calls into question the sophist's central claim that by sophistry he is made secure.[78]

If, however, we recast these sentences only slightly, we can see them quite differently. Socrates can endure the public's scorn, indeed, and as tyrant (philosopher-king) would not have to depend on the public at all. Protagoras is a creature of public opinion; in a democracy he would have to prevail with his rhetoric over opposing rhetors and convince the Assembly or the jury of the justice of his cause, just as Pericles had to continue to persuade of his excellence in governing in order to continue being chosen to do so.

Plato against Pericles

There is a moment in the *Protagoras* that appears there almost as a tossed-off remark but that serves for me as an important contextual clue. At one point, upon beginning to narrate his response to the Sophist and orator, Socrates relates:

So Protagoras concluded this lengthy exhibition of his skill as a speaker. I stayed gazing at him, quite spellbound, for a long time, thinking that he was going to say something more, and anxious to hear it; but when I saw that he had really finished, I collected myself with an effort, so to speak and looked at Hippocrates. "Son of Apollodorus," I said, "I am most grateful to you for suggesting that I should come here; for what I've learnt from Protagoras is something of great importance. Previously I used to think that there was no technique available to men for making people good; but now I am persuaded that there is. I've just one small difficulty, and it's obvious that Protagoras will explain

---

for Ps.-Xenophon by the hegemonic political authority of those who are necessarily inferior, both morally and culturally, over their betters" (*Political Dissent*, 17).

78. Coby, *Socrates*, 97.

it too without any trouble, since he has explained so much already. Now if you went to any of the orators about this question, you would perhaps get a similar speech from Pericles, or from some other able speaker; but if you ask them any question, they are no more capable of answering or asking anything themselves than a book is. Ask them anything about what they've said, no matter how small a point, and just as bronze, once struck, goes on sounding for a long time until you take hold of it, so these orators spin out an answer a mile long to any little question." (328d5–329a4).

Socrates does his best Peter-Falk-as-Colombo ("Everything you say makes perfect sense, Protagoras," and then, turning to leave and over his shoulder: "I've just got one little question, Mr. P.").[79] Plato is out here to skewer both Protagoras and Pericles, but why Pericles? This is not a random thrust. Pericles, in addition to being Thucydides' champion, is the best of the democrats, and is also the leader most closely associated with Protagoras. At least in legend, Pericles chose that Sophist to prepare a constitution for the new Athenian colony at Thurii in Italy. Hippocrates, furthermore, wishes to be trained for the life of the democratic polis, so attacking Pericles is very much to the point of Plato's protreptic discourse, indeed. If he hopes to win Hippocrates from the life of the democracy to the secluded, alienated life of the philosopher-prince, then discrediting both Protagoras and Pericles could not be more apposite. The terms under which the attack on Pericles (and, by implication, notwithstanding Socrates' ironic praise of him, on Protagoras) is carried out are precisely those favoring the use of lengthy speeches or dialogues in discursive practice.

Pericles' famous Funeral Oration in Thucydides is an eloquent defense of rhetoric and persuasion as the praiseworthy form and goal of public speech, and with this a defense of democratic speech in which experts debate and the citizenry decide:

Our constitution does not copy the laws of neighboring states; we are rather a pattern to others than imitators ourselves. Its administration favors the many instead of the few; this is why it is called a democracy.

79. For another example of this rhetorical technique in Socrates, see *Theaetetus* 145d1.

If we look to the laws, they afford equal justice to all in their private differences; if to social standing, advancement in public falls to reputation for capacity, class considerations not being allowed to interfere with merit; nor again does poverty bar the way; if a man is able to serve the state, he is not hindered by the obscurity of his condition. (2.37)[80]

Although some readers have taken the statement that "its administration favors the many instead of the few; this is why it is called a democracy" (καὶ ὄνομα μὲν διὰ τὸ μὴ ἐς ὀλίγους ἀλλ᾽ ἐς πλείονας οἰκεῖν δημοκρατία κέκληται) to mean that democracy serves the interests of one group, "the many," and oppresses another group, "the few," it is more naturally read in my view as meaning that in a democracy decision making is in the hands of the majority and not in the hands of a small and powerful subgroup, the oligarchy. A far better translation, then, is Edward M. Harris's: "The Athenian political system 'is called a democracy because the management of affairs is not in the hands of a few but in the hands of the majority.'"[81] Harris has, moreover, cited and successfully refuted a group of scholars who take the passage not as praise for democracy, but as the promotion, rather, of an aristocracy of talent. Through close analysis of the syntax and structure of the Greek, Harris convincingly argues that, there being three parts to the democracy, Thucydides is enumerating for us the democratic aspect of all three: in deliberation in the council and Assembly the will of the majority of all citizens prevails; in the law courts, in private disputes, all are equal before the law; and in magistracies all are equally eligible without regard to class or economic status but based only on merit.[82] In my opinion, then, there can be little doubt that Harris is correct in asserting that "a proper understanding of the structure of thought in the passage reveals that Pericles is not contrasting the

80. Thucydides, *The Landmark Thucydides: A Comprehensive Guide to the Peloponnesian War,* ed. Robert B. Strassler, introd. by Victor Davis Hanson, trans. Richard Crawley (New York: Free Press, 1996), 112.

81. Edward M. Harris, "Pericles' Praise of Athenian Democracy: Thucydides 2.37.1," *Harvard Studies in Classical Philology* 94 (1992): 161. See discussion of (and philological rejection of) alternatives at 163–64. Harris is by no means alone in his interpretation. As he points out on the following page, he is supported by Kurt Raaflaub and Jacqueline de Romilly, among others.

82. Harris, "Pericles' Praise," 162. Harris's argument directly contravenes Ober, *Political Dissent,* 86–87, whose interpretation is in this instance simply not convincing to me.

democratic facade of Athenian government with its aristocratic reality, nor introducing a modification to the general principle of equality by pointing to the importance of merit in election to office. On the contrary, Pericles is drawing a sharp distinction between Athenian democracy and Spartan oligarchy."[83] Indeed, the merit that assures that all citizens have the possibility of being elected to a magistracy is much more democratic than the Spartan one in which magistrates are chosen only from a single group.[84]

Harris's argument can be supported from another direction. Pericles rather precisely delineates the role of expertise and merit in a democratic system and explicitly marks the function of nonexpert voters in decision making. Thucydides writes: "Our public men have, besides politics, their private affairs to attend to, and our ordinary citizens, though occupied with the pursuits of industry, are still fair judges of public matters; for, unlike any other nation, we regard the citizen who takes no part in these duties not as unambitious [*apragmona*] but as useless, and we are able to judge proposals even if we cannot originate them; instead of looking at debate/speeches [*logoi*] as a stumbling-block in the way of action, we think it an indispensable preliminary to any wise action at all" (2.40).[85] John Finley has argued "that when Pericles states his firm confidence in debate and in the capacity of all citizens both to interest themselves in the city and to think clearly of its affairs (2.40.2), he is answering exactly the arguments which the Theban Herald in the *Suppliants* (409–425) makes against democracy. The latter says that the oratory of the politicians leads the masses astray and that the poor in any case lack the time and ability for politics. . . . Clearly then the question was crucial in the contemporary debate on democracy, and when Pericles defends the fitness of the masses for government, one must see in his words not merely the faith of a convinced democrat but the line of argument actually pursued in the Periclean Age by the advocates of a democratic system."[86] Plato in his sharp contrast between dialectic and speech

83. Harris, "Pericles' Praise," 162.

84. On Sparta's government, see G. E. M. de Ste. Croix, *The Origins of the Peloponnesian War* (Ithaca, N.Y.: Cornell University Press, 1972), 125–51.

85. Thucydides, *Landmark*, 113.

86. John H. Finley, *Three Essays on Thucydides* (Cambridge, Mass.: Harvard University Press, 1967), 22. Note that I am not taking any position at all on Thucydides' own ideology.

making, to the detriment of course of the latter, decisively rejects Pericles' precise description of democratic speech in the Funeral Oration that we have just read, one in which experts debate and well-informed nonexperts judge. We see here how Socrates' conversation with Protagoras, seemingly on the near-private level of the search for Truth, can be read as well, nay ought to be read as well, as a strong comment on political theory and as a rejection of the very premise of Athenian democracy.

The term ἀπράγμονα (literally, "free from business") is charged. Hobbes wittily translated this phrase as "for we only think one that is utterly ignorant therein, to be a man not that meddles with nothing, but that is good for nothing."[87] The point, in any translation, is that what in other places is a compliment, to be ἀπράγμων, is not so at Athens, where to be uninvolved in political life is to be deemed useless. Perhaps better would be to say that the adjective is still a compliment, even at Athens, but would not be applied there to one who is ignorant and uninvolved in public affairs.[88] Considering that this term is precisely that which philosophers used of themselves in praise of their life without striving for power, prestige, and money, it is, at least arguably, a highly marked criticism of those good-for-nothing men that Thucydides is remarking. For instance, in Xenophon's *Memorabilia* 3.11.16, we find Socrates describing himself as precisely that:

> "Ah!" said Socrates, making fun of his own leisurely habits, "it's not so easy for me to find time. For I have much business to occupy me, private and public; and I have the dear girls, who won't leave me day or night; they are studying potions with me and spells."

The rhetoric here is a bit tricky: Socrates is speaking ironically, making fun (*episkôptôn*) of his own leisurely habits (*tên hautou apragmosunên*), yet it seems nevertheless quite clear that that is the way that he (and others) would have praised his life, similar to the way that "scholar" comes from *skhole* and scholars are, in Hebrew, praised as בטלנים, idle (usually useless) people. The point can be made stronger:

---

87. Thucydides, *The Peloponnesian War: The Complete Hobbes Translation,* with notes and a new introduction by David Grene (Chicago: University of Chicago Press, 1989), 111.

88. For further discussion of this point, see Simon Hornblower, *A Commentary on Thucydides,* vol. 1, *Books I–III* (1991; repr., Oxford: Clarendon Press, 2003), 305.

for Socrates to be ironic about his *apragmosunên,* it would normally have to be a term of praise. For Thucydides' Pericles, on the other hand, such praise of elite uninvolvement in the life of the polis is anathema; it is the moral responsibility of every citizen to engage with the democracy and its decision making.

Although Pericles' statement "we are able to judge proposals even if we cannot originate them" is textually uncertain and can be translated in various ways,[89] it seems clear to me that its general import is the same in all versions: there is at Athens, as at other cities and even oligarchies, a distinction between men who primarily pursue the city's affairs and those who primarily engage in other activities. The former become more expert and are thus best at formulating and presenting policy, but the latter are, nonetheless, capable, entirely so, of judging correctly between well formulated and presented policies.[90] This utterance cannot, in my humble opinion, be taken on any stretch to mean that "Thucydides [is] making Pericles claim that the democracy is actually not fully participatory at all, but run by an élite."[91] Rather, Thucydides reveals here his (or at any rate Pericles') clear approbation of the free discussion of all citizens, in the form of their listening to speeches by "experts" who make proposals and counterproposals and then deciding on the merits of those proposals.[92]

89. Hornblower, *Commentary,* 305.

90. See too for this interpretation Gregory Vlastos, "The Individual as Object of Love in Plato," in *Platonic Studies* (Princeton, N.J.: Princeton University Press, 1981), 16n43.

91. Hornblower, *Commentary,* 305. Here is not the place for technical textual discussion, but the other possible translation leads to an even stronger approbation of participatory democracy. Hence it is enough for my argument to show that even the version that suggests a distinction between those who formulate and present policies for discussion and those who competently judge between them is not at all an attack on (or even qualification of) participatory democracy. Yunis too thinks that Hornblower is wrong here (Harvey Yunis, *Taming Democracy: Models of Political Rhetoric in Classical Athens* [Ithaca: Cornell University Press, 1996], 76n40).

92. This is exactly the process that Thucydides shows as "working" in the Mytilenian Debate. (I will discuss this point elsewhere; for the moment let suffice my caution that I am *not* claiming that Thucydides was a supporter of the democracy, but he was not an opponent of the democracy. Of that I am certain.) This seems, moreover, to have been a commonly held account of democracy, namely that what citizens do best is "judging." See on this point Maurice Pope, "Thucydides on Democracy," *Historia* 37 (1988): 285: "a glimpse here into a fifth century democrat's handbook." Note how sharply Plato attacks this notion. Aristotle, on the other hand, fully approbates it. Cf. *Politics* III. xi. 1–2 (1281b). For a sense of how widespread this topos is, note that it comes up again in the famous speech of Athenagoras in Thucydides vi. 39.1; and see discussion in A. H. M. Jones, *Athenian Democracy* (Baltimore: Johns Hopkins University Press, 1986), 54–55.

Aspasia's Funeral Oration, the *Menexenus*

There seems to be a dual political motivation for Plato's propaganda. The first and lower aspect of this is academic rivalry and competition with other teachers, notably Isocrates. The other motive that we can ascribe to Plato is both more serious (less venal) and more dangerous, for it goes beyond the question of academic prestige and success and involves the very foundations of the Athenian polity. The arts of speaking were most significant in the Assembly and law courts, both public institutions of the democracy, and Plato was an implacable opponent of democracy and supporter of oligarchy, in part owing to the experiences of his family at the time of the restoration of the democracy. For Plato, philosophy could not be so teachable, for then it could not be restricted to a tiny elite of philosopher-kings. Hence philosophy has to be absolutely split off from that other known as sophistic or rhetoric. There is little reason, however, to imagine that the preponderance of Athenian thinkers accepted Plato's odd and antidemocratic notions that ran counter to the traditions of Athens. The *Protagoras,* more than anything else, can be read (I propose) as a move in the great Athenian controversy about democracy. From this point of view, the attack on Pericles is anything but unmotivated, but rather a key to the whole project of the dialogue. In order to understand in a more nuanced way what it is that drives Socrates' seemingly almost gratuitous jibe at Pericles, we need to attend to one of Plato's strangest of texts, the dialogue *Menexenus,* which parodies the Thucydidean funeral oration.

It is by now almost a commonplace that Thucydides in writing Pericles' Funeral Oration was highly influenced by rhetors and especially Gorgias. Thucydides' closeness and indeed indebtedness to the Sophists has been argued by H. D. Rankin.[93] Proctor has further commented on these sophistic connections:

Dionysius of Halicarnassus, a perceptive critic, complained that not a few of what he called the theatrical figures of speech affected

93. H. D. Rankin, "Thucydides: Sophistic Method and Historical Research," in *Sophists, Socratics, and Cynics* (London: Croom Helm, 1983), 98–121. I would suggest that this point weakens considerably Ober's case for Thucydides as sharp critic of democratic knowledge and of rhetoric, cf. Ober, *Political Dissent,* 77–79.

by Gorgias—his matching clauses, assonances, plays on words and
antitheses—were to be found in Thucydides.... "Puerile," μειρακιῶδη,
was his word for both of these [Pericles' last speech and Hermocrates'
speech in VI]. He also took exception to the style of the famous chapters on revolution (III.82–83), with which most modern readers are
well content, saying that Thucydides here "began to dramatise"—
ἀρξάμενος ἐπιτραγῳδεῖν.

That the craze for ornamentation was no mere flash in the pan is
shown by the fact that Plato thought it worth while to parody it—
in the *Epitaphios* attributed by Socrates to Aspasia in the *Menexenus*
and in the peroration of Agathon's speech in the *Symposium*, which
Socrates is made to pick on as peculiarly "Gorgiastic."... That Thucydides certainly did not escape its influence in the three years before
he left Athens is attested by Marcellinus and the anonymous writer
whose biography of Thucydides has come down to us with his; and it
has indeed left unmistakable traces in his style.[94]

Given indeed Plato's disdain for Gorgias as expressed in his eponymous dialogue as well as in the two moments mentioned by Proctor,
it is not surprising that Plato, too, expresses views that are the exact
opposite of Thucydides' Periclean peroration in the Funeral Oration.
Plato, in this most unusual of dialogues, the *Menexenus*, gives us a funeral oration, presented as having been written by Aspasia, Pericles'
lover and the mother of his children. Although it is not an uncontro-
versial point in interpretation, many scholars have seen this piece as a
parody of Pericles' own Funeral Oration, among them such notables
as E. R. Dodds and Nicole Loraux.[95] Since the text being parodied in
this dialogue is the Thucydidean Funeral Oration of Pericles, and this
parody of Pericles is put in the mouth of none other than his beloved

94. Dennis Proctor, *The Experience of Thucydides* (Warminster, Wilts., England: Aris &
Phillips, 1980), 39.

95. E. R. Dodds, introduction to *Gorgias: A Revised Text, by Plato* (1959; repr., Oxford:
Oxford University Press, 2002), 23–24; Proctor, *Experience*, 6; Nicole Loraux, *The Invention
of Athens: The Funeral Oration in the Classical City* (Cambridge, Mass.: Harvard University
Press, 1986), 311–27; M. Pohlenz, *Aus Platos Werdezeit* (Berlin: Weidmann, 1913), 264–92;
A. E. Taylor, *Plato: The Man and His Work* (London: Methuen, 1960), 42. Incidentally, it
is not beside the point to remark that if Pericles' Funeral Oration were already a sort of
self-parody in Thucydides as Ober holds, Plato ought to have been less moved to parody it
himself. This is, of course, not in any sense a knockout punch to Ober's reading, but it is, I
think, suggestive.

Aspasia, this would seem to be a crucial text for my purposes of arguing that Plato's invention of *philosophia*/dialectic is as much about politics as it is about metaphysics.

One key to the interpretation of the *Menexenus* is in the character of Aspasia, lover/wife of Pericles and a brilliantly educated woman. We have records of a Socratic dialogue by Aeschines in which Aspasia is Socrates' teacher in matters erotic. In the *Menexenus*, Socrates is clearly made to treat us to his view of funeral orations in general:

> Actually, Menexenus, in many ways it's a fine thing to die in battle. A man gets a magnificent funeral even if he dies poor, and people praise him even if he was worthless. Wise men lavish praise on him, and not at random but in speeches prepared long in advance, and the praise is so beautiful that although they speak things both true and untrue of each man, the extreme beauty and diversity of their words bewitches our souls. For in every way, they eulogize the city and those who died in battle and all our forebears, and even us who are still alive, until finally, Menexenus, I feel myself ennobled by them. I every time stand and listen, charmed, believing I have become bigger, better-born, and better-looking on the spot. (234c)[96]

The contrast between seductive, flattering, beautiful language that is untrue, and spontaneous, unbeautiful language that carries truth is very well known to us from the *Symposium*, another work in which Gorgias's rhetoric and encomia in general are explicitly thematized and attacked. Menexenus gets the joke, of course, and remonstrates with Socrates for always making fun of rhetors. In the *Menexenus*, Aspasia is charged with having written Pericles' own Funeral Oration and then with having composed one of her own out of the "leftovers" from that one (236b). Reginald E. Allen, following a couple of hints in Aristotle, which he takes to represent the view of the Academy, suggests that "rhetorical flattery is the theme of the *Menexenus*."[97] I agree with Allen, as well, that there is no question at all but that "the speech

96. Plato, *Euthyphro, Apology, Crito, Meno, Gorgias, Menexenus,* trans. Reginald E. Allen, The Dialogues of Plato (New Haven: Yale University Press, 1984), 329.

97. Reginald E. Allen, "Comment, Menexenus," in Plato, *Euthyphro, Apology, Crito, Meno, Gorgias, Menexenus,* trans. Reginald E. Allen, The Dialogues of Plato (New Haven: Yale University Press, 1984), 320.

of Aspasia is base rhetoric," a parody of that which is delightedly to be mocked.[98] For E. R. Dodds the *Menexenus* is a (parodic) example of the practice that the *Gorgias* excoriates in theory: "Both of them convey the same criticisms of Athenian democracy and Athenian foreign policy, though the expression is direct in one case, ironical in the other."[99] And for Loraux, the *Menexenus* "is the only work of the classical period devoted explicitly to exorcizing the official oration."[100]

After mocking the whole enterprise and genre, Socrates proceeds to deliver to his young friend that very oration of Aspasia's, comparing the performance to taking his clothes off and dancing naked for Menexenus. "Aspasia's" Funeral Oration is a reductio ad absurdum of Pericles' own. The falsehoods of "hers" are so ridiculous in order to point up the slyer falsehood of his. Now insofar as Pericles' oration is the very zenith of Athenian democracy for Thucydides, nothing could be more marked with respect to political theory than Plato's contempt for this speech.[101] Once again, citing the precise formulation of Nicole Loraux: "In attacking the funeral oration Plato is again attacking Athenian democracy, and in one of its most solemn practices. Democratic is the rule that gives the poor man a magnificent tomb and accords a fine speech to the commonplace man redeemed by a fine death (*Menexenus* 234c2–4). Democracy is also the collective character of the epitaphioi: for all the same destiny, for all, the same oration; and against this egalitarianism the advocate of geometrical

---

98. Allen, "Comment, Menexenus," 320. Allen proceeds to dismantle any claim to the contrary that would "affirm its excellence as a specimen of Greek oratory." As Allen puts it, "The speech is no doubt good of its kind, but its kind is not good: it is base rhetoric. Rhetoric which aims at the good of the soul must aim also at truth, or so the *Gorgias* claims, and if the *Menexenus* conforms to the accepted structure of a funeral oration, that structure is itself the product merely of knack and experience in achieving a desired effect" (321). Loraux makes the same point, commenting that it is not so much the content "which is that of the traditional funeral oration but the presence of such terms as *dokein* or *phainesthai,* which undermine the statement that follows them, exposing the oration as a parody. . . . It would be pointless to try to see the Platonic epitaphios as a 'reasonable funeral oration'; I would therefore oppose all the serious readings of the *Menexenus,* although they are based on a tradition going back to antiquity." Loraux, *Invention,* 325.

99. Dodds, *Gorgias,* 24.

100. Loraux, *Invention,* 312.

101. It is fascinating to learn that a much later tyrant of Greece, Metaxas in the twentieth century, forbad the study of Pericles' Funeral Oration in schools, as I learn from Loraux, *Invention,* 5. I think he well understood something about Thucydides that some scholars miss.

equality protests."[102] We see already how politically fraught the opposition of debates to dialectic is for Plato, and in his taking of the exact
opposite stance to Thucydides in his evaluation of Pericles, Plato is
signifying his posture on the democratic question, as well, thus fully
clarifying his seemingly unmotivated jibe at Pericles with which I began this piece of the text.[103] For Plato, as the *Menexenus* makes clear,
the corruption of the Sophists and of sophistic rhetoric is bound up
hand and foot with his disdain for democracy and cannot be sepa-
rated from it. The *Protagoras,* I hope to have shown, in its seemingly
unmotivated attack on Pericles articulates clearly the interface between epistemology and political theory.

The Politics of Protagoras

A bit more close reading of the *Protagoras* will enhance this point further. After interrupting Protagoras's attempt to make his arguments
via an analysis of a poem by Simonides (an attempt, in which, by the
way, Protagoras was trying to keep to the question-and-answer form
dictated by Socrates) (342a), Socrates (with the help of the ever-faith-
ful Alcibiades) once again bullies Protagoras into assuming the position of answerer in the dialectic (348c). Just before entering into the
passage, Socrates bamboozles Protagoras into agreeing that "measur-
ing" of pleasure and pain is an exact science, a *tekhnē* that has within it
epistēmē.[104] It is here that the element of coercion enters into the Platonic speech situation, for as T. H. Irwin has pointed out, following
Richard Rorty, it is precisely the claim for absolutely objective "truth"
that introduces the element of coercion into philosophical discourse.

102. Loraux, *Invention,* 314–15.

103. This line of thinking about the connection between the *Menexenus* and the
Symposium will be further expounded in chapter 7 below. On the opposition of dialogue to
rhetoric, see also Lucian, *Twice Accused,* 28, in which Rhetoric insists that "the Syrian" not
be allowed to make a speech in his defense, since he has abandoned her for Dialogue. The
possibility of a defense in dialogue is, of course, quite absurd. Lucian of Samosata, "The
Double Indictment," in *Lucian III,* with an English translation by A. M. Harmon, 8 vols.,
Loeb Classics (London: W. Heinemann, 1913–67), 141.

104. I think my language is not too strong (although it is, to be sure, aggressive). At
several occasions in the dialogues, Socrates' enemies (again, not too strong) compare him
to some sort of creature who stuns or poisons his victims. Most memorably, there is the
image of the torpedo fish in the *Meno* 75c8ff. Socrates himself, à la Plato, is more likely to
compare himself to a gadfly who wakes Athenians up!

"The misguided philosopher wants anyone who claims knowledge to come to him for a certificate of legitimacy, because he can tell them when a claim will be justified. He can tell them this because he knows what conditions a claim or method must satisfy if it is to reveal to us the way the world is. The way the world is is the way it objectively is, in logical independence of our beliefs and desires about how it is. The principles of misguided philosophy satisfy Nozick's conditions for being coercive, since they tell rational people what they have to believe, like it or not."[105] This misguided philosopher could very well be, then, a character sketch of Socrates, and Protagoras the very type of the "anyone who claims knowledge." On this reading, what so irks Plato about Protagoras is precisely his powerful unsettling of the epistemological conditions for such coercion in his famous "The human being is the measure" dictum.[106]

Socrates begins his final attack by returning to what is, after all, the theme of the whole conversation by asking Protagoras once again, as in the beginning, whether he holds that "wisdom, soundness of mind, courage, justice, and holiness" are five separate things that are all parts of excellence (*arete*) or whether they are five names for what is essentially the same thing.[107] Protagoras concedes that he has become convinced that four of these parts of virtue are similar to each other (and presumably entail one another) but that courage is quite independent of the rest, for there are "men who are totally irreligious, unjust, wanton, and ignorant, but very courageous" (359b). The rest of the dialogue consists of questions and answers in which Protagoras is completely defeated by Socrates on this last point (359c–360d).

Socrates leads off by recalling Protagoras's distinction between courage and the other parts of virtue and remarks at how surprised he was by it.[108] Socrates "proves" that whatever the actions of men at

---

105. Irwin, "Coercion," 51. See also Richard Rorty, *Philosophy and the Mirror of Nature* (Princeton, N.J.: Princeton University Press, 1980), 177; and Irwin's discussion there.

106. For further discussion on this, see Schiappa, *Protagoras*, 117–33, and a host of other scholars cited there.

107. I am not entering here into the excellent philosophical discussions about what Plato might have meant by sameness and difference here, which are beside my point and can be easily followed in the commentaries on the *Protagoras*.

108. I shall be partly following Coby's lucid paraphrase of the argument here (Coby, *Socrates*, 166–72), in spite of drawing nearly directly opposing conclusions from it.

war, for instance, whether bold or fearful, they are always caused by knowledge or lack of same. Socrates reaches the conclusion by asking Protagoras whether cowards go toward things that inspire confidence and the courageous toward things that inspire dread.

Socrates then builds on his above-discussed (admittedly fallacious and perhaps deliberately so) conclusion that *akrasia* (moral weakness) is equivalent to mere ignorance.[109] If people do not "give into themselves" out of moral weakness but always calculate their best interests, some wisely and some foolishly, then no one goes toward that which is truly fearful in the long run. Since he has manipulated Protagoras previously into assenting to these propositions, the latter cannot but agree to that which is now derived from them as premises. It could be said that Socrates preserves some degree of intellectual integrity with his proviso "if that demonstration was correct," knowing full well that it wasn't, but that very qualification is calculated to go by Protagoras very quickly and lightly here.

Socrates' conclusion seems, then, ineluctable: "But now everyone, coward and courageous alike, goes for what he is confident about, and in this way, at any rate, cowards and courageous go for the same things." Protagoras cannot tolerate this violation of common sense: "'But, Socrates,' he said, 'the things that cowards go for are exactly the opposite of those that the courageous go for. For instance, courageous men are willing to go to war, but cowards aren't.'" In order to refute this palpably correct observation, Socrates now mobilizes another of his tricky conclusions from the previous discussion, to wit, the equally fallacious claim that "the noble, the good, and the pleasant are three terms designating the same thing, namely maximum pleasure and minimum pain." If that be the case, then the next conclusions follow as night follows day:

"Is it praiseworthy to go," I said, "or disgraceful?"

"Praiseworthy."

"So if it's praiseworthy, we agreed previously that it is good; for we agreed that all praiseworthy actions are good."

109. Coby, *Socrates*, 167. See also G. R. F. Ferrari, "Akrasia as Neurosis in Plato's *Protagoras*," *Proceedings of the Boston Area Colloquium in Ancient Philosophy* 6 (1990): 115–39.

"That's true; I remain of that opinion."

"You are right," I said. "But which of them is it you say are not willing to go to war, though that is something praiseworthy and good?"

"Cowards," he said.

"Well, now," I said, "if it's praiseworthy and good, is it also
pleasant?"

"Well, that's what was agreed," he said.

"So cowards are unwilling, in full knowledge of the facts, to go for
what is more praiseworthy and better and pleasanter?"

"But if we agree to that," he said, "we shall contradict our previously agreed conclusions."

"And what about the courageous man? Does he not go for what is
more praiseworthy and better and pleasanter?"

"I have to agree," he said.

Protagoras here has reluctantly agreed to a proposition that seems
to him contrary to good sense and experience, namely that going to
war, since it is good and noble, must also be pleasant.[110] Since the
practice of courageous men who go to war has been predicated as
everything positive—goodness, nobility, and even pleasantness—the
courageous could not possibly be frightened by shameful fears nor
made brave by foolish and shameful boldness:

"Now in general, when a courageous man is afraid, his fear is not something disgraceful, nor his confidence when he is confident?"

"That's right," he said.

"And if not disgraceful, are they not praiseworthy?"

He agreed.

"And if praiseworthy, good as well?"

"Yes."

"Now by contrast the fear and the confidence of cowards, madmen,
and the foolhardy are disgraceful?"

---

110. I rather think that Protagoras would almost have grounds for a suit of slander
against Coby, who writes here, "Of the nobility and goodness of courage, he replied, 'You
speak truly, and always it seems so to me.' This was the Protagoras of old speaking, urging
self-sacrifice on others while reserving pleasure for himself; it was the 'safe' reply (351d)"
(Coby, Socrates, 167).

He agreed.

"And is their confidence disgraceful and bad for any other reason than ignorance and error?"

"It's as you say," he said.

Protagoras, it seems, is now so confused by Socrates' rapid argument that he cannot even see how he is being manipulated. He is dispirited, not, on my reading, because he sees that he is about to lose a contest, but because he senses that Socrates is maneuvering him toward a conclusion that profoundly violates his sense of how things are. For Socrates, of course, that is a consummation devoutly to be wished. Plato's entire epistemology is based on the assumption that what people believe is at best only appearance and false consciousness. He is the very ideal type of Rorty's "misguided philosopher." But Protagoras has no such elitist presuppositions.

The relentless juggernaut proceeds:

"Well, now, do you call what makes a man a coward, cowardice or courage?"

"I call it cowardice," he said.

"And didn't it turn out that they are cowards as a result of their error about what is to be feared?"

"Certainly," he said.

"So it's in consequence of that error that they are cowards?"

He agreed.

Even Coby, the most blatant apologist for Socrates that I have found in modern writing, elegantly skewers Socrates' conclusion here, showing, for instance, that it might very well lead to the conclusion that "it follows that what is courageous behavior for the general (a rational determination that warfare is more pleasurable than painful) may well prove cowardly behavior for his troops—which leaves one with the comic possibility of a general courageously leading a charge and his troops courageously running for cover."[111]

But the logic is inexorable:

111. Coby, *Socrates,* 169.

"And you agree that what makes them cowards is cowardice?"

He assented.

"So cowardice proves to be error about what is to be feared and what isn't?"

He nodded.

If it is cowardice that makes men cowardly, and it is error that makes men cowardly, then it follows that cowardice is error. Socrates goes on:

"But now," I said, "the opposite of cowardice is courage."

"Yes."

"Now wisdom about what is to be feared and what isn't is the opposite of error about that."

At that he nodded once again.

"And error about that is cowardice?"

With great reluctance he nodded at that.

"So wisdom about what is to be feared and what isn't is courage, since it is the opposite of error about that?"

At this he wasn't even willing to nod agreement, but remained silent. And I said, "What's this, Protagoras? Won't you even answer yes or no?"

"Carry on yourself," he said.

"I've only one more question to ask you," I said. "Do you still think, as you did at the beginning, that some men are altogether ignorant, but very courageous?"

"I see that you insist, Socrates," he said, "that I must answer. So I'll oblige you; I declare that from what we have agreed it seems to me impossible." (359c–360d)

It's all over but the crowing. I find that this dénouement quite bears out Barrett's verdict that "Plato gives Protagoras the attitude of a rehabilitated rebel who has learned the right way and the right words to say."[112] With this bon mot, Barrett helps me nail down the

---

112. Barrett, *Sophists,* 60. It should be stated that Irwin, "Coercion," is largely an attempt to show that in the *Gorgias* Plato partly corrects for defects in the earlier elenctic method that render it coercive, but even Irwin (72–73) is not entirely sure of his success in this enterprise. Whatever Irwin's conclusions about the possibility of a noncoercive dia-

point of this chapter, alluding, as he does, to the Melian Dialogue. Plato at his most *spoudaios,* as I believe he is in the *Protagoras,* is deeply committed to an attack on a mode of speech, on a speech genre, if you will—the debate or speech in the Assembly. This objection carries with it an entire epistemology which is, at the same time, a political theory. On the one hand, Plato holds that there is absolute Truth somewhere out there in the Formosphere, and even though it is extremely difficult, nigh impossible, to discover, it is there beyond the flux of phenomena and experiences. Since only that Truth can give a meaningful basis to ethical action, only those who have access to it (or, at any rate, who seek it), shall have power in the polis, and democracy, as well, falls victim to oligarchy. If Protagoras is, as Farrar claimed compellingly, "the first democratic theorist," then Plato is, if not the first—surely not the first—an antidemocratic theorist, not least, or perhaps even most, in his slanderous attack on the Sophists Protagoras and Gorgias.

The essence of Athenian democracy hangs on the ability of the Athenian citizens who are not experts and not even adepts in political *tekhnē* to nevertheless hear and understand opposing speeches about justice (*dissoi logoi*) and to make just decisions on that basis. We see better now why this issue will be such a fraught one for Plato, appearing as it does in the *Protagoras* in the discussion of taking on a referee between Protagoras and Socrates and in the *Gorgias* and the *Symposium* in the figures of the theatrical competition and the rhetorical competition (to be discussed below).

The *Gorgias* is a similar dialogue to the *Protagoras* in that in it a virtual caricature of one of the most important Sophists is set up as a straw man and shot down in the service of the promulgation of (monological) dialogue over rhetoric and debate. Oddly enough, however, it is in this dialogue that Plato shows us (on my reading) his self-perception of the cracks in his own epistemological foundationalism as well.

---

lectic might be, it seems clear that *in practice* Socratic speech was coercive and criticized as such by democrats (Callicles!), and that is what is crucial for my argument here.

3

"Confound Seriousness with Laughter":
On Monological and Dialogical Reading—
the *Gorgias*

In an essay professing to advise students on how to get the most out of college, the conservative pundit David Brooks wrote recently:

> Read Plato's "Gorgias." As Robert George of Princeton observes, "The explicit point of the dialogue is to demonstrate the superiority of philosophy (the quest for wisdom and truth) to rhetoric (the art of persuasion in the cause of victory). At a deeper level, it teaches that the worldly honors that one may win by being a good speaker . . . can all too easily erode one's devotion to truth—a devotion that is critical to our integrity as persons. So rhetorical skills are dangerous, potentially soul-imperiling gifts." Explains everything you need to know about politics and punditry.[1]

Despite a century of research findings and explication to the contrary (since Nietzsche), this way of thinking about the place of Gorgias (and of sophism generally) in our culture is still

---

1. David Brooks, editorial, "Harvard-Bound? Chin Up," *New York Times*, 2 March 2006.

dominant. (I, of course, giving similar advice to students would suggest: read Gorgias.) Accepting the caricature drawn by Plato, George
and Brooks seem able to understand Gorgias only as a charlatan who
was cynically aware that what he taught was nothing but a means to
achieve victory in debate, without regard for truth (and in service of
the adept's own power and pleasure).[2] In this chapter, I wish then
to explore two ways of reading Plato, one that takes fully seriously
and at (highly critical) face value his attack on Gorgias and the other
Sophists, and one that attends to an at least incipient, if not more,
voice of internal critique within Plato himself, the vaunted "second
accent" of the heteroglossic or dialogical text. The point is precisely
that neither reading is the correct one, but rather that Plato's texts
manifest an intention to be read with such dead seriousness in one
moment but to be heard as qualifying themselves at another. With
this chapter, then, I begin to develop a dialogical reading of Plato's
corpus.

In the *Gorgias,* one of Plato's main objectives is the very invention
of *rhētorikē* in order to set it up as the other of *philosophia.* A distinguished historian of philosophy has written: "It was the widening
gulf between rhetoric and reality which led Plato in the *Gorgias* to
contrast rhetoric and philosophy, and to condemn the practice of the
first, and then later in the *Phaedrus* to argue in favour of a reformed
rhetoric based on dialectic and psychology as a possible servant of
philosophy."[3] Was it indeed? To my way of reading (learned from
other and better scholars than I, notably Nightingale and Schiappa),
Plato actually "invented" rhetoric as a way of establishing the dis-
tinctiveness and sole value of his notion of thinking, so there could
have been no widening gulf between a "rhetoric" that had not yet
been invented and a putative reality. In other words, rhetoric as a
discipline separate from philosophy did not exist until Plato drew
the distinction and created the binary opposition.[4] In order to get

2. For a good summary of what we know about Gorgias, see Scott Porter Consigny,
Gorgias: Sophist and Artist, Studies in Rhetoric/Communication (Columbia: University of
South Carolina Press, 2001).

3. G. B. Kerferd, *The Sophistic Movement* (Cambridge: Cambridge University Press,
1981), 78.

4. Edward Schiappa, "Did Plato Coin *Rhētorikē?*" *American Journal of Philology* III
(1990): 457–70.

a better sense of what it is that I am pushing against, let me cite the formulation of one of the more influential of traditional historians of rhetoric, George Kennedy, who writes, "The most important and most influential of the critics of rhetoric was Plato, especially in the dialogue *Gorgias*."[5] Thus for Kennedy there was an existing entity called "rhetoric" already in place for Plato to criticize. Kennedy, who simply takes Plato's dialogues as somehow a true story (and not the literary fictions that they almost patently are), argues that since the dialogue is set in the late fifth century and Gorgias and Polus both accept the term *rhētorikē,* therefore it must have existed earlier than Plato. The fallaciousness of this inference hardly needs to be argued.[6] The invention of the word and the concept of "rhetoric" is, I believe, intimately bound up in the reinvention of the word and the concept of "philosophy" by Plato, for whom the definition of that term indicates a willingness to "challenge the hold of the concrete over our consciousness, and to substitute the abstract."[7] We can see, then, that the very definition of rhetoric and philosophy as each other's others (much like the later terms "heresy" and "orthodoxy") is bound up in what we would call a philosophical question itself, namely the insistence on a realm of abstract or ideal existence, that which is constituted by the Platonic "ideas" or "forms," exactly that which Gorgias had denied. "Plato," remarks Nightingale, "was born into a culture which had no distinct concept of 'philosophy,' in spite of the fact that various kinds of abstract and analytic thinking had been and were being developed by the Presocratics, the mathematicians, dif-

5. George A. Kennedy, *Classical Rhetoric and Its Christian and Secular Tradition from Ancient to Modern Times* (Chapel Hill: University of North Carolina Press, 1980), 7.

6. Cf. Charles H. Kahn, *Plato and the Socratic Dialogue: The Philosophical Use of a Literary Form* (Cambridge: Cambridge University Press, 1996), 2, who gets this just right, stating the intention "to situate Plato in his own time and place, and thus to overcome what one might describe as the optical illusion of the dialogues. By this I mean Plato's extraordinary success in recreating the dramatic atmosphere of the previous age, the intellectual milieu of the late fifth century in which Socrates confronts the Sophists and their pupils. It is difficult but necessary to bear in mind the gap between this art world, created by Plato, and the actual world in which Plato worked out his own philosophy." See his harsher words on p. 3 for scholars who mistake the dramatist for a historian.

7. Eric Alfred Havelock, *Preface to Plato* (Cambridge, Mass.: Harvard University Press, 1963), 281. Or see Charles Kahn's formulation: "My interpretation is to this extent unitarian, in that I contend that behind the literary fluctuations of Plato's work stands the stable world view defined by his commitment to an otherwordly metaphysics and to the strict Socratic moral ideal." Kahn, *Plato and the Socratic Dialogue*, xv–xvi.

ferent kinds of scientists, and the Sophists. Previous to Plato, these intellectuals, together with poets, lawgivers, and other men of skill or wisdom, were grouped together under the headings of *'sophoi'* and *'sophistai.'*"[8]

As I have suggested, there are two kinds of political moves embedded in Plato's monological dialogues. In addition to the politics of Athens, we can also discern a more conventional kind of politics, namely academic rivalry. (When Henry Kissinger was asked why he was leaving Harvard for the State Department, he is reported to have answered that he was tired of politics.) As Charles Kahn has put it, "The intellectual world to which Plato's own work belongs is defined not by the characters in his dialogues but by the thought and writing of his contemporaries and rivals, such as the rhetorician Isocrates and the various followers of Socrates."[9] It is on this view quite plausible to read the *Gorgias* as primarily a covert attack not so much on Gorgias the teacher, as on Isocrates the (alleged) pupil of Gorgias and true

8. Andrea Wilson Nightingale, *Genres in Dialogue: Plato and the Construct of Philosophy* (Cambridge: Cambridge University Press, 1995), 10.

9. Kahn, *Plato and the Socratic Dialogue*, 2; and Schiappa similarly remarks:

There were good reasons for Plato to invent the term *rhētorikē*. The *Gorgias* was written at about the same time as the *Menexenus*, a piece in which Plato also attacked *rhetorike*—despite providing what came to be regarded by the Athenians as a good example of a funeral oration. The combined target of the *Gorgias* and the *Menexenus* was nothing less than the most important public speaking practices in Athens: defense in the law courts, speaking in the assembly, and the important political act of eulogizing the war dead. If Plato could identify the "product" of his rival Isocrates' training as something unnecessary or undesirable, so much the better for the reputation of Plato's school. Gorgias, it should be remembered, was the teacher of Isocrates, hence a dialogue on public discourse titled *Gorgias* that included thinly veiled references to Isocrates would easily have been recognized in the fourth century as an attack on the training afforded by Isocrates. It is significant, I think, that the portion of the dialogue devoted to "What is rhetoric?" begins with an exchange between the *students* of Gorgias and Socrates (Polus and Chaerephon), perhaps symbolically paralleling the conflict between Isocrates and Plato. The portions of the dialogue concerned explicitly with the nature of *rhētorikē* involve Gorgias; afterward his character fades from the dialogue. If, as I have conjectured, *rhētoreia* was a novel term associated with the training offered by Isocrates, then Gorgias' explicit declaration at 449a5 that he teaches the art of oratory (*rhētorikē*) would have been a clear signal to fourth-century readers that the target of the passage was Isocrates.

Edward Schiappa, *Protagoras and Logos: A Study in Greek Philosophy and Rhetoric* (Columbia: University of South Carolina Press, 1991), 45. See also discussion in Samuel IJsseling, *Rhetoric and Philosophy in Conflict: An Historical Survey* (The Hague: M. Nijhoff, 1976), 9–10.

rival of Plato. We get something of what was at stake for these two rivals in reading Isocrates' own words on the subject:

> Since it is not in the nature of man to attain a scientific knowledge (ἐπιστήμην) by which, once we possess it, we would know what to do or say, I consider those men wise who are able by means of con-jecture/opinion (ταῖς δόξαις) to hit upon, for the most part, what is best; and I call those men "philosophers" who are engaged in the stud-ies from which they will most quickly achieve this kind of wisdom. (*Antidosis* 271)[10]

Now, of course, the oppositions between *epistēmē,* Truth, and *doxa,* opinion, are precisely the fundamental opposition that consti-tutes Plato's entire invention of philosophy as opposed to rhetoric.[11] Isocrates' direct target here is his rival teacher Plato.

Thus, at least one of Plato's motives was his rivalry, for prestige, for power, with Isocrates. This comes out as well at the end of the *Phaedrus* in which Isocrates is directly addressed.[12]

The work of Nightingale has been an important guide to me in the formulation of the hypotheses which I will be exploring in this chap-ter as throughout. As Nightingale has written, "In addition to looking at Plato's dialogues in the context of intellectual history, we need to interpret them in the context of social history."[13] What precisely is the social history that is so relevant here? Plato was deeply and person-ally implicated in the enormous and enormously painful changes that took place within his lifetime in the social, political, and economic structures of democratic Athens. The dénouement of the Pelopon-nesian wars occasioned a devastation in morality and morale that en-gendered enormous emotions. In part, I would suggest, Plato's entire lifework is dedicated to overturning the Athenian worldview that is exemplified best (however critically and painfully) by Thucydides,[14]

---

10. Translation as given in Nightingale, *Genres in Dialogue,* 28, and see her discussion there as well.

11. This is the major thrust of Nightingale's argument.

12. James A. Coulter, "*Phaedrus* 279a: The Praise of Isocrates," *GRBS* 8 (1967): 225–36.

13. Nightingale, *Genres in Dialogue,* 9.

14. Kahn, *Plato and the Socratic Dialogue,* xv.

clearly an important and explicit nemesis for Plato.[15] One of the most important steps in that overturn of traditional Athens was the discrediting of Gorgias which he set out to perform in the eponymous dialogue. In order to set up this point, I will first perform a reading of the remains that we have of some of Gorgias's actual texts to better see both what Plato was opposing and how he was caricaturing or satirizing a serious intellectual opponent.

Will the Real Gorgias Please Stand Up?

Plato's discipline was not born like Athena full-grown out of Zeus's head, but had a normal gestation and birth. It grew out of debates at least a generation earlier than Plato and even than his teacher Socrates. As the highly distinguished scholar of Plato Gregory Vlastos has written:

> The antecedents of this view can be discerned a generation or more before Socrates, in the dawn of metaphysics in Greece, when epistemology, still in its infancy, is not yet a fully articulated discipline and its doctrines are set forth in oracular prose (as in Heraclitus) or in poetic form (as in Empedocles and Parmenides). To illustrate from Parmenides: his implicit acceptance of indubitable certainty as the prerogative of the philosopher's knowledge shows up in the fictional guise of divine revelation in which he presents his metaphysical (and even his physical) system. . . . The appeal is throughout to critical reason, not to faith; the goddess does not say "Close your eyes and believe," but "Open your mind and attend to the 'strife-encompassed refutation' I offer." But the hierophantic trappings of the argument attest the certainty its author attaches to its conclusion.[16]

Parmenides, in the fragments that we have remaining of his work, seems to make a distinction between that which is true or real (*aletheis*), which persuades automatically, as it were, and our perceptions or received opinion, which do not persuade but virtually force us to

---

15. I hope to develop this argument elsewhere.
16. Gregory Vlastos, *Socratic Studies,* ed. Myles Burnyeat (Cambridge: Cambridge University Press, 1994), 54–55.

believe things that are wrong. He is thus making a clear distinction between persuasion and force or compulsion.

As Mi-Kyoung Lee has put it:

In his poem, Parmenides lays claim to a kind of knowledge not attained by ordinary mortals, the way to which is revealed to him by a goddess who presents him with a choice between the way of persuasion and the way of δόξα or ordinary human opinion (DK 28 B1.28–30, B.2 4–8); the latter she says is deceptive and should be avoided. Parmenides' special twist on the theme is that truth must be attained by the active use of reason.[17]

In other words, Parmenides is the first promulgator of the notion of rational compulsion, which is persuasion and not truly compulsion, as analysis of his poem will bring out.

Parmenides' little work *On Nature* is divided into two parts. The first discusses the world of "truth" or "reality," the world of *logos,* while the second concerns itself with the world of illusion, *kosmos,* the world of the senses, and the erroneous opinions of humankind founded upon them:

The one—that [*it*] *is,* and that [*it*] *cannot not be,*
Is the path of Persuasion (for it attends upon truth):
The other–that [*it*] *is not* and that [*it*] *needs must not be,*
That I point out to you to be a path wholly unlearnable,
For you could not know what-is-not (for that is not feasible),
Nor could you point it out.[18]

Now the foundation of what will be called later on (after Plato) philosophy comes as well from Parmenides, who further writes, "because the same thing is there for thinking and for being"[19] and then "the same thing is for thinking and [is] that there is thought; For not without

17. Mi-Kyoung Lee, *Epistemology after Protagoras: Responses to Relativism in Plato, Aristotle, and Democritus* (Oxford: Oxford University Press, 2005), 39.

18. David Gallop, *Parmenides of Elea: Fragments, a Text and Translation with an Introduction, Phoenix: Journal of the Classical Association of Canada* suppl. vol. 1 (Toronto: University of Toronto Press, 1984), 55.

19. Gallop, *Parmenides of Elea,* 57.

what-is, on which [it] depends, having been declared, Will you find thinking . . . "[20] There should be a perfect correspondence, it would seem, between rational thought and the real, "objective," *aletheis* structure of Being, of the universe. As François Jullien has recently put it, "As is well known, philosophy turned to that which is stable and unchangeable in its quest for truth; that which is true only became absolute truth when it became linked with being (in other words, philosophy only emerged by becoming ontological). It is even possible to identify the point at which it did so. In lines 3–4 of the second fragment of Parmenides, philosophy emerges from its religious context and declares itself to be the understanding of being qua being; and the path according to which '[it] is, and [it] cannot not be' is the path that 'attends upon truth.'"[21] The goddess (Athena) in speaking to Parmenides recognizes, however, that rational persuasion of what is true or real, which ought to persuade simply and completely, does not always do so (or perhaps does not do so very often or maybe even ever). She distinguishes between *logos* and *kosmos*. *Logos* here means the reasoning, the exclusively logical, rational character of truth in contrast to the *kosmos* of the words. The Greek word *kosmos* means that which is ordered or harmonious and by extension anything that is adorned. Hence develops easily the meaning of illusion (cf. our word "cosmetics"). The goddess says: "Here I stop my trustworthy speech [*Logos*] to you and thought about Objective Truth. From here on, learn the subjective beliefs of mortals; listen to the deceptive ordering of my words [Kosmos]." Robert Wardy explains, "Just as a painted face deceives the onlooker, so the goddess's phrase suggests the disturbing possibility that a *kosmos* of words . . . might mislead precisely in that these words wear an attractive appearance of superficial order masking essential incoherence."[22] The goddess goes on to describe such a *kosmos,* namely a construction very similar to the philosophical positions held by Parmenides' contemporaries, the position that was considered "orthodox" at the time of Parmenides' activity, one that is "stunningly complex and complete," but a fabrication, a *kosmos* of words, as any account of the world other than the goddess's

---

20. Gallop, *Parmenides of Elea,* 71.

21. François Jullien, "Did Philosophers Have to Become Fixated on Truth?" trans. Janet Lloyd, *Critical Inquiry* 28, no. 4 (2002): 810.

22. Robert Wardy, *The Birth of Rhetoric: Gorgias, Plato, and Their Successors,* Issues in Ancient Philosophy (New York: Routledge, 1996), 13.

own (i.e., Parmenides') *logos* must be. The reasons, according to the goddess, for uttering such falsehoods, for constructing such *kosmos,* is "so that no one will outstrip you in judgment, / so that no mortal belief will outdo you." There seems to be a striking contradiction, then, within Parmenides' own position. On the one hand, he speaks of an absolute truth which everyone would immediately recognize as such when its *logos* is laid out by rational argument; but, on the other hand, he seems to speak of an equally persuasive falsehood which persuades by the same means and without a criterion to tell the difference. First of all, while Parmenides is insisting that the power of *logos* as truth is so transparent that it needs, in fact, no force, no authority to make it so, he puts his own discourse into the mouth of a goddess, thereby belying his own claims.[23] Secondly, truth/reality is defined as that which is persuasive, but the *kosmos* is also deceptive, therefore likely to deceive, to persuade, so then what criterion has been offered for telling the difference between one persuasive argument and another? Parmenides through his opposition of persuasion to compulsion, problematic as it is, was setting the stage for Plato's opposition of philosophy to rhetoric. He found a worthy opponent in the Sophist Gorgias, who perceiving this contradiction, chose to live within it rather than seek to escape it.

On Nature; or What Is Not[24]

The title of one of Gorgias's works extant (at least in epitome): *On What Is Not or On Nature* is already parodic of Parmenides' title *On*

---

23. See also Jullien, "Did Philosophers," 808, on this relation. The same paradox can be found at the end of the *Gorgias* (see Nightingale, *Genres in Dialogue,* 87), which will be further discussed below.

24. For the Greek texts of Gorgias and Protagoras, I cite Hermann Diels and Walther Kranz, *Die Fragmente der Vorsokratiker, Griechisch und Deutsch* (Zürich: Weidmann, 1966). For translation, I am citing the excellent work of Michael Gagarin and Paul Woodruff, *Early Greek Political Thought from Homer to the Sophists,* ed. and trans. Michael Gagarin, Cambridge Texts in the History of Political Thought (Cambridge: Cambridge University Press, 1995), having closely consulted as well Hermann Diels and Rosamond Kent Sprague, *The Older Sophists,* ed. Rosamond Kent Sprague (Columbia: University of South Carolina Press, 1972); and for the *Encomium to Helen* also Douglas M. MacDowell, ed. and trans., *Encomium of Helen by Gorgias* (Bristol: Bristol Classical Press, 1982). Finally for Sextus, I cite Sextus, *Against the Logicians,* ed. and trans. Richard Arnot Home Bett, Cambridge Texts in the History of Philosophy (Cambridge: Cambridge University Press, 2005).

Nature.[25] Nature was generally considered that which is, as is evident in the title of a book written by Parmenides' pupil Melissus called *On Nature or On What Is.* Gorgias sets out, it seems, to overturn Parmenides. And he does so on the grounds of something that we might call common sense. Gorgias's tenets in this text are traditionally described as threefold. Here is Sextus Empiricus's summary:

> Gorgias of Leontini belonged to the same troop as those who did away with the criterion, but not by way of the same approach as Protagoras. For in the work entitled *On What Is Not* or *On Nature* he sets up three main points one after the other: first, that there is nothing; second, that even if there is [something], it is not apprehensible by a human being; third, that even if it is apprehensible, it is still not expressible or explainable to the next person.[26]

The interpretation of these sentences has been much contested,[27] but historian of rhetoric Richard Enos has provided a compelling interpretation of these seemingly nonsensical statements.[28] It would seem, at first glance, that Gorgias is denying the existence of the empirical, physical world, but not only would this be an absurd position, it would contradict everything else we know about his thought. In fact, however, it seems that Gorgias is, through this statement, asserting that there is nothing *but* the physical world. In this he is the disciple, as it were, of no less than Heraclitus, who, according to Cynthia Farrar, "chose fire, transition, paradox, conflict, as the essence of the universal order, . . . because they are characteristics of the world men

25. MacDowell cleverly suggests a modern analogue in the form of a text entitled *Thirteenth Night; or, What You Won't.* MacDowell, *Encomium of Helen by Gorgias,* 11.

26. Sextus, *Against the Logicians,* 15. There are many problems with the text of the testimonia to this work, which is known from two ancient paraphrastic sources: *Against the Logicians* of Sextus Empiricus as cited here and from pseudo-Aristotle's *Melissus, Xenophanes, and Gorgias* 979a11–980b21. For the general, broad interpretation being advanced here, these textual issues do not matter. For excellent discussion, see Edward Schiappa, *The Beginnings of Rhetorical Theory in Classical Greece* (New Haven [Conn.]: Yale University Press, 1999), 134–36.

27. Sextus, *Against the Logicians,* 15n35.

28. Until quite recently, taken as nonsensical or "sophistry" by most historians of philosophy (such as E. R. Dodds, ed., *Gorgias: A Revised Text by Plato* [1959; repr., Oxford: Oxford University Press, 2002], 7–8).

[*sic*] actually experience."[29] Gorgias is, therefore, intellectually most comparable to Protagoras, as we have seen him in the previous chapter. According to Enos's account, what Gorgias is denying is precisely existents in the philosophical (that is Parmenidean, hence Platonic) sense, essences, ideas or forms, that enable speech of essences.[30] This interpretation is strongly supported by Kahn's classic demonstration that *einai* is not a semantic match for English "to be." Where, in English, as Schiappa explains Kahn, I can say "I exist," while knowing that I have been born and will die, in ancient Greek, or at any rate, in the Greek of Parmenides, such a statement cannot be made, since to exist is neither to come into being nor to end. Greek *gignesthai,* glossed usually as "to become," but most frequently used in Greek where we would use forms of "to be," exhibits this semantic nuance well.[31] Gorgias claims that no essences exist, but only the physical reality that we see and touch. As Enos puts it, "Platonic notions of ontological 'essences' . . . were absurdities to Gorgias. He viewed humans as functioning in an ever changing world and manufacturing ideas that lose their 'existence' the instant they pass from the mind of the thinker. Accordingly, ideals attain existence only through the extrapolations of the mind and are dependent upon the referential perceptions of their creator. As such, they cannot exist without a manufactured antithesis or anti-model. By their very nature, they can form no ideal at all since each individual predicated ideals based on personal experiences."[32]

The latter two of Gorgias's three points are closely related to the

29. Cynthia Farrar, *The Origins of Democratic Thinking: The Invention of Politics in Classical Athens* (Cambridge: Cambridge University Press, 1987), 39.

30. This interpretation seems certainly supported by the other extant ancient paraphrase of Gorgias's text, in which the first clause is οὐκ εἶναί φησιν οὐδέν, which translates best as "there is no 'to be'"; he says that it is nothing, or, perhaps, as Schiappa would have it, "there is no be-ing," Schiappa, *Beginnings of Rhetorical Theory,* 133. This version of Gorgias's fragment is found in pseudo-Aristotle's *On Melissus, Xenophanes, and Gorgias* 979a12–13.

31. Schiappa, *Beginnings of Rhetorical Theory,* 145.

32. Richard Leo Enos, *Greek Rhetoric before Aristotle* (Prospect Heights, Ill.: Waveland Press, 1993), 81–82; *pace* Consigny, *Gorgias,* 35. I don't think that this position commits Enos to identify in Gorgias an "empiricist" epistemology according to which "we may perceive [the world] empirically through our sensory 'pores' and describe [it] accurately with a scientific discourse." Enos may or may not hold such a view elsewhere, but taken on its own, his account of Gorgias could as easily lead to an antifoundationalist as an empiricist position.

first. Based on his fundamental sensibility or understanding that the only objects of human cognition are sense perceptions, Gorgias simply argues that even if there were some essence or idealities, there is no way that humans could perceive and understand them. In other words, we have here a statement of the limitations of human knowing because of the "*human media* of understanding—sense perceptions."[33] Beyond the positive experience of humans lie only the extrapolations of the mind, once again a system of representation or signification in which nothing exists except by virtue of that which it is not (Saussure before Saussure). Gorgias's third tenet is, then, simply a further statement about the inability of human language to communicate even sense perceptions, let alone whatever truths about reality that it might have been able (again contrary to plausibility) to divine. As must be obvious, Gorgias's rhetorical, or sophistic, thought leads us in very different directions from the thought of philosophy, as Plato had defined it. Plato desired to discover, and believed he could, truths that would be always true without reference to speakers, hearers, or situations. Gorgias's thought leads us to understand that we must allow "for the contingencies of interpretation and human nature that are inherent in any social circumstances, which inherently lack 'ideal' or universally affirmed premises."[34] Gorgias's views clearly reflect a strong theoretical opposition to Platonic philosophy, as a discipline per se. Since all of Western philosophy has been read as "footnotes to Plato," à la Whitehead, this very opposition has been marked, following Plato, as mere charlatanism, searching for success rather than truth. But there is no reason not to imagine an expanded sense for philosophy in which the very critique of Truth (rhetoric/sophism) is internal to the enterprise of thought and not a discarded externality. A philosophy that would be, rather, footnotes to Gorgias. Read this way, Gorgias anticipates no less than Nietzsche!

I think that it has not been emphasized enough how precisely Gorgias's three points dog the steps of Parmenides,[35] who had written, as we saw above: "The one: that it is and it is impossible for it not to be.

---

33. Enos, *Greek Rhetoric*, 82, emphasis original.
34. Enos, *Greek Rhetoric*, 73.
35. For an exception, Schiappa, *Beginnings of Rhetorical Theory*, 143.

This is the path of persuasion, for it accompanies Objective Truth [*Aletheia*]. The other [*Doxa*]: that it is not and it necessarily must not be. That, I point out to you, is a path wholly unthinkable, for neither could you know what-is-not (for that is impossible), nor could you point it out." Gorgias's denials are precisely denials or reversals of each one of Parmenides' points. There is nothing; you don't know it; and, indeed, you can't point it out. Gorgias's views, thus, clearly reflect a strong theoretical opposition to Parmenidianism.

The Encomium to Helen

Gorgias's most famous text, *The Encomium to Helen* (D-K 3)[36] stands at a crux in the development of Greek and thus Western discourse and textuality.[37] It also occupies the border between poetry and prose and between magical language and *tekhnē*.[38] In its latter guise, it is in the control, so to speak, of its employers and thus subject to self-reflexivity. An important point to be emphasized, and one that Susan Jarratt articulates eloquently, is that seeing the discourse of the Sophists and especially Gorgias's great text as liminal in this way does not mean that it is a stepping-stone from one state to another, nor that it represents progress with respect to what came before nor a primitivity with respect to what would come after. It is foundational, I would argue, in its raising of a set of philosophical dilemmas from which we have not yet escaped or found solutions to, problems having to do with agency, persuasion, seduction, and force. As *tekhnē,* it is required to reflect on the conditions of its operations and especially their moral effects: "In order for Gorgias's rhetoric to escape the accusation of amoral manipulation, it would need to bring the conditions under which persuasion was effected before the audience itself as a subject for consideration. In the *Encomium of Helen,* Gorgias engages in just such a public exploration of the power of *logos*—a force com-

36. MacDowell, *Encomium of Helen by Gorgias.*

37. To the best of my knowledge, it is both the first prose encomium (which disturbed Isocrates, who claimed that it was not "truly" an encomium) and the first encomium to a woman.

38. Jacqueline de Romilly, *Magic and Rhetoric in Ancient Greece,* The Carl Newell Jackson Lectures (Cambridge, Mass.: Harvard University Press, 1975), 16.

ing to be seen in the mid-fifth century Greek *polis* as rivaling the fate of the gods or even physical violence in its power."[39] Jarratt provides a compelling account of Gorgias's project in his *Encomium to Helen*. In brief, her reading is that for Gorgias *logos,* in this case, persuasive speech—that which will later be called rhetoric—is a drug, indeed, and like drugs can bring either death and disease or life and health. If, as we have seen in his *On Nothing,* Gorgias radically denies the possibility of discovery and communication of Truth, he nevertheless believes that we do communicate with each other: "Gorgias, in other words, recognizes and inquires into the psychological conditions of assent for the individual who participates in the rhetorical scene of democracy. In choosing Helen to exonerate from blame, he suggests that the private, internal process of granting assent to the deceptions of language can have a public impact."[40] Jarratt continues to make her most significant point, arguing that according to Gorgias, "this process is not guided by the 'rational' intellect. In his story of Helen's abduction, language is parallel with forces of violence, love, and fate, all of which exceed the bounds of rational containment. Gorgias calls that emotional experience in the space between reality and language 'deception' (*apate*). *Though once again a Platonic concept of commensurability between word and thing will interpret this term pejoratively, Gorgias empties it of its moral charge, like Nietzsche in his redefinition of 'lies.'*"[41]

I would like to build on Jarrat's suggestive comments on the *Encomium* and move toward a deeper appreciation of its import by reading it, like *On Nature,* as a kind of parodic response to Parmenides and especially a critique (almost a precisely formal deconstruction in the full Derridean sense) of the binary opposition of persuasion to compulsion on the one hand and of the notion of *rational* compulsion through *logismos,* logic, on the other. On my reading, the question that Gorgias sets, the dilemma that he raises, is whether or not there is truly something called persuasion that is different from force, whether or not, that is, there can be a rhetoric that nonetheless leaves

39. Susan C. Jarratt, *Rereading the Sophists: Classical Rhetoric Refigured* (Carbondale, Ill.: Southern Illinois University Press, 1991), 57. See Romilly, *Magic and Rhetoric,* 3–22.

40. Jarratt, *Rereading,* 55. There is, indeed, something very Santayanan in this description, or so it seems to these untutored ears.

41. Jarratt, *Rereading,* 55, emphasis added. See also Thomas G. Rosenmeyer, "Gorgias, Aeschylus, and *Apate,*" *American Journal of Philology* 76 (1955): 225–60.

its recipient free to choose between different positions and thus subject to moral and criminal judgment. At the same time that Gorgias
will argue that the beauty (*kosmos*) of speech is truth, he denies that
anyone knows or can know truth (as we have seen above in the discussion of his *On Nothing*), and there follows from this a deeply dialogical
text, produced by an elegant paradox, which we can follow through a
closer reading.

The Helen in question is, of course, Helen of Troy; she whose beautiful face allegedly "launched a thousand ships and burnt the topless
towers of Illyrium," a classical case, it would seem, of blaming the (female) victim, and this is precisely Gorgias's theme. In the beginning
of the *Iliad*, we find Helen already in Troy, opening up the obvious
question of how she got there, and whether she is culpable or not. As
Gorgias himself, says, "Who it was or why or how he took Helen and
fulfilled his love, I shall not say. For to tell those who know something
they know carries conviction, but it does not bring pleasure." What
is important for Gorgias is rather to investigate Helen's motivations
for journeying to Troy. It is characteristic, of course, that such fundamental questions of will and culpability are debated in antiquity on
the bodies of women (and especially raped women; cf. Lucretia). This
may be the earliest attestation indeed of the topos by which women
are being read entirely out of the realm of thinking subjects by being
made "good for thinking with."[42]

Gorgias wishes to exonerate Helen of any blame that has been attached to her person and name by pejoratively marking it "as single-
voiced, single-minded conviction [ὁμόφωνος καὶ ὁμόψυχος] [that has]
arisen about this woman" (2). He is, moreover, to do this by introducing "reasoning" (λογισμόν) into the debate. The term *logismos* is not,
it seems, a common word in the fifth century, and where it occurs
(Democritus, Aristophanes, Thucydides), it means reasoned logical
thought but not necessarily the truth. As Vessela Valiavitcharska (following Schiappa) has put it, "The word λογισμός is not unequivocally

42. Cf. Susan Biesecker, "Feminist Criticism of Classical Rhetorical Texts: A Case
Study of Gorgias' *Helen*," in *Realms of Rhetoric: Phonic, Graphic, Electronic*, ed. Victor J.
Vitanza and Michele Ballif (Arlington, Tex.: Rhetoric Society of America, 1990), 67–82;
Andy Crockett, "Gorgias's Encomium of Helen: Violent Rhetoric or Radical Feminism?"
Rhetoric Review 13, no. 1 (Autumn 1994): 71–90. See also Ann Bergren, "Language and the
Female in Early Greek Thought," *Arethusa* 16 (1983): 69–95.

connected with truth, although it may be used to reflect logical reasoning or careful analysis. But if a *logos* combined with λογισμός is not necessarily a truthful *logos*—yet Gorgias explicitly purports to reveal the truth—what kind of *logos* is a true *logos*?"[43] In the first paragraph of his text, Gorgias twice mentions "truth." In the very first sentence, in a list of that which is "ornament" (κόσμος) to various entities, such as wisdom as the ornament of a mind and excellence (ἀρετή) as the ornament of an action, "truth" (ἀλήθεια) is listed as the ornament of a speech. In order, then, for Gorgias's own speech, this very text, to be a good one it must be adorned with truth. Note that Gorgias's use of the term *kosmos* is deliberately provocative with respect to Parmenides, who had used it to delineate the false or merely decorative (cf. cosmetic) aspect of rhetoric,[44] while Gorgias uses it precisely to refer to the truthfulness of a *logos*. We certainly cannot interpret Gorgias's own use of *kosmos* as evincing this negative sense, given the other examples of *kosmos* that he lists, which are all manifestly positive. The text becomes quickly more complicated by the end of the first paragraph, for one is enjoined to praise a speech that has the *kosmos* of truth, and, claims Gorgias, a speech blaming Helen would be an untrue, lying speech (τοὺς δὲ μεμφομένους ψευδομένους). Gorgias wishes, then, to produce a speech that has the *kosmos* of truth by freeing the slandered woman from blame.

To accomplish this purpose, he adduces four possible causes for her actions: (1) being forced by gods and their desires; (2) being forced (raped) by a man; (3) being persuaded by speeches (λόγοις πεισθεῖσα); and (4) being captivated by desire (ἔρωτι ἁλοῦσα). In the first two

---

43. Vessela Valiavitcharska, "Correct *Logos* and Truth in Gorgias' *Enconomium of Helen*," *Rhetorica* 24, no. 2 (2006): 153.

44. I am using the term "rhetoric" here to refer to persuasive speech and not a theory of discipline of rhetoric, which certainly, as Schiappa has eloquently proven, did not yet exist in the fifth century; Schiappa, *Beginnings of Rhetorical Theory*. This distinction will answer, as well, Schiappa's objections to the notion that the *Helen* is about rhetoric (119–20). Once again, to be clear, I suggest that the *Helen* is a discourse on the practice of speech making, not on rhetoric as a discipline. For fifth-century attacks on that practice, we need look no further than Thucydides' Mytilenian Debate, in which *rhetores*, not rhetoric, are attacked and defended. Schiappa's own discussion of the *Helen* adds much to understanding of the place of that text in the history of thinking, arguing that "From the standpoint of intellectual history, it is arguably the case that Gorgias' questioning of a taken-for-granted dichotomy [between persuasion and force] is a more important step in developing new modes of inquiry than any particular claim that Gorgias makes about *logos, pethō*, or *biā*." Schiappa, *Beginnings of Rhetorical Theory*, 128–29.

cases, we have Compulsion (Ἀνάγκη), which even on Parmenides' view would certainly free a person from responsibility. The question that will really interest Gorgias in this text about speech is whether having been persuaded by speech is the same as compulsion, in which case Helen is blameless on this account as well, or whether it is different from compulsion, in which case her free choice would condemn her. Gorgias, of course, wishes to argue the former possibility. He beautifully writes of the power of speech:

> If speech [*logos*] persuaded and deluded her mind, even against this it is not hard to defend her or free her from blame, as follows: speech is a powerful master and achieves the most divine feats with the smallest and least evident body. It can stop fear, relieve pain, create joy, and increase pity. How this is so, I shall show; and I must demonstrate this to my audience to change their opinion. (*Encomium* 8–9)

The last sentence, usually glossed over by commentators, is both exceedingly puzzling and exceedingly important. The Greek reads: ταῦτα δὲ ὡς οὕτως ἔχει δείξω, δεῖ δὲ καὶ δόξῃ δεῖξαι τοῖς ἀκούουσι. Although Gagarin and Woodruff take the last clause to mean "change their opinion," this is something of a smoothed-over paraphrase of an ambiguous phrase. Sprague gives, "It is necessary to offer proof to the opinion of my hearers," thus translating more literally but still yielding the sense of Gagarin and Woodruff's translation. Instead, however, of taking the dative in which the word "opinion" is cast as indirect object, MacDowell translates the dative instrumentally: "I must prove it by opinion to my hearers." This seems to me at least a highly attractive option, and it is the one that I am going with here, recognizing full well that it is not ineluctable. Gorgias seems to be saying, at first glance, that he will need to do two separate things, prove the matter through *logismos* (logically), on the one hand, and on the other prove it via opinion for his listeners. This seems to be the way that Segal, for instance, reads the text, thus justifying his position that Gorgias knows that there is absolute truth but knows that he must deceive to persuade the hoi polloi.[45] His version then would

---

45. Charles Segal, "Gorgias and the Psychology of the Logos," *Harvard Studies in Classical Philology* 66 (1962): 99–155.

have Gorgias accept Parmenides' and Plato's terms but reverse them cynically (as Plato portrays him in the eponymous dialogue). This interpretation of Gorgias's words would lend support to those who accuse him of insincerity, of knowing that there is truth but recognizing that he must lie to persuade his listeners (something like a "noble lie" perhaps [to be read with heavy irony]). I would like to suggest a different interpretation of the relationship of the two clauses to each other, namely that the second clause explicates the first clause: I must prove this, and, moreover, do so via the opinion of my listeners, that is, by using what they already believe (more literally "through opinion to my listeners").[46] This latter interpretation, which does, after all, make much more sense of the text, is important—if not absolutely crucial—for my argument, for according to this reading, Gorgias refuses to make a distinction between "the Truth" and opinion.

Gorgias goes on to construct his proof, which seems to follow best on this interpretation. He argues that since human beings do not and cannot possess memory of the past and understanding of the present and foreknowledge of the future, they must depend on opinion. He argues, then, that belief being slippery and unreliable (ἡ δὲ δόξα σφαλερὰ καὶ ἀβέβαιος οὖσα),[47] those who employ it have slippery and unreliable success. Therefore, Helen is blameless, since "persuasion expelled sense; and indeed persuasion, though not having an appearance of compulsion, has the same power" (12). This is, I would suggest, a direct challenge to Parmenides' distinction between persuasion and compulsion. Persuasion, and thus Parmenides' "rational compulsion," is merely compulsion by other means. Helen is, therefore, exonerated of having been seduced on the same grounds as those who would have exonerated her had she been raped. Gorgias declares at this point (after first going through the argument for her own sexual desire as compulsion, as well) that he has succeeded in his original aim, to exonerate the blameless Helen: "to dispel injustice of blame and ignorance of belief." He has, moreover, produced a speech (λόγος).

But at the same time, there is a deep paradox in Gorgias's demonstration, as, I suppose, he himself realizes. The paradox is formed

46. This construal of the syntax is accepted by both Sprague and Gagarin/Woodruff in their translations, even though they interpret the sentence differently in other respects.

47. For this translation of the two terms, see MacDowell, *Encomium of Helen by Gorgias*, 25.

through the following moves. In order to exonerate Helen he persuaded us, his listeners, that rhetoric is something that removes the
power of decision as completely as physical force, and that, to put it
sharply, every seduction is a rape, including the seduction of Helen.
But, if he successfully persuades us that that is the case, he has undermined any moral force that his own art of persuasion has claimed
and thus its very power to exonerate, to be an encomium at all. For he
has indicated that he also must prove his point using belief or opinion, just as the seducer does. Let me put this another way to make it
clearer. Segal argues that the text is an encomium of Helen and also
an encomium of *logos* (rhetoric *avant le lettre*), and so it would seem to
be, as Segal puts it, a "kind of advertisement of his skills."[48] However,
insofar as the text succeeds as a defense of Helen, it fails as a defense
of or advertisement for the (moral) value of *logos*—and this is Gorgias's stated goal: to display the κόσμος of speech, its truthfulness—
having argued that *logos* is a drug the use of which constitutes coercion and not persuasiveness, whether for good or ill.

The simplest way, perhaps, of articulating this self-contradiction is
to say that Gorgias intends that his speech will demonstrate the power
of speech, by convincing us either of Helen's innocence or of speech's
potency, a potency akin to divine power, physical force, and seduction.
If Helen is innocent owing to the power of speech, then we are duped
into believing in her innocence by the power of the same speech that
exonerates her. If Helen's seduction is rape owing to the inexorable
power of her seducer's words, then our seduction is as well.

If we are not simply to take Gorgias as a kind of moral nihilist and
cynic, in the modern sense (as many, to be sure, do), we almost must
read this text in this paradoxical fashion, for he tells us four things
that seem mutually incompatible: (1) that the excellence of speech is
truth and that he intends to tell truth and dispel falsehood; (2) that
he must prove his argument by using *doxa;* (3) that *doxa* is not reliable
(and this is why Helen was compelled and should be blameless); and
(4) that he has succeeded in his task. If he is not simply conceding that
he is a deceiver, that his first statement of intent was a lie, and that all
speech is deceit, as many interpreters and most notably Segal would
have it, then the paradox, even the *aporia* of the relation of speech to

48. Segal, "Gorgias," 102.

"truth" comes to the fore in the text. If Gorgias's text persuades us that Helen is innocent, it does so by convincing us that persuasion is the same as compulsion. But our having been persuaded that this is the case is equally a matter of compulsion and equally based on opinion or belief. Ergo, our having been persuaded is equally unreliable, and perhaps, then, Helen is guilty. We can't know truth—nothing *is*— and even if we did, we could not communicate it to others. Inter alia, this reading has the beneficial effect of making the *Helen* compatible with the *On Nature*. Not only through parody[49] but through paradox (the paradox is the therapy—not the antidote—of the orthodox), Gorgias's text makes a brilliant case for undecidability. In calling his own text a plaything (παίγνιον), he is, I suggest, employing his own principle that "one should demolish one's opponents' seriousness by humor, and their humor by seriousness,"[50] but he is both protagonist and antagonist in this dialectic! I think that this interpretation is supported at least somewhat by the very form of Gorgias's final sentence in the *Helen,* in which, to be exact, he writes in a nice example of asyndetic antithesis: "I wished to write an account that would be, on the one hand, Helen's encomium, on the other, my own plaything."[51] At one and the same time, a genuine vindication for Helen and a plaything for him. The text is thus a self-consuming artifact, as it were, one that he calls a "plaything," not because he is not dead serious in this enterprise—it is one of the greatest of ethical and political inquiries that there could be—but because the way that he chooses to lay bare this issue, to enter the *aporia* (blind canyon), is via a paradox that eats its own tale (*sic*). George Kennedy captures this meaning precisely, I reckon, when he writes that "Gorgias *plays at* undercutting a serious purpose in the speech."[52] Gorgias is only playing at undercutting his seriousness with play; he is also undercutting his plaything with seriousness. He thus shows the way, in this text, toward a dialogism in which a thesis and an antithesis are not in a dialectical relation that leads toward a synthesis, but in a relation of calling each other into question and leaving each other forever in place, as well; neither pole

49. See Consigny, *Gorgias,* 30.

50. Gorgias as cited in Aristotle, *Rhetoric* 1419b4–5.

51. ἐβουλήθην γράψαι τὸν λόγον Ἑλένης μὲν ἐγκώμιον ἐμὸν δὲ παίγνιον.

52. George A. Kennedy, trans., *On Rhetoric: A Theory of Civic Discourse by Aristotle* (New York: Oxford University Press, 1991), 288n, emphasis added.

taking precedence over the other. Self-refutation, here, is raised to an epistemological principle.

From one generic point of view, then, Gorgias's text seems most closely related to Zeno's paradoxes or the paradox of the Liar,[53] and Gorgias was, of course, a familiar of Zeno. An even stronger comparison would be to the famous paradoxical law case attributed to Protagoras by Aulus Gellius.[54] According to that story, Protagoras took a pupil in rhetoric, Euathlus by name, who promised to pay the teacher after winning his first court case. Since the student seemed not willing to pursue his career, thus leaving Protagoras bereft, Protagoras sued him, claiming that either way he would collect. If Euathlus lost the case, he would pay by law, and if he won, he would have fulfilled the terms of the contract and be required to pay on that account. Euathlus, according to the tale, countered that in either case, he would not have to pay, for if he won, the court would have absolved him of payment, while if he lost, the contractual terms would release him from payment. The court, according to some reports, went home and didn't return for a hundred years. According to at least one interpretation, Protagoras's goal in this wily scheme was not to win the case and collect his fees but something much more important than that, namely, to demonstrate his holding that, as paraphrased by Seneca, "one can take either side on any question and debate it with equal success—even on this very question, whether every subject can be debated from either point of view."[55] This brings us close to my interpretation of the paradoxical play of the contemporary Gorgias, namely that through his *paignion,* his toy, he is demonstrating to us, as well, the deep paradoxicality involved in the distinction, so crucial to Parmenides, between force and persuasion.[56] Some support for this conjecture about the meaning of *paignion* may be found in the report

53. For one example of the use of paradox in philosophical argument, see Jon Moline, "Aristotle, Eubulides and the Sorites," *Mind* 78, no. 2 (July 1969): 393–407.

54. Aulus Gellius, *The Attic Nights of Aulus Gellius,* trans. John Carew Rolfe, Loeb Classical Library (Cambridge, Mass.: Harvard University Press, 1967), i:405–9. Interestingly, there is a version of this story in which the protagonists are the apocryphal Corax and Tisias, alleged founders of rhetoric theory in Sicily. Schiappa, *Beginnings of Rhetorical Theory,* 5–6.

55. Lucius Annaeus Seneca, *Ad Lucilium Epistulae Morales,* ed. and trans. Richard M. Gummere, Loeb Classical Library (Cambridge, Mass.: Harvard University Press, 1961), ii:375.

56. John Poulakos has already noted that by calling the speech a *paignion,* Gorgias would have been undermining its possibility of service simply as an advertisement for himself and

that Monimus of Syracuse, one of the early Cynics, wrote "trifles
[*paignia*] blended with covert seriousness," and that these *paignia* were
"early examples of the 'seriocomic' style [*spoudogeloion*]."[57] Demetrius,
moreover, reports the existence of a seriocomic style a century or so
later than Gorgias's time;[58] and on the evidence of the *Encomium of
Helen,* we might well say that Gorgias had anticipated it brilliantly.

Andrea Nightingale provides further insight that will be helpful
in arguing this point. She locates Gorgias's *Encomium* among a genre
of paradoxical encomia that is fairly well attested at the time, arguing that this form of encomium originated in the late fifth century
and was particularly popular in the fourth. In addition to the Gorgias
text, she sees as examples of this genre Isocrates' *Busiris* and his own
Helen as well as the praise of the lover who does not love in the first
speech of the *Phaedrus* (attributed, of course, to Lysias). Nightingale
cites, as well, many other examples of this genre in which eulogies
are composed for salt, bumblebees, "pots, pebbles, and mice."[59] Now
what is most important for my purposes here is the explanation she
gives for the production of such texts, namely that they serve to rela-
tivize values. She cites Rosalie Colie on the significance of paradox in
general in discourse:

> One element common to all these kinds of paradox is their exploita-
> tion of the fact of relative, or competing, value systems. The paradox
> is always somehow involved in dialectic: challenging some orthodoxy,
> the paradox is an oblique criticism of absolute judgment or absolute
> convention.[60]

---

rhetorical training. John Poulakos, "Gorgias' *Encomium* to Helen and the Defense of Rhetoric," *Rhetorica* 1 (1983): 3. Cf. in a somewhat different vein, Consigny, *Gorgias,* 30.

57. R. Bracht Branham and Marie-Odile Goulet-Cazé, eds., *The Cynics: The Cynic Movement in Antiquity and Its Legacy,* Hellenistic Culture and Society 23 (Berkeley: University of
California Press, 1997), 10–11.

58. Demetrius, *Demetrius on Style: The Greek Text of Demetrius, De Elocutione,* ed. W. Rhys
Roberts (Hildesheim: G. Olms, 1969), 151, referring to Crates and the Cynics. On Crates,
see Anthony A. Long, "The Socratic Tradition: Diogenes, Crates, and Hellenistic Eth-
ics," in *The Cynics: The Cynic Movement in Antiquity and Its Legacy,* ed. R. Bracht Branham,
Marie-Odile Goulet-Cazé, Hellenistic Culture and Society 23 (Berkeley and Los Angeles:
University of California Press, 1997), 28–46.

59. Nightingale, *Genres in Dialogue,* 100–101.

60. Rosalie L. Colie, *Paradoxia Epidemica: The Renaissance Tradition of Paradox* (Princeton: Princeton University Press, 1966), 10.

Nightingale has completely comprehended the importance of this insight for understanding the paradoxical encomium of ancient Greece as well. The point is not only, as hostile witnesses would have it, to advertise the skills of a teacher of rhetoric who can turn dross into gold and make the weaker case *appear* the stronger, but to convey the relativity of all claims to truth, including his or her own. If I am not mistaken, Gorgias's *Helen* is the oldest example that she cites of "the 'paradoxical' encomium," which was "a eulogy for a person or thing that was generally held to be unpraiseworthy if not despicable."[61] In Gorgias's text, as I hope to have shown, the paradox and its meaning are carried out on several levels—most overtly in the choice of topic, the invention of (or entry into) the genre of the paradoxical encomium itself—but are reproduced in the very *logismos* of the piece at several levels, as I have tried to expose in my reading. In his antiphilosophical discourse, his parodic and paradoxical campaign against Parmenides (as I read him), Gorgias is suggesting that Truth is itself a coercion, for if it persuades automatically, as Parmenides had claimed, then there is no distinction between persuasion and force. In contrast, Gorgias implies, I think, a much more relativist notion of "true *logos*" as being the product of a weighing of alternatives and a choosing of what seems the best one under the current circumstances. As we saw in the last chapter, Protagoras also, in his insistence that knowledge is only through human perception, and thus necessarily mutable, strongly counters Parmenides' notions of absolute and unchanging Truth.[62] To this image of Gorgias as serious thinker, we must now oppose Plato's caricature of him in the "iambic"—not formally so, of course—dialogue called the *Gorgias*.

"How well Plato knows to satirize [ἰαμβίζειν]!"—Gorgias

What is striking about Plato's dialogues and, while it hardly goes unremarked, not sufficiently noted, is how often Socrates' arguments are simply (and fairly obviously) fallacious. Since this point is going to function in this book not so much as a stick with which to beat Plato

---

61. Nightingale, *Genres in Dialogue*, 100.
62. For Protagoras as also responding to Parmenides, see Farrar, *Origins*, 46.

but as a key to a novel reading of his work as satire, this section will commence by documenting this claim.

Socrates' Sophistical Refutations

I will begin by exposing what I take to be a fairly transparent example of fallacious and brow-beating argumentation on the part of "Socrates" in dialectic with "Gorgias."[63] Socrates has compelled Gorgias—as he repeatedly does with this and other interlocutors—to answer only yes or no to his questions.[64] The subject is the definition of rhetoric:

> SOCRATES: Come, then. You say you have knowledge of the rhetorical craft, and that you can make someone else a rhetor. Which of the things that are is rhetoric really about? For instance, weaving is about the production of clothes, isn't it?
> GORGIAS: Yes.
> SOCRATES: And isn't music about the production of melodies?
> GORGIAS: Yes.
> SOCRATES: By Hera, Gorgias, I do admire your answers; you answer as briefly as anyone could.
> GORGIAS: Yes, Socrates; I think I do it reasonably well.
> SOCRATES: You're right. Come, then, answer me in the same way about rhetoric too. It is knowledge about which of the things that are?
> GORGIAS: About speech [*logos*].
> SOCRATES: What kind of speech, Gorgias? The kind that explains the treatment to make sick people well?
> GORGIAS: No.
> SOCRATES: Then rhetoric is not about all speech.
> GORGIAS: No, true enough.

63. The scare quotes are to remind us once more that we are talking about characters in a Platonic novel, not the historical figures on which they are more or less loosely based. I shall abandon them with their potential for annoyance of the reader after this one reminder.

64. This technique of control became a virtual tradition in Western life in the practice of the courtroom, where witnesses are forced to answer only yes or no to questions that they wish to nuance or complicate.

SOCRATES: But still it makes men powerful [*dunatos*] at speaking.

GORGIAS: Yes.

SOCRATES: And at understanding the things they speak about?

GORGIAS: Certainly.

SOCRATES: Now does the medical craft we've just mentioned make people powerful at understanding and speaking about the sick?

GORGIAS: Necessarily.[65]

SOCRATES: Then apparently medicine as well is about speech.

GORGIAS: Yes.

SOCRATES: Speech about diseases, that is.

GORGIAS: Certainly.

SOCRATES: And isn't gymnastics too about speech, about the good and bad condition of bodies?

GORGIAS: Yes, quite.

SOCRATES: And indeed the other crafts too are this way, Gorgias; each then is about the speech which is about the thing which each craft is the craft of.

GORGIAS: Apparently.

SOCRATES: Then why ever don't you call the other crafts rhetorical, when they are about speech, since you call whatever craft is about speech rhetorical? (449d–450b)[66]

Socrates' argument is fallacious on the very face of it. The confusion seems to be about two different senses of *logos:* (1) speech, in the sense of *parole* and (2) discourse or even doctrine. Medical science is not designed, of course, to increase the ability of its practitioners to produce effective speech, not at all; it *is* designed to make them think better about the conditions of bodies and how to ameliorate them. From this confusion, assented to by Gorgias, endless self-refutations result. Gorgias is made to distinguish between that which is mostly craft of the hands and that which is entirely *logos,* such that only the latter qualifies as *rhētorikē tekhnē,* only to be tripped up on arithmetic and other such theoretical arts of thinking. There is not the slightest recognition here

65. Modified from Irwin's "It must." The Greek is Ἀνάγκη.

66. Terence Irwin, translated with notes by, *Gorgias by Plato* (Oxford: Oxford University Press, 1979), 16. I have modified Irwin's presentation (with each speech on a separate line), following rather the way that Dodds presents the Greek, to give a better sense of the rapidity of *brachyologia.*

of the possibility of metalanguage, of rhetoric being speech about language itself. Plato, I would assume (charitably and realistically) was certainly aware of the fallaciousness of Socrates' elenchus of Gorgias here. (I'd even bet that, unlike Plato's caricature, the "real" Gorgias could have sorted this out.) It is, in a sense, the very palpability of the fallacy that produces one of the great dilemmas of Platonic writing.[67] I'll proceed by asking a rhetorical question of my own.

Is Socrates ever refuted in the dialogues of Plato? Analysis of an important interchange in the *Gorgias* between Socrates and Gorgias's disciple, the rhetor (and teacher of rhetoric) Polus, will help to answer this rhetorical question in the negative. Although I can't prove this deductively (I don't know the entire Platonic corpus well enough), an exemplary instance of mock refutation, when Socrates becomes the questioned and not the questioner, will go some way inductively toward making my point.[68] We are at a moment in the *Gorgias* in which that figure, having been thoroughly twisted in knots by Socrates, is "rescued" by his pupil Polus:

> POLUS: Really, Socrates? Is what you're now saying about rhetoric what you actually think of it? Or do you really think, just because Gorgias was too ashamed not to concede your further claim that the rhetor also knows what's just, what's admirable, and what's good, and that if he came to him without already having this knowledge to begin with, he said that he would teach him himself, and then from this admission maybe some inconsistency crept into his statements—just the thing that gives you delight, you're the one who leads him on to face such questions—who do you

---

67. See Kenneth James Dover, ed., *Symposium by Plato* (Cambridge: Cambridge University Press, 1980), 145, speaking of Socrates' speech in the *Symposium:* "Throughout this section (204c7–206a13) Plato uses the art of rhetoric more subtly than when he is caricaturing the verbal sophistries of others (e.g., 196c3–d4; *Euthyd.* 276a–b) but no more honestly." Cf. too Kevin Corrigan and Elena Glazov-Corrigan, *Plato's Dialectic at Play: Argument, Structure, and Myth in the* Symposium (University Park: Pennsylvania State University Press, 2004), 104–5. I don't find Dover's judgment "extreme," but exactly to the point. This, of course, only sharpens the Platonic dilemmas.

68. I can also rely on such an authority as Richard Robinson, *Plato's Earlier Dialectic* (Oxford: Clarendon Press, 1953), 7, who writes, "[The Socratic elenchus] is so common in the early dialogues that we may almost say that Socrates never talks to anyone without refuting him." And this, of course, despite Socrates' declarations in *Gorgias* 458a that he prefers being refuted to refuting!

think would deny that he himself knows what's just and would teach others? To lead your arguments to such an outcome is a sign of great rudeness. (461b)[69]

We can be even more perspicacious than Polus in identifying the problem here. Polus, of course, doesn't entirely "get it," for so Plato wishes to portray him, but Plato has indeed also let us see the great fallacy in Socrates' argument analyzed just above.

It is not just that Gorgias was "ashamed" to admit that his practice doesn't make people better; he is actually tricked into the contradiction. Let us see how:

GORGIAS: Well, Socrates, I think that if someone in fact doesn't know these things, he will learn them also from me.

SOCRATES: Hold it there—you're speaking well. If you make anyone a rhetor, he must either know in advance the just and unjust things, or later, having been taught them by you.[70]

GORGIAS: Quite.

SOCRATES: Well now; is someone who has learnt carpenter's things a carpenter, or isn't he?

GORGIAS: Yes, he is.

SOCRATES: And isn't someone who has learnt musical things a musician?

GORGIAS: Yes.

SOCRATES: And isn't someone who has learned medical things a doctor? And in other cases, analogously, isn't a man who has learnt each of these things such as his knowledge makes him?

GORGIAS: Quite.

SOCRATES: Then according to this account isn't also the man who has learned just things just? (460a–c)

69. Donald J. Zeyl, trans., "The *Gorgias* by Plato," in *Plato on Rhetoric and Language: Four Key Dialogues,* introduction by Jean Nienkamp (Mahwah, N.J.: Hermagoras Press, 1999), 98. My only modification of this translation is to change Zeyl's "orator" and "oratory" to "rhetor" and "rhetoric," which I will do throughout when citing his translation. On this passage and the difficulties of the Greek and their significance, see Dodds, *Gorgias,* 221: "This sentence caused the older editors much perplexity. But most of the difficulties disappear once it is realized that Polus 'is sputtering with indignation and anacolutha,' as Shorey put it."

70. Translation slightly modified from Irwin.

And a just man will only do the just, etc. From here Gorgias's self-contradiction inevitably follows, as before he had argued that the teacher is not responsible for the misuse the pupil makes of his technical training. But, of course, Socrates' argument is totally fallacious— "sophistical" as one writer would have it. First of all, it is dependent on a category error; indeed, the honest rhetor can desire and aim to teach the student ethics, but the primary matter of the teaching is a *tekhnē*. Builders, musicians, and certain doctors can use their technical knowledge for bad ends, whatever efforts have been made by their teachers to teach them ethics (justice), as well. Why not insist that the professors of medicine be held responsible for their failure in training doctors, since some of them participate in torture of prisoners or executions? Secondly, Socrates has tacitly, even surreptitiously, introduced a new premise here, namely that knowing what is just automatically produces a just person. I have no doubt that Socrates really held this to be true, but it is not simply a given that must be accepted for all philosophical conversation, unless, of course you want to talk to *this* man, Socrates. As a well-known ethicist, upon being caught in some seemingly unethical private behavior is reported to have said: you wouldn't expect a professor of mathematics to become a triangle! All the more so, when the professor is a professor of rhetoric, not ethics, however much he might, and not just out of shame, seek to teach ethics to his pupils as well. By forcing this concession, which, in fact, is a proposition that needs proving in the argument, indeed is the question itself, Socrates is begging the question in the full technical sense of that fallacy, namely requiring (or even requesting) his opponent to concede the very question at hand.

This passage is emblematic of the sort of intellectual problems that Plato proposes to us, of what it is that makes his texts endlessly interpretable. Socrates seems (always) to be Plato's hero but frequently engages in conduct that is unheroic indeed, using false logic and manipulation to twist his opponents into knots and force them to concede that which they firmly, clearly, hold to be false. (This is the very definition, according to Parmenides and others, of what false compulsion [ἀνάγκη] accomplishes as opposed to persuasion [πειθώ].) The most die-hard of Platonic apologists argue that Socrates is allowed to use these methods of falsehood in order to discredit his opponents because they are, indeed, the charlatans that Socrates

(Plato) claims them to be, and all is fair in the war on the intellectual terrorism of the Sophists.[71] Here's an egregious example: Plochmann and Robinson write of Polus's excited and angry response, "The entire colloquy starts when Polus, breathless and a little uncoordinated in his utterances, interrupts to ask *whether Socrates has just expressed his real opinion of rhetoric,* without saying exactly which one of the many hints that Socrates has supplied he, Polus, is concerned about."[72] But Socrates has just, one sentence above, declared, "But now, as we subsequently examine the question, you see for yourself too that it's agreed that, quite to the contrary, the rhetor is incapable of using rhetoric unjustly and of being willing to do what's unjust."[73] To me, it is obvious that it is to this declaration of Socrates'—that the rhetor cannot be unjust—that Polus is skeptically responding. This seems to me so obvious that I would venture to say, somewhat impertinently, that it is only Plochmann and Robinson's overly "friendly" reading of the *Gorgias* that prevents them from seeing it.

Polus knows full well that Socrates does not, in fact, mean it. Socrates, of course, will not allow his opponents to say other than that which they truly believe to be true, but he himself constantly manipulates by speaking insincerely, and Polus knows this. Writers of Plochmann and Robinson's ilk refer over and over to Polus's (and Gorgias's) ineptitude in dialectic as both questioners and answerers without realizing (or pretending not to realize) that Socrates' practice is arbitrary and coercive per se. Obviously, I, at any rate, find this a highly suspect form of special pleading. If we don't allow Socrates such a privileged position, a genuine paradox results: Plato seems to be giving us a portrait of the philosopher as a young (and even older) man in which he either in good faith or in bad faith presents false and manipulative arguments solely for the purpose of defeating the Sophists. If Socrates' arguments are intended in good faith, then he is stupid; if they are in bad faith, then he becomes, as it were, that

71. Notably Patrick Coby, *Socrates and the Sophistic Enlightenment: A Commentary on Plato's Protagoras* (Lewisburg, Pa.: Bucknell University Press, 1987). See Gene Fendt and David Rozema, "Have We Been Nobly Lied To?" in *Platonic Errors: Plato, a Kind of Poet* (Westport, Conn.: Greenwood Press, 1998).

72. George Kimball Plochmann and Franklin E. Robinson, *A Friendly Companion to Plato's Gorgias* (Carbondale: Southern Illinois University Press, 1988), 54, emphasis original.

73. Zeyl, "The *Georgias*," 98.

which he claims his opponents are. The paradox is heightened even
more when the very accusation of this is put firmly (and accurately) in
the mouth of such a Sophist. Polus may be reduced to barely articulate sputtering, but the point he makes is spot-on.[74] Gorgias had been
asked to reflect on the possibility of a trained rhetor using rhetoric
for ill, and he had allowed that this was possible. Later he had been
asked if rhetoric were an "unjust thing," to which he answered that
it is used for speeches about justice. Finally, he was asked, if a pupil
came to him and knew nothing of justice, would he teach it, and he,
of course, agreed he would, thus allegedly refuting his own premise
that rhetoric could be used for injustice. (Is there, indeed, any form
of wisdom that while striving for the good cannot be turned to evil?
Had Socrates not heard of Darth Vader—whose activities, we know,
were in the distant past?) Every force has a dark side. Gorgias has
been trapped in a contradiction owing to a concession that he really
needn't have made (and, moreover, one that could be applied just as
easily to Socrates' own teaching, as well. See the case of Alcibiades!).
Although Dodds in the name of the great Wilamowitz suggests that
the notion of a barely articulate professor of rhetoric is what is being
pilloried here, it is at least as strongly the case that the professor of
Truth is being shown up as a duplicitous dialectician as well. We will
need to carry this thought all the way until the end of the book, when
an attempt to read this paradox will be essayed. Until then I will play
it as it lays, as it were, reading Plato's Socrates as the power broker,
the (en)forcer that he seems to be.

After some discussion about the necessity, in Socrates' view, that
Polus not engage in *makrologia* (long speech) but only in dialectic, Polus chooses to be the questioner, to get a chance, so to speak, to refute
Socrates (an opportunity at which, of course, he will fail). Here's how
the text goes:

> SOCRATES: So now please do whichever of these you like: either ask
> questions or answer them.
> POLUS: Very well, I shall. Tell me, Socrates, since you think Gorgias
> is confused about rhetoric, what do you say it is?
> SOCRATES: Are you asking me what *craft* [*tekhnē*] I say it is?

---

74. Robinson, *Plato's Earlier Dialectic*, 27; but see too Dodds, *Gorgias*, 220.

POLUS: Yes, I am.

SOCRATES: To tell you the truth, Polus, I don't think it's a craft at all.

POLUS: Well then, what do you think rhetoric is?

SOCRATES: Something of which you claim to have made a craft in your treatise that I have just read.[75]

POLUS: What do you mean?

SOCRATES: I mean a skill picked up by experience [empirical skill].[76]

POLUS: So you think rhetoric is an empirical skill?

SOCRATES: Yes, I do, unless you say it's something else.

POLUS: A skill for what?

SOCRATES: For producing certain gratification and pleasure.

POLUS: Don't you think rhetoric's an admirable thing, then, to be able to give gratification to the people?

SOCRATES: Really, Polus! Have you already discovered from me what I say it is, so that you go on to ask me next whether I don't think it's admirable?

POLUS: Haven't I already discovered that you say it's a skill?

SOCRATES: Since you value gratification, would you like to gratify me on a small matter?

POLUS: Certainly! (462b–e)[77]

Now, of course, the Platonic apologists, including the best of them, such as Dodds, gloss this exchange as Plato mocking the "rhetorician's ineptitude at the philosopher's game of dialectic,"[78] but, of course, Polus didn't volunteer to play that game at all. He wanted to play his own game, which Socrates refused. Moreover, it is hardly the case that Socrates plays here according to his own rules, which only allow yes or no answers. Why, after all, does not "admirable" follow from "gratification and pleasure"? Finally, Socrates, when asked what he takes rhetoric to be, doesn't even answer that in a short manner,

75. Translation modified from Zeyl following Dodds's analysis; Dodds, *Gorgias,* 99.

76. This is my own translation of *empeiria,* capturing the nuance of the untheorized, and perhaps untheorizable. The usual translation "knack" doesn't work, insofar as a knack in English refers not to something learned but something innate: "He's got a knack for cooking" is not the same thing as "He learned cooking by watching his mother and trial and error" (which is what *empeiria* means).

77. Zeyl, "The *Gorgias,*" 99–100 (modified as noted).

78. Dodds, *Gorgias,* 223.

as he and his "method" would demand, but discursively goes somewhere else entirely in his disingenuous and mocking request that Polus gratify him.

A Dialogue in One Voice

In the next section then of the colloquy, Socrates hilariously "instructs" his young interlocutor in the art of dialectic:

> SOCRATES: Ask me now what craft I think cookery is.
> POLUS: All right, I will. What craft is cookery?
> SOCRATES: It isn't one at all, Polus. Now say, "What is it then?"
> POLUS: All right.
> SOCRATES: It's a skill. Say, "a skill for what?"
> POLUS: All right.
> SOCRATES: For producing gratification and pleasure, Polus.
> (462d–e)[79]

Without going any further in detail in this colloquy, let alone in the dialogue as a whole, this sequence alone seems to me to establish (and never mind for the nonce that all I know I know from Plato here) precisely the undialogical nature of Socrates' dialectic. Both sides are scripted: when Socrates is the questioner he leads his interlocutors in such way that they must answer in a certain way; when, perchance he is the "answerer," he tells them precisely what to ask him in order to get his way.

Socrates, moreover, continues in this vein for a while, browbeating Polus for not knowing in advance what questions he is supposed

---

79. Zeyl, "The *Gorgias*," 100. Zeyl translates ὀψοποιία as "pastry baking," while our "friendly" readers of Plato translate "catering" (Plochmann and Robinson, *Friendly Companion*, 58) to indicate that it is a useless form of gratifying with no nutritional value, as they say explicitly. The word is rare, but basing myself on a fairly explicit context in Xenophon's *Memoirs* (3.14.5), I would say that it means the preparation of all the things eaten with bread at an Athenian meal: meat, fish, cheese, sauces, everything but the bread itself. In Xenophon, Socrates is reacting to a certain member of the company who eats only the other food and doesn't take bread with it. Liddell and Scott translate ὄψον as "properly, cooked meat, or, generally, meat, opp. to bread and other provisions," noting as well that it signified anything eaten with the bread, and, at Athens, frequently referred to fish. Accordingly "pastry baking" is possibly the worst translation possible and "cookery" (which appears in many translations), the best.

to ask Socrates in order to elicit the answers that Socrates wishes to give. Soon enough we find Socrates dictating to Polus: after having declared that rhetoric belongs to the genus of "flattery," Socrates demands of Polus that he ask (in order to find out what rhetoric is) "what part of flattery I say rhetoric is." If this is not an instance of "begging the question," I hardly know what is, and, moreover, it involves deceit and manipulation of the weaker party. Polus could hardly know that Socrates means to produce a category called flattery (κολακεία)—which, indeed, Dodds describes as more discreditable than flattery, being more on the order of brown-nosing—and to place rhetoric as well as cookery in this category.[80] This category or practice called flattery, we are then generously informed by Socrates, has four parts: rhetoric, cookery, cosmetics, and sophistry. The arbitrariness of this procedure, its coerciveness emblematized by Socrates now dictating not only the answers, but the questions that Polus must ask, fully exemplifies, in my opinion, the fatally nondialogical nature of Platonic dialogues or Socratic dialectics (or best put, I think, the Socratic dialectics within the Platonic dialogues).

I can go even further in this demonstration. After having stated arbitrarily that rhetoric is a species of flattery or pandering, Socrates invites Polus to refute him. Polus, quite reasonably, asks him then whether the reason that rhetors are held in low esteem in their cities is because they are flatterers. Socrates, as usual, deflects the question and answers the one he would have wanted to be asked, claiming that rhetors are held in no regard at all in their cites (466a–b). Polus responds by saying, "What do you mean, they're not held in any regard? Don't they have the greatest power in their cities?" Socrates says, no they don't have any power, because power is something good for the person who has power, and since, after all, there is no guarantee that rhetors or tyrants will know what is best for them, they truly have no power at all. The ensuing sequence is, once again, remarkable:

SOCRATES: I say, Polus, that both rhetors and tyrants have the least power in their cities, as I was saying just now. For they do just about nothing they want to, though they certainly do whatever they see most fit to do.

80. Dodds, *Gorgias*, 225.

POLUS: Well, isn't this having great power?

SOCRATES: No; at least Polus says it isn't.

POLUS: I say it isn't? I certainly say it is!

SOCRATES: By Zeus, you certainly don't!, since you say that having great power is good for the one who has it.

POLUS: Yes I do say that.

SOCRATES: Do you think it's good, then, if a person does whatever he sees most fit to do when he lacks intelligence? Do you call this "having great power" too?

POLUS: No, I do not.

SOCRATES: Will you refute me, then, and prove that rhetors do have intelligence, and that rhetoric is a craft, and not flattery? If you leave me unrefuted, then the rhetors who do what they see fit in their cities, and the tyrants, too, won't have gained any good by this. Power is a good thing, you say, but you agree with me that doing what one sees fit without intelligence is bad. Or don't you. (466d–467a)[81]

I could go on citing this passage, but I will stop. Socrates is unrefutable because he simply never allows his basic assumptions to be challenged. If rhetoric is defined as being part of the same genus as cookery; if exercising power without full epistemic knowledge of essences (as Socrates demands just a bit later on) is necessarily injustice, necessarily miserable; and if Socratean knowledge is possible, if only to a very few, then, well of course, there is only one possible conclusion: rhetoric is bad, as Socrates has already told us, and the only possible just rulers, those who would truly have power, would be an oligarchy of philosopher-kings. The yellow brick road to Kallipolis is fully paved here. Whether one agrees with Socrates philosophically or no, there is, I think, no defense for the position that there is genuine dialogue here in which different views are given a hearing. Socrates will always win when playing by his rules. The reason that Socrates is irrefutable is because he assumes and demands assent to the propositions that there is something called Truth, that it is discoverable only through dialectic, and that a search for justice is possible only via knowledge of the Truth; these are precisely the

---

81. Zeyl, "The *Gorgias*," 103.

propositions that rhetoric, as I have shown in my discussions of the "real" Gorgias and Protagoras above, would contest.

The Dialogue as Covert Critique of Socrates

The most astonishing thing, however, to observe in the entire *Gorgias* is that it is Plato who exposes openly the fallacy (deliberately, I would think) of Socrates' "dialogues," or "discussions," and, after having shown us Polus realizing this, puts the insight again into the mouth of the least attractive of all the characters in the dialogue, one Callicles:

> Socrates, I think you're grandstanding in these speeches, acting like a true crowd pleaser. Here you are, playing to the crowd now that Polus has had the same thing happen to him that he accused Gorgias of letting you do to him. For he said, didn't he, that when Gorgias was asked by you whether he would teach anyone who came to him wanting to learn rhetoric but without expertise in what's just, Gorgias was ashamed, and out of deference to human custom, since people would take it ill if a person refused, said that he'd teach him. And because Gorgias agreed on this point, he said, he was forced to contradict himself, just the thing you like. He ridiculed you at the time, and rightly so, as I think anyhow. And now the very same thing has happened to him. And for this same reason I don't approve of Polus: he agreed with you that doing what's unjust is more shameful than suffering it. As a result of this admission he was bound and gagged by you in the discussion, too ashamed to say what he thought. (482c–e)[82]

Callicles is on to something here. His words, I suggest, are not being presented in order to expose him (although, as I have hinted, it is hard to approve of his moral positions, but that is not the point). Rather, Callicles reveals here the force by which Socrates compels his interlocutors to misstep. As Callicles suggests, over and over again in these dialogues, Socrates simply asserts a position, rather browbeating his opponent to assent to it. He then catches this opponent in a contradiction between the opponent's truly held position and the

---

82. Zeyl, "The *Gorgias*," 120.

consequences of the premise that Socrates has shamed him into assenting to, without there being any logical reason to force that assent.
This is what Socrates calls Polus refuting Polus. However, since these
premises are only asserted and not demonstrated in any way, and since
they contradict the premises of the other's very arguments, the fact
that Socrates can confuse or compel his opponents into assenting to
the opposite of the positions they truly believe in is as unreliable a
form of proof as the general consensus to which they appeal at first.
There is no dialogism in the dialectic or discussions of Socrates; if
there be dialogism in Plato, it is precisely in the straightforward presentation of these accusations from outside the system as it were. We
shall have to figure out what to make of *that,* and figuring it out will be
one of the main burdens of the rest of this book.

Callicles goes on to analyze the fallacy of Socrates' argument even
more sharply:

> Although you claim to be pursuing the truth, you're in fact bringing
> the discussion around to the sort of crowd-pleasing vulgarities that
> are admirable only by law and not by nature. (482e)[83]

Callicles has really, in my view, drawn a bead on Socrates here.
Socrates treats aspects of conventional Athenian morality as well as
the law itself as if they were natural kinds. The point does not necessarily lead to the conclusions of Callicles,[84] horrifying ones, in their
way as terrible as the arguments of the Athenians in the Melian Dialogue, but it does point up once again how Socrates is constantly,
almost ubiquitously, begging the question. Plato, it might be said,
couches the horrific doctrine of nature raw in tooth and claw as a norm
in the mouth of the rhetor Callicles, while Thucydides puts it into the
form of philosophical dialogue. Plato is thus critiquing rhetoric while
Thucydides is critiquing dialogue, but, in turn, Callicles' critique of
Socrates' methods (putting aside the content of Callicles' thought) is

---

83. Zeyl, "The *Gorgias,*" 120: ὦ Σώκρατες, εἰς τοιαῦτα ἄγεις φορτικὰ καὶ δημηγορικά,
φάσκων τὴν ἀλήθειαν διώκειν, ἃ φύσει μὲν οὐκ ἔστι καλά, νόμῳ δέ. Perhaps better is Jowett:
"For the truth is, Socrates, that you, who pretend to be engaged in the pursuit of truth,
are appealing now to the popular and vulgar notions of right, which are not natural but
only conventional."

84. Dodds, *Gorgias,* 264–65.

telling. Socrates may not have any dialogue in his dialectics, but Plato does in his texts when he allows such an eloquent and persuasive critique of the whole process of dialectic, indicting its tricky and demagogic ways. As Jonathan D. Pratt has recently put it to me: "It seems to me that Plato's non-coercive treatment of the reader depends precisely on his willingness to show us how coercive Socratic method can be, for otherwise we would have nothing more to go by than Socrates' egalitarian mystifications. The pornographic glimpse of Socrates' work on his interlocutors is oddly liberating when experienced at the textual level."[85] We do not need to accept Callicles' notion that the law of nature is "might makes right" and that everything is permitted to the strong, but we do need to realize that the laws/customs of a community may not be just, and that, in any case, they are the product of convention and not a natural fact and cannot, therefore, produce the epistemic knowledge vaunted by Socrates. The critique or counterposition that Callicles proposes requires answering and refutation by Socrates but, predictably, it won't get that either.

After some ironic praise designed to set Callicles up for a fall, Socrates proceeds with the following piece of dialectic. Since the text is long and full of logical non sequiturs and fallacies, I will cite it broken up with brief comments as I go (citation at end of sequence):

SOCRATES: ... Please restate your position for me from the beginning. What is it that you and Pindar hold to be true of what's just by nature? That the superior should take by force what belongs to the inferior, that the better should rule the worse and the more worthy have a greater share than the less worthy? You're not saying anything else, are you? I do remember correctly?

CALLICLES: Yes, that's what I was saying then, and I still say so now, too.

SOCRATES: Is it the same man you call both "better" and "superior"? [Πότερον δὲ τὸν αὐτὸν βελτίω καλεῖς σὺ καὶ κρείττω;] I wasn't able then, either, to figure out what you meant. Is it the stronger [ἰσχυροτέρους] ones you call superior, and should those who are weaker take orders from the one who's stronger? That's what I think you were trying to show then also, when you said that large

85. Jonathan D. Pratt, personal communication, September 2008.

cities attack small ones according to what's just by nature, because
they're superior and stronger, assuming that *superior, stronger,* and
better are the same. Or is it possible for one to be better and also
inferior and weaker, or greater and more wretched? Or do "better" and "superior" have the same definition? Please define this
for me clearly. Are *superior, better,* and *stronger* the same or are they
different?

CALLICLES: Very well, I'm telling you clearly that they're the same.

Socrates is catching Callicles here in an ambiguity of Greek that
Callicles is simply not acute enough to spot. There are three partially
overlapping Greek terms here: *Beltiō* means "generally better" in the
moral sense (but can also mean "aristocratic" as in our usage of "the
best people"); *kreittō* is ambivalent; it can mean "better" in the moral
sense but it can also mean "stronger," while *isxuros* unambiguously
means "stronger." So *beltiō* means *kreittō* and *kreittō* means *isxuros,* but
beltiō does not mean *isxuros,* and Callicles is not smart enough to see
how he is being manipulated (he will see it and cry havoc when he perceives the results later). On this initial fallacy, Socrates will continue
to build with great élan.

SOCRATES: Now aren't the many superior by nature to the one?
They're the ones who in fact impose the laws upon the one, as you
were saying yourself a moment ago.

CALLICLES: Of course.

SOCRATES: So the rules of the many are the rules of the superior.

CALLICLES: Yes, they are.

SOCRATES: Aren't they the rules of the better? For by your reasoning, I take it, the superior are the better.

CALLICLES: Yes.

Since, as Socrates has compelled Callicles to agree that the more
powerful are ipso facto the better and, since the many do, in fact (in
the democracy) make the rules and are therefore the powerful, then
the many must, indeed, be the best. If so, then, of course, their rules
must be the rules of the better, as well, and therefore it follows as the
night follows the day that

SOCRATES: And aren't the rules of these people admirable by nature, seeing that they're the superior ones?

CALLICLES: That's my view.

SOCRATES: Now, isn't it a rule of the many that it's just to have an equal share and that doing what's unjust is more shameful than suffering it, as you yourself were saying just now? Is this so or not? Be careful that you in your turn don't get caught being ashamed now. Do the many observe or do they not observe the rule that it's just to have an equal and not a greater share, and that doing what's unjust is more shameful than suffering it? Don't grudge me your answer to this, Callicles, so that if you agree with me I have my confirmation from you, seeing that it's the agreement of a man competent to pass judgment.

CALLICLES: All right, the many do have that rule.

Perhaps, indeed, the many have such a rule in Athens at a certain moment, but since Callicles has been bamboozled into agreeing that the many, being the most powerful, are therefore the superior, and their laws are superior as well (and this, by nature, since it is by nature that the best rule, and the best, we have already established, are the most powerful by nature), then

SOCRATES: It's not only by law, then, that doing what's unjust is more shameful than suffering it, or that it's just to have an equal share, but it's so by nature, too. So it looks as though you weren't saying what's true earlier and weren't right to accuse me when you said that nature and law were opposed to each other and that I, well aware of this, am making mischief in my statements, taking any statement someone makes meant in terms of nature, in terms of law, and any statement meant in terms of law, in terms of nature.

It is not at all surprising to me that Callicles at this moment bursts out with "This man will not stop talking nonsense!" since, as I hope to have shown, this refutation is fully sophistical in the Aristotelian sense of *sophistai elenchoi* (sophistical refutations), and hardly a move in it is valid.

If anything, Socrates' practice of argument proves precisely that might makes right—that the superior man deserves to rule by any means necessary (and this is, after all, Plato's—no rule of the many for him—political theory). As Callicles so well puts it:

> tell me, Socrates, aren't you ashamed, at your age, of trying to catch people's words and of making hay out of someone's tripping on a phrase? Do you take me to mean by people being *superior* anything else than their being *better*? Haven't I been telling you all along that by "better" and "superior" I mean the same thing? Or do you suppose that I'm saying that if a rubbish heap of slaves and motley men, worthless except perhaps in physical strength, gets together and makes statements, then these are the rules? (488b–489c)[86]

Indeed! A sophistical refutation at its best. No rhetorical trickster could have done better. Now, of course, Socrates himself admits to Callicles that he didn't really mean what he said here, but was just trying to reduce his position that the better are the stronger to absurdity. It needs to be remembered that this position was one that was put into Callicles' mouth by Socrates. Moreover, it is necessary at the same time to realize that Callicles' critique of Socrates' own fallacy of equating the cultural with the natural for the purposes of defeating Polus has never been answered and indeed was merely swept aside in a flurry of misdirection. But it's not quite over yet. A bit later in the conversation, we receive one more hint that Socrates' discourse is not quite what it's cracked up to be (by Plato, by Socrates). Callicles has been arguing that it is not the lack of desire that constitutes happiness (that is, according to him, being dead or a stone) but the satisfaction of desire, thus even one who has an itch and scratches it (a lewd suggestion put forward by Socrates) also is happy. At this point, Socrates interjects:

> SOCRATES: What if he scratches only his head—or what am I to ask you further? See what you'll answer if somebody asked you one after the other every question that comes next. And isn't the

---

86. Zeyl, "The *Gorgias*," 124–25.

climax of this sort of thing, the life of the *kinaidos,* a frightfully
shameful and miserable one?[87] Or will you have the nerve to say
that they are happy as long as they have what they need to their
hearts' content?

CALLICLES: Aren't you ashamed, Socrates, to bring our discussion
to such matters?

SOCRATES: Is it I who bring them there, my splendid fellow, or
is it the man who claims, just like that, that those who enjoy
themselves, however they may be doing it, are happy, and doesn't
discriminate between good kinds of pleasures and bad? Tell me
now too whether you say that the pleasant and the good are the
same or whether there is some pleasure that isn't good.

---

87. All translations including Zeyl give here "catamite," which is wrong. In order to
make his case that the disciplined ascetic life is happier than that of the man who has
desires and can fulfill them, Socrates invokes the example of the *kinaidos,* the pathic male,
the adult male who desires anal penetration (494e). Socrates here surely displays some
characteristic *kinaidophobia* (see Amy Richlin, "Not Before Homophobia: The Materiality
of the *Cinaedus* and the Roman Law Against Love Between Men," *Journal of the History of
Sexuality* 3, no. 4 [April 1993]: 523–73) of his own (and his own culture), but all of the translators and commentators that I have seen get this wrong and in their own homophobic
ways. The correct Latin translation for *kinaidos* is not "catamite" but *cinaedus,* as illustrated
in the title of Amy Richlin's essay, while "catamite" derives from Latin *catamitus,* apparently a borrowing of Etruscan *catmit* as a corrupted form of the name Ganymede. The
catamite is indeed the boy in a pederastic relationship, a far cry from the pathetic male
Socrates invokes. Having mistranslated the word, the commentators then go on a field
day of further misinterpretation: "Back to the catamite, whose body is not a stone, yet
may be quite passive with no special desires. The only advantage for him would be money,
not his own satisfaction. So long as money is paid, the satisfaction he provides another
man's body is unlimited"; Plochmann and Robinson, *Friendly Companion,* 149–50. These
friendly companions go on, moreover, to write about "the catamite, a sad little boy whose
succession of patrons resembles the life of the insatiate bird," contradicting themselves
and everything we know about Greek culture as well (146–47), for, of course, as we know
well from the *Symposium,* if nowhere else, the boy is indeed not supposed to receive physical gratification, which would be shameful, but he is not doing what he is doing for money
either, which would be even more shameful, but rather to provide gratification for someone who is teaching, guiding, mentoring him. Secondly, reading it this way completely
distorts the metaphor, since the metaphor refers to one who is never satisfied but always
experiencing pleasure, which is hardly the case of the boy catamite. Plochmann and Robinson have to do some fancy footwork to get out of that one. Zeyl gets this wrong as well,
if not quite so egregiously, when he glosses *kinaidos* as the "passive partner (especially boy)
in homosexual practices," which may or may not be an adequate definition of "catamite"
in English usage (he cites an English dictionary) but hardly defines the *kinaidos,* who is
an adult male who precisely does get pleasure from being penetrated and is portrayed as
insatiable and shamefully dishonored by Socrates, in accord with the common negative
prejudices about such men. For these distinctions, see David M. Halperin, *How to Do the
History of Homosexuality* (Chicago: University of Chicago Press, 2002).

CALLICLES: Well, to keep my argument from being inconsistent if I say that they're different, I say they're the same.

SOCRATES: You're wrecking your earlier statements, Callicles, and you'd no longer be adequately inquiring into the truth of the matter with me if you speak contrary to what you think.

CALLICLES: You do it too, Socrates. (494c–495b)[88]

Socrates, indeed, does do it, as I hope by now to have shown. The terms of the critique that I would develop against Socrates' practice are right there, then, in the text, and despite Socrates' immediate protestation that he speaks insincerely only by mistake and should be called on it, speaking so "ironically" is the very hallmark of Socratean discourse.

But again, I emphasize, we know all this only owing to one thing: Plato has let us know it. He has given us Socrates' fallaciousness (and cannot not have known that he was purveying fallacies);[89] he has even given us the key to unlock these fallacies in the critiques of Socrates' practices on the part of both Polus and Callicles. There is a double-voicing in Plato's texts that demands interpretation in some way or another, that has to be read. I propose, therefore, a dialogical reading of Plato's apparently monological dialogues, a reading for the tension and the heterogeneity and not for harmonizing.

Monological or Dialogical Reading

As we have seen, monological readers of Plato, philosophical scholars for the most part, see these fallacies as well but explain them away as something that Socrates is permitted to do, since his opponents are almost by definition morally inferior men, and all is fair in the love of wisdom and war against sophistry. If we are not prepared to admit such arguments, then what can we make of Plato's—to my mind—blatant inclusion and thematization of Socrates' fallacies? My tentative answer lies precisely in the distinction between Socrates and Plato, but not the conventional one that draws a distinction between the "real" Socrates, represented or not in Plato's dialogues (or

88. Zeyl, "The *Gorgias*," 130–31.
89. Robinson, *Plato's Earlier Dialectic,* 21–34.

his early ones at any rate) and the real Plato, with the Socrates of the later dialogues being Plato's "mouthpiece." Rather I propose drawing a distinction between Socrates as Plato's hero and the author Plato throughout the corpus. The reason that this distinction is not frequently made is that Plato seems (and is) so invested in Socrates as hero of his new intellectual program that it is difficult to imagine him presenting Socrates critically,[90] even mockingly—such that the views of "Socrates" in each dialogue are taken by very respectable scholars to be a transparent reflection of Plato's at the time of writing. This is surely a correct perception, but what, then, do we do with all of this seemingly critical material on Socrates (again if we do not assume that Socrates is permitted everything as he is the superior man, à la Callicles)? In the end, I will try to interpret Plato within this paradox, to argue that in some sense the paradox itself is the meaning of Plato, the insistence both on the ultimate value of philosophy, as well as the allowing of a totally incongruous voice of critique.

To recapitulate, one version of an answer to the Platonic question would indict (or praise) all of Plato's writing as a massive, noble lie and a kind of spiritual test. One who sees the explicit voice of critique of Socrates that is presented in such interventions as those of Polus and Callicles and assents to these critiques is only demonstrating that he or she is in the same category of misguided intellects as these figures themselves who cannot see the greater and higher purpose of Socrates' paradoxical fallaciousness. One elegant statement of this interpretation is that of Fendt and Rozema, who write:

> Consider a mimesis *that does to the audience or reader something like what the thing itself would do:* a bust of Socrates with piercing ironic gaze that makes the viewer ask himself what he is doing staring so intently into a block of stone; a dialogue constructed so that the effect of the dialogue on the reader is the effect Socrates had on his fellow citizens in life: stunning their overactive mouths to silence, their brains to acknowledgment of ignorance or stupidity, and then self-examination; similarly, a tragedy that raises the emotions of pity and fear that events

90. Cf. Mark Jordan, "Flesh in Confession: Alcibiades beside Augustine," in *Toward a Theology of Eros: Transfiguring Passion at the Limits of Discipline,* ed. Virginia Burrus and Catherine Keller (New York: Fordham University Press, 2006), 23–37, a landmark paper to which I shall return.

like those in the tragedy would raise in life. If the dialogue, when it comes into contact with a reader, performs a mimesis of Socrates coming into contact with a Greek in the agora, it may well be that the Socrates in the dialogue is not necessarily saying what Socrates (much less Plato) believed or said, for what is required in order *accomplish the effect of Socrates* may be something entirely different from and indifferent to a record of the *beliefs* or dialogues—generic or specific—*of* either *Socrates* or *Plato*.[91]

The point of it all is to expose them/me by any means necessary: "The dialogue raises questions, places us in puzzles, vexes and pummels with good and bad logic—not necessarily or always in the same way to us as to Hippias. How readers respond to these puzzles and vexations—indeed what they consider the puzzles and vexations to be—reveals something about the reader, just as what may well have been pesky about Socrates was that he made his interlocutors reveal things about themselves."[92] Once again we find here an interpretative practice according to which Socrates cannot lose, for all opposition only reveals the reader (like the dialogue partners in "Greece") as stupid or ignorant. Thus, thinking as I do that Polus and Callicles are somehow right in their refusal to be pummeled by bad logic only reveals me to be Polus, or worse, Callicles. I prefer not to accept this interpretation, either in its negative acceptation, namely as an indictment of Plato's undemocratic temper,[93] or in its positive reading, namely as a defense of elite truth against the great unwashed.

From my perspective, we are led rather to think about a systematic double-voicing in the Platonic writing, a level of self-contradiction as remarkable, I hope to show by the end of this book, as anything in ancient literature. This double-voicing of Plato's writing will help us understand this literature in another way entirely from conventional readings. This point can be put even more starkly. Plato's hero, Socrates, on these readings, is the teacher furthest from dialogical

91. Gene Fendt and David Rozema, *Platonic Errors: Plato, a Kind of Poet* (Westport, Conn.: Greenwood Press, 1998), 4, emphasis original.

92. Fendt and Rozema, *Platonic Errors*, 5.

93. Karl Raimund Popper, *The Open Society and Its Enemies* (London: Routledge & K. Paul, 1962).

thinking and dialogical practice that almost could be imagined. His practice is arbitrary in many ways, dependent systematically on fallacy and particularly on begging the question and confusing and browbeating his opponents, who are frequently presented as not as intelligent or clever (δεινός) as he is. Now come the two contradictory propositions I have adumbrated above: Plato seems thoroughly aware of these antidialogic characteristics of Socratean discourse and Plato seems to approve of Socrates throughout the corpus too. Monological readers of Plato, assuming that Plato fully approves of Socrates' practice, produce apologies, sometimes fairly gross ones, for the practice. But they capture an important, indeed necessary, insight as well: Plato is certainly aware of the fallacies and lets us see them, but surely his project as a whole is dependent on a strong affirmation of Socrates and his difference from the Sophists. The dialogism that I find in the dialogues is not where it is usually sought, in the interactions between speaking characters, between Socrates and his interlocutors. Rather there is an ongoing dialogue between Plato the "author" and the speech of his hero, Socrates, throughout the corpus. This dialogical relation between Plato and Socrates takes different forms at different stages, but it is dubious and highly implausible to imagine (as so many do) that in some set of the dialogues, for instance, the alleged "early" dialogues, *Protagoras* and *Gorgias,* we have something like the "real" Socrates, while later, he is reduced to Plato's "mouthpiece." As Debra Nails has memorably put it, "Mouthpiece Schmouthpiece."[94] Please note that I am totally reversing the usual topos that "Socrates"—some "real" Socrates—was a truly dialogical thinker, speaker, interlocutor, while Plato has undermined this dialogicality. I find it difficult to read *any* of Plato's Socratic texts in this way, certainly not, as I hope to have shown, the *Protagoras* or the *Gorgias.* This reading of the *Gorgias,* then, opens up the possibility of another way of interpreting the Platonic corpus, one much more attentive to the elements of the *spoudogeloion* in his writings, long before that form was supposed to appear on the scene.

94. Debra Nails, "Mouthpiece Schmouthpiece," in *Who Speaks for Plato: Studies in Platonic Anonymity,* ed. Gerald A. Press (Lanham, Md.: Rowman & Littlefield, 2000), 15–26.

Crude Contradiction: Plato's "Second Accent"

SOCRATES: Are you asking a question or beginning to declaim some
speech?
POLUS: I'm asking; I'm asking. (466b)

The systematic fallaciousness of Socratic argument has been laid
out eloquently by Richard Robinson in a nearly seventy-year-old book
that is justly regarded as a classic. As Robinson writes, "The statements [of Socrates] that he is 'seeing whether the answer is true' are
insincere."[95] Robinson demonstrates — in a very different way than
mine but reaching nearly identical results — that "the picture we have
so far obtained of the Socratic elenchus is by no means a favorable
one." He elaborates on the point: "This elenchus involved persistent
hypocrisy; it showed a negative and destructive spirit; it caused pain
to its victims; it thereby made them enemies of Socrates," and then,
asks the question that demands to be asked: "The question thus arises
what Plato conceived to be the justification of the elenchus. For what
end was it worth while to be so destructive and insincere, and to incur
so much enmity?"[96]

Denying, as I think we must, that Plato seeks to discredit Socrates,
Robinson attempts to answer this great question, or rather these great
questions, via explicit citations from the Platonic corpus in which the
elenchus is described as having a therapeutic function of demonstrating to the supposed (or self-supposed) knower that he or she knows
nothing, in order to prepare the way for the attainment of knowledge, on the assumption that false knowledge is an impossible barrier
to the acquiring of true knowledge.[97] Robinson, himself, however,
points out that Socrates rarely actually convinces his interlocutor that
he is wrong, but rather that he has merely been outfoxed, outmaneu-
vered, stung by a stingray (Meno), or bound and gagged (Gorgias).[98]
Robinson, nevertheless, is persuasive in his judgment that "the aim
of the elenchus is to wake men out of their dogmatic slumbers into
genuine intellectual curiosity. The conviction of one's own ignorance

---

95. Robinson, *Plato's Earlier Dialectic,* 9.
96. Robinson, *Plato's Earlier Dialectic,* 10.
97. Robinson, *Plato's Earlier Dialectic,* 12–13.
98. Robinson, *Plato's Earlier Dialectic,* 17.

involves and includes some dim realization of the difference between knowledge and all opinions whether false or true. In other words, the notion of the elenchus contains a germ of the Platonic conception of knowledge as absolutely distinct from opinion. The elenchus does not directly give a man any positive knowledge; but it gives him for the first time the *idea* of real knowledge, without which he can never have any positive knowledge even if he has all the propositions that express it."[99] This might, indeed, provide some kind of answer to the question of why Socrates is willing to be unpleasant and to anger his discussants, but in my opinion, in no way, shape, or fashion does it justify the use of fallacy, insincerity, and misdirection in the procedure.

We can make one of two choices now in a sort of diaeresis:[100] either Plato recognized the fallaciousness of much of Socrates' argument or he did not. Robinson clearly asserts the second of these alternatives. Utilizing a strict methodology (and not an impertinent one by any means) to avoid anachronism in the history of philosophy, he argues that many things that seem to follow from Socrates' statements and arguments as articulated by Plato may not have so followed to Plato himself, not, of course, because Plato was incapable of seeing the point, but because human thought had not yet progressed to the point where it was possible to see it even for a Plato: "But both Goodrich and the expungers [nineteenth-century commentators on Plato who attempted to explain what appears to us a 'logical monstrosity'] assumed that Plato's logical views were like ours in a point in which they are not. Even in mathematics, even in logic, the human race changes its opinions from age to age."[101] The assumption, however, that Plato just did not see what seem to us—even to the very untrained of us, namely me—as gross inadequacies in the argument may make good history, but it surely makes for a much weaker text. It is, moreover, I think, contradicted by Plato's placement of explicit remarks on Socrates' fallaciousness in the mouths of his defeated opponents. If they could sense it, even if not quite able to precisely articulate what was wrong, surely Plato could see it too. Or better put, if Plato could put it in their mouths then necessarily he had seen the point.

99. Robinson, *Plato's Earlier Dialectic,* 18.

100. I. M. Bochenski, *A History of Formal Logic,* trans. and ed. Ivo Thomas (Notre Dame, Ind.: University of Notre Dame Press, 1970), pp. 35–39.

101. Robinson, *Plato's Earlier Dialectic,* 32.

This question comes up explicitly in the commentatorial tradition in the *Gorgias*. There is an obvious "sophism" in Socrates' argument against Polus at 474–476, in the sense of a "refutation" that is conducted by an unthematized double meaning in a word. Socrates gets Polus to concede that something which is less "useful" (ὠφέλιμος) is less good and, therefore, seems to catch him in a contradiction by papering over the distinction between useful and thus good for the polis, and useful and thus good for the individual. Polus had claimed that it is better to be unpunished than to be punished, but since punishing wrongdoers is more "useful" and thus "better" than leaving them unpunished, and since the more useful is better, then how can it be better to be unpunished than to be punished? By eliding this distinction, and confusing Polus in doing so, Socrates drives Polus to a self-contradiction by which he declares the same thing good and not good. There has been much discussion in the literature as to whether *Plato* was aware of this contradiction, with, once again, many scholars coming down on the side of logical form simply being undeveloped in Plato's time and thus a Plato unable to see the fallacy. I am inclined to agree, however, with Dodds, who writes that "it is not easy to believe with T. Gomperz and others that Plato was wholly unconscious of the equivocation. . . . It looks rather as if he was content at this stage to let Socrates repay the Sophists in their own coin, as no doubt Socrates often did."[102] As Leslie Kurke has recently shown, this coin is of a very Aesopian sort of minting, one in which, as in the Aesopian narratives, any kind of trickery is permitted in order to force the opponent to confess that he is wrong.[103] This alleged Platonic "contentedness," which I have pointed out as a feature of the *Protagoras* as well, seems to me a devastating indictment of Socratic practice. "Paying in their own coin," if indeed it is that and not Socrates himself simply behaving as the sort of Sophist that he condemns, debases entirely the coinage of Socrates' sincerity and "say what you mean" demands on others. Only special pleading will gainsay this point.[104] In other words, Plato is either a fool, a knave, or a critic of Socrates.

102. Dodds, *Gorgias*, 249.

103. Leslie Kurke, "Plato, Aesop, and the Beginnings of Mimetic Prose," *Representations* 94 (Spring 2006): 26. See also her excellent discussion of this matter on p. 31.

104. A point of view that I do not accept is that Socrates is portrayed as simply trying, by any means necessary, to break down the self-confidence of his interlocutors with a view

Whatever Plato was, he was not a fool, so our only two options are knave or critic.

Let us assume, then, that Plato knew, more or less, what he was doing. This gives us another forking path: either he was doing something fundamentally dishonest (for good or bad reasons), or he was not. According to the first path (the knave), the Platonic corpus performs a gigantic "noble lie," according to which, the end of getting Athenian intellectuals to abandon the moral premises on which Athenian society was built was so vital (for good or bad reasons from our point of view) that it justified the means, even when the means were very far from an approach to truth at all. I will make Patrick Coby a synecdoche for this line of interpretation. For Coby, who provides a strong reading of the *Protagoras* as a whole, this consequence represents the exposure of the falsity and hypocrisy of Protagoras's sophistic position, even while mobilizing some very knowingly fallacious argumentation on Socrates' part. Plato, in other words, is intentionally rendering Socrates' arguments fallacious in order to model how the philosopher ought to deal with those who oppose him, some version of a noble lie. It is remarkable to me that even the sharpest apologists for Socrates, those who love him almost as Alcibiades did, see this too; they just think Socrates is justified in these "noble lies," because

---

to then rebuilding them in another direction (rather like Luther's theology of the function of the law). Thus, as Krabbe, for instance, would have it:

> To what types of conversation (or: dialogue) did dialectic originally refer? On the practical side, one may take the Socratic dialogues as instances of dialectic exchanges. On the face of it, a Socratic dialogue most often aims at getting at the truth of some matter by answering a question like "Is X Y?" or "What is X?" (Richard Robinson, 1970, p. 49). Thus the dialogue would be a type of cooperative inquiry aiming at (philosophical) knowledge. However, the practice of these "inquiries" displays many features of persuasion dialogues and even of eristic quibbling. Moreover, the Questioner (most often Socrates) displays a technique of refutation of a definitely more personal character than needed for a disinterested use of *reductio ad absurdum* arguments in objective proof. In Socratic elenchus, it is the Answerer himself who is refuted, not just his thesis. Elenchus, though painful, is supposed to have beneficial effects on the soul of its victim. According to Richard Robinson (1970, p. 15): "In order to make men virtuous, you must make them know what virtue is. And in order to make them know what virtue is, you must remove their false opinion that they already know. And in order to remove this false opinion, you must subject them to elenchus." Thus the ultimate purpose of these dialogues seems to be educational. (Erik C. W. Krabbe, "Meeting in the House of Callias: Rhetoric and Dialectic," *Argumentation* 14, no. 3 [2000]: 207.)

I think it hardly would be "educational" to use precisely the techniques alleged of the opponents, the Sophists, in order to convince folks to abandon sophism!

in some sense, he is absolutely right.[105] Plato has shown his hand here quite dramatically: to allow a true debate, in which each side gets to present its point of view in a planned and expansive manner, and in which the decision between them is made by third parties observing the debate, is to allow for the possibility that Socrates might lose; this is, of course, precisely the risk of democracy. Note that on this reading, on this version of Plato, the success of the enterprise is predicated on one of two results: either we do not see the fallacies and are taken in by the noble lie for its allegedly noble purposes, or, we do and thus collaborate with the noble liar because we too share his political and moral convictions.

Certain "continental" philosophical readings of Plato offer a much more sophisticated and attractive version of this line of reasoning. Although, in truth, I came to John Sallis very late in the process of writing my book, and, moreover, am not in deep intellectual sympathy with his mode of reading (and am fairly antipathetic to some of his epigones' work), I find his writing empowering for describing my own project of reading. Sallis makes the most excellent point that when we read Plato, "to read carefully includes also taking care to ask about the reading itself and not just plunging precipitously into what is to be read, losing ourselves, as it were, in it as though it were obvious what is required on the part of a reading in order for it to be adequate to the dialogues. The reflective question must not be suppressed, least of all at the beginning. Thus, even to begin reading carefully includes being prepared to learn, in the wake of such questioning, that simply reading the dialogues is no simple affair at all."[106] It is the purpose of this entire book in some nontrivial way to address that complexity of the affair of reading Plato and the Talmud, indeed to engage the reflective question and the self-reflexive question of

---

105. Thus, for instance, Coby shows brilliantly that the moment the chairs are reversed and Protagoras is the questioner and Socrates the questioned, "Socrates promptly entangles himself in his own answers, and like Protagoras, seeks refuge in a long, confounding speech—a preposterous *epideixis* of poetry criticism," and, therefore, "the present offer to instruct Protagoras on the proper way of answering appears like comic braggadoccio." Coby is, of course, right, then to seek what advantage this exchange might have brought for Socrates (and certainly for Plato), but the answer, in my view, only further exposes Socrates' "sophistical" manipulation (Coby, *Socrates*, 94–95).

106. John Sallis, *Being and Logos: Reading the Platonic Dialogues* (Bloomington: Indiana University Press, 1996), 1–2.

the two texts. The differences between our intellectual/reading strategies emerge in what I take to be (modestly I hope) my attempt to read the dialogues both from within their project and from outside it (an outside that I conceive of Plato himself inscribing). If Sallis can claim—sharply, very sharply—"It is not a matter of seeking Plato's opinions at all, for philosophy is what is fundamentally at issue in the dialogues, and philosophy is never a matter of someone's opinions; it is rather that decisive transcending of opinion through which man is subordinated to a higher measure in such a way that, thereby, it is established that man is not the measure of what is," then I wish to query precisely that very claim about philosophy and opinion, to raise the question, heretically, of whether, indeed, the human is not the measure. I wish, as it were, to give voice to Protagoras in a dialogue with Plato, a dialogue that raises the question of both the transcendence of opinion and the "higher measure"; indeed, by the end of the book, I will claim that Plato himself sanctions such a dialogue. Such a dialogue is a dialogue with philosophy, not a dialogue within philosophy. Plato himself, I think, bids us to dismiss Protagoras as totally as Sallis does (not to mention Francisco Gonzalez),[107] but at the same time Plato finds a way to call us to attend to Protagoras as well, to allow for the possibility that the human is, indeed, the measure. He does so, I will argue in the last chapter, through the comic, occasionally grotesquely comic, narratives in which the dialogues of high seriousness are set. My own heuristic model (and perhaps not only heuristic) for this alternative mode of reading Plato—one that, inter alia, does not leave out the politics of it all—is the Talmud, in which as I shall argue we find a dialogue *between* the Torah (the Rabbis' name for their *philosophia*) and a sharp and unanswered voice of critique from without/within, as well, that is "the arena of almost every utterance [in which] an intense interaction and struggle between one's own and another's word is being waged."[108]

In the rest of this book, I purpose, therefore, to pursue the third

107. Francisco J. Gonzalez, "Giving Thought to the Good Together: Virtue in Plato's *Protagoras*," in *Retracing the Platonic Text*, ed. John Russon and John Sallis (Evanston, Ill.: Northwestern University Press, 2000), 113–54.

108. Mikhail Bakhtin, *The Dialogic Imagination: Four Essays by Mikhail Bakhtin*, ed. Michael Holquist, trans. Michael Holquist and Caryl Emerson, University of Texas Press Slavic Series (Austin: University of Texas Press, 1981), 348.

option, one in which Plato both knew what he was doing and expected us to see it as well. This reading sees in the Platonic corpus not
a noble lie, indeed no lie at all, but finally something much more cred-
itable, a Platonic critique of his own most deeply held convictions,
a deep dialogicality that subsists under the powerful monologism
represented in the dialogues themselves, qua dialogues. As much as
I agree that he is an unqualified supporter of "Socrates" and the program of philosophy; as much, indeed, as it is Plato's own program, I
propose a partially new strategy for reading Plato, namely one also allowing "the appearance of a second accent [that] would inevitably be
perceived as a crude contradiction within the author's world view."[109]
In a move that will be repeated several times in the rest of this book,
indeed becoming the central argument of the book, I suggest reading
Plato as advancing with dead seriousness, absolute commitment, and
by any means necessary his program of *epistēmē,* dialectic, and Athens-
Become-Kallipolis. At the same time, he is allowing us to hear that second accent, that crude contradiction, a voice that throws the whole
system into doubt but is not allowed, nevertheless, to undermine it.
This, I shall propose, is where dialogue may be found in the Platonic
writing. So neither fool nor knave, Plato in my reading is a critic, a
self-critical critic of his own most intensely held convictions.

I will suspend my reading of Plato now for three chapters, for in
order to more fully open a way through the aporia I have reached
in these Platonic readings, I am going to go a strange route through
a text a thousand years later than Plato and from another country,
the Babylonian Talmud, which is, of course, the single great literary
product of the Rabbis of the late-ancient Sasanian Jewry and the
single most important document for all of later rabbinic Judaism as
well. Through the mediating figure of Lucian, a second-century Syrian writing in Greek, I hope to excavate and illuminate the perhaps
clearer and rougher double-voicing of the Talmud and then bring that
reflected light back to bear on a reading of what I take to be perhaps
Plato's most crucial text, the *Symposium,* in which the principle of
spoudogeloion is most richly and directly explored within the Platonic
corpus.

---

109. Mikhail Bakhtin, *Problems of Dostoevsky's Poetics,* ed. and trans. Caryl Emerson,
Theory and History of Literature (Minneapolis: University of Minnesota Press, 1984), 82.

4

Jesting Words and Dreadful Lessons:
The Two Voices of the Babylonian Talmud

Introduction: Hellenism in Jewish Babylonia; or, What Are Plato and the Babylonian Talmud Doing in the Same Book?

This book imagines, hypothesizes, a cultural relationship, not merely a typological parallelism, between Plato and the Babylonian Talmud. This is a controversial point. It is commonly held among scholars and learned lay folk alike that while the Palestinian Rabbis were in dialogue (and dispute) with Christians and other Hellenists, the Rabbis of Babylonia were in cultural contact with them only secondarily through the medium of their interaction with Palestinian Rabbis and their literature and traditions.[1] I am proposing, however, that

---

1. For instance, even the very savvy Joshua Levinson considers only the question of the depth and intensity of the Hellenism in Jewish Palestine. "The Tragedy of Romance: A Case of Literary Exile," *Harvard Theological Review* 89, no. 3 (July 1996): 227. See, however, Abraham Wasserstein, "Greek Language and Philosophy in the Early Rabbinic Academies," in *Jewish Education and Learning Published in Honour of Dr. David Patterson on the Occasion of His Seventieth Birthday,* ed. Glenda Abramson (Chur, Switzerland: Harwood Academic Publishers, 1994), 221–31. A very recent exception is Richard Kalmin, who treats other aspects of Western connections for Babylonian rabbinism (*Jewish Babylonia between Persia and Roman Palestine* [Oxford: Oxford University Press, 2006]). For a more extensive form of my argument here, see Daniel Boyarin, "Hellenism in Rabbinic Babylonia," in *The*

the Babylonian Rabbis had a Hellenism of their own. At this point a caveat must be entered, lest I be misunderstood. By asserting that Babylonian rabbinic culture was a Hellenistic culture, I am not in the least denying profound Iranian impact on the culture as well. Recent work in this field, primarily by Yaakov Elman and under his aegis, is exploring and exposing the richness of reading the Bavli (as I shall call the Babylonian Talmud, following tradition) through Iranological lenses as well.[2] Insofar as a Hellenism is by definition a "mixed" culture, there is, however, not the slightest contradiction in reading the Bavli as one articulation of Hellenism. Nor would Elman think so either. As he has noted, following James R. Russell, "influences" from one culture do not preclude in any sense "promiscuous intermingling with material from another tradition."[3] Sasanian Babylonia was a Babel of cultures, including the Persian, Eastern Christian, Mandaean, and Jewish, as well as Manichean cultures and religions. The argument for a Babylonian rabbinic Hellenism is especially compelling with respect to matters not known from Palestinian rabbinic traditions. These, at least arguably, only enter the rabbinic textual world at a period and in a stratum of the Babylonian Talmud in which impact from Palestine is considerably less likely than interaction with the local milieu of trans-Euphratian Christian Hellenism.

In a very important discussion, Shaye Cohen has pointed to the Hellenism in Jewish Babylonia, noting that the very structuration of the rabbinic academies there, resembling the Hellenistic philosophical schools with their successions of "heads," is not to be found in rabbinic Palestine, and, therefore, "perhaps then the parallels between patriarchs and scholarchs tell us more about the Hellenization of Babylonian Jewry in the fourth and fifth centuries than about the

---

Cambridge Companion to Rabbinic Literature, ed. Charlotte Fonrobert and Martin Jaffee (Cambridge: Cambridge University Press, 2007), 336–63.

2. Yaakov Elman, "Acculturation to Elite Persian Norms," in *Neti´ot Ledavid: Jubilee Volume for David Weiss Halivni,* ed. Yaakov Elman, Ephraim Bezalel Halivni, and Zvi Arie Steinfeld (Jerusalem: Orhot Press, 2004), 31–56; Yaakov Elman, "Middle Persian Culture and Babylonian Sages: Accommodation and Resistance in the Shaping of Rabbinic Legal Traditions," in *Cambridge Companion to Rabbinic Literature,* ed. Charlotte Fonrobert and Martin Jaffee (Cambridge: Cambridge University Press, 2006). See too Kalmin, *Jewish Babylonia.*

3. Elman, "Acculturation to Elite Persian Norms," 32.

Hellenization of Palestinian Jewry in the second."[4] My arguments tend to support the position of Shaye Cohen fairly vigorously, albeit not in terms of Hellenistic "influence," nor even yet in terms of "Hellenization"; rather, I suggest we consider Babylonian Jewish culture as itself a Hellenism, or more nuancedly, as a vibrant participant in Richard Kalmin's "rudiments of a partly shared elite culture [which] may have been emerging in Syria and Mesopotamia, perhaps a refinement of a rudimentary shared non-elite culture which had existed earlier."[5] This emergence involves the development of a shared intellectual culture that flows through the Roman East and the Sasanian West, an international style, if you will.[6]

The ways that I imagine such cultural exchange, namely between Christian or "pagan" Greek-writing intellectuals and Babylonian Jewish intellectuals, are drawn from the models and methods of folkloristic research.[7] Diffusion among cultures of motifs, stories, sayings, proverbs, legends is, of course, a very well-known phenomenon, intensively studied since the nineteenth century. I certainly do not imagine Babylonian Rabbis *reading* Platonic dialogues—there just

---

4. Shaye J. D. Cohen, "Patriarchs and Scholarchs," *Proceedings of the American Academy of Jewish Research* 48 (1981): 85. See now too Adam H. Becker, *The Fear of God and the Beginning of Wisdom: The School of Nisibis and Christian Scholastic Culture in Late Antique Mesopotamia,* Divinations (Philadelphia: University of Pennsylvania Press, 2006), 14–15. Further, Abraham Wasserstein has adumbrated such a result, arguing, "The Jews were as susceptible to the lure and influence of Hellenism as their gentile neighbours. This is no less true of the Aramaic-speaking Jews in Palestine and Babylonia than of those of their co-religionists who, living in Asia Minor or in Egypt, or in Greek-speaking cities in Palestine and Syria, had either adopted Greek speech or inherited it from their forebears." I thank Shamma Boyarin for bringing this essay to my attention. It is important to point out that Wasserstein emphasizes as well the common Hellenistic world of the rabbis and of Syriac-writing Christians; "Greek," 223.

5. Kalmin, *Jewish Babylonia,* 174.

6. For a recent and very effective challenge to the notion of "influence" in the study of late-ancient Jewish cultures, see Michael L. Satlow, "Beyond Influence: Towards a New Historiographic Paradigm," in *Jewish Literatures and Cultures: Context and Intertext,* ed. Anita Norich and Yaron Z. Eliav, Brown Judaic Studies 349 (Providence, R.I.: Brown Judaic Studies, 2008), 37–53.

7. For such models in their richest application to rabbinic texts, see Galit Hasan-Rokem, *The Web of Life—Folklore in Rabbinic Literature: The Palestinian Aggadic Midrash Eikha Rabba,* trans. Batya Stein, Contraversions: Jews and Other Differences (Stanford: Stanford University Press, 2000); and Dina Stein, *Memrah, Magyah, Mitos: Pirke de-Rabi Eliezer le-or Mehkar Ha-Sifrut Ha-Amamit* (Jerusalem: Hotsaat sefarim a. sh. Y. L. Magnes, ha-Unversitah ha-Ivrit, 2004).

isn't evidence for that for the seventh century, even though a century or two later they certainly were—but rather that literary modes and religious ideas reached them via the modes of diffusion of the kinds of literatures that we design as folklore. This does not mean, of course, that they were not elite products. Recent folkloristic scholarship assumes that "folkloristic" modes of production and dissemination occur at all levels of society and culture capital. This would provide a model to explain at least partially Kalmin's "shared elite culture." Such disseminated products are then subject to another well-studied process known as ecotypification, in which they undergo transition and are modified to fit better the cultural situation of their new environment.[8]

Finally, it is important to realize that written culture becomes transmuted into oral culture and then back again by such means over and over and over again. Some recent work on early Islam will help to demonstrate this point. In a lucid and compelling account, Uwe Vagelpohl has discussed the problems attending "the philological outlook," defined by him as "a tendency to look at the translation movement as a philological phenomenon in isolation from its political and intellectual contexts,"[9] or, in other words, exclusive attention to written texts. As Vagelpohl makes clear, "one consequence of the 'philological outlook' is the centrality accorded to the *textual* transmission of Greek thought."[10] Vagelpohl goes on to explain that in addition to actual texts translated from Greek into Syriac and into Arabic, there are other means by which Greek wisdom was transmitted to the East. Arguing that "we cannot explain every Grecism and every instance of terms and ideas apparently inspired by a Greek source, whether directly or indirectly," he claims that we must postulate "a certain amount of oral communication across linguistic boundaries and 'para-translational' phenomena which leave less conspicuous traces in a literary tradition than the outright translation of texts."[11] Since the particular historical,

8. Daniel Boyarin, "Virgins in Brothels: Gender and Religious Ecotypification," *Estudios de literatura oral* 5 (1999): 195–217.

9. Uwe Vagelpohl, *Aristotle's Rhetoric in the East: The Syriac and Arabic Translation and Commentary Tradition,* Islamic Philosophy, Theology and Science, vol. 76 (Boston: Brill, 2008), 1–2.

10. Vagelpohl, *Aristotle's Rhetoric,* 3.

11. Vagelpohl, *Aristotle's Rhetoric,* 5.

linguistic, and cultural system of which Vagelpohl writes is substantially the same one as that of the Babylonian Talmud (with Greek materials diffusing eastward via Syriac-speaking Christians),[12] albeit a couple of centuries later, the phenomena of which he speaks, are, in my view, very plausibly postulated for the later layers of the textual/cultural processes that gave rise to the Bavli. As Louise Marlow has stated, "The assimilation of Hellenism into the culture of the eastern Mediterranean in the course of the sixth and seventh centuries foreshadowed the permeation of Islamic thought by Classical Greek and NeoPlatonic social ideas."[13]

Dimitri Gutas points out that it is extremely difficult to prove oral transmission, since, almost necessarily, it has not left a written record.[14] Gutas also makes the excellent point that what would be transmitted by such posited or hypothesized oral means is not full philosophical doctrines but rather short and poignant sayings and anecdotes, precisely the sort of material I see as revealing the Bavli's Hellenism.[15] Some scholars wish to deny any explanatory value to that

12. As Vagelpohl explains, "In pre-Islamic Palestine, Syria and Iraq, Greek learning was mainly transmitted through the various Christian churches of the area. Many of the Christian scholars trained in the convents and churches that were part of the local educational system(s) were familiar enough with Greek to read Greek literature in the original but their native language was Syriac, a dialect of Aramaic that had become the dominant language of scholars and merchants in the 'Fertile Crescent' in the wake of the spread of Christianity." Vagelpohl, *Aristotle's Rhetoric*, 15. Given, for instance, that the Targum to the Proverbs is simply the Peshitto transliterated into Hebrew characters, can we doubt that Jewish "scholars and merchants" found Syriac culture accessible? Further: "At the time of the Islamic conquest, the centers of Greek scholarship in the eastern part of the Roman Empire and western Persia were Edessa, Nisibis, Seleucia (near Ctesiphon) and Gundīsāpūr (all of them dominated by Nestorian denomination)" (16).

13. Louise Marlow, *Hierarchy and Egalitarianism in Islamic Thought,* Cambridge Studies in Islamic Civilization (New York: Cambridge University Press, 1997), 44. Vagelpohl's book has been invaluable to me both for his own insights and for sending me to this reference and several others cited in these paragraphs as well.

14. Dimitri Gutas, "Pre-Plotinian Philosophy in Arabic (Other Than Platonism and Aristotelianism): A Review of the Sources," in *Aufstieg und Niedergang der römischen Welt: Geschichte und Kultur Roms im Spiegel der neueren Forschung Teil 2, Bd.36, Tbd.7, Principat Philosophie, Wissenschaften, Technik Philosophie (systematische Themen; indirekte Überlieferungen; Allgemeines; Nachträge),* von Wolfgang Haase/herausgegeben von Wolfgang Haase und Hildegard Temporini (Berlin: De Gruyter, 1994), 4947.

15. I am, accordingly, not claiming anything like the "maximalist" version of a "hidden tradition," as anatomized by Gutas, "Pre-Plotinian Philosophy," 4945–46. But neither am I convinced that the "minimalist" position that Gutas dismisses is as trivial as he would have it be. Why indeed are "borrowed adages and similarities in outlook not among the constitutive elements of a high civilization" (4945)?

which cannot be demonstrated positively[16] (in this camp among Jewish scholars would E. E. Urbach),[17] assuming always internal cultural development until proven otherwise. For my taste, in contrast, it is quite enough that we have parallels to such transmission avenues to make the explanatory value of hypothesizing them rich and telling when particular puzzling textual phenomena in the Bavli are illuminated thereby.[18]

An example that seems quite compelling to me is the idea of *anamnesis*. For Plato, famously, the fetus knows all truth but forgets it upon birth, so learning is remembering (*Meno* 86b). For the Rabbis, equally famously (if in more limited circles), an angel teaches the fetus the whole Torah and then makes him/her forget it on birth, so all learning of Torah is remembering (Nidda 30b). For another example of the same consonance, witness the Seventh Letter, in which Plato writes: "I do not . . . think the attempt to tell mankind of these matters a good thing, except in the case of some few who are capable of discovering the truth for themselves with a little guidance" (341b). One should compare this to the famous clause in the Mishna that one teaches esoterica only to "one who is wise and understands of himself," on which the Bavli remarks that "we give into his hands the chapter headings alone" (Ḥagiga 13a). These parallels are too specific to be mere chance, and they bespeak some cultural channels, by no means necessarily written, by which Platonic *stories* and maxims reached the Rabbis of Babylonia. Thus, it is not implausible to imagine by this means that even Platonic motifs, let alone Lucianic or Petronian ones, became part of oral culture, were transmitted to the Babylonian Rabbis through the medium of oral transcultural transmission, and then reappeared in writing within the Bavli itself, having undergone a sort of sea-change (or perhaps desert-change) en route.[19]

Another significant factor in the increased "Hellenizing" of the Babylonian Rabbis may very well be the increased movement of Syriac Christian sages after 489 AC after the bishop of Edessa was given

16. In this category falls Gutas himself; "Pre-Plotinian Philosophy," 4944–49.

17. Ephraim E. Urbach, *The Sages: Their Concepts and Beliefs,* trans. Israel Abrahams (Jerusalem: Magnes Press, 1975), 246–48.

18. See Vagelpohl, *Aristotle's Rhetoric,* 5n13.

19. Cf. Michael G. Morony, *Iraq after the Muslim Conquest,* Princeton Studies on the Near East (Princeton, N.J.: Princeton University Press, 1984), 7–11.

permission to close down the theologically suspect "School of the Persians" in that city. Its adherents, thereupon, fled over the Persian border and founded their school at Nisibis.[20] Isaiah Gafni has argued that the founding of this East Syrian (formerly known as "Nestorian") school in Nisibis had a big impact on the formation of the rabbinic schools in that area.[21] This perspective has the potential to lead to revolutionary new ways of conceiving the history of Babylonian rabbinic Judaism,[22] insofar as one of the outstanding features of these Syriac-speaking and writing Christian scholars and teachers was their concern with Greek (and especially Neoplatonic) philosophy. It is important to note that in areas very close to the centers of production of late-ancient Babylonian rabbinic culture, an Aramaic-speaking and writing Christian community was increasingly articulating its religious thought on the basis of Greek philosophy, just as Christian writers had been doing, if somewhat earlier, in the Greek-speaking West. The geographical center of authority for the Babylonian Jews is in Maḥoza (Syriac Maḥoze, a section of Seleucia-Ctesiphon, the Sasanian capital), the site of the Catholicos of the East Syrian church. As Becker has put the point, "Jews and Christians in Mesopotamia spoke the same language, lived under the same rulers, practiced the same magic, engaged in mystical and eschatological speculation, and shared scriptures as well as a similar fixation on the ongoing and eternal relevance of those scriptures. They developed similar institutions aimed at inculcating an identity in young males that defined each of them as essentially a *homo discens,* a learning human, or rather, a *res discens,* a learning entity, since learning was understood as an essential characteristic of their humanity."[23] Given these considerations,

20. Becker, *Fear of God,* 2.

21. Isaiah Gafni, "Nestorian Literature as a Source for the History of the Babylonian *Yeshivot,*" *Tarbiz* 51 (1981–82): 567–76 (in Hebrew). For the significance of Nisibis (trans-Euphratian Antioch) as a center of Jewish learning, see Aharon Oppenheimer, Benjamin H. Isaac, and Michael Lecker, *Babylonia Judaica in the Talmudic Period,* Beihefte zum Tübinger Atlas des Vorderen Orients (Wiesbaden: L. Reichert, 1983), 328–31.

22. See Becker's remarks relating how changing legends of origin in Mesopotamia about Syrian monasticism were homologous with the institutional changes also taking place. So as the East Syrian monastic practices became Egyptianized, "the memories of early Syriac monasticism and its indigenous origins were completely erased. The culmination of this may be seen in the Mār Awgēn tradition, which held that monasticism was brought to Mesopotamia by Eugenius the Egyptian." Becker, *Fear of God,* 175.

23. Becker, *Fear of God,* 5.

Becker adumbrates—but in concert with the scope of his project does not develop the particulars of—the importance of this shared culture for the formation and content of the Babylonian Talmud. Vagelpohl, moreover, has identified Seleucia-Ctesiphon and Nisibis as being "at the time of the Islamic conquest" two of "the centers of Greek scholarship in the eastern part of the Roman Empire and western Persia."[24]

My considerations above of the plausibility of a joint cultural milieu, or at least of the possibility of cultural contact between the authors of the Bavli and late Hellenistic literary and thought forms, are meant to be just that, an argument for the inherent plausibility of such a milieu, not a proof for its existence. Given this inherent plausibility of such a cultural environment, my question is: does positing it help me produce a hypothesis to account for previously unexplained anomalies in particular texts or in the entire corpus? If I can account for anomalies in a text, small or large, by relating them to a particular historical-literary context, and if there does not seem to be an alternative explanation that can explain such anomalies, I will offer this reading as a hypothesis. Should someone find another way of reading the text that accounts for more of the text on fewer assumptions, that interpretation would be preferable to the one I offer here. Failing that, my readings should provide evidence for the hypothesis of extensive cultural contact and interaction between the Rabbis of late Babylonia and the Greco-Christian cultural world. The "method" is to imagine a different place, a hypothesized Republic of Letters, in which a series of textual readings can be imagined to lodge. It is vital, of course, that this new metanarrative not violate the more or less assured results of historians to date, but it surely can go beyond the hypotheses and conclusions that they draw upon these findings.

The Talmud's Monological Dialogues

It is at least arguable that the second most vauntedly dialogical of texts from antiquity—after Plato—is the Babylonian Talmud. The Bavli has become almost a poster child for the dialogical text. Countering perhaps an earlier (nineteenth-century) representation of

24. Vagelpohl, *Aristotle's Rhetoric*, 16.

the Talmud as severe and repressive, many twentieth-century critics (including the writer of these lines) saw in the apparent open-
endedness of the talmudic dialectic a version of pluralism or some
kind of near-deconstructive undecidability. Certainly, as I have argued above, and as many have argued before me, the Bavli bespeaks
numerous individual voices. But I have changed my mind that such a
plethora of voices necessarily constitutes a dialogical text.

Bakhtin has most clearly described the monologism inherent in
represented dialogue in his essay "Discourse in the Novel." In this
essay, he argues that a "rhetorical double-voicedness" may sometimes
be "unfolded into an individual dialogue, into individual argument
and conversation between two persons," but since the exchanges
belong to a "single unitary language," they are not diverse in speech
or language even when the parties are arguing with each other. As
he comments, "Such double-voicing, remaining within the boundaries of a single hermetic and unitary language system, without any
underlying fundamental sociolinguistic orchestration, may be only a
stylistically secondary accompaniment to the dialogue and forms of
polemic. The internal bifurcation (double-voicing) of discourse, sufficient to a single and unitary language and to a consistently monologic
style, can never be a fundamental form of discourse: it is merely a
game, a tempest in a teapot."[25] I maintain in this book that the Bavli
is indeed a dialogical text but that the dialogue in the text is not to
be found where it has been sought, between the voices of the different speakers, "not from *individual* dissonances, misunderstandings or
contradictions."[26] Rather, it arises in the "internal dialogism of authentic prose discourse, which grows organically out of a stratified
and heteroglot language," that "cannot ultimately be fitted into the
frame of any manifest dialogue, into the frame of a mere conversation between persons."[27] In this chapter, I will be making an argument about the Babylonian Talmud similar to the one I have made
with respect to Plato, namely that *in its dialectic,* the Bavli is anything
but dialogical.

25. Mikhail Bakhtin, "Discourse in the Novel," in *The Dialogic Imagination: Four Essays
by Mikhail Bakhtin,* ed. Michael Holquist, trans. Michael Holquist and Caryl Emerson,
University of Texas Press Slavic Series (Austin: University of Texas Press, 1981), 325.
  26. Bakhtin, *The Dialogic Imagination,* 325.
  27. Bakhtin, *The Dialogic Imagination,* 326. See too p. 330.

In a forthcoming book, Barry Wimpfheimer has treated the Talmud from a Bakhtinian perspective.[28] In my own reading of the Talmud, I shall be both building on Wimpfheimer's account and ultimately modifying it in a certain direction as well. Wimpfheimer notes
the drive for coherence that motivates the talmudic text: "While the
Bavli takes the structural form of a multi-vocal debate, the drive for
coherence is the true energy behind Talmudic conversations. In fact,
the words 'Talmud' and 'gemara'—words that would later become
synonyms for the Bavli—refer in the rabbinic lexicon to the practice
of juxtaposing contradictory assertions and dialectically resolving
their contradictions."[29] The effect, in terms of the "Talmud" in this
sense of dialectical resolutions of contradictions, is to produce, albeit by very different means, a form of dialogue as ultimately monological (on Wimpfheimer's reading) as that of Plato himself (on my
reading).[30] Indeed, the famous refusal of the Babylonian Talmud to
allow any resolution to its dialectic (similar to the *aporetic* dialogues
of Plato) does not constitute openness or pluralism as I see it now,
but a similarly monological protreptic that maintains that all Truth—
in this case figured as the revelation at and from Sinai of the oral
Torah—can be found only via the truth procedures, oral Torah, and
in the institution which is the sole possessor of the oral Torah and its
methods, the rabbinic House of Study. Thus while the detailed and internally directed questions of halakhic practice are endlessly debated
with the utmost of seriousness, no possible challenge to the system
itself may be brooked. In this sense, the dialectic of the Talmud (the
sugya) is not dialogical; it is monolingual. The talmudic dialectic is no
more dialogical than the Platonic and for largely the same reason: in

28. Barry Wimpfheimer, *Telling Tales out of Court: Literary Ambivalence in Talmudic Legal
Narratives,* Divinations: Rereading Late Ancient Religions (Philadelphia: University of
Pennsylvania Press, forthcoming). I am grateful for the privilege of reading this book prior
to its publication. It needs to be said that the extent to which this chapter is in conversation with Wimpfheimer is greater than can be marked in specific footnotes.

29. Wimpfheimer, *Telling Tales,* introduction.

30. In reading Wimpfheimer's work, I noticed at one point that he referred to previous scholars who have claimed that the Midrash and Talmud are themselves, ipso facto,
dialogical works in the Bakhtinian sense, and looking to see who that scholar was and to
cite him or her as a ground to my own claims about the monologicity of these texts in
their represented dialogues, I discovered, of course, myself. So I am my own fall guy. The
present work represents a virtual volte-face from my earlier, and as I now think, naively
celebratory positions.

both there is one abstract consciousness, one "profile of rationality," by which all opposition is nulled.[31] For Plato, of course, that is *philosophia,* as we have seen, while for the Talmud it is that rabbinic profile of rationality named oral Torah, together with its midrashic and other modes of reasoning. I am not claiming that Platonic philosophy is translatable into talmudic Torah, but rather that they function in two very different cultural environments in analogous ways.

A few introductory words about the composition of the Talmud may prove helpful here. The bulk of the Babylonian Talmud consists of a particular kind of dialectic in which two opposing views on a given topic in halakha are presented and then an argument is pursued in which each of the two *amora'im* (named post-Mishnaic speakers) tries to topple the view of the other by contradicting it with authoritative texts which are explained away in turn. More often than not, the "conversation" ends with neither side defeating the other, but all contradictions to either side neatly explained away in more or less convincing fashion. Although the "fiction" of the Talmud is that these are the records of living conversations that actually took place, it is clear, rather, that they are the product of artfully constructed rhetorical composition practices that make use of existing halakhic sayings in order to construct the dialectic, which is glued together with connective materials, questions that various sayings are made as if to answer, and contradictions made up out of originally independent sayings. This is the specific authorial "hand" that has taken the utterances (ממרות) of the *amora'im* and turned them into conversations and especially dialectics, in large part by juxtaposing them one to the other (even if the speakers were continents and centuries apart). These anonymous authors have also frequently added questions to which the utterances were allegedly an answer, objections that they allegedly refute. All of this connective material that builds the dialectic of the *sugya* out of the *memrot* is called (traditionally and by scholars) the *stam* or *stamma.*

Among Bakhtin's achievements is the articulation of the notion of the monologic dialogue, that is, the represented dialogue in a text,

---

31. For an almost directly opposite account of the Talmud, see Sergei Dolgopolsky, *What Is Talmud? The Art of Disagreement* (New York: Fordham University Press, 2009); he is surely at least as "right" as I am.

that when analyzed can be shown to encode only the point of view of the "author." I hope to show here that the talmudic dialectic produced by the *stamma* works to produce such monological dialogue, in which, "even when one is dealing with a collective, with a multiplicity of creating forces, unity is nevertheless illustrated through the image of a single consciousness: the spirit of a nation, the spirit of a people, the spirit of history, and so forth."[32] In the case of the Talmud, of course, this single consciousness can best be seen as the "spirit" of Torah, that is, of a particular practice of devotional study that organizes the whole world of value and meaning from alpha to omega around the determination of correct practice, halakha, allowing no other consciousness, neither Jewish nor gentile, to have independent existence. As Bakhtin characterizes such monologism, "Everything capable of meaning can be gathered together in one consciousness and subordinated to a unified accent; whatever does not submit to such a reduction is accidental and unessential."[33] This would undoubtedly be an extreme way of describing the talmudic dialectic; in some senses it is too chaotic and not clearly under anyone's control (even the limited control that an author exercises) to quite produce a unified accent, but in a strong sense, this is, nevertheless, an important descriptive tool for understanding the talmudic dialectic in the sense that the Bavli is a protreptic (in *this* sense exactly analogous to Plato's dialogues) for a way of life, the life of the House of Study. It is, moreover, a useful way of thinking about the fate of those intractable stories in the Talmud which are a major part of my topic in this book; they are for the Talmud "whatever does not submit to such a reduction," and has, therefore, been treated by the tradition as "accidental and unessential."

The Babylonian Talmud, even more than the Palestinian,[34] is a scholastic document produced largely to convince folks that the way of life of the oral Torah, the way of the Rabbis, is the only way toward appropriate behavior toward God and humankind (equivalent only in this functional sense to Platonic philosophy). This is, moreover, the

32. Mikhail Bakhtin, *Problems of Dostoevsky's Poetics,* ed. and trans. Caryl Emerson, Theory and History of Literature (Minneapolis: University of Minnesota Press, 1984), 82.

33. Bakhtin, *Problems of Dostoevsky's Poetics,* 82.

34. On this point, see Richard Kalmin, "The Formation and Character of the Babylonian Talmud," in *The Cambridge History of Judaism,* vol. 4, *The Late Roman-Rabbinic Period,* ed. Steven T. Katz (Cambridge: Cambridge University Press, 2006), 840–77.

way that the Talmud has been read and used for a millennium and a half. Rather than suggesting that this is the way the Talmud invites itself to be read exclusively, I offer the idea that there is a strongly monologizing voice within the Talmud that serves as the impetus of such a reading, a reading that turns ultimately all that is authoritative into halakha. I will refer to the ideology of this voice as "legism."[35] Concomitantly, as I will argue below, there is a second voice in the Talmud, one scarcely attended to, that resists not only legism but nomism altogether (or better put, the rabbinic program tout court). My representation of the ways that the Talmud inhibits and closes off dissent from that program is thus to be taken less as a description of the Talmud than as a move against monological reading practices with respect to the Talmud and a move toward a dialogically holistic reading. In other words, pulling the dialectic out of its context is intended as a heuristic way of isolating a language, a prominent, dominant language in the Talmud that illuminates and is, in turn, illuminated by a deeply discordant other language that is there too.

While perhaps in the earliest stages of his thinking, Bakhtin had identified dialogue between characters in the novel as an instance of dialogism, it quickly became clear to him that not only does dialogism not rest exclusively in the dialogues of characters, it is most often resisted in such dialogue, which is, after all, entirely under the control and within the plane of the discourse of the author. Without being more absolutist than Bakhtin—there is some measure of dialogism perhaps in the dialectic—I, nonetheless, propose that such nondialogical represented dialogue (or dialectic) is as characteristic of the talmudic *sugya* as it is of Plato's dialogues. I offer, therefore, that in the *sugya*, at least as much as in the Platonic dialogue, the author, the *stamma*, "cram[s] everything into one abstract consciousness," as Bakhtin puts it.

The monologism of the talmudic *sugya* does not generally consist of the kind of power play that we find, for instance, in the *Protagoras*, being rather something more like the *Symposium* in its strategies. That is, it is not so much that one voice in the dialogue is crushed as

35. The term "legism" is drawn from the literature of Confucianism in precisely this sense as one of the schools of Confucianist thought. As Borges remarked (I don't remember where), the Chinese and the Jews are the only peoples on earth who tried to legislate for every moment of life.

Protagoras's is, but rather that the voices in the represented dialogue are brought under the full control of the *stamma*, author of the *sugya*, at every moment. (No one is allowed to introduce any dangerous substances into the valise of the *sugya*.) This kind of monological dialogue is rather closer to Bakhtin's account of nondialogical dialogue, in which "the unconfirmed ideas are distributed among the heroes, no longer as signifying ideas, but rather as socially typical or individually characteristic manifestations of thought. The one who knows, understands, and sees is in the first instance the author himself. He alone is an ideologist."[36] The role of the author of the rabbinic dialectic thus provides a perfect fit for the Bakhtinian notion of the monological dialogue. Indeed, the Rabbis themselves imagine God as the author of all of their words.

A Divine Conversation: The Single Shepherd and the Consolidation of Rabbinic Hegemony

It was David Stern among modern critics who first showed how deeply antithetical to dialogue in the Bakhtinian sense is the alleged plurality of voices in rabbinic literature in general, including in the Talmud. Stern demonstrated as well the explicit effort of the *stamma* to harmonize away any possibility of genuine dissent: "The conclusion of such a discourse is, of course, a powerful and tendentious support for rabbinic hegemony. . . . [T]he citation of multiple interpretations in midrash is an attempt to represent in textual terms an idealized academy of rabbinic tradition where all the opinions of the sages are recorded equally as part of a single divine conversation. Opinions that in human discourse may appear as contradictory or mutually exclusive are raised to the state of paradox once traced to their common source in the speech of the divine author."[37] Stern discusses at length a talmudic passage in which it is explicitly claimed that all of the opinions of all of the Rabbis are all equally sanctioned by God, as it were:

36. Bakhtin, *Problems of Dostoevsky's Poetics*, 82.
37. David Stern, *Midrash and Theory: Ancient Jewish Exegesis and Contemporary Literary Studies*, Rethinking Theory (Evanston Ill.: Northwestern University Press, 1996), 37.

Should a man say: Since some pronounce unclean and others pronounce clean, some prohibit and others permit, some declare unfit
and others declare fit—how then shall I learn Torah? Therefore Scripture says: All of them "were given by one shepherd." One God gave
them, one leader (i.e., Moses) proclaimed them from the mouth of the
Lord of all creation, blessed be He, as it is written, "And God spoke
all these words" [Exodus 20:1; my emphasis]. Therefore make your
ear like the hopper and acquire a perceptive heart to understand the
words of those who pronounce unclean and the words of those who
pronounce clean, the words of those who prohibit and the words of
those who permit, the words of those who declare unfit and the words
of those who declare fit. (TB Ḥagiga 3a–b)

The Bavli is actually quite outspoken here about its ambitions. By
insisting that all sides in the debate are correct, it completely vitiates
the power of genuine debate and dissent. That is, a true challenge
to these practices from outside the rabbinic community is impossible, given the Bavli's claim that all are the words of the Living God,
all were given by one Shepherd. Everyone must incline his/her ears
like hoppers and accept the Rabbis' words as divine. Thus are the
Talmud's opposing rabbinic opinions brought clearly under Bakhtin's
dictum that in a monological dialogue "unity is nevertheless illustrated through the image of a single consciousness," the spirit of the
rabbinic oral Torah. This is, as I am arguing, the actual practice of the
halakhic dialectic of the Talmud. Anything but dialogical, the Bavli's
sugya is a classic instance of a Bakhtinian monological dialectic, of
which as we have seen, he writes: "Dialogue and dialectics. Take a dialogue and remove the voices . . . remove the intonations . . . carve out
abstract concepts and judgments from living words and responses,
cram everything into one abstract consciousness—and that's how
you get dialectics."[38]

That to this day it is nearly impossible to imagine a world of committed Jewish practice in late antiquity that was not rabbinic, or even
not fully rabbinic, is a measure of the success of these rhetorical and
literary practices in convincing readers that there is no authentic Jew-

38. Bakhtin, *Problems of Dostoevsky's Poetics,* xxxii, citing Bakhtin's Jottings of 1971.

ish voice outside the House of Study. And yet historical scholarship does force us to consider this as at least a possible reality. In another literary context, Tim Whitmarsh has reminded us that "the various constituent voices that are to be found in dialogue with each other in the novel can be, on their own terms, authoritarian; that there is no ultimate closure or resolution does not necessarily detract from their forcefulness."[39] Indeed, as suggested by Stern, we could go even a step further and propose that it is the ultimate nonclosure of the talmudic *sugya* that guarantees the forcefulness of the ideological authority of the ultimately single-voiced dialectic.

When considered from another point of view, this is simply the character of dialectic per se. The halakhic (legal) dialectic of the Babylonian Talmud by itself is as profoundly monological as Plato's in that it brooks no real challenge to its possession of the oral Torah, the guaranteed, if admittedly only partly comprehended, definitive God's truth. This is, indeed, a given of its very use of dialectic, and, moreover, this is the primary definition and telos of dialectic itself. As Erik Krabbe has written, "The primary purpose of dialectic (in the narrower sense), as being mostly concerned with inquiry, is to attain at a truth of some sort, whereas that of rhetoric, as being concerned with persuasion, is to arrive at a shared opinion."[40] Still less is the purpose of dialectic the airing of and exposure of difference. To be sure, what is crucial is the "truth of some sort" toward which dialectic drives. I will repeat and repeat again that I am, of course, not claiming that the epistemology of the Bavli is in any direct way comparable to that Plato. But it is the case, in my view, that the function of the talmudic dialectic is very similar to that of Plato in that both are inquiries based on a single and singular concept of rationality (different in each case). Like Plato's Academy, the Rabbis' House of Study is vaunted as the only possible venue for the discovery of truth.

I have found three general methods through which the *stamma* monologizes or reduces the potentially dialogical to the monological. The first is by constructing dialectical encounters out of different state-

39. Tim Whitmarsh, "Dialogues in Love: Bakhtin and His Critics on the Ancient Novel," in *The Bakhtin Circle and Ancient Narrative*, vol. 3, ed. R. Bracht Branham, Ancient Narrative (Groningen: Barkhuis Publishing and the University Library of Groningen, 2005), 109.

40. Erik C. W. Krabbe, "Meeting in the House of Callias: Rhetoric and Dialectic," *Argumentation* 14, no. 3 (2000): 211.

ments made in different contexts, thus turning what might have been dialogue into dialectic; the second is by harmonizing different opinions in such wise that their power to be distinct is bleached out of them; and the third is via a mode of appropriation through which voices that potentially challenge the entire halakhic system of authority and normativity are defanged, their potential to challenge having been staved off by being assimilated into the halakhic system. I will exemplify each of these quite prevalent talmudic strategies with one example.

Dialogue into Dialectic: Monologizing the *Sugya*

In the first Mishna of the second chapter of Ketubbot, we are told of a situation in which there is contention between a woman and her divorcing husband or between a widow and her deceased husband's heirs as to her status at the time of the marriage. If the marriage was a first marriage, she is entitled to a payment of two hundred *zuz* at the time of dissolution of the marriage for either cause, while if it was a remarriage she may only collect one hundred. The Mishna informs us:

> If there were witnesses that she went out [to the wedding procession] in a *hinuma* with her hair uncovered, she may collect two hundred [in accordance with a first marriage]. Rabbi Yoḥanan ben Beroqa: Even the distribution of toasted grains is a proof.

The Mishna adduces two customs that were practiced only at a first wedding (neither of which was understood even by the time of the Bavli), so if the divorcée or widow can produce witnesses who remember that one of these practices was engaged in at the wedding, she is entitled to the reimbursement suitable for the dissolution of a first marriage.

To this the Talmud objects:

> Shouldn't he [the author of the Mishna] be concerned that she will produce witnesses in this court and collect and then again produce her *ketubba* in another court and collect again?

If we allow a widow to collect on the basis of the testimony of witnesses to the marriage, objects the *stamma,* then she could pull out

her marriage contract in another court and successfully sue for the
payment on dissolution of marriage there as well.

To respond to this question, the *stamma* cites a Palestinian
authority:

> Said Rabbi Abbahu: This demonstrates that we write a quitclaim [and
> give it to the husband or his heirs].

The question of the quitclaim is a contested one at other sites in the
Talmud. The controversy turns on whether or not in cases of a debt
being paid the court should provide the former debtor with a document which proves that he has paid the debt, lest he be sued again for
the same obligation. Rabbi Abbahu is made to answer the question,
arguing that since our Mishna seems to create an impossibly unjust
situation if we don't assume that a quitclaim is afforded the paid-off
debtor, it is clear that the court must provide such a document.

But of course, this being the Talmud, his argument is not allowed
to stand:

> Said Rav Pappa: We are speaking of a place where no *ketubba* is
> written.

Rashi (the great eleventh-century commentator on the Talmud)
explains that Rav Pappa's view is that the court should not ever give a
quitclaim document to a paid-up debtor, for then the burden of proof
would shift to him, and if suit is brought for an unpaid debt, it will be
his obligation to prove that he paid it. This seems to Rav Pappa inherently unfair, given the general rabbinic presumption that the one who
is seeking to receive money must prove his or her claim. Rav Pappa,
accordingly, opines that the Mishna in which the woman collects by
adducing witnesses refers to a situation in which the local custom is
not to actually write a *ketubba* document but to rely on the prevailing
conditions for marriages set by the court, and accordingly she would
not be able to produce her *ketubba* in another court to collect again
(since she does not have one).

Although the *sugya* goes on, this is enough for me to make my point
here. What is important to realize is that despite this *sugya*'s fiction
of being a conversation—a question asked, one answer given, an an-

tithetical answer given—this *sugya* is, in fact, like most, an artificial literary construction. For one thing, the participants in this apparent controversy lived a century and thousands of miles apart (Abbahu in Palestine in the third century; Pappa in Babylonia in the fifth). For another thing, it is not at all clear, Rashi's commentary notwithstanding, that Rav Pappa is, in fact, answering the question. He could, just as well, have simply been interpreting the Mishna as applying in a situation where there is no documentary *ketubba,* thus explaining the need for witnesses altogether. He is not, on that assumption, making a comment, then, on the question of quitclaims. Furthermore, since it is the author of the dialectic who constructed this entire controversy, we don't even really know to what Rabbi Abbahu's comment was originally attached, or whether, indeed, it even referred to the situation of the Mishna. In fact, the *stamma* itself bruits this possibility immediately afterward, thus showing how constructed and hypothetical was the first contextualization of Rav Pappa's statement. My point is not, of course, that there is in this case any deep ideological stake involved; in fact, almost the opposite: the point is stronger because there isn't anything at stake, but rather the *sugya* shows precisely how the living voices of rabbinic (amoraic) commentators were made in particular times and places in response to particular conditions, and texts are transformed to become examples of Bakhtin's "dialectic," wherein the author "carve[s] out abstract concepts and judgments from living words and responses." The point is not that there is no difference between Rabbi Abbahu's and Rav Pappa's views; the point is rather that there is no difference between Rabbi Abbahu and Rav Pappa (the *sugya* would suffer nothing if they were exchanged), and, moreover, precisely that there is hardly anything of moment at stake in this disagreement.

This dialectic remains lively and compelling to be sure (myriads of people even today—including me—find endless delight in following the logic and resolving the logical difficulties of this incredible text, the Babylonian Talmud), but I insist on the point that it is not and cannot be cited as an example of some kind of pluralism or dialogue in the weak sense of people listening to each other or being tolerant. Something other than a vaunted pluralism is at stake and at hand in the famous production of the endless and endlessly unresolved conversation across time and space of the Talmud, namely the consolida-

tion of rabbinic power. By confronting rabbinic disagreement and do-
mesticating it such that it becomes a series of distinctions that make
no difference, the Talmud reaffirms and re-enforces the point that all
the rabbinic words add up to the will of the one Divine Shepherd. The
point is not so much that no one is ever right (and that, therefore,
a genuine pluralism of opinion is imagined), but that no one is ever
wrong, as long as he (*sic*) is in the right institution. (I am not ascribing malevolent intent or evil results to this consolidation of power
to which I happily submit myself; I am more concerned not to see
it watered down into something that is intellectually jejune and plays
false to the historical meanings of the texts in their socioreligious
contexts.)

Rescuing Apostates: Much Ado about Nothing

Another way in which the talmudic *sugya* reduces any real dissent is
by construing arguments in a sense in which there turns out to be no
real difference between the positions. The following text illustrates
the means through which the author of the dialectic turns what has
the potential to be real (and significant) disagreement into an argument about virtually nothing:[41]

> Rabbi Abbahu taught before Rabbi Yohanan: Gentiles and shepherds,
> one does not help them out nor throw them in, but the *minim* [Jewish
> heretics] and the *delatores* [informers] and apostates [to paganism],[42]
> they would throw them in and not help them out.
>
> He said to him, but I teach: "*all* of the losses of your brother" [Deu-
> teronomy 22:3] to add the apostate, and you have said: they would
> throw them in.
>
> Delete from here "the apostates!"

41. I discuss the same text elsewhere to somewhat different ends. Daniel Boyarin,
Border Lines: The Partition of Judaeo-Christianity, Divinations: Rereading Late Ancient
Religions (Philadelphia: University of Pennsylvania Press, 2004), 197–200.

42. משומד, following the mss. According to the brilliant interpretation of Shlomo Pines
that a משומד is one who has become a "pagan," it follows that *minim,* Jewish-Christians, are
in a much worse category than Jews who have become "pagans." This is an excellent example of how muddying the categories is the greatest threat of all. See Shlomo Pines, "Notes
on the Parallelism between Syriac Terminology and Mishnaic Hebrew," in *Yaakov Friedman Memorial Volume* (Jerusalem: Institute for Jewish Studies, 1974), 209–11 (in Hebrew).

The text begins with Rabbi Abbahu citing a tannaitic teaching to the effect that if idol worshipers and shepherds (considered thieves) should fall into a hole, while we should not push them in, neither should we rescue them; the second category of *minim, delatores* (Judas Iscariots), and apostates ought to be pushed into a hole without rescue. To this Rabbi Yoḥanan objects that the verse that enjoins saving the lost objects of one's brother includes even brothers who are apostates,[43] so how is it possible that Jews are commanded to endanger the apostates' lives? The answer is that apostates are to be entirely removed from the list of those to be thrown into pits. Notice that at this point in the talmudic text—which may indeed reflect the earlier text on which the *stamma* of the dialectic is performing "his" monologizing operations—we have a sharp point of disagreement. Are the apostates included in the category of the worst deviants who are to be put to death, or are they in the category of "brothers," to whom one returns a lost object? Effectively, moreover, by citing the authoritative Rabbi Yoḥanan and emending Rabbi Abbahu's tradition, the hypothetical earlier Talmud has decided the question in favor of the latter option: apostates are indeed "brothers."

We see here, accordingly, the clear difference of the layers of the talmudic text and of talmudic textual practice, for the *stamma* cannot leave this conclusion alone.[44] This *stamma* cannot, it seems, tolerate such a situation of rational resolution of a question. The text continues:

> But he could have said to him: This is talking about an apostate who eats non-kosher meats out of appetite, and that refers to an apostate who eats non-kosher meats out of spite.
>
> For it is said: the apostate Rav Aḥa and Ravina disagree about him. One said, an apostate out of appetite is an apostate, and for spite is a *min,* while the other said, even for spite he is still an apostate, and what is a *min?* Someone who worships an idol [i.e., a Jew who worships an idol]. He thought that one who eats non-kosher meats out of spite is a *min.* (TB Avoda Zara 26b)

43. By virtue of the addition of the word "all."

44. This example would seem then to support the notion of a more continuous process (or at any rate historically layered one) of the production of the *sugya* than the single-event model promulgated by Halivni in recent works. David Halivni, "Aspects of the Formation of the Talmud," *Sidra* 20 (2005): 68–116 (in Hebrew).

The Talmud asks: why did Rabbi Abbahu so readily accede to the emendation of his text in response to Rabbi Yoḥanan's objection? He had a better way out. He could have said that there are two kinds of apostates. In the case of the one who eats nonkosher meats out of appetite, we still consider him a "brother" and we rescue his lost object, and a fortiori his person, but an apostate who eats nonkosher meats demonstratively, to "spite," to make a religious point, that is the one whom we not only do not redeem but indeed are enjoined to endanger. To this the answer is that Rabbi Yoḥanan was of the opinion that such a one who eats nonkosher meats in order to spite the Jewish Torah is not an apostate but a *min*. The Talmud, that is, the *stamma* of the dialectic *sugya*, backs this point up by citing an amoraic (later rabbinic, in this case very late Babylonian) argument as to the definition of the apostate and the *min*. Note how the meaning of the term *min* is transformed as well from the earlier to the later stratum of the *sugya*.

The tannaitic (early rabbinic) text projects a clear hierarchy of "evil-doers." Gentiles and shepherds are obviously of a higher status than the *minim*, the apostates, and the *delatores*. In the course of Rabbi Yoḥanan's intervention, apostates, whatever they are, are raised not only into a higher category than the *minim* and the informers but even into a higher category than the gentiles, for the latter are neither rescued nor endangered, while the former are rescued as well. However, the most important aspect of the talmudic discussion (the *sugya*) is its production of a new and seemingly important category distinction not known from the earlier amoraic text, a distinction between two types of apostates. This distinction is between apostates for appetite, the typical case being one who is desirous and sees nonkosher meat and eats it, and apostates "for spite," those who choose to disobey the laws of the Torah out of religious conviction (someone like Saul of Tarsus, for instance). At this point, the *stamma* of the dialectic *sugya* says these latter are to be considered *minim*. *Min* is thus a category that is constructed ideologically, even when that ideological difference manifests itself behaviorally; it is the ideological difference that constitutes the *min*. Finally, according to one of the views of the two *amora'im*, it is an even stronger ideological difference that constitutes *minut* (the category of being a *min*), namely an improper belief in God. According to the first view, a Christian would be considered a *min* even if she had no defects in her theological doctrine, *except for the very fact of her ideological refusal to keep the commandments, which is, itself, a theological statement,* and the case remains undecided.

At first glance, it would seem that the lack of resolution of such a significant question does indeed project an agreement to disagree, a form of epistemological pluralism. I note, however, that in either view, a person who refuses to keep the commandments for ideological reasons (such as Paul), whether called an apostate or a *min,* fits into the category of the worst deviants, who are subject to righteous murder. Any distinction in their nomenclature, which in the end is all the *sugya* claims, makes no difference whatsoever. On one view they are killed as apostates, on the other as *minim.* We are told that Rabbi Yoḥanan, who places apostates in a very high category indeed, means only the apostates for appetite, so we take them out of the category of those to be executed, because apostates for ideology have been transferred into the category of *minim,* anyway. The other position leaves the apostates, meaning the apostates for ideology, in the category of those to be executed; it just does not call them *minim.* Surely to the potentially (or rather theoretically) to-be-executed ones the precise rubric under which they are being executed hardly makes a difference. Thus, while our reconstructed early (pre-*stamma*) *sugya* resolves the question of the status of the apostate, it does so while keeping the actual original controversy alive as a distinction that would make a difference. The Babylonian Talmud keeps a simulacrum of distinction alive, while completely defanging it. Total harmony is thus achieved, in effect, with only the appearance of dialogue preserved.

Turning the Tables

It is, however, in the direct representation of conversation between the rabbinic cultural system and its others (similar in this sense to the dialogues that we find in a novel between different characters with different ideological viewpoints) that we find the more directly oppressive moves that are similar to the Socratic ones of the Platonic corpus. In these representations of others, the Talmud almost explicitly acts like Socrates does in Plato's dialogues with respect to the Sophists. Here we will find the Talmud conjuring up its others precisely to shore up the center of its hegemonic truth, just as Plato produces sophistry in order to reinforce *philosophia.*

Not infrequently, the "others" are represented in encounters with the rabbis in which a challenge to the rabbinic system is offered and summarily dismissed by one of the rabbis. A complex instance of this neutralization of voices from outside the rabbinic system in the Bavli is one in which the voice from outside the system is named and transformed into a voice from inside. In other words, even more important than defeating the content of the voice from outside is to obviate its externality, to domesticate it and bring it under the purview of the real rabbinic project, the subsumption of all power and knowledge for Jews under the regime of their oral Torah. Consider the following passage from tractate Nedarim:

> Rabbi Yoḥanan ben-Dahavai said, The ministering angels told me, Why are there lame children? Because they [their fathers] turn over the tables [have intercourse with their wives on top]. Why are there dumb children? Because they kiss that place. Why are there deaf children? Because they talk during intercourse. Why are there blind children? Because they look at that place.

Rabbi Yoḥanan ben-Dahavai's utterance is not couched in the language of the forbidden and the permitted; that is, it is not halakhic language, but rather the language of some other regime of power/knowledge, signified by its origin in the angelic realms. Rabbi Yoḥanan—*not* the same as R. Yoḥanan ben-Dahavai—later transforms the words of that earlier Rabbi Yoḥanan by dissenting from his words as if from a halakha that the angels communicated through him:

> Rabbi Yoḥanan said, These are the words of Rabbi Yoḥanan ben-Dahavai, but the sages say, Anything that a man wishes to do [together] with his wife, he may do. A [halakhic] parable is to meat that comes from the shop. If he wishes to eat it with salt, he may; roasted, he may; boiled, he may; braised, he may. And similarly fish from the store of the fisherman.

And then:

> Amemar said, Who are the ministering angels? The rabbis, for if you say literally, *ministering angels,* then how did R. Yoḥanan say that the

law is not like R. Yoḥanan ben-Dahavai? After all, angels certainly know embryology!

Through his reinterpretation of the "angels" as a metaphorical representation of "our rabbis," Amemar dramatizes the transformation of the conflict in this text from a contest over power between different forms of authority, different modes of power/knowledge, into a normal rabbinic controversy within the same kind of *epistēmē,* the realm of Torah, the realm of the Rabbis themselves. This brings what might have otherwise been an issue outside the purview of halakha under the controlling consciousness of the Rabbis and their Torah. Amemar does this by converting the "angels" of the earlier text into ordinary rabbis. The use of "the sages" (*ḥakamim*) and "the rabbis" (*rabbanan*) here marks this subtle shift, since both designate the same group. It should be emphasized, thus, that Amemar only renders explicit what was implicit in R. Yoḥanan's dissent, wherein the latter transforms the angelic knowledge into an ordinary rabbinic opinion of Yoḥanan ben-Dahavai.

The narrative continues with "actual cases," precedents, legal narratives that both illustrate and buttress the point made in the preceding section:

> A certain woman came before Rabbi [R. Yehudah Hanasi], and said to him, Rabbi: I set him a table, and he turned it over. He said to her, *My daughter, the Torah has permitted you;* and I, what can I do for you?
>
> A certain woman came before Rav. She said to him, Rabbi, I set him a table, and he turned it over. He said, How is the case different from fish? (Nedarim 20a–b; emphasis mine)

Quite understandably, this passage has usually been read by scholars as a sort of rudimentary rabbinic *scientia sexualis,* or at least as an *ars erotica,* one, moreover, that is particularly obnoxious in its disregard for women's sexual rights over their own bodies. The fish metaphor is particularly complex. The point of the statement is that just as fish, if it is kosher, can be cooked and eaten in any way one desires, so too sex; that is, there are in the Torah no restrictions on sexual acts between legitimate couples. At the same time, however, there is no denying the undertone in the text as well; it is certainly the case that the body of the woman, as it were, is being spoken of in an objectifying and potentially degrading fashion. This is particularly brought to the fore if we compare it with a passage in Plutarch's *Amatoria:* "Aristippus . . . replied to the man who denounced Laïs to him for not loving him: He didn't imagine, he said, that wine or fish loved him either, yet he partook of both with pleasure."[45] I shall not be downplaying this potentially degrading element if, at the same time, I suggest that there are even more compelling political forces at work here, that the text represents part of a talmudic project of takeover and disenfranchisement of *all* sources of traditional and competing religious authority among Jews, including the authority of women's traditions. It is not an accident that so many of these crucial narratives of struggles over power and authority are connected with sexuality, because they are implicated in struggles against sites of women's traditional power/ knowledge. The struggle for rabbinic authority is, in part, a campaign for control of women's bodies and sexuality. Or perhaps (especially given the paucity of evidence for actual women's power in the pre-rabbinic period), we should reverse this narrative of cause and effect and suggest, instead, that the opposite vector is more tenable: the campaign for control of sexuality was an instrument in the struggle for rabbinic authority, and the narrative here of female agency now being superseded by rabbinic control is an instrument in that struggle, which is, of course, against other men. This would make this narrative a rabbinic analogue to the great Athenian narratives of former female control displaced by men.[46] A related point has been made by Ishay Rosen-Zvi: "The [talmudic] text creates a figure of the Evil Instinct as omnipotent and omnipresent, and stories that describe a totalitarian Instinct lead to a totalitarian regime [regimen]."[47]

45. Plutarch, "Amatorius," in *Moralia IX,* trans. Edwin L. Minar (Cambridge, Mass.: Harvard University Press, 1961), 317. I am grateful to Simon Goldhill for bringing this passage to my attention. It should not be thought that this is Plutarch's own view.

46. See Froma Zeitlin, *Playing the Other: Gender and Society in Classical Greek Literature,* Women in Culture and Society (Chicago: University of Chicago Press, 1996). I have been stimulated to think this way in the light of a very pointed question asked of me by my colleague Sharon Marcus, on the occasion of presentation of a version of this work at UC Berkeley's Center for the Study of Sexual Culture.

47. Ishay Rosen-Zvi, "The Evil Instinct, Sexuality, and Forbidden Cohabitations: A Chapter in Talmudic Anthropology," *Theory and Criticism: An Israeli Journal* 14 (Summer 1999): 70–71 (in Hebrew). This is a very important article about which I intend to say more in future work.

The term "turning the tables" can most likely be identified as vaginal intercourse with the woman on top.[48] Most interpretations of the narratives of the two women who come to the rabbis complaining of having "set the table," which the husband then overturned, and the rabbis' refusal to intervene, understand this as rabbinically sanctioned marital sexual abuse. The full context, however, suggests another interpretation. This is, I suggest, a text primarily about the acquisition of rabbinic power and the rabbis' struggle with other forms of Jewish authority, and not principally "about" sex or sexual abuse at all. According to Rabbi Yoḥanan ben-Dahavai, one of the sexual practices proscribed by the "angels" is precisely the activity that the two women claim their husbands desired. Moreover, according to this "angelic" eugenics, intercourse in this position produces damaged children. Although this is the only evidence I have for this claim, I would suggest that this nascent embryology represents a form of popular Jewish pietistic practice of sexual hygiene, one that would have been the province of men (not, however, of the rabbinic party), as well as of women. The complaint of these wives is not that their husbands wished to engage in a painful or distasteful form of sex, but that they wished to engage in intercourse that the old mores of the Jews considered improper and dangerous to the fetus.[49] The responses of Rabbi and Rav do not, therefore, counsel submission to abuse, which would indeed indicate that the wife is either the husband's sexual property or a "consumable,"[50] but rather assert the sole authority of "Torah" over any other kind of religious leadership, whether angelic or traditional, including the traditional power/knowledge of women. If the Torah does not prohibit an activity, no other source of authority has any jurisdiction over Jewish behavior, according to the rabbis; neither angelic nor popular, including women's culture. Moreover, in the re-

48. If for no other reason than if it be interpreted as anal intercourse, it is hard to imagine where the allegedly deformed babies would come from.

49. Typical, if judicious in his formulation, is Satlow, who writes: "From this passage, it is again not clear what activity is being performed. Clearly, though, these women do not like it." Michael L. Satlow, "'They Abused Him Like a Woman': Homoeroticism, Gender Blurring, and the Rabbis in Late Antiquity," *Journal of the History of Sexuality* 5, no. 1 (1994): 24. I am suggesting here that their "not liking it" might very well be read as the product of a normative regime, stricter than that of the rabbis, rather than individual taste.

50. The alimentary metaphors are perhaps less unsavory when they are read against the semantic field of the Song of Songs.

sponse of the rabbis to the women, the exclusion of women from the "Torah" is enacted and made explicit. The Torah, the rabbinic House of Study, disciplines and protects (or not, as it chooses) the religious lives of women and their *'Am Ha'areṣ* husbands to boot.

One could read Amemar's later intervention (interpreting the angels as Rabbis) as a further step in the same process of denial of all power/knowledge outside of the rabbinic collective. The ultimate issue is not what kind of sex Jews will engage in, but who gets to decide: angelic (that is, mantic) authorities, women's tradition, or the "Torah" (the Rabbis). This seems to me a plausible construal of the text in that it renders the actual "cases" into illustrations of the principle articulated by Rabbi Yoḥanan. Rabbi Yoḥanan, together with Rabbi and Rav, are surely central figures in the narrative of the rabbinic rise to domination. Deploying in this text precisely these three crucial culture heroes in the struggle against alternative sources of authority indicates the centrality of the encoded narrative in telling the story of the rise of the rabbinic *epistēmē*. Once again, I reiterate that nothing that I am arguing here, of course, diminishes the salience of the fact that here, as so often, the battle between men for power is being carried out across the discursive bodies of women.[51]

Through such discursive means, as we can see, the authors of the Talmud disarm (if not as thoroughly as they would have liked) the forces within normative Jewish culture that resist the patterns of rabbinic legism, of Torah as legal rules. There are other ways of talking about normative behaviors and expectations other than rules, but the later Rabbis, or better, the *stamma* of the dialectic *sugya,* seek to transform all those other manners of normative speaking into a language of halakha and halakha alone. As Wimpfheimer has written, "Within the normative world, the discourse of legal rules is a language spoken and understood by adherents and interpreters. But it is not the only such language nor the only one capable of justifying or mandating behavior. If only for this reason, rules of law are always connected to the

51. For just two clear examples of this cultural phenomenon, see Virginia Burrus, "The Heretical Woman as Symbol in Alexander, Athanasius, Epiphanius, and Jerome," *Harvard Theological Review* 84 (1991): 229–48; Kate Cooper, "Insinuations of Womanly Influence: An Aspect of the Christianization of the Roman Aristocracy," *Journal of Roman Studies* 82 (1992): 150–64.

exercises of power that authorize and enforce them. Those exercises of power are negotiations among cultural languages within which legal meaning is broadly constructed."[52] Going beyond the explicit conflict of different sources of authority as demonstrated in the presumably earlier narratives about Rav and Rabbi, the *stamma*'s insistence that these "angels" are not an alternative, competing source of norms but only other rabbis—rabbis who can be declared wrong—manifests the legism that characterizes the tendency of the *stamma* according to Wimpfheimer. Moreover, as demonstrated by this example, it is palpably the case that the rabbinic legism is *not* always more strict and rigid than the other Jewish discourses of normativity. Sometimes yes; sometimes no. What distinguishes this work of the *stamma* of the *sugya* is rather bringing all value, normativity, practice under the sway of "Torah," the discursive rules and practices of the rabbinic "Academy." On the other hand, and at the very same time, we can begin to see here how such incorporation of another voice (the voice of the angels, the voices of the women), already threatens the monologizing hegemony of the *stamma* and of his agent, the oral Torah.

Carnival Seriousness

Wimpfheimer writes, "The Bavli as a concrete text before us contains legal texts written in different genres,"[53] that is, apodictic law, legal dialectic, and narrative precedents. From this perspective, focusing on the legal nature of the text, it is certainly the case that

> arguably the defining feature of Talmudic legal discourse (and the one that accounts for the term "Talmud" within the Talmud itself) is the exercise of ensuring the congruence of disagreeing canonical legal texts. The Stamma specializes in juxtaposing conflicting texts and resolving the conflict through distinction; post-Talmudic commentaries continue this process, with subsequent generations of scholars expanding the boundaries of the canonical texts that demand coherence.[54]

52. Wimpfheimer, *Telling Tales*, end of chapter 1.
53. Wimpfheimer, *Telling Tales*, introduction.
54. Wimpfheimer, *Telling Tales*, chapter 1.

Wimpfheimer notes that even within halakhic material itself, there are several genres incorporated within the Talmud, notably the dialectic and the precedent, short narratives that illustrate a halakha in action, as it were, as it was enacted or adjudicated by a known rabbinic authority. As in many analyses of Plato in which that author is seen as successfully reducing the heterogeneity of incorporated genres, Wimpfheimer convincingly adduces such cases with respect to the Talmud and at least one of its incorporated genres, the *ma'ase*, the narrative of halakhic behavior, which not infrequently, were it left on its own, would contradict the very norms (or even more, the norm-making) of the "Talmud" itself.

For thousands of years, beginning within the Talmud, continuing with the medieval commentaries, and into modern research,[55] the persistent tension, if not contradiction, between the dialectic and the precedent within the context of a single *sugya* has frequently been remarked. The example itself is lively and appropriately comic. In Megilla 7b, we find the following text:[56]

> Rabbah said, one is obligated to become intoxicated on Purim until one does not know [the difference] between "cursed is Haman" and "blessed is Mordekhai."
>
> Rabbah and Rav Zeira made the Purim feast with one another. [After Rabbah had gotten drunk], he went and slaughtered Rav Zeira. [When he was sober, or in the morning] Rabbah prayed for Rav Zeira and brought him back to life.
>
> A year later, [Rabbah] said to [Rav Zeira], "Let the master come and let us make Purim [together]. [Rav Zeira] said to [Rabbah], "miracles do not happen every time."[57]

Perhaps the first thing that might be noticed is that we have here a tale in which a rabbi is killed by another one and then resurrected, and upon his resurrection is understandably quite wary of further contact with his murderer/resurrector. This theme, surely drawn from the reserves of a stratum of the popular grotesque, allows for

---

55. Eliezer Segal, *Case Citation in the Babylonian Talmud: The Evidence of Tractate Neziqin*, Brown Judaic Studies (Atlanta, Ga.: Scholars Press, 1990).

56. Extensively discussed by Wimpfheimer in his introduction.

57. Translation modified from Wimpfheimer, *Telling Tales*.

the Talmud to represent various modes of exaggerated rabbinic behavior. Here Rabbah has expressed what is taken certainly within the
talmudic tradition as a legal obligation, namely that on Purim there is
an obligation on each and every Jew to get drunk, thus celebrating the
reversals of victor and victim, oppressor and oppressed, that mark
the day as the Jewish Carnival. This is followed in the Talmud by a
comic narrative in which this prescription having been carried out to
the letter by its author, tragedy ensues, only redeemed and rendered
comic by miraculous means. The panhalakhic rabbinic tradition has
seen these two texts, the dictum and the narrative, as contradicting
each other by rendering each an absolute prescription, thus the dictum requires extreme drunkenness while the story would seem to forbid it. Various resolutions to this "contradiction" have been bruited,
one prescription being deemed as having displaced the other or the
two harmonized in such wise that the story simply limits the application of the dictum. The humor, needless to say, has been lost entirely.
As Wimpfheimer writes of one such resolution: "Rabbenu Ephraim
is not content to understand this as a debate between two equally
strong texts with different opinions. Rather, the later narrative text
with its dire consequences overwhelms the legal dictum and elimi-
nates its mandated behavior even as optional behavior; the legal narrative has changed the law from mandate to prohibition"—literally
Prohibition. In other words, the rabbinic tradition has completely
flattened the difference in voice between the dictum and the story.
Wimpfheimer, however, comments: "Inasmuch as the story comments on the practice of becoming inebriated, it does not appear to
undermine or contradict the practice. After all, if the violence of year
one were to impact the behavior of year two, Rav Zeira would not
have to rely on a miracle. It is precisely the expectation that the two
rabbis will perform their Purim feasts in exactly the same manner as
previously that yields the reader's laughter following Rav Zeira's retort. The story's comedy, in other words, draws energy from its play
with the expectations of mandate."[58] Rabbenu Ephraim's attempt to
harmonize by making the story overwhelm the dictum thus fails on
Wimpfheimer's reading. Wimpfheimer goes on to explicate this text
richly as playing out in itself the very tension between nomos and

58. Wimpfheimer, *Telling Tales.*

narrative: on the one hand, the whole point of Rabbah's dictum is to "enforce," as it were, the necessity to burst all bounds on Purim; on the other hand, the very fact of such enforcement is the enactment of a bound. This paradox within the Law is the one that generates the narrative as well.

On Wimpfheimer's reading, then, a "framework that uniquely authorizes the discourse of prescriptive rules as the primary discourse of reading—the primary discourse for cultural meaning" has been made to simply overwhelm and thoroughly monologize the dialogicality that such a genre of heterogeneity as the *ma'ase* could have introduced into the talmudic text. While showing that this monologizing reading becomes strongest in the post-talmudic commentatorial tradition, Wimpfheimer unambiguously locates the monologizing impulse in the work of the *stamma:* "Thus the incoherence of Talmudic legal narrative is often the basis, either within the Stam or in post-Talmudic commentary, for explicit attempts to force the narratives into coherence with legal precedent. Where the rules framework syllogizes the narratives into statutes, the Talmudic dialectic energy ensures that these incongruent narrative statutes can be made coherent with legal precedent." And the *stamma* does seem to be enforcing such a monologizing reading, at least when read in the fashion in which I have read Plato and focusing hard on the halakhic material, whether rule or narrative precedent. As Wimpfheimer puts it, "The hermeneutic itself reflects a claim to power for the rules of law and the rabbis who both legislate and adjudicate them. By focusing on the ways in which legal narratives are ill-fitted for inclusion within this rules-centered discourse, I hope to highlight the extent to which such a discourse is severely limited by its own self-interest in monopolizing authority: how it never allows itself to be contextualized in light of other discourses and certainly not to be subservient to them."[59] This alleged refusal of the halakhic discourse to allow itself to be contextualized by non-rule-centered and even antinomian languages constitutes the monologism of the *stamma* according to Wimpfheimer. Wimpfheimer argues that it is the very work of the "Talmud" precisely to remove incongruity and incoherence between different voices and different elements within the legal discourse. I offer, therefore, this

---

59. Wimpfheimer, *Telling Tales,* introduction.

case as well as evidence that in the dialectical *sugya,* at least as much as in the Platonic dialogue, the author, the Talmud, attempts to monologize the potentially dialogical.

While there is much, much indeed, with which I would agree in Wimpfheimer's analysis of this *sugya,* there is a point of disagreement between us that I need to unfold in order that the thesis of this book be made clearer. What Wimpfheimer successfully shows is how the tradition of reception of the Talmud reduces here all potential for dialogism to a monologism by turning the nonhalakhic normative statement produced by the story into a halakhic statement; the latter is then taken to counter the statement of the halakha by Rabbah, such that then we need to choose between them what to write in our codebooks. What I find unconvincing in his analysis of this case, however, is the attempt to see this reduction of the dialogism within the text of the Talmud itself. We have seen such, explicitly, in the *sugya* of turning the tables just analyzed above, where the normative voices of "the angels" and women's traditions have been unambiguously reinscribed as halakhic opinions of "the rabbis" in order to dismiss them, but that is much less (if at all) the case here. Indeed in the case of Megilla, I would suggest the defensibility of quite a different reading of the *sugya,* one that will render it a vade mecum to the presentation of the dialogism that I find in the Bavli, that is, not a dialogism of so-called differences of opinion within the halakha, but a challenge to the whole system of halakha.

Paying attention to the ritual context of this little *sugya* will help advance this reading. The context is Purim, the day in which the Jews celebrate their defeat of the enemy who would have destroyed them entirely. The celebrations of this day are all under the carnivalistic sign of "It is upside down" (ונהפוך הוא). One could easily say that Rabbah's attempt to normativize the Carnival by rendering a halakhic obligation to drink to the point of losing control of the opposition between the good and the evil, is an overturning of halakha itself. The very halakhic norm is, on that reading, carnivalistic, turning the halakha into a Carnival halakha, analogous to the parodic Purim Torah and Purim rabbi of later rabbinic traditions and practices. Furthermore, the narrative continuation, with its own particularly carnivalistic elements (miraculous resurrections are always mock pathos), continues the Carnival *sugya* by presenting itself as a mock *ma'ase* that contradicts. Another way of putting it would be to say that the story exemplifies what happens when you take yourself too seriously, when a charge to rejoice and let loose becomes turned into a sort of grim obligation, hemmed in by a precise measurement of how much one must let loose in order to fulfill the obligation. The joke is on the reader, and the reader who takes it all seriously (nearly all readers within the tradition) is the one who doesn't get the joke. Far from being an emblem of the monologization of the *stamma* (a process which I have learned about from Wimpfheimer's work and with which I largely agree), I would see this *sugya,* then, as a brilliant example of a certain potential for a dialogical undermining—but *not* displacing, much like Carnival itself—of that powerful force for monologization that characterizes the Bavli, by and large.

In his key essay, the famous "Discourse in the Novel," Bakhtin delineates more richly how such dialogism works. Although his argument is long and complex, I shall try to summarize it here. Dialogism in the artistic prose text is always a refraction of the author's language produced, "incorporated," and "organized" in different forms. Dialogism appears in the ratio (too formal a word) between the author's language and "the background of normal literary language, the expected literary horizon"; "every moment of the story has a conscious relationship with this normal language and its belief system, is in fact set against them, and set against them *dialogically:* one point of view opposed to another, one evaluation opposed to another, one accent opposed to another." This dialogism between the author's language and an other language is achieved in different ways; one is the presence of a narrator: "The author is not to be found in the language of the narrator, nor in the normal literary language to which the story opposes itself . . . but rather, the author utilizes now one language, now another, in order to avoid giving himself up wholly to either of them; he makes use of this verbal give-and-take, this dialogue of languages at every point in his work, in order that he himself might remain as it were neutral with regard to language, a third party in a quarrel between two people (although he might be a *biased* third party)."[60] It is under the sign of this Bakhtinian insight that I will pursue here my further analysis of the Bavli, considering the pious/"serious" language

---

60. Bakhtin, *The Dialogic Imagination*, 314, emphasis original.

of the Bavli and its wild and grotesque languages as the true "verbal give-and-take [*šaqla wetarya*]" of the Bavli. Let us understand the dialectic of the *sugya* and even the "normal" aggada as the language of one "narrator" of the Talmud, he whom I will be pleased to call the *stamma* of the *sugya,* while the language of the acerbic, corrosive, bizarre legendary narratives is another such language and narrator. The *stamma* of the Talmud would be, then, the overall author of the Talmud as the neutral—but *biased*—third party whose own language is always dialogized by the languages of these other narrators and with respect to them and the normative language. Working out and specifying this thesis vis-à-vis the Babylonian Talmud will be the project of the rest of this chapter and the next two. In the next section of this chapter (incorporating the story of our eponymous obese rabbis), I endeavor to provide an extended example of this double-voicing, this dialogism, within the Bavli.

"Monstrous Conjugations of Foreign Parts": The *Stamma* Meets the Grotesque

Chapter 7 of the talmudic tractate Baba Metsia, begins with the following Mishna and attendant discussion:

> One who hires workers and said to them to come at sunrise and depart at sunset: If it is a place where it is not customary to come at sunrise and work until sunset, he may not compel them. Where it is customary for the employees to get food, the employer must comply. In places where it is customary to furnish them with sweetmeats, he must do so, and all according to the custom of that country.
>
> It happened with R. Yoḥanan b. Matia that he said to his son: "Go and hire laborers for us." He did so and agreed that they should be given food. And when he came to his father, he said to him: "My son, even if you should provide them with meals like the banquets of King Solomon at his time, you will not have fulfilled your obligation, as they are children of Abraham, Isaac, and Jacob. Rather, before they begin their work go and tell them that they may claim of me only bread and beans." Rabban Shim'on ben Gamaliel said: It was not necessary at all [to stipulate], as all must be done according to the custom of the country. (Baba Metsia 83b)

According to the Mishna, the principle that a day laborer's conditions cannot be worsened by a contractual agreement is absolute. Whatever the local custom is, that is determinative, notwithstanding what the employer has stipulated at the time of employment. The anecdote that follows is a seeming contradiction to this principle as the Talmud itself remarks later on. It is placed in the Mishna here in order to communicate Rabban Shim'on's dismissal of it and thus to emphasize, once more, the inviolability of the principle of the Mishna that one may not contract with day laborers to worsen their conditions vis-à-vis local practice and custom. It doesn't matter what the employer says; the conditions that apply are the local ones in practice. This, of course, protects day laborers from being coerced to accept inferior conditions out of their (frequently desperate) need for the work.

The Talmud now begins its commentary on this text:

Gemara: Is this not self-evident? [i.e., that he may not worsen their conditions beyond the norm] No, it's a case where he offered to pay more than their [customary] wages. What might you have thought [if the Mishna had not spoken]? That he could say to them that the reason that I increased your wages was with the intent that you would come earlier and leave later. The Mishna teaches us that [this is not the case], as they may answer him, saying: The fact that you added to our wages was in order that we do especially good work for you.

This is a typical initial discussion of a Mishnaic passage by the *stamma*. The ideology of the *stamma* is that every word in the Mishna must contribute new information in two ways. First of all, there must be no redundancy in the sense of repetition of the same proposition, or even a proposition that could seemingly be deduced from a proposition uttered elsewhere in the Mishna. The second kind of redundancy is when the Talmud objects that the very point of the Mishna is so obvious as not to need articulation at all. If the Talmud deems the statement of the Mishna as obvious in the sense of self-evidently correct, it will also object as it has here. The typical response to that, as we find here, is to elaborate a particular situation in which it is not at all obvious, since there are two potentially different ways of looking at the matter, and the Mishna is then reckoned to be telling us which of these to choose.

The Talmud continues with a comment by a third-century Palestinian *amora:*

> Resh Lakish said: The day laborer goes home from work on his own time, but he goes to work on the employer's time, as it is written, "When the sun rises, they leave and go hide in their lairs; man goes then to his work, to his labor until evening" (Psalms 104:22–23).
>
> [But to what purpose was this statement?] Let them observe the custom of that city? He is referring to a new city. But even then let him observe the custom where they come from? He means when the laborers were hired from different cities with different customs. And if you wish, he refers to a case in which he told them that they should work in the manner of a worker in the Torah [and not local custom].[61]

Resh Lakish derives from the verse of the Psalm a midrashic conclusion. Given that the unit of payment for a day laborer is sunrise to sunset, if the verse says that at sunrise the laborer goes to his work, the indication is that the morning travel time is covered by the employer, but if, as the verse continues, he is to work until sunset, then he travels home after dark, on his own time. The *stamma* queries the necessity of this statement, since the Mishna already requires that everything be in accordance with the custom of the place, rendering Resh Lakish's statement both otiose and perhaps even wrong, depending on local practice. The Talmud then offers two alternate resolutions of this difficulty. Both indicate a situation in which the force of custom is vitiated, either because there is no custom in that place, a new city of heterogeneous population, or because the workers and the employer have agreed to follow the custom of the "Torah" and not local custom in their labor practices. In either of these cases, it becomes necessary to determine the "law" via Resh Lakish's Midrash, that is, his deriving from the verse of the Psalm his conclusion about travel to and from work.

Notice, however, how incompatible and politically/ethically at odds these two resolutions are. The first one maintains the Mishna's

---

61. This translation, suggested to me by Steven Fraade, is superior to "in accordance with the law of the Torah" for כפועל ראודייתא.

absolute primacy of local custom over any other legislating authority,
remarking that Resh Lakish's midrashic principle comes into effect
only when there is absolutely no local custom on which to rely. The
second resolution completely vitiates the Mishna's principle (and
thus its absolute protection of day laborers as vaunted by Levinas)
by indicating that the employer can set other parameters ("according to the Torah") as a condition of employment. The first indicates
that the force of Resh Lakish's "Torah"-based determination of the
workday comes into play only in a place without established custom,
while the second—much more radically—says that an agreement to
follow the custom described in "Torah" may *replace* the local custom.
Although seemingly casually snuck in here as a second resolution to
a fairly recondite problem, in fact this second resolution is a symp-
tom of the enormous shift in rabbinic Jewish culture marked by the
monologization of Jewish practice as halakha by the *stam*. As part of
that very process, looser forms of discourse, conversation, maxims,
even proverbs, are transformed, as we have seen above, into absolute,
cut-and-dried legal imperatives and prohibitions. "Torah" is in many
such relays within the Bavli a code name for the attempted rabbinic/
halakhic takeover of all authority for religious practice from local
custom and traditional custom, whether to the side of stringency or
leniency, as we have seen in the case of the angelic *ars amatoria* of the
previous section.

It follows that this latter resolution to the difficulty, to the effect
that the parties have "agreed" to follow the Torah and not custom,
completely undermines the very principle of the Mishna that all goes
according to custom. If the employer may specify to his employees
that he is imposing Torah law on them instead of local custom as a
condition for their employment, even where there is a local custom,
the Mishna's principle that all goes according to local custom has been
displaced. This talmudic intervention (together with many other similar ones) would ultimately have a transforming effect on Jewish society, namely precisely the ultimate production of the "Torah"—that
is, the Talmud—as a kind of universalistic voice from nowhere which
alone has authority and power in Jewish practice. Where, historically,
before the success of this power play, local communities (let us say
in North Africa) could resist the central authorities in Babylonia by
countering the force of the Talmud with local practice, after the shift,

resistance was futile.[62] What had begun as a fairly innocent comment by Resh Lakish ends up being in this fashion an undermining of such dialogism as exists at the earlier stages of the rabbinic formation. In the earlier form, the Rabbis' own authority was limited by the authority of custom and its replacement with a higher authority, the authority of the rabbinic institution, analogously to the way that the Platonic institution sought to supersede and control the *paideia* of the Athenians, bespeaking a monologization of that earlier form. In this very late passage—the one in which the objection to Resh Lakish is raised and refuted—we can observe the strong drive toward monologization of the halakha, toward its ultimate subsumption under the category of Torah (= Midrash) and thus the full control of the rabbinic authority. This case is then similar to Plato's relationship to the genres of Greek literature[63] and supports the characterization of the production of the dialectic as monologizing—a monologicity which, as we have seen, has worked to deeply strengthen the rabbinic institution.

According to my reading, then, this *sugya* provides a most powerful exemplification of the practice of the *stamma* in pulling all normativity in and under the single language of the rabbinic halakha, allowing, as in the examples given above (especially of the angels) no other source of authority or normativity to hold sway.

As if to further solemnize the occasion, the Bavli's text continues with a piece of uplifting aggada:

> Rabbi Zeira expounded, and some cite it that it was Rav Yosef who repeated it: What is it that is written, "You bring darkness and it is night, the night in which all the beasts of the forest trample"?—These are the wicked in it [the world] who are like the beast of the forest; "the son will shine and they be gathered and in their dwellings they will lie down"—"The son will shine," for the righteous; "they will be

62. This shift in the balance of power to the Talmud was to take, however, centuries to be effective. In an unfortunately as yet unpublished book of extreme importance, Talya Fishman argues that it is only in the early Middle Ages and in Ashkenaz that the *stamma* of the Talmud wins the day, as it were, and the text (the Torah) becomes a higher authority than local practice, which had prevailed until then. There is a real cultural struggle personified here.

63. See Andrea Wilson Nightingale, *Genres in Dialogue: Plato and the Construct of Philosophy* (Cambridge: Cambridge University Press, 1995).

gathered," the wicked to Hell; "and in their dwellings they will lie down"—There is not even one righteous person who does not have a dwelling of his or her own [in heaven]. "The person will go out to work"—The righteous will go out to receive their reward [the word "work" means both the activity and the payment], "and to his labor until evening"—One who has completed his labor until evening [that is, remained righteous until death].

What we have here is a perfect little example of what the Talmud itself calls aggada, homiletical readings of scripture, one which needs for this context no further glossing. The same verse has been used in two ways within the *sugya,* once halakhically, to produce a certain legistic norm, and once aggadically, to support such norms with theological underpinnings. Commonplace readings aside, there is no difference in tone, however, between the halakha and the aggada per se. One can see in both a strong centripetal force for bringing the Jews,[64] all of the Jews in ambition, under the authority of the rabbinic definitions of righteous behavior according to their halakhic traditions and halakhic piety.[65] Here certainly we see how the rabbinic halakha and aggada, far from being in tension, as frequently held by certain pundits and scholars,[66] are actually in astonishing harmony with each other. Discordant, dissident, or critical voices will have to be sought elsewhere than in the distinction between halakha and aggada.

Once again, I emphasize, I don't wish to be heard as identifying this as a fault or flaw in rabbinic piety; it is, I believe, a sincerely held molding of the spiritual and the ethical life together. The Talmud,

64. For a very helpful account of the use of the terms "centripetal" and "centrifugal" in Bakhtin, see Michael Holquist, "Glossary," in *The Dialogic Imagination,* 425.

65. Bakhtin writes: "These forces are *the forces that serve to unify and centralize the verbal-ideological world.* Unitary language constitutes the theoretical expression of the historical processes of linguistic unification and centralization, an expression of the centripetal forces of language. A unitary language is not something given [*dan*] but is always in essence posited [*zadan*]—and at every moment of its linguistic life it is opposed to the realities of heteroglossia. But at the same time it makes its real presence felt as a force for overcoming this heteroglossia, imposing specific limits to it, guaranteeing a certain maximum of mutual understanding and crystallizing into a real, although still relative, unit—the unity of the reigning conversational (everyday) and literary language, 'correct language.'" Bakhtin, *The Dialogic Imagination,* 270.

66. Notably, the Zionist poet Hayyim Nahman Bialik, whose famous essay, *Ha-Hala-khah Veha-Agadah* (Jerusalem: Ma'aritse-ha-halakhah, 1917), is still being read far too often.

however, does bring into relief a centrifugal force as well, one introduced by the inclusion of the biographical, and especially grotesque,
legends in the same work as that which includes both legal genres,
the halakhic *sugya* (the non-narrative legal dialectic), the legal narrative, and the pious aggada.[67] In other words, I suggest that the *stamma*
produces a real dialogism at one level even while shutting it down at
another, or, as I shall begin to argue in the next section (and more
fully develop in the next chapter), there are, in effect, two *stammas,*
two authorial entities within the Babylonian Talmud (whether or not
the same people are behind them historically is irrelevant here).

Another one of Bakhtin's lapidary utterances will be helpful here:
"At the same time when major divisions of the poetic genres were developing under the influence of the unifying, centralizing, centripetal
forces of verbal-ideological life, the novel—and those artistic prose
genres that gravitate toward it—was being historically shaped by the
current of decentralizing, centrifugal forces. At the time when poetry
was accomplishing the tasks of cultural, national and political centralization of the verbal-ideological world in the higher official so-
cio-ideological levels, on the lower levels, on the stages of local fairs
and at buffoon spectacles, the heteroglossia of the clown sounded
forth. . . . There developed the language of the *fabliaux* and *Schwänke*
of street songs, folksayings, anecdotes, where there was no language-
center at all, where was to be found a lively play with the 'languages' of
poets, scholars, monks, knights and others, where all 'languages' were
masks and where no language could claim to be an authentic, incontestable face."[68] Bakhtin further argues there that the heteroglossia
of the "low genres" was "parodic, and aimed sharply and polemically
against the official languages of its given time. It was heteroglossia
that had been dialogized."[69] For the Talmud, then, the monologizing
force that produces the *sugya* qua *sugya* with both its halakhic and aggadic (homiletical) elements is equivalent to Bakhtin's metaphorical

67. In truth, from the point of view of folklore genres, these grotesques are hardly
"legends," as I don't suppose that anyone was meant to "believe" them in the sense of
taking them seriously as something that really happened. I use "legends," therefore, in a
purely nontechnical sense. See Linda Dégh and Andrew Vázsonyi, "Legend and Belief,"
in *Folklore Genres,* ed. Dan Ben-Amos, Publications of the American Folklore Society 26
(Austin: University of Texas Press, 1976).

68. Bakhtin, *The Dialogic Imagination,* 273.

69. Bakhtin, *The Dialogic Imagination,* 273.

"poetic" voice, while the narratives of our rabbinic heroes' wild and wooly adventures is the equivalent of the language of the *fabliaux* and their congeners, as we are about to see. In the grotesque biographical legend, when juxtaposed to the halakha and the aggada, as we shall see here in a moment, the entire epistemological enterprise of the discovery of and enactment of God's will through halakha and dialectic is called into question, but *not* thereby undermined.[70] What is, at least for me, most striking about this particular part of the Bavli is the way that its most severely monologizing voice, the one I have just been exposing, and its wildest, most carnivalesque and grotesque countervoice are bound so intimately, cheek by jowl, within the single literary context.

The Eponymous Narrative: A Rabbilaisian Tale

Epitomizing the argument so far: Wimpfheimer has suggested that the *stamma* has been wrongly undertheorized: "To traditional students of the Babylonian Talmud, the Bavli's anonymous voice is nearly invisible. Though the anonymous warp and woof of Talmudic question and answer is ubiquitous on every Bavli page, this material has been treated by traditional readers as if it is necessary but supplemental—the unnoticed air that allows the attributed statements and rationale of named *tannai'im* and *amora'im* to breathe. The anonymous voice of the Bavli is only (and rarely) attributed agency within traditional Talmudic commentaries if such agency resolves a difficult exegetical problem. In traditional exegesis, the *Stam HaTalmud* is a poor stepchild—remembered rarely and only for blame."[71] The direction that I am offering is subtly different from this, although it builds on

70. This is a significantly different approach to the questions involved than the one we find in Robert Cover, "The Supreme Court 1982 Term: Foreword; Nomos and Narrative," *Harvard Law Journal* 97 (1983): 4–68, in which biblical narratives that seem to violate the norms of the Law are treated as revelatory exceptions rather than a genuine dialogical challenge to the rule of that very nomos by narrative. As Cover writes, "To be an inhabitant of the biblical normative world is to understand, first, that the rule of succession can be overturned; second, that it takes a conviction of divine destiny to overturn it; and third, that divine destiny is likely to manifest itself precisely in overturning this specific rule" (22). This is very different from the proposal I am making with respect to the Talmud.

71. Wimpfheimer, *Telling Tales*.

his insight. I propose that there is a strong panhalakhic (and thus monolingual) voice in the Talmud, identifiable most clearly but not absolutely with the implied author who produces the *sugya* out of its disparate earlier materials. This voice, which Wimpfheimer has clearly identified and described, authorizes and gives rise to the monological reading practices of the Jewish Middle Ages and beyond. While Wimpfheimer suggests, rightly I think, that the voice of the *stamma* deserves more attention, I would add that there is more than one voice within that very "anonymous" layer that we call the *stamma*. Wimpfheimer's *Stam HaTalmud* is what I would call the *stamma* of the *sugya,* the implied author of the individual units of text called *sugyot* (I make no claims here as to how, when, or why the *sugya* came into being). However, another level of production of the text, the work of the author behind the Talmud as a whole, is produced within the Bavli through the inclusion of the antithetical biographical/legendary material. This operates as a countervoice that dialogizes the *sugya*. The two languages—the language of the *sugya* and the language of the comic, the fantastic, and grotesque—carve out a space for each other and illuminate each other, as in the Bakhtinian account of heteroglossia.

Let us turn, then, to the comic sequel to the debate about day laborers' rights and its uplifting aggadic homily. After that homily growing out of the Mishna with its sincere plea that human beings should not be made to work at night like preying beasts, we continue:

Rabbi El'azar the son of Rabbi Shim'on met up with a certain officer of the king who used to catch thieves. He asked him, "How do you prevail over them? Aren't they compared to animals, as it is written 'at night tramp all the animals of the forest'?" (Ps. 104:20). . . . Said [the rabbi] to him, "Perhaps you are taking the innocent and leaving the guilty." [The policeman] said to him, "How shall I do it?" [The rabbi] said to him, "Come; I will teach you how to do it. Go in the first four hours of the morning to the wine-bar. If you see someone drinking wine and falling asleep, ask of him what his profession is. If he is a rabbinical student, he has arisen early for study. If he is a day-laborer, he has arisen early to his labor. If he worked at night, perhaps it is metal smelting [a silent form of work], and if not, then he is a thief and seize him." The rumor reached the king's house, and he said, "Let him who read the proclamation be the one to execute it."

This passage enters the text owing to an association between the verse cited about the animals tramping at night and Resh Lakish's very serious argument using that same verse to prove that humans oughtn't be made to work at night. It is thus seamlessly incorporated into the associative flow of the talmudic pericope just like other material of very different tone and theme. In contrast to traditional and postmodern harmonizing and moralizing readings of this passage, I can make sense of it only as deeply parodic in its stance toward rabbinic truth procedures. A representative of that very community (the community of "us") is shown here proposing both ridiculous and palpably pernicious logic in his advice to the policeman. A logical procedure for determining guilt is proposed that would be just as likely to catch new fathers as night raiders in its net. And this is presented as having been so impressive to the local representative of the empire that our good rabbi himself is hired as chief of police.

From this point on, the text is thus not an assertion of its own practices but rather a critique of the forms of epistemological certainty that subtend these practices. Rabbi El'azar's logical deduction with its concomitant certainty must be read, I suggest, as parodic of the practices of rabbinic deduction. In a kind of reductio ad absurdum, the text lets us know that a criterion of truth leads to the deaths of innocents; it is Rabbi El'azar's search for absolute righteousness through absolute truth that leads to that gross injustice. As the text explicitly remarks of the clever rabbi, he is, in his epistemic certainty of who and what is good and evil, not a revolutionary at all but a *moser*, a collaborator with tyranny. He becomes the policeman, and has his own epistemological criteria by which he decides who it is that he will send to his death. When we see it in the Hellenistic context of its own time, it fits beautifully into the world of the *spoudogeloion* and the Menippean satire. This point is neither philological nor historical, but literary and interpretative. The text, like Menippean satire itself, is precisely a critique of and not an affirmation of the view that there are those who know what goodness is, a critique of both philosophical and halakhic *epistemai*. It is a critique, that is to say, of the very monologizing rabbinical power consolidation that so much of the Talmud would seem to vaunt.

Gut Feelings; or, Epistemology in the Operating Theater

Our little picaresque continues with the following anecdote raising even sharper rabbinic doubts about rabbinic epistemologies:

> One day a certain laundry man met him [Rabbicop], and called him "Vinegar son of Wine" [wicked son of righteous father; his father was none other than the saintly Rabbi Shim'on bar Yoḥai who wrote the Zohar some thousand years later!]. He said, "Since he is so brazen, one can deduce that he is wicked." He said, "Seize him." They seized him. After he had settled down, he went in to release him, but he could not. He applied to him the verse, "One who guards his mouth and his tongue, guards himself from troubles" (Proverbs 21:23). They hung him. He stood under the hanged man and cried. Someone said to him, "Be not troubled; he and his son both had intercourse with an engaged girl on *Yom Kippur*." In that minute, he placed his hands on his guts, and said, "Be joyful, O my guts, be joyful! If it is thus when you are doubtful, when you are certain even more so. I am confident that rot and worms cannot prevail over you." (Baba Metsia 83b)

The rabbi's absolute certainties lead here to gross and irreversible injustice on a matter of life and death. True enough, the text retrieves the rabbi's honor, as it were, by indicting the victim of other capital crimes, but surely this does not vindicate his deduction that the man was a thief. The text has now entered fully into a late-antique world of the grotesque and satirical in which the gut instincts of the rabbi— and we will see that these are prodigious guts indeed—are sufficient to justify sentences of death.

The sequence ends with a brilliant rabbinic self-parody:

> "I am confident that rot and worms cannot prevail over you." But even so, he was not calmed. They gave him a sleeping potion and took him into a marble room and ripped open his stomach and were taking out baskets of fat and placing it in the July sun and it did not stink. But no

fat stinks. It does if it has red blood vessels in it, and this, even though it had red blood vessels in it, did not stink.

After relating this extraordinarily over-the-top story of a scientific experiment by which the rabbi could actually test and prove the ability of his guts to tell the truth, an objection of pure talmudic form is raised. The fat-in-the-sun test is not a good test, since fat never stinks. Having raised an objection (*qushya*) in the dialectical style, the resolution (*teruṣ*) is classically talmudic as well. A particular circumstance is cited with respect to this situation that makes it exceptional and thus a good test case. Note how similar in form the objection and resolution are to the canonical versions of both in the "serious" halakhic part of the *sugya*. There too, an objection is resolved by discovering a particular situation to which a (seemingly general) proposition can be limited.[72] In this case, however, it has highly comic effect. As already mentioned, we have slipped in the course of a paragraph from the important and ethical reflections of the early part of the text to a grotesque parody of everything that the Rabbis hold true and holy, their study of Torah with its logical content and form.

The Jewish Silenoi

The Talmud has not yet exhausted its store of grotesque commentary on these rabbinic guts. Remarking of our good rabbi and a colleague of his of similar bodily proportion, the Talmud, deadpan, informs us:

When Rabbi Ishma'el the son of Yose and Rabbi El'azar the son of Rabbi Shim'on used to meet each other, an ox team could walk between them [under the arch formed by their bellies] and not touch them.
　A certain matron said to them, "Your children are not yours."
　They said, "Theirs [our wives' bellies] are bigger than ours."
　"If that is the case, even more so!"
　There are those who say that thus they said to her: "As the man, so is his virility." And there are those who say that thus did they

say to her: "Love compresses the flesh." (Babylonian Talmud, Baba Metsia 84a)[73]

There is no question but that this account of literally "gargantuan" rabbis—that very emblem makes my point—inscribes this piece of the Talmud in the same cultural tradition that gives us Rabelais's "Pantagruelism." Not only is this anecdote strange and bizarre in its representation of rabbinic bodies, it also incorporates yet another moment of talmudic self-parody. The communication of alternative traditions for the retort of the rabbis to their matronly tormentor can surely be read as a mock-heroic version of the talmudic custom of providing alternative traditions in matters of high moment. A great parallel for this in tone would be Rabelais's "In that year the kalends were fixed by the Greek date-books, the month of March was outside Lent, and mid-August fell in May. In the month of October, I believe, or perhaps in September—if I am not mistaken, and I want to take particular care not to be—came the week so famous in our annals, that is called the Week of Three Thursdays," followed by the scientific explanation of this prodigy and then a discourse on enormous body parts and the birth of Pantagruel.[74]

Here too later rabbinic voices have sought to reduce the strangeness of this anecdote by providing moralistic explanations. A striking parallel from the second-century Philostratus, a new Sophist who incorporates elements of the menippea in his work, will, I think, illuminate it and place it within its cultural context without diluting its bizarre comedy. In his *The Lives of the Sophists,* Philostratus relates the following legend about one of his heroes:

> When this Leon came on an embassy to Athens, the city had long been disturbed by factions and was being governed in defiance of established customs. When he came before the assembly he excited universal laughter, since he was fat and had a prominent paunch, but

73. For longer discussion of this passage in its context, especially insofar as it concerns gender and sexuality, see Daniel Boyarin, *Carnal Israel: Reading Sex in Talmudic Culture,* The New Historicism: Studies in Cultural Poetics 25 (Berkeley: University of California Press, 1993), 200–206.

74. Rabelais, *The Histories of Gargantua and Pantagruel,* ed. and trans. J. M. Cohen, Penguin Classics 147 (Harmondsworth, Middlesex: Penguin Books, 1955), 171.

he was not at all embarrassed by the laughter. "Why," said he, "do ye laugh, Athenians? Is it because I am so stout and so big? I have a wife at home who is much stouter than I, and when we agree, the bed is large enough for us both, but when we quarrel not even the house is large enough." Thereupon the citizens of Athens came to a friendly agreement, thus reconciled by Leon, who had so cleverly improvised to meet the occasion."[75]

The narratives are strikingly similar: a Sophist/sage is made fun of owing to his obesity, and in each case, the response is that his wife is even fatter than he is. In the talmudic version, the sexual slur is made directly, while in Philostratus it is only alluded to, but in both cases, the response is that where there is love, there is room in the bed! I find it difficult to escape the conclusion that whatever the precise lines of transmission, and they could be legion, these two narratives are so close as to demonstrate their genetic connection.

In my opinion, this text, in fact, provides a proverbial smoking-gun proof of the claim that Babylonian rabbinic literature is part and parcel of an expanded late-ancient Hellenism. The talmudic version of the story contains a deep infelicity, an ungrammaticality that can be shown to be the product of transformations of the text from its Philostratian source (or, more likely, a common source for both of them). When the *matrona* in the talmudic version challenges the rabbis with the taunt that their children could not be theirs, they seem to answer her that their wives are even fatter than they are, to which her obvious response is: in that case you certainly weren't able to have intercourse with them! The question that arises immediately is what on earth did they have in mind in answering her thus in the first place, a question to which the Talmud, uncharacteristically for once, does not provide an answer (indeed it doesn't raise this obvious question). This problem, it suffices to note, has exercised talmudic interpreters ever since, with many and various unsatisfying answers provided

---

75. Wilmer Cave France Wright, ed. and trans., *Philostratus: The Lives of the Sophists; Eunapius: Lives of the Philosophers* (Cambridge, Mass.: Harvard University Press, 1998), 15. For possible connections between Philostratus and the (Palestinian) rabbis, see E. E. Halevy, *Amoraic Aggadot: The Biographical Aggadah of the Palestinian and Babylonian Amoraim in the Light of Greek and Latin Sources* (Tel Aviv: Tel Aviv University Press, 1976), 13–20, in Hebrew.

(the most recent of which may have been my own baroque attempts). However, if we recognize how the text transforms its original, then the problem is solved (at least diachronically). For Leon, the introduction of his wife's stoutness is an integral part of his rhetoric. He is precisely trying to make the point that although he is obese and his wife even more so, when there is harmony and love between them the bed is big enough for the two of them. The rabbinic version has turned this rhetoric into sexual banter and threatened its coherence. Instead of the introduction of the wives' obesity being an enhancement of the incongruity of the two fitting the bed, it has been transformed into an attempt at a refutation of the challenge to such fitting. As such, it is lame. Finally the element which was the climax of Leon's little parable for the Athenians, namely the harmony that enables the incongruous to live together, is now transformed into an answer to the obvious question of the *matrona* as to how these fat rabbis with even fatter wives make love at all. We can see all of the elements of the "original" within the Babylonian transformation and thus (as very rarely) actually delineate a line of transmission. My point is not to argue that in general rabbinic texts are "influenced" by Greco-Roman texts, but to use this particular incidence as evidence for a claim of cultural interdependence between the Sasanian East and the Byzantine West in late antiquity sufficient to understand and make plausible my attempts to read the Bavli within the context of literary and cultural moves taking place in that broader context, namely the invention and promulgation of Menippean satire and related genres, as well as the general taste for such indecorous miscellaneous texts as the "Attic Nights" and the "Learned Diners." Reprising the points that I have made in the introduction to this chapter, I would emphasize that it is not specific texts and their influence, certainly not the transmission of written texts, that I have in mind, but rather the oral, "folkloristic" transmission of elite cultural narratives and especially of a certain seriocomic satirical style.

As an emblem of this satirical dialogicity, we find the immediately following coda to our narrative in what is surely one of the most sensational, if not shocking, passages in the Talmud. As if in order to demonstrate the principle that a man's virility is in proportion to the size of his belly, the Talmud offers the following information on a group of notoriously fat rabbis:

Said Rabbi Yoḥanan, "Rabbi Ishma'el the son of Yose's member was like a wineskin of nine kav [approximately five gallons]; Rabbi El'azar the son of Rabbi Shim'on's member was like a wineskin of seven kav." Rav Pappa said, "Rabbi Yoḥanan's member was like a wineskin of three kav." And there are those who say: like a wineskin of five kav. Rav Pappa himself had a member which was like the baskets of Hipparenum. (84a)

Note that we have a kind of ladder form here. In each case, the rabbi who reports on the penis size of his colleagues has his own exposed by the next speaker, and the *stamma* concludes it all with the extravagance of Rav Pappa's own equipment. To clarify the point: the argument is not that we find an element of the incongruous grotesque here because sexuality is broached in such a direct and seemingly crude manner—that easy acceptance of the lower bodily aspects of the human, or even preoccupation with them, is practically a defining characteristic of the Bavli as a whole—but rather that the grotesque emerges in the fantastic, wildly exaggerated presentation of these rabbinic corpora: penises that are five gallons large, indeed![76]

Every single one of these rabbis functions within halakhic dialectic as the most serious and dedicated of seekers after truth. If all one knew of our fat rabbis is the narrative of their capacious bodies and genitalia, one would hardly expect to find either of them figuring in such serious contexts as the following:

R. Yoḥanan said: What is it that is written: "The Lord gave [happy] tidings; they are published by heralds, a numerous host" (Psalms 57:12)? This implies that each and every word emanating from the mighty God was given in seventy languages. The school of R. Ishmael, however [adduced the same from another passage]: It is written: "Is not thus my word like the fire? saith the Lord, and like a hammer that shatters the rock?" (Jeremiah 23:29). As the hammer that strikes emits

76. Upon the occasion of my presentation of this material at Yale University on 17 November 2008, that is, just before it went to press, David Quint commented that these enormously large rabbis with gigantic phalloi are also a powerfully self-aggrandizing figure. I hadn't thought of it that way, but think that it's compatible with the double meaning of a figure like Pantagruel, as well. The grotesque and the superhuman are very close to each other here.

a multitude of sparks, so is every word emanating from the Holy One, blessed be He, given in seventy different languages.

R. Ḥananel bar Pappa said: It is written: "Hear! for of noble things will I speak" (Proverbs 8:6). Why are the words of the Torah compared to a noble? To inform us that inasmuch as a noble has in his power the disposal over life and death, so have also the words of the Torah. This is similar to what Rava said: To those who walk in the right ways of the law, it is an elixir of life, but to those who pursue not the right way, it is the poison of death. (Shabbat 88b)

To be sure, we don't quite have Rav Pappa here, but we do have his eldest son together with Rabbi Yoḥanan delivering words of the highest solemnity and sacrality, as well as of terror and dread (for those who are not included in the "right way of Torah").[77] Here's one more example of such lofty Torah which has not one but two of our ithyphallic rabbis in it:

Said R. Yehudah in the name of Rav, "One who treats the Sabbath as enjoyment is given everything his heart desires, because it is written: And enjoy yourself in the Lord, and he will give you the wishes of your heart" (Psalms 37:4). What is meant by "enjoy"? From the passage: "If thou call the Sabbath an enjoyment" (Isaiah 58:13) we can deduce that the "enjoyment" means Sabbath.

With what ought the Sabbath be enjoyed? Said Rav Yehudah, the son of Rav Samuel bar Shilath, in the name of Rav: "With a dish of beets, large fish, and garlic-heads." But R. Ḥiyya bar Ashi said in the name of Rav: "Even with any dish whatever prepared especially for the Sabbath." What does "any dish whatever" mean? Said Rav Pappa: "Even small fish fried in oil."

. . . .

R. Yoḥanan said in the name of R. Shimʿon bar Yoḥai: "If the Israelites were to keep two Sabbaths in succession as they should, they would immediately be released from exile, for it is written: 'Also the

77. I could have chosen myriad other passages, even ones that do include Rav Pappa himself with Rabbi Yoḥanan. I chose this one owing to its inherent thematization of "nobility." For discussion of the meaning of the phrase in about seventy languages, see Azzan Yadin, "The Hammer and the Rock: Polysemy and the School of Rabbi Ishmaʾel," *Jewish Studies Quarterly* 9 (2002): 1–17.

sons of the stranger, that join themselves unto the Lord, to serve
him, and to love the name of the Lord, to be unto him as servants,
every one that keeps the Sabbath by not violating it, and those who
take hold of my covenant' (Isaiah 56:6) and immediately afterwards
it is written (verse 7): 'Even these will I bring to my holy mountain.'"
(Shabbat 115b)

We are very far here from accounts of the sizes of penises and rough
bantering about sexual prowess, love, and obesity. And it needs to be
emphasized, for my own presentation in this book necessarily distorts
this effect, that the vast majority of the matter of the Talmud is more
like this than like narratives of fat rabbis and their penises. Most of
the Talmud—an enormous most—is more like the beginnings of our
sugya (the serious part before the fat rabbis passage), in which the details of a position are discussed with all the pleasures and exclusions
implicated by a scholastic tradition. The tradition has been reading
well in attending primarily to this dominant voice, and it would be a
deeply apologetic move to suggest anything else. It is vitally important that we attend to each and both of the Talmud's two voices with
equal care—each one alone and the two of them together—because
otherwise we will entirely miss the way that each of these languages
of the Talmud carves out a space for the other to appear within. The
"serious" voice is not properly apprehended without paying attention
to the comic, for the Talmud is, assuredly, a serious book. A millennium and more of interpreters can't be entirely wrong, not by any
means. Bakhtin has, once more, provided the words I need: "The image in such cases reveals not only the reality of a given language but
also, as it were, its potential, its ideal limits and its total meaning conceived as a whole, its truth together with its limitations."[78] And this
is because "in an intentional novelistic hybrid, moreover, the important activity is not only (in fact not so much) the mixing of linguistic
forms—the markers of two languages and styles—as it is the collision
between differing points of views [*sic*] on the world that are embedded in those forms."[79] The dominating language of the Talmud *is* the

78. Bakhtin, *The Dialogic Imagination,* 356.
79. Bakhtin, *The Dialogic Imagination,* 360.

language of the serious dialectician who guides Jews to the only true way to live according to God's will; this is the language in which it can be said that it doesn't quite matter whether or not one keeps the Sabbath in this way or that, as long as one follows the rules of discourse set by the Rabbis for making that decision. This is, to my mind, not only not pluralism but not even dialogue, any more than the dialogue of the characters within a philosophical dialogue is truly dialogical.

But at the same time, something else, I contend, has been missed—missed, as so often, because the means to account for it have been lacking—namely the presence of a second accent, a contradictory voice within the fabric of the Bavli. At the very same moment that the Talmud is aggrandizing the Rabbis and the rabbinic institutions and practices, the study of Torah and the House of Study, it is also, through these Menippean narratives, letting us see into the self-doubts and internal critique of those persons, practices, and institutions themselves.

Indeed the story sequence that I have been presenting here goes on and on and on. Our good Rabbi El'azar, still unsure of himself after the great fat massacre, prays for terrible illnesses and sufferings to come upon him with which to atone for his sin. Each night his wife puts sixty felt pads under him and in the morning sixty vessels of blood and puss are removed from under him. She cooks him sixty dishes of figs every day to restore his strength. One day she hears him praying for these illnesses to come at night, and realizing that he wills them, becomes angry and leaves, saying that he is decimating her patrimony. Miraculously enough, sixty sailors bring him sixty purses up from the sea and make him the sixty dishes of figs. We are thus reminded how enormous this man (and his wife) are, if it takes sixty strapping sailors to replace her cooking every day. Finally the rabbi ends up back in the House of Study, where he performs a gargantuan feat of halakhic legerdemain, rendering pure—and not with a miracle—sixty women with a flux. A character more like Pantagruel with his enormous body, enormous physical needs, and finally also enormous intellectual capacity to match, can hardly be imagined. The simultaneous grotesquing and aggrandizing implied by his fantastic proportions seem, to this reader, almost precisely an instance of Pantagruelism, and the rest of the story is written on the book of *Carnal*

Israel.[80] This is surely enough, I hope, to make palpably clear the truly Rabelaisian look and feel of this astonishing text and its—and its fellows'—necessary impact on how we ought (or at any rate, might very well) read the Talmud. I want to thus propose that the double-voicedness of the Babylonian Talmud inscribes it in a literary tradition that flourished in the Mediterranean world in the first few centuries after Christ, notably in Lucian, and then had progeny down to Rabelais (and from thence, perhaps, to Herman Melville, for example).

We should not make the error of assuming that the division between voices which I am positing for the Bavli is between halakha and aggada, for there is, indeed, as we have seen, much very serious aggada, as well as, arguably at least, some satirical (or self-reflective in a semiparodic manner) halakhic texts as well.[81] Indeed, I find it a mistake to use the term *aggada* in the way we have become accustomed to for the last thousand-odd years. *Aggada* should be reserved, as it is in the Talmud itself, for homilies, and especially homilies on the Torah.[82] These grotesque legends are, however, something else. It is more often than not in these stories about its heroes, the Rabbis, that the Bavli finds it easiest to elaborate its uncertainties about its own practices and, in Menippean fashion, to put them to the test. I will complete this chapter with a further rich and very nearly explicit story that exemplifies this point.

The Weakness of Rabbi Yoḥanan: On the *Stamma*'s Self Reflection

The Bavli self-reflectively (and self-reflexively) represents explicitly (or very nearly so) the nondialogical nature of its own dialectic, characteristically via the apparatus of a rather gruesome pseudobiographical story found in tractate Baba Qamma 117a–b:

> A certain man wished to point out the straw of his neighbor [to the Sasanian officials]. He came before Rav. He [Rav] said to him: Do not show it! Do not show it! He [the certain man] said: I will show it; I will

---

80. Boyarin, *Carnal Israel,* 219–25.

81. Wimpfheimer, moreover, has compellingly dismantled this conventional opposition as an analytic tool. Wimpfheimer, *Telling Tales.*

82. Defending this point would take much more space than I can afford here, but I do think it is eminently defensible.

show it. Rav Kahana, who was sitting before Rav, tore out the man's windpipe. Rav read over him the verse "Your sons have fainted; they lie at the head of every street, like a wild bull caught in a net" [Isaiah 51:20]. "Just as with this wild bull that once it has fallen into the net, one does not have mercy on it, so also the property of Israel, once it has fallen into the hands of the gentiles, no one has mercy on it."

As promised, a rather grim beginning to this story. A Jew defiantly intends to point out property of a fellow Jew to the authorities, who would surely confiscate it. Rav Kahana, upon hearing this intention so definitively repeated, murders the man. Rav justifies this murder by a midrashic use of a verse that refers to the wicked sons of the Israelites who are lying in the streets like hunted wild bulls. By sleight of tongue, Rav derives from this a (very doubtful) halakhic principle that one who would cause a fellow Jew's property to be stolen counts as a collaborator (usually reserved for collaborators in dealing of death) and, therefore, is legitimately subject to summary execution. The situation is, as we should expect, entirely fictional. It is, of course, quite impossible to imagine a "real" situation in which a Jew intending to betray a fellow would come to the rabbinic court to ask permission to do so.

The narrative continues:

Rav said to him: "Kahana, until now [our rulers] were Persians who don't care about murder, but now they are Greeks who do care about murder, {and they will cry 'murder, murder!'"}.[83] Get up and run away to the Land of Israel and take a vow not to raise any objections to Rabbi Yoḥanan [in his talmudic lessons] for seven years. He went and found Resh Lakish sitting and summing up the lesson of the day to the Rabbis. He said to them: "Where is Resh Lakish?" They [the rabbis] said: "Why?" [= Who's asking?]. He said to them this difficulty and that difficulty; this refutation and that refutation. They went and told Resh Lakish. Resh Lakish went and told Rabbi Yoḥanan: "A lion has come up from Babylonia. Prepare tomorrow's lesson very carefully!"

83. The curly braces indicate that this phrase is not in most mss. On this phrase, see Shamma Friedman, "The Further Adventures of Rav Kahana: Between Babylonia and Palestine," in *The Talmud Yerushalmi and Graeco-Roman Culture III*, ed. Peter Schaeffer (Tübingen: Mohr/Siebeck, 2002), 249n16; and earlier literature cited there.

Although hopelessly confused in the details — there were no Greek rulers of Babylon in this time, of course — the story does seem to reflect a memory of a shift in regime from the Parthian to the Sasanian empires. The picture is scarcely amended by the manuscript versions that reverse the order of Greeks and Persians, since the Parthians would hardly have been thought of as Greeks either. Since the story clearly is told in and from a Babylonian perspective, perhaps the indirection is intentional, but this blatant ahistoricity serves to underline the fictionality of the account, as does the fact that impossibilities of chronologies in the lives of the rabbis are comprehended.[84] In any case, Rav Kahana is advised by his mentor to escape to Palestine to safety from the wrath of the "Greeks" in Babylonia.[85]

The story, of course, is not finished yet:

> On the morrow, they sat [Rav Kahana] in the front row before Rabbi Yoḥanan. He said the lesson and [Rav Kahana] didn't raise any objections. He went on with the lesson and no objection. They moved him back seven rows and sat him in the last row. Rabbi Yoḥanan said to Resh Lakish: "The lion that you spoke of has become a fox."
>
> He [Rav Kahana] said: "Let it be the will [of God] that the seven rows will be in place of the seven years that Rav commanded me. He got up on his feet and said, "Would the master repeat the lesson?" He [Rabbi Yoḥanan] said the lesson and he [Rav Kahana] raised objections. They put him in the front row. Rabbi Yoḥanan was seated on seven cushions; they took one cushion out from under him. He went on with the lesson and [Rav Kahana] objected, until they had pulled out all of the cushions from under Rabbi Yoḥanan, and he was seated on the ground.

This story has been well analyzed in the context of the complex patterns of hierarchy and humiliation involved in the Babylonian practice of dialectic in the yeshiva. Already at the beginning of the last century it was recognized that the story, while ostensibly about

---

84. See on this Friedman, "Further Adventures of Rav Kahana," 251.

85. Incidentally, the Tosafists (twelfth-century France, Germany) recognize the impossibility of assuming Greek rule in Babylonia on grounds of other talmudic texts (with seemingly no knowledge of the history at all).

third-century Palestine, at least in its current recensions in the Bavli, clearly reflects the realia of the Babylonian yeshiva. In more recent work, it was established beyond doubt that many of the narrative elements are best paralleled by sixth-century Sasanian motifs, thus further establishing its provenance in the postamoraic time of the *stamma*. The conclusion of these accounts is that the story is a late (postamoraic) representation of the Babylonian yeshiva of that period, and that its purpose is to aggrandize the Babylonians' ways of study of Torah over the those of the Palestinians.[86]

These readings are undoubtedly correct, and especially with respect to their Babylonian polemical thrust. What I think has been not noticed—not least by me—until now is how over the top the story is, even as a representation of such conflict and hierarchical structure. The silence of the new guest in the yeshiva is sufficient to have him demoted from a place of honor in the front row to the very last row, and then, when he can no longer stand it and shows his intellectual power, it is the aged Rabbi Yohanan, leader of the rabbis of Palestine at the time, who is humiliated until he is sitting on the earth. There is no reason to regard this story as anything but invention. While it obviously, as nearly all scholars have recognized, does not represent anything realistic about Palestinian yeshivas of the third century, it would be a mistake to read it as a realistic representation of the life of a Babylonian yeshiva of the sixth century, either. It must be read, I think, as a fictional rendering of the life even of that latter institution. As such, I think, it is a highly satirical and critical representation of that life.

This direction of reading is brought out more compellingly in the grotesque ending to the story:

---

86. Isaiah M. Gafni, "The Babylonian Yeshiva as Reflected in Bava Qamma 111a," *Tarbiṣ* 49 (1980): 292–301 (in Hebrew; English summary pp. v–vi); Daniel Sperber, "On the Unfortunate Adventures of Rav Kahana: A Passage of Saboraic Polemic from Sasanian Persia," in *Irano-Judaica: Studies Relating to Jewish Contacts with Persian Culture throughout the Ages*, ed. Shaul Shaked (Jerusalem: Ben-Zvi Institute, 1982), 83–100; Shamma Yehuda Friedman, "Towards the Historical Aggada in the Babylonian Talmud," in *The Saul Lieberman Memorial Volume*, ed. Shamma Friedman (New York: Jewish Theological Seminary, 1993), 119–64 (in Hebrew); Adiel Schremer, "'He Posed Him a Difficulty and Placed Him': A Study in the Evolution of the Text of TB Bava Kama 117a," *Tarbiṣ* 66, no. 3 (April-June 1997): 403–15 (in Hebrew; English summary p. viii); Friedman, "Further Adventures of Rav Kahana."

Rabbi Yoḥanan was an old man and his eyelids drooped. He said to them: "Raise up my eyelids that I might see him!" They raised them up with a small silver toothpick. He saw that he [Rav Kahana] had split lips [perhaps a harelip?]. He thought that he was laughing at him. He [Rabbi Yoḥanan] became furious and [Rav Kahana] died. The next day he [Rabbi Yoḥanan] said to the Rabbis: "Did you see what that Babylonian did!?" They said to him: "His way is thus" [i.e., he has a harelip]. He entered into the cave [where Rav Kahana was buried]. He saw that a snake was blocking it. He said to it: "Snake, snake, Open your mouth and let the master come into the disciple," and he [snake] did not open. "Let the colleague come into the colleague," and he did not open. "Let the disciple come into the master," and he opened for him. He [Rabbi Yoḥanan] prayed and resurrected him [Rav Kahana]. He [Rabbi Yoḥanan] said to him: "Had I known that this is the way of the master, I would not have gotten angry; now let the master come to us [to study]." He said to him: "If you are able to pray that I will not die again, I will come, and if not, I won't, because once the hour is passed, it is passed" [= I can't count on another miraculous resurrection]. He [Rabbi Yoḥanan] woke him and stood him up and asked him everything about which he had a doubt, and he [Rav Kahana] resolved them for him. And this is what Rabbi Yoḥanan was used to saying: "They say it is yours, but it is theirs." (Baba Qamma 117a)

This text represents, then, a perfect example of Menippean satire in the sense in which I shall be developing it through the next several chapters; on the one hand, it aggrandizes its own practices and institutions; on the other hand, it presents sharp critique (and parody) of those same practices and institutions at the very same time and in the very same moment. It writes itself into that tradition most clearly by being a story of death and miraculous resurrection in bathetic circumstances. It is, then, a Pantagruelian figure of its own, the giant who represents the power and gargantuan self-regard of a discourse as well as its grossly exaggerated and criticized dimensions (the jealousies and envies of the hierarchical yeshiva). This narrative, precisely to the extent that it represents *Babylonian* practice (albeit post-talmudic), is highly self-critical as well. The dialectic, in other places represented as an irenic search for truth—much like the disinterested search for truth that Socrates himself declares—is here represented as having deadly effect. In the portrayal of the deadliness of rivalries and jealousy within the rabbinic academy (academies of a sort that seem only to have existed toward the end of late antiquity and then only in Babylonia),[87] our story rivals the more famous one of Rabbi Yoḥanan and Resh Lakish in which the former also kills his rival with a look, following the latter's challenge to his hegemony.[88] In that story as well, the absolutely hierarchical nature of the Babylonian dialectic is made manifest. After Resh Lakish dies, Rabbi Yoḥanan passionately desires him back, for "he would ask twenty-four objections and I would answer with twenty-four refutations, and between him and me the matter would be clarified." The nature of dialectic, per se, is made absolutely clear through this description. One dominant voice presents and defends his position. No other possibility is comprehended. Indeed, in the story, it is when Resh Lakish dared to present his own opinion that he was effectively killed, as is Rav Kahana by a glance of Rabbi Yoḥanan's. We have here an elegant illustration of Krabbe's point about dialectic as the deliverer of truth. Hardly a dialogue between opinions, the Bavli's dialectic is thus represented by the Bavli itself (or at any rate this late narrative strand within the Bavli) as a procedure of inquiry in which the opinions of the master are clarified via the objections of the disciple. It is in such a moment of self-doubt, of self-reflection, self-interrogation, and self-critique that, I think, we find the key to the incorporation of the grotesque biographical material in the Talmud.

My argument is, then, that the grotesque and harshly self-critical biographical legends, when read together with the "serious" incorporated genres of halakhic dialectic, legal story, and uplifting aggada, produce a dialogical text, a text that both advances its program and recognizes its failure (the failure of all human endeavor—shades of Kohellet), precisely the kind of mixed bag that we find in such as Lucian and Petronius, that is in the literature called Menippean, and this is where my discussion will take us next.

---

87. David M. Goodblatt, *Rabbinic Instruction in Sasanian Babylonia*, Studies in Judaism in Late Antiquity 9 (Leiden: E. J. Brill, 1975).

88. Friedman, "Towards the Historical Aggada," demonstrates that the Rav Kahana story is a kind of imitation of the one about Resh Lakish. See also Schremer, "He Posed," 411–12, on this comparison.

5

"Read Lucian!"

Menippean Satire and the Literary World of the Babylonian Talmud

For Bakhtin, there is a force, "the clamping principle," which binds all of the heterogeneous elements "into the organic whole of a genre."[1] If the Talmud is an "organic whole," it will look, I think, like a very rotund rabbi, with various and very large organs sticking out crudely—almost obscenely—sometimes, as organic perhaps as a fish-horse or a goat-stag, to quote Lucian on his own works. I am attempting, in part, to theorize and historicize a persistent intuition I have had in my forty years of reading Talmud, an intuition that it somehow best fits, in world literature, with precisely the satirical dialogues of Lucian, *The Satyricon,* with *Gargantua and Pantagruel, Tristram Shandy,* and *Moby Dick.* We have just seen that however dominant the dialectical *sugya* is in the Talmud and however large it looms in the history of talmudic reception, it is by no means the entire matter of the Talmud, for narratives such as those of our eponymous obese clerics appear as a kind of minor obbligato in the Talmud that is deeply threatening to the decorum of the entire text.

---

1. Mikhail Bakhtin, *Problems of Dostoevsky's Poetics,* ed. and trans. Caryl Emerson, Theory and History of Literature (Minneapolis: University of Minnesota Press, 1984), 134.

In these narratives within the Talmud we find its very heroes (and to a lesser extent even biblical heroes) nearly burlesqued and the talmudic dialectic parodied and rendered absurd. This type of fantastic (and sometimes—but not always—comic) biographical legend, analogous writ large to the hiccups of the Platonic text, has caused commentators no end of difficulty.

The Talmud's Two Anonymouses; or, Where Is the Jewish Agency?

Richard Kalmin has argued against the notion that the halakha and aggada belong to the same editorial stratum, since the aggada comprises, as he puts it, "many talmudic stories [that] are extremely uncomplimentary toward their rabbinic protagonists."[2] Kalmin's solution to this "problem" is to state explicitly that the redactors of the Talmud were faced with traditional material from other sources hostile to their rabbinic heroes, and that they were constrained against their will to include such material simply because it was traditional. This strikes me as a thoroughly implausible account on both historical and literary grounds for how the Talmud came to be so heterogeneous. Arguing against this view is the fact that the legendary material, including some of the most antithetical in tone and content to the halakhic, is frequently integrally related to it in terms of the flow of the *sugya*. Secondly, it is impossible to imagine that the redactors of the Babylonian Talmud labored under constraint to include all the traditional materials circulating among the Jews; they obviously exercised choice and agency. Third, there are clearly aggadic cycles that are later than the halakhic materials and refer to them and so are too, palpably, part of the final redactorial efforts of the *stamma*.[3]

At the same time, Kalmin is absolutely right to point to the extreme tensions between "the overwhelmingly prosaic, legal preoccupations of these commentators throughout the Talmud" and the tone of sharp critique frequently articulated in the wildly creative aggada. This is, indeed, precisely the point I make here; the question is rather

2. Richard Kalmin, "The Formation and Character of the Babylonian Talmud," in *The Cambridge History of Judaism,* vol. 4, *The Late Roman-Rabbinic Period,* ed. Steven T. Katz (Cambridge: Cambridge University Press, 2006), 845.

3. See essays collected in J. L. Rubenstein, ed., *Creation and Composition: The Contribution of the Bavli Redactors to the Aggadah* (Tübingen: Mohr/Siebeck, 2005).

whether we conclude from this, as he does, that "the anonymous editors of the Talmud are very unlikely candidates for authorship of the Talmud's brilliantly artistic, dramatically gripping, and ethically and theologically ambiguous narratives."[4] I think not, any more than we would conclude from the widely divergent generic tonalities of Rabelais that he couldn't have written the entire text, or that Melville had to include the chapters on the whale because they were traditional materials that he couldn't ignore. Or for that matter, that the author of the *Republic* could not possibly have penned the *Symposium*. I would question, moreover, Kalmin's characterization of the *sugya* as unartistic; these highly rhetorical, structured compositions manifest, rather, a great deal of literary art, as much, I warrant as the "stories." Taking the same materials in mind and recognizing that they are all parts of one book, the Talmud, the question is rather: what does it mean to have such deeply antithetical materials in the same book?

Galit Hasan-Rokem in her book *Tales of the Neighborhood* asks a question similar to mine (and Kalmin's), namely, why are there "folk narratives" embedded in the talmudic text?[5] She comes, however, to a somewhat different answer than I will. Her practice of focusing on these narratives forces us to pay attention to the necessary distinction between the text as it has been read traditionally and a different kind of reading. She asks us "to disentangle that [rabbinic] literature from its traditional immurement in the confines of the synagogue and the academy (*bet-midrash*), a restriction largely created by later interpretative practices and academic discourse."[6] Hasan-Rokem proposes "a fundamental principle of the interpretation of folk narratives in Rabbinic literature":

Reading Rabbinic stories as folk narratives often associates them with worldviews and ideas that make it difficult to harmonize them with what has traditionally—and in my view at least partly mistakenly— been understood as *the* Rabbinic worldview. Their explication as an inherent part of the Rabbinic text, however, highlights ideas in them

4. Kalmin, "Formation," 846.
5. Galit Hasan-Rokem, *Tales of the Neighborhood: Jewish Narrative Dialogues in Late Antiquity,* Taubman Lectures in Jewish Studies (Berkeley: University of California Press, 2003).
6. Hasan-Rokem, *Tales of the Neighborhood,* 9–10.

that become particularly concretized and reinforced by the Rabbinic context.[7]

Hasan-Rokem rightly, in my opinion, rejects such interpretations that would argue that the Rabbis included these utterances in their works in order to attract a wider audience (or variations of this theme)—explanations that recall the genial and harmless accounts of Pantagruelism in Plato's texts discussed above.[8] For Hasan-Rokem herself, the inclusion of this material indicates simply that the rabbinic community itself was *not* a scholastic world to the degree that we are used to thinking of it as such, but was open to the marketplace, the tavern, even the brothel. She, accordingly, seeks an "integrative interpretation of the Rabbinic text that includes the folk narratives in it."[9] Hasan-Rokem is primarily speaking of the midrashic literature of Palestinian Rabbis, while I, of course, am dealing in this book with the Babylonian Talmud, a closely related but, I think, quite different sort of text.

While I find Hasan-Rokem's analysis a tremendous step forward from any previous attempt to read (or more generally ignore) the incongruity even of the talmudic text (which is, as I've just remarked, not really her purview), I hope to move one step further. To put the point concisely, I would suggest that a fuller reading of the Bavli has to account precisely, also, for the fact of rabbinic "immurement" in the overweening "Torah" of the House of Study, while also reading the practices in the texts that resist such immurement. The expressed rabbinic ideal, after all, is of one who "kills himself in the tent of Torah." Building, then, on Hasan-Rokem's work, I want to take it in a slightly different direction, in a less irenic mode perhaps, in a direction in which what is dramatized is the Rabbis' self-reflexive ambivalence about their own hegemonic practices via the mobilization (or even invention) of a particular set of literary practices and genres. The lens of the (anti)genre of Menippean satire provides one way of focusing on and responding to the heterogeneity of the Bavli.

Hasan-Rokem focuses our attention on the ethnographic aspect

7. Hasan-Rokem, *Tales of the Neighborhood,* 21.
8. Hasan-Rokem, *Tales of the Neighborhood,* 60–61.
9. Hasan-Rokem, *Tales of the Neighborhood,* 21.

of rabbinic literature and on the inclusion of folk narrative as a way of "implementing a common search for identity under markedly diverse circumstances."[10] In contrast, but not sharply so, my focus is more narrowly on the House of Study itself, to put it somewhat metaphorically. Concentrating on the Babylonian Talmud, I see a much more scholastic community, a text of intellectuals, of Sages (Sophists), and ask, why did they produce a literature like this, inter alia? What was at stake for them in incorporating blocks of a genre of (folk) literature that seems not only incompatible but betimes even distinctly hostile to their worldview and represented self-image? What kind of book is a Babylonian Talmud? To my way of thinking, the richest answer comes from the world of Menippean satire, the literary style that *by definition* combines seemingly contradictory elements. This is the textual form (genre?) whose very name, *satura,* meaning a kind of pudding or sausage of mixed aliments, indicates such incongruous interminglings. For me, then, the operative questions are not so much of elite and folk but of the intercutting and undercutting of antithetical genres. I don't, therefore, refer to the narrative material as "folk narrative," while at the same time I recognize, of course, at least one of its sources in that which people call folk literature. For the purposes of the analysis that I wish to make, the comparative question is not so much how the "folk" material lines up with other "folk" material, but rather how these sophisticated intellectuals make texts and how the texts they make appear in the light of the texts of other roughly contemporaneous intellectuals.

Hasan-Rokem has to be right that the ways that we interpret the Bavli are largely the product of later "interpretative practices and academic discourse," if only because such practices and discourse seem so incapable of making sense of the whole sausage. But at the same time, I resist an interpretation that simply dismisses such later interpretive practices, since there are, as I have argued in the previous chapter, powerful forces for such monological reading within the text itself in its "serious"—"dreadful"—voice. Reading for the serio-comic demands that we pay attention to the serious *qua* serious with its drive toward monologicality as well as the counterdrives within the text, reading them indeed, as Hasan-Rokem would have us do,

10. Hasan-Rokem, *Tales of the Neighborhood,* 59.

as one text but certainly not as one harmonious or organic text. I have tried to read the Bavli in a double fashion, first paying attention to its drive toward the monological voice and authority of the oral Torah and once again reading for the textual elements that are heterogeneous with respect to that very enterprise. In certain respects, Hasan-Rokem echoes Nachman Krochmal's distinction between normative aggada and aggada of the "uneducated," which Krochmal argued was *mistakenly* included in the aggadic corpus by Babylonian scribes in the sixth century.[11] Yet, there are sharp differences between Krochmal and Hasan-Rokem. Krochmal, who is responding to the Enlightenment figures of his day (who mock the outlandish statements of the aggada), *bemoans* the inclusion of this material and seeks to diminish its importance. For Hasan-Rokem, the rabbis, who consciously sought to appropriate folk literature to aid in their presentation of culture, were unaware of the often radical antiestablishment concepts embedded within this material. It is we, in this view, who are now fortunate enough to have a window into the world of the margins.[12] In short, for Hasan-Rokem and Krochmal alike, these elements surreptitiously got into the aggada through the back door and subverted the rabbinic establishment. Their respective appraisals of this alleged situation remain, of course, directly opposed.

My dual goal is to avoid marginalizing the "bizarre" aggada by treating it as something other than the text in which it is found and to eschew harmonizing by understanding its force as only that which entered the text willy-nilly (either its texts as in Krochmal or its subversive meanings as in Hasan-Rokem). My reading will propose rather to see such strange interludes as another language within the text, as in Bakhtin's account of certain kinds of texts as machines for the mutual illumination of discordant languages. Instead of seeing the grotesque stories as somehow or other extraneous to the main business of the Talmud, I am offering a reading of the Talmud as Menippean satire in which both languages, the language of Torah and the

---

11. Jay M. Harris, *Nachman Krochmal: Guiding the Perplexed of the Modern Age,* Modern Jewish Masters Series (New York: New York University Press, 1991), 292–97. Saul Friedman called my attention to this discussion.

12. This formulation has been much informed by an unpublished paper by Saul Moshe Friedman. I am grateful to him for allowing me thus to paraphrase from his Ph.D. exam paper.

language of the grotesque, are brought into contact with one another with deep purpose.

Closely related to the Menippean satire in Bakhtin's account is the novel, so another way of approaching the question of the antithetical materials in the Bavli is to think of the Talmud as a novel, as presented by Bakhtin: "Authorial speech, the speeches of narrators, inserted genres, the speech of characters are merely those fundamental compositional unities with whose help heteroglossia [*raznorečie*] can enter the novel; each of them permits a multiplicity of social voices and a wide variety of their links and interrelationships (always more or less dialogized)."[13] Whether or not, then, this piece of Talmud or that is quoted from other, "earlier" sources, the question is about the heterogeneous text that we have before us. It is almost identical, I think, to the great questions about Plato and his use of literary materials deeply antithetical to his ostensible primary point, the absolute primacy of dialectic (philosophy) over rhetoric (sophism) and poetry (epic and drama).[14] To put it bluntly, I propose that we shift from source-and-influence criticism with respect to the Talmud, or even from a literary criticism that treats only individual units and incorporated genres of text as autonomous,[15] to a literary criticism imbued with the concept of intertextuality (which is, in turn, derived directly from the Bakhtinian notion of heteroglossia, as will become clearer anon). By considering the Bavli under the rubric of Bakhtin's understanding of the novel, we may begin to approach its multiple genres and authorships in new ways.

13. Mikhail Bakhtin, "Discourse in the Novel," in *The Dialogic Imagination: Four Essays by Mikhail Bakhtin*, ed. Michael Holquist, trans. Michael Holquist and Caryl Emerson, University of Texas Press Slavic Series (Austin: University of Texas Press, 1981), 263. Holquist helpfully glossed this: "[The novel] is thus best conceived either as a supergenre, whose power consists in its ability to engulf and ingest all other genres (the different and separate languages peculiar to each), or not a genre in any strict, traditional sense at all. In either case it is obvious that the history of what might be called novels, when they are defined by their proclivity to display different languages interpenetrating each other, will be extremely complicated" (xxix).

14. Andrea Wilson Nightingale, *Genres in Dialogue: Plato and the Construct of Philosophy* (Cambridge: Cambridge University Press, 1995).

15. I am thinking here of the groundbreaking work of Yonah Fränkel, such as his *Readings in the Spiritual World of the Stories of the Aggada* (Tel Aviv: United Kibbutz Press, 1981) (in Hebrew). This corresponds to Bakhtin's remark that "sytlistic analysis is not oriented toward the novel as a whole, but only toward one or another of its subordinated stylistic unities." Bakhtin, *The Dialogic Imagination*, 263.

Reading Bakhtin himself, however, is itself not uncomplicated. One reading of Bakhtin (or perhaps, one strand of Bakhtin's writing) would lead us to assume that the author is not in control of her text and that the alien words enter, as it were, of their own agency, the agency of the language itself, that is, all the anonymous and unknown usages of the word prior to this text. It is this reading that produces the Kristevan or more broadly deconstructive version of intertextuality. On this reading, the Talmud, like any other text decentered from any authorial consciousness or agency, contains somehow the contradictory registers and dialects, if you will, of the very language itself, the language that speaks the text and its author. We would understand the Talmud as embodying such crude contradictions as part and parcel of its very existence as literature, as discourse, as human language, only perhaps more overtly so than some other forms of Western belles lettres. The "alien" word is not a product of anyone's agency, but creeps in or inhabits the text simply by virtue of the text having been composed in a language with all its cacophony of registers and usages. The second accent appears, as it were, of itself; the language of jarring contradictions speaking the text and thus the author.[16]

Another reading of Bakhtin—actually another strand in Bakhtin's writing—seems to imagine authors who are capable of harboring a word and the word that challenges that word at one and the same time without seeking harmonization or closure or decision, and who can, moreover, build such dialogue into the text at its deepest structural levels. The first reading does not distinguish between genre and genre, text and text, author and author with respect to intertextuality, by definition, since there are no authors or texts on its lights. The latter does draw a distinction, for instance, notoriously between Tolstoy and Dostoevsky, and ascribes a degree of agency to the author in the making of the text that is denied in the first, deconstructive interpretation of Bakhtin.

On this view, which I find deeply attractive, an author has agency (even a multiple author, even an implied author) in the production

16. See too Chana Kronfeld, "Intertextual Agency," in *Ziva Ben-Porat Jubilee Volume,* ed. Michael Gluzman and Orli Lubin (Tel Aviv: Tel Aviv University Press, 2008) (in Hebrew), on this issue.

of the dialogical text. The Talmud, consonant with the accents of its broad literary context, manifests a deep commitment to a set of ideals and perhaps even to a search for truth, imagined as God's will, while at the same time incorporating within its textual world a voice as strident as any Menippean satire, a voice that would corrosively deny any such ideals and any such searches, reducing them to the itches and scratches of a human body. Tales of grotesque bodies of rabbis and the bizarre, fantastic, and betimes disreputable behavior of some of the greatest heroes and even "saints" of the Bavli, nearly unique within rabbinic literature to the Babylonian Talmud, resist the closure of Torah and the absolute presentation of the Rabbis and the rabbinic institution, even of the oral Torah itself, as the locus of life according with the will of God. This stratum within the Babylonian Talmud has, in a very Bakhtinian manner, to do with the body and its nether parts, with elimination, sex, and lust, but also with extreme conduct borne of envy and jealousy. With rare exception, such as the sixteenth-century Polish commentator, Maharsha, little attempt has been made even to harmonize these materials at all, and they have been, for the most part, simply explained away or ignored.[17]

In one of his pronouncements on the Talmud with which I heartily agree, Levinas writes, "The Talmud is not a simple compilation—whatever some otherwise enlightened spirits might think—of folkloric memories in a contingent order, but there is an inner movement in this text, that its arrangement is ordered by its meaning, that it is meaningful."[18] The producer of this "inner movement," however much I differ from Levinas as to its character, is the final "author" of the Talmud of whom I have been speaking. I thus consider the text of the Talmud entire, including even the "wildest" of aggada as incorporated in the Talmud by this—at least implied—"author" and thus integral to the "work" as a whole. Once we have made this shift, we will find the monological thrust of the halakhic nondialogue dialo-

17. Maharsha himself remarks that the reason the Talmud tells us this is to indicate that although these rabbis all had enormous penises and presumably lust to match, they were, nonetheless, able to control themselves and be holy and ascetic rabbis! All previous commentators whom I have read take the word "members" to mean stomachs, arms, legs—anything but penises.

18. Emmanuel Levinas, *Nine Talmudic Readings,* trans. Annette Aronowicz (Bloomington: Indiana University Press, 1990), 104.

gized by the very presence in the same textual context of the aggadic genres that are most alien and even antithetical to it.

It follows, as I have begun to argue in the previous chapter, that at least two implied "authors" must (and can) thus be kept apart from each other: the anonymous author (*stamma*) who constructs the dialectic of the *sugya* and the anonymous author (*stamma*) who incorporates the dialectic together with those grotesque narratives about the sages to which Krochmal and many others have called our attention. The first author, the *stamma* of the dialectic *sugya* (including most genres of what is now called aggada as well), produces the single voice (accent) of the serious, of the *spoudaios* in the Talmud, while the second author, the *stamma* of the Talmud, has allowed a "second accent, a crude contradiction," to invoke Bakhtin's terminology once again, to enter the text; "his" is not the "second accent," but it is "he" who has allowed the second accent to appear. It is this second "author" who makes the Talmud both *spoudogeloios* and Menippean. We need to consistently distinguish between the (implied) author of the dialectic as the one dominant genre within the Talmud and the implied author of the Talmud as an entire work. From a slightly different point of view, we could claim that the dialogicality of the Talmud is the dialogue between the two anonymous authors, a monological voice that seeks to bring all under the purview of the system called oral Torah and another *stamma* that allows cracks to appear in the fabric of that very system. This distinction will be necessary as we continue in our reading of the Talmud.

The historical author(s) of the dialectic of the *sugya* need not be, although I believe they are, quite late. This is a subject on which there is much controversy.[19] On the other hand, the "author" of the Talmud must be, by definition, late, so to speak, because until "he" did "his" work there was no Talmud (as we know it) and afterward there was. Some scholars, including me in past work, have been very concerned to identify actual human groups behind this authorial activity. My

---

19. The alternative view, supported lately most strongly by Robert Brody in a series of forthcoming publications, argues for a continuous process of such production of the *sugya*, which was, after all, the traditional account also. I think that some of the confusion in the discussion is owing to conflating the two literary functions (both known as *stamma*), one which arranged the *sugya* out of disparate sayings and stories and one which produced the whole book of the Talmud out of these and other types of material as well.

project here is more literary, inquiring into the *stamma* not so much as a historical construct of a real author(s) of the Talmud, but as a literary structure within the Talmud, the implied *stamma,* if you will. Whatever the historical considerations for or against the particularities of the first usage of the notion of the anonymous, this second usage must be accepted, because without it there is no text at all. Unless we make the very strong assumption that the Talmud is a virtually aleatory collection of materials that were by and large formed elsewhere and elsewhen and then incorporated into a fairly random anthology, we can—and must—ask why different materials appear together in the Talmud and what the meaning is of the work of whoever placed them together there. Bakhtin's "clamping principle" of the Talmud is called or operated by that literary function that talmudic scholars have for a millennium called the *stamma.*

The anonymous author of the Talmud is precisely the absence of author. On Barthes's famous account:

> We know now that a text is not a line of words releasing a single "theological" meaning (the "message" of the author-God) but a multidimensional space in which a variety of writings, none of them original, blend and clash. The text is a tissue of quotations drawn from the innumerable centers of culture. Similar to Bouvard and Pécuchet, those eternal copyists, at once sublime and comic and whose profound ridiculousness indicates precisely the truth of writing, the writer can only imitate a gesture that is always anterior, never original. His only power is to mix writings, to counter the ones with the others, in such a way as never to rest on any one of them.[20]

We don't need to adopt (and I won't) quite so rigorous (*rigor*ous *mortis*) a notion of authorial nonagency in order to recognize how apt a description this is of the "writer" of the Talmud; indeed, this is precisely the stance or subject-position of the *stamma.* The author of the Talmud, as opposed to the author of the dialectic sugya (together frequently with its legal narratives), is not to be understood, then, as

---

20. Roland Barthes, "The Death of the Author," in *The Death and Resurrection of the Author?* ed. William Irwin, Contributions in Philosophy 83 (Westport, Conn.: Greenwood Press, 2002), 6.

"author" in the sense of a control on interpretation, "a point where
contradictions are resolved."[21] Rather, I would suggest, this author is
exactly the opposite, that is, the point of an opening to a self-aware
contradictoriness, in which there is no resolution, the consciousness
or (ascribed) agency that produces the dialogical text. It seems that if
we don't appeal to such a construct, then it will be impossible even to
see incongruity in the text. To be clear, no judgment is being offered
here at all as to the historical status of these two implied authors in
and of the Talmud; just as in a film where the director/auteur may or
may not be the same person as the editor, so too for the Talmud.

I consider the anonymity of the *stamma* as a necessary literary function, as precisely that which brings the Talmud into being, as it were,
as the Old Blind Homer of the Talmud. What we learn from Simon
Goldhill is that in order for a text to function as discourse there *must*
be an anonymous "clamping principle," a *stamma.* The *stamma* would
not then be a specific or particular feature of the Talmud but rather
a token of a type animating all narrative discourse. As I have been
suggesting through these pages, the kind of authority that such an
author or clamping principle inhabits is equivalent to what modern
theoreticians of the novel call the implied author of the text.[22] The
"real" author of the novel has to disappear into this literary function
in order for novelistic discourse to exist. And similarly, whoever the
rabbis were who produced the *stamma* had to disappear themselves
into the Talmud, now identifiable with precisely their anonymous
voice. "Plato" is constituted in the Platonic dialogues by a very similar disappearance of Plato.[23] The name "The Talmud" or *Stamma de
Talmud* becomes, on this analysis, semiotically equivalent to "Plato"
or "Lucian" (who explicitly plays with this convention).[24]

Barthes, once again, has proposed an even more radical option, for

21. Michel Foucault, "What Is an Author?" in *The Death and Resurrection of the Author?*
ed. William Irwin, Contributions in Philosophy 83 (Westport, Conn.: Greenwood Press,
2002), 16.
22. Wayne C. Booth, *The Rhetoric of Fiction* (Chicago: University of Chicago Press,
1983).
23. Kevin Corrigan and Elena Glazov-Corrigan, *Plato's Dialectic at Play: Argument, Structure, and Myth in the* Symposium (University Park: Pennsylvania State University Press,
2004), 21–22.
24. Simon Goldhill, "Becoming Greek, with Lucian," in *Who Needs Greek? Contests in
the Cultural History of Hellenism* (New York: Cambridge University Press, 2002), 60–107.

which the "clamping principle" is the reader and not any kind of author function at all. As Barthes writes:

> A text is made up of multiple writings, drawn from many cultures and entering into mutual relations of dialogue, parody, contestation, but there is one place where this multiplicity is focused and that place is the reader, not, as was hitherto said, the author. The reader is the space on which all the quotations that make up a writing are inscribed without any of them being lost; a text's unity lies not in its origin but in its destination. Yet this destination cannot any longer be personal: the reader is without history, biography, psychology; he is simply that *someone* who holds together in a single field all the traces by which the written text is constituted.[25]

For Barthes then the "clamping principle" is that which he calls "the reader." This is the case in another sense for Foucault as well, who claims that "the author is not an indefinite source of significations which fill a work; the author does not precede the works; he is a certain functional principle by which, in our culture, one limits, excludes, and chooses; in short, by which one impedes the free circulation, the free manipulation, the free composition, decomposition, and recomposition of fiction."[26] My suggestion, in some contrast to this, is to offer the author of at least some texts as the principle that allows the text to manifest "crude contradiction" and "second accents"; the author being the one who brings the discordant voices together. Note that this description of the author is almost exactly the one that Barthes himself gives with his description of the author whose "only power is to mix writings, to counter the ones with the others, in such a way as never to rest on any one of them." This seems to me, *pace* Barthes, considerable power indeed. One author who answers to this description is of course the voice of the *stamma* who puts the Talmud together (note the present tense), gives us the Talmud that we have as a book, that is the author of the Talmud.

Arguing for a holistic reading of the Talmud neither precludes polyvalence and the possibility of multiple modes of interpretation

25. Barthes, "The Death of the Author," 7.
26. Foucault, "What," 21.

nor denies historical layering in the text, a historical layering that is
of great value (in other scholarly, hermeneutic contexts) to uncover.
A recent essay by Elliot R. Wolfson has articulated this point sharply
and clearly throughout, but especially in the following remarks:

> I would propose that plurivocality and fragmentariness need to be
> kept distinct. Too often, it seems, they are confused, and one assumes
> that the former automatically implies the latter. To argue for a plu-
> rality of voices, however, does not necessarily mean that all we have
> are fragments. The overarching sense of the whole may, in fact, rever-
> berate only through a polyphony of voices. In the case of the zoharic
> text, it is possible, in my opinion, to apply a "holistic analysis," even
> if we entertain the possibility of multiple layers at the compositional
> level. The poststructuralist approach that I have adopted both allows
> for these different strata and maintains that there is an overall system
> that engenders the particulars.[27]

The same applies to the Talmud as to the Zohar. In the Talmud
for sure, "the overarching sense of the whole may, in fact, reverberate
only through a polyphony of voices."

An important point of departure for a reading of the whole is the
"anonymity" of the Talmud. We literally have no idea who produced
the text that we have in front of us (or when, or where, although we
can take some — quite contentious — quite educated guesses at these).
Rather than a historical problem to be overcome (or not, as the case
may be), we can see this strong version of anonymity as the very thing
that makes the Babylonian Talmud — the Talmud.[28] Analogously to
the ways that, as Simon Goldhill has shown, figures such as Plato
and Lucian hide themselves in their texts anonymously, as it were,
so the *stamma* of the Bavli can be read as such a hidden authoring
voice.[29] Note again that I am making no claims as to whether or not

27. Elliot R. Wolfson, "Structure, Innovation, and Diremptive Temporality: The Use
of Models to Study Continuity and Discontinuity in Kabbalistic Tradition," *Journal for the
Study of Religions and Ideologies,* special issue, *Reading Idel's Works Today* 6, no. 18 (2007): 156.

28. This was a point made to me by Virginia Burrus nearly a decade ago which has
proven very fruitful for me.

29. Although I have learned much from such scholars as David Halivni and Shamma
Friedman on this, I differ from them in that I am not concerning myself (at least not
here and now) with the actual history and reconstructed persons who produced the *stam,*

the author of the *sugya* and the author of the Talmud have different biographical/historical authors or the same. Either way, however, we must consider each author/*stamma* as its own voice entering into dialogue with the other.

If, as Bakhtin has put it, "the novelistic hybrid is *an artificially organized system for bringing different languages in contact with one another, a system having as its goal the illumination of one language by means of another, the carving out of a living image of another's language,"*[30] and if the Talmud itself is, as I have proposed, such a system as well, then it would be an error to reduce that system of languages to a single monological discourse. It is not, accordingly, so much the polyphony potential in narrative that produces dialogism in the Talmud, but the yoking of the narrative with the halakhic dialectic, like an ox with a donkey, in the talmudic field that renders the Talmud a dialogical text. I am suggesting that the languages of the halakhic *sugya* and of the "wild" biographical legend are deeply antithetical and thus in dialogue with each other. The positing of a historically grounded genre of literature—whether in the end we call it "novel" or not—in which one could, and I would, read the Talmud seems powerfully compelling.

Bakhtin writes of an earlier scholar of Dostoevsky, "Had [Leonid] Grossman linked Dostoevsky's compositional principle—the unification of highly heterogeneous and incompatible material—with the plurality of consciousness-centers not reduced to a single ideological common denominator, then he would have arrived in earnest at the artistic key to Dostoevsky's novels: polyphony."[31] While Grossman had located the polyphony of Dostoevsky in the "conversation" or "quarrel" in the diegesis itself—and we have learned to be suspicious of such dialogue—Bakhtin locates it rather in "the yoking of highly heterogeneous and incompatible material," arguing that this yoking, the antidecorum or grotesque character of the (Dostoevskian) text itself, is what produces the polyphony. If there were ever a set of texts in

---

the so-called *Stamma'im*. See also in this comparative and theoretical regard, Gian Biagio Conte, *The Hidden Author: An Interpretation of Petronius' Satyricon,* Sather Classical Lectures (Berkeley: University of California Press, 1996).

30. Bakhtin, *The Dialogic Imagination,* 361. Virginia Burrus has discussed the relation of Bakhtin's hybridity to that of Homi Bhabha in her "Mimicking Virgins: Colonial Ambivalence and the Ancient Romance," *Arethusa* 38 (2005): 51.

31. Bakhtin, *Problems of Dostoevsky's Poetics,* 17.

which heterogeneous and incompatible material are yoked, the rabbinic literature is it, and especially the Babylonian Talmud. In what
remains of this chapter, I shall show how late-ancient heteroglossic
texts, texts that explicitly and implicitly thematize the incongruous,
and especially the genres known as Menippean, provide the best models for an understanding of the Babylonian Talmud as a whole text.

Bakhtin's account of the literary category (genre/genres) of what
the Hellenistic world terms *spoudogeloion* as a genus of genres at the
end of classical antiquity and in the Hellenistic/Roman period proves
a highly productive instrument for describing the Babylonian Talmud
as a literary text. Bakhtin lays out three major characteristics of late
ancient seriocomic text types. The first of these is that rather than
dealing with the absolute past of myth and legend, "the subject of serious representation" is presented "on the plane of the present day, in a
zone of immediate and even crudely familiar contact with living contemporaries." The bulk of the talmudic literature is, indeed, about the
lives and opinions of the Rabbis, "living contemporaries," as it were.
Secondly, "the genres of the seriocomical do not rely on *legend* and do
not sanctify themselves through it." Instead they rely on experience
and free invention. This continues the first point; there is virtually
nothing of the "mythical"—which is what Bakhtin seems to mean by
"legend"—in tone in the rabbinic literature and especially the Talmuds, in this case in either Talmud. It is, however, the third characteristic identified by Bakhtin that makes the seriocomical most relevant
for the study of the Bavli in particular, namely "the deliberate multistyled and hetero-voiced nature of all these genres." The decorum, the
stylistic unity, that characterizes the serious genres of epic, tragedy,
epideictic rhetoric, lyric (and, I would add, the law) are all rejected in
favor of a "multi-toned narration," in which we find "a mixing of high
and low, serious and comic." Broad use is made of "inserted genres—
letters, found manuscripts, retold dialogues," multilinguality, and singly, doubly, triply masked authors.[32] With respect to the Menippean

---

32. Bakhtin, *Problems of Dostoevsky's Poetics,* 108. See too p. 118, where the point is made
again in slightly different terms. For a quite different, but interestingly parallel, account
of absolute difference between epic and novel, see José Ortega y Gasset, "The Nature
of the Novel," *Hudson Review* 10 (1957): 14–15. Ortega y Gasset, like Bakhtin, considers
genre to be of great ideological significance: "The Epic, for example, is not the name of a
poetic form but of a basic poetic content which reaches fulfillment in the process of its

satire, perhaps the most relevant of the genres for the Talmud, Bakhtin
writes, "The presence of inserted genres reinforces the multi-styled
and multi-toned nature of the menippea; what is coalescing here is a
new relationship to the word as the material of literature, a relationship characteristic for the entire dialogic line of development in artistic prose."[33] While not manifesting all of these characteristics, certainly not in equal degree, the Babylonian Talmud seems to appear best
as a literary *work* when seen in the context of this literary milieu, as an
instance of this form of literary taste. I think and hope to persuade that
Menippean satire and the related genres of late Hellenism provide an
illuminating lens through which to read the Babylonian Talmud.

Although, as I have mentioned, there has been much discussion
in the halls of classical academe as to the actual historical validity of
Bakhtin's identification of a specific genre (or rather in the scope he
claims for it),[34] there can be no doubt, I think, that he has captured
in his descriptions something vital and vitally important in the literary taste or mood of late antiquity, a certain knowing breaking of
decorum, a mixing together (whether organically or not; I think not)
of that which had been kept carefully apart before. What we have
here is not so much genre as a literary and even cultural mood.[35] Seen
in that light, we could consider the "collisions" of which Bakhtin
speaks between the "lofty" and the "slum naturalism" of the menippea as a system that has as its goal the illumination of one language
by another, or dialogism in its most powerful sense. The literary taste
reflected by this widespread cultural form in the *Kulturgebiet* is especially characterized by violations of decorum, by the yoking together
of that which in other times and places would be kept distinct. The
essential aspect of this set of literary practices is that it is the product

---

expansion or manifestation. Lyric poetry is not a conventional idiom into which may be
translated what has already been said in a dramatic or novelistic idiom, but at one and the
same time a certain thing to be said and the only way to say it fully" (11–12). I shall discuss
these points further in chapter 8 of this book.

33. Bakhtin, *Problems of Dostoevsky's Poetics,* 118.

34. *Bakhtin and the Classics,* ed. Robert Bracht Branham, Rethinking Theory (Evanston,
Ill.: Northwestern University Press, 2002); *The Bakhtin Circle and Ancient Narrative,* ed.
Robert Bracht Branham, Ancient Narrative (Groningen: Barkhuis Groningen University
Library, 2005). Both of these collections of essays are uncommonly rich and important,
but see especially Branham's "The Poetics of Genre: Bakhtin, Menippus, Petronius," in
The Bakhtin Circle and Ancient Narrative, 3–31.

35. This point was clarified for me by Burrus, "Mimicking Virgins," esp. pp. 50–51.

of intellectuals, and the intellectuals themselves are also the subjects and objects of its narratives.

Fish-Horses and Goat-Stags: The Late Ancient Poetics of the Incongruous

Lucian, more than most writers before such postmoderns as Laurence Sterne, seems acutely self-consciously aware of his transgressive project. There are two things that render Lucian's works (or at least some of them) bee-orchids or centaurs (to anticipate Lucian's own terminology below): The first is the deliberate mixing of genres. This textual practice is elaborated by Lucian in a little text entirely dedicated to this theme, "To One Who Said 'You're a Prometheus in Words.'"[36] In this text, the speaker, Lucian, is responding (as the title suggests) to one who has compared him to Prometheus. He cleverly deflects the compliment, if indeed it was meant as a compliment, comparing rather the interlocutor, a lawyer, to Prometheus: "Yet how much more just would it be to compare to Prometheus all you people who win fame by fighting real battles in the courts! What you do is truly alive and breathing and, yes, its heat is that of fire." Meanwhile Lucian presents himself with ironic—if not mock—modesty as a mere entertainer: "So it's occurring to me to wonder whether you are calling me Prometheus as the comic poet called Cleon Prometheus. He says of him, you remember, 'Cleon's a Prometheus after the event.'"

But now, a (hypothetical) voice comforts Lucian by informing him that it was his Promethean originality to which the panegyrist referred. After referring to marvels and wonders of originality brought to Egypt by Ptolemy, including camels, Lucian remarks:

> I am afraid that my work too is a camel in Egypt and people admire its bridle and its sea-purple, since even the combination of those two very fine creations, dialogue and comedy, is not enough for beauty of form if the blending lacks harmony and symmetry.[37]

---

36. Lucian of Samosata, "To One Who Said 'You're a Prometheus in Words,'" in *Lucian VI*, with an English translation by A. M. Harmon, 8 vols., Loeb Classics (London: W. Heinemann, 1913–67), 418–27.

37. Lucian of Samosata, "Prometheus," 427.

This is a highly sophisticated reflection on creativity and originality. Having been called a Prometheus, the very type of the creative artist (we refer even today to a Promethean creator), Lucian protests that he is only a bricoleur, and the appearance of creativity is only the placing of things in a context in which they have never been, like a camel in Egypt. Moreover, on that occasion the Egyptians notoriously admired the trappings of the camel and not the camel itself, as Lucian fears his readers will admire his work for its outside beauty and novelty and not see its potential flaws.

This sentence is then followed by the remarkable passage in which Lucian explicitly describes his work as a monstrous combination of erstwhile enemies, dialogue ("Socrates") and comedy (Aristophanes). Lucian mocks those who would see him as original, for as he says, his originality consists in the making of fish-horses and goat-stags. Lucian clearly indicates his awareness of what he is doing in his mixtures of genres, in his production of these hybrid forms. He is deliberately confounding not only Socrates in the *Phaedrus,* with his famous demand that discourses (*logoi*) have an organic shape with middles that are in proportion to their extremities, but also Horace, who wrote that "the poetic body must avoid the monstrous conjugation of foreign parts."[38]

In a characteristically hilarious piece, known in English as the "Double Indictment" (or "Twice Accused"), Lucian produces precisely such a monstrous copulation. Even at Lucian's late date, dialogue and rhetoric were considered two mutually exclusive opposing principles and discursive practices with directly opposing ideological entailments. After a brilliant opening speech from Zeus about how busy the gods are, Zeus decides to go ahead anyway and try a bunch of outstanding court cases, including two related ones: *Rhetoric v. the Syrian* and *Dialogue v. the Syrian,* the Syrian (thematized as anonymous)[39] being, of course, none other than Lucian himself.[40] It is quite clear

38. This analysis makes problematic Bakhtin's earlier assumption that what seems incongruous to modern eyes was not so in antiquity; Mikhail Bakhtin, *Rabelais and His World,* trans. Hélène Iswolsky (Bloomington: Indiana University Press, 1984), 108–9. Lucian, at any rate, seems exquisitely aware of the chimera he creates.

39. Goldhill, "Becoming Greek."

40. Lucian of Samosata, "The Double Indictment," in *Lucian III,* with an English translation by A. M. Harmon, 8 vols., Loeb Classics (London: W. Heinemann, 1913–67), 113.

from the content of these two lawsuits, one by Rhetoric for Lucian having loved her and left her for Dialogue and one by Dialogue for Lucian having dragged him down into the dirt, that these are considered binary opposites in Lucian's world, one associated with sophism and the other with *philosophia.*

By taking the very metier of the philosophers, the dialogue, and using it to produce (Menippean) satires, Lucian is at once undermining the dignity of this "most serious" of discursive forms in the sociolect of his time and also using it precisely against its own devoted practitioners, the philosophers. He has Dialogue accuse him:

> I was formerly dignified, and pondered upon the gods and nature and the cycle of the universe, treading the air high up above the clouds where "Great Zeus in heaven driving his winged car" sweeps on; but he dragged me down when I was already soaring above the zenith and mounting on "heaven's back," and broke my wings, putting me on the same level as the common herd. Moreover, he took away from me the respectable tragic mask that I had, and put another upon me that is comic, satyr-like, and almost ridiculous. Then he unceremoniously penned me up with Jest and Satire and Cynicism and Eupolis and Aristophanes, terrible men for mocking all that is holy and scoffing at all that is right. At last he even dug up and thrust in upon me Menippus, a prehistoric dog, with very loud bark, it seems, and sharp fangs, *a really dreadful dog who bites unexpectedly because he grins when he bites.*
>
> What is most monstrous of all, I have been turned into a surprising blend, for I am neither afoot nor ahorseback, neither prose nor verse, but seem to my hearers a strange phenomenon made up of different elements, like a Centaur.[41]

This is a typically Lucianic bit of urbane humor. "Dialogue," which is not only the literary genre but also a cipher for its most prominent exponent, "Socrates," was formerly dignified and serious. His pursuits were so lofty that he was above the clouds, but, lately Lucian has dragged him down, mixed up his high seriousness with comedy, with *geloion,* with cynicism, and even, perish the thought, with Aristo-

---

41. Lucian of Samosata, "The Double Indictment," 147 (emphasis mine). On this text, see too Goldhill, "Becoming Greek," 72–73.

phanes. Part of the humor in this is, of course, that Socratic floating among the clouds already mixes him up with Aristophanes. But the most awful fate of all for Dialogue is to have been turned into a baggy monster, neither fish nor fowl, but a hybrid such as a centaur.

This complaint is seconded in the satirical dialogue "The Fisherman," in which no less than Diogenes goes on the attack. Speaking to Philosophia, he rants:

> What is worst of all, in doing this sort of thing, Philosophy, he shelters himself under your name, and he has suborned Dialogue, our serving-man, employing him against us as a helper and a spokesman. Moreover, he has actually bribed Menippus, a comrade of ours, to take part in his farces frequently; he is the only one who is not here and does not join us in the prosecution, thereby playing traitor to our common cause.[42]

I think it important to note that in both of these citations, Lucian is explicitly projecting himself as accused of having suborned, not only Dialogue, but Menippus the Cynic himself (and thus Diogenes' colleague). This suggests, at least probably, that Lucian sees himself as the inventor of the Menippean dialogue (not, of course, the Menippean satire per se; that was, at least, current from Varro). Why does Lucian suborn Dialogue and bribe Menippus? To what end? Whatever levels of irony or indirection there are in this text, it is hard not to consider it under the sign of an authorial agency, albeit represented as a prisoner on the block. "Lucian" has certainly, it seems, committed literary crimes. Although somewhat discredited in the most recent scholarship, the humanist insight that what characterizes Lucian's work is a combination of humor and serious intent (comparing him to Voltaire) seems to me discerning.[43] I have ideas, however, about

42. Lucian of Samosata, "The Dead Come to Life, or the Fisherman," in *Lucian III*, with an English translation by A. M. Harmon, 8 vols., Loeb Classics (London: W. Heinemann, 1913–67), 43.

43. Joseph William Hewitt, "A Second Century Voltaire," *Classical Journal* 20, no. 3 (December 1924): 132–42; but note also Bywater's comment: "As for the hackneyed comparison between him and Voltaire, Prof. Bernays very rightly maintains that the comparison is superficial, and in every way unfair to Voltaire. Lucian lacked among other things the varied knowledge, the intellectual sincerity, the revolt at injustice and oppression of the great Frenchman; and his ambition was to end his days as a Roman official." I. Bywater,

how this plays out in Lucian different from the older interpretations, which tended to think in terms of either *dulce et utile* or to argue that Lucian's satire is directed against certain philosophies and not others to which he is deemed to cleave.[44] In my view, Lucian's invention of Menippean satire is precisely in service of a dialogical, deeply anti-logistic involvement with philosophy.

The assault on philosophy is palpable. Lucian's entire dialogue "Lives for Sale" consists of bitter mockery of every single one of the philosophical schools of his day, without exception. And the "philosophers," it seems, responded in kind (at least in fictional kind), as Lucian himself records at the very beginning of his "The Fisherman":

> Pelt, pelt the scoundrel with plenty of stones! Heap him with clods! Pile him up with broken dishes, too! Beat the blackguard with your sticks! Look out he doesn't get away! Throw, Plato; you, too Chrysippus; you too; everybody at once! Let's charge him together.

"Socrates" is the speaker! A more direct statement of enmity between "Lucian" and philosophy/philosophers seems hardly possible.

According to Joel Relihan, the point of it all is to indict those who believe that they have vision enough to understand human society and right its wrongs, but are sadly mistaken in their conviction.[45] Those who think they have the answers are far more dangerous than those who know they don't. This can be exemplified (if not fully justified) by reference to a passage in Lucian's *Icaromenippus*. Menippus has managed to rise to heaven, where he is being conducted on a guided tour by Zeus. Zeus, having complained that the people are no longer sacrificing to him but to other gods, continues: "Consequently, you can see for yourself that my altars are more frigid than the Laws of Plato or the Syllogisms of Chrysippus" (τοιγαροῦν ψυχροτέρους ἄν μου τοὺς βωμοὺς ἴδοις τῶν Πλάτωνος νόμων ἢ τῶν Χρυσίππου συλλογισμῶν)

"Bernays' Lucian and the Cynics," *Journal of Hellenic Studies* 1 (1880): 302. Without rendering any judgment pro or con about fairness to Voltaire, about whom I know next to nothing, this strikes me, nevertheless, as a judgment most unfair to Lucian, whom I would in any case compare rather to that other great Frenchman, Rabelais.

44. For discussion, see A. S. Alexiou, "Philosophers in Lucian" (Ph.D. diss., Fordham University, 1990), 10, microfilm.

45. Joel C. Relihan, *Ancient Menippean Satire* (Baltimore: Johns Hopkins University Press, 1993), 30.

(24.24).[46] This comment, rendered by a brilliant double meaning, plays on the physical meaning of frigidity (the altars) and the moral meanings, haughty, formal but empty (the philosophers). The great ethical philosophies are implicitly being accused of providing no virtue at all but only frigid speculation that does no work in the world; this is a complaint that is particularly ironic given that still in Lucian's time, the prime importance of a philosophy was as a way of life.[47] Witness Lucian's own texts, a satirical comparison of philosophies, called *"Lives* for Sale" (emphasis mine).

Lucian is not, however, a mere impeacher of philosophy. In texts such as "Zeus Catechized," it has been long noted, Lucian presents a sober and very praiseworthy cynic philosopher. Even more to the point is his unambiguously positive portrayal of Demonax, his teacher, also a cynic. As Eunapius wrote, "Lucian of Samosata, a man serious in his pursuit of laughter, wrote a life of Demonax, a man of that time, and in that work and very few others was completely serious."[48] A. S. Alexiou's recent dissertation on Lucian starkly poses the dilemma: "Sometimes Lucian presents the philosopher in glowing terms, and at other times most negatively. Why is this so?"[49] Another scholar, Susan Prince, has shown that even Lucian's critique of Plato is not without its ambivalences: "Lucian builds his most positive portraits of knowledge and other appropriate epistemological attitudes out of terms and images he borrows from one of Plato's most famous and extended statements about philosophical knowledge, in the sequence of the Sun, the Line, and the Cave in *Republic* 6–7. This sequence is not without its own fantastic premises, in the Cave analogy,

---

46. Lucian of Samosata, "Icaromenippus, or the Sky-Man," in *Lucian II,* with an English translation by A.M. Harmon, 8 vols., Loeb Classics (London: W. Heinemann, 1913–67), 311.

47. Pierre Hadot, *What Is Ancient Philosophy?* (Cambridge, Mass.: Harvard University Press, 2002).

48. The Loeb gives, "Lucian of Samosata, who usually took serious pains to raise a laugh, wrote a life of Demonax, a philosopher of his own time, and in that book and a very few others was wholly serious throughout." Wilmer Cave France Wright, ed. and trans., *Philostratus: The Lives of the Sophists; Eunapius: Lives of the Philosophers* (Cambridge, Mass.: Harvard University Press, 1998), 349. See too Lawrence Giangrande, *The Use of Spoudaiogeloion in Greek and Roman Literature* (The Hague: Mouton, 1972), 99; and R. Bracht Branham, *Unruly Eloquence: Lucian and the Comedy of Traditions,* Revealing Antiquity (Cambridge, Mass.: Harvard University Press, 1989), 26–27.

49. Alexiou, "Philosophers in Lucian," 1.

but it also has serious commitments to a higher alternative world of the Forms, the objects of real knowledge transcendent over the world of material and change which we all think we know. In *Icaromenippus,* in particular, Menippus' ascent into a good epistemic state does, despite the fantasy of its presentation, also enable him the sort of real, serious knowledge we find Lucian endorsing routinely in more straightforward ways throughout his corpus as well as here, knowledge of the real nature of human life beneath its deceits."[50] This discrepancy has been so striking that Jakob Bernays proposed a change of heart on Lucian's part with the prophilosophy texts coming from an earlier period in his life, before he turned against the philosophers and especially the cynics.[51] Our explanatory tastes run different from those of the nineteenth century, preferring as we do to allow such *dissoi logoi* to persist in an author and his or her corpus rather than arbitrarily harmonizing through hypothetical biographical tallyings. C. P. Jones has perhaps articulated this paradox most sharply: "Lucian's treatment of philosophy is at once a central feature of his works and one of the most paradoxical. When he aims his satire at targets such as religious belief or magic, he often does so by making philosophy their defender or representative; when he mocks vices like hypocrisy or venality, he often incorporates them in philosophers. Yet in other works he claims an interest in philosophy or praises individual philosophers . . . "[52] This double movement of praise and blame at once is exactly what we have been defining as the major trait of Menippean satire. In other words, I am suggesting that Lucian chose (or

50. Susan Prince, "The Discourse of Philosophy in Lucian's Fantastic Worlds," typescript (Cincinnati, 2007). I am grateful to Professor Prince for giving me permission to read and cite this essay prior to its publication.

51. Jakob Bernays, *Lucian und die Kyniker. Von Jacob Bernays. Mit einer Übersetzung der Schrift Lucians über das Lebensende des Peregrinus* (Berlin: W. Hertz, 1879), 48–52. See discussion in Alexiou, "Philosophers in Lucian," 30.

52. C. P. Jones, *Culture and Society in Lucian* (Cambridge, Mass.: Harvard University Press, 1986), 24. Jones, himself, comes to some rather counterintuitive conclusions, writing, "Lucian's treatment of the various schools, therefore, is more nuanced than would be expected if his knowledge came solely from books. Certainly many of his jokes are found in earlier writing, not only comedy but epigram. It does not follow, however, that because his typical philosopher has a long beard and knitted eyebrows, he is cut out of paper: that would only be likely if Lucian's picture differed greatly from that drawn by his contemporaries, which is not the case" (31–32). To my mind, the argument should exactly be reversed; it is the fact that Lucian's descriptions are so nearly identical to those of his contemporaries that suggest strongly that he is manipulating stereotypes and topoi.

invented!) the *Menippean* dialogue precisely because it is a medium for articulating the "second accent," the "crude contradiction" of which Bakhtin speaks. Only a suborned, Menippean dialogue can speak crude contradiction, and not the dignified, philosophical dialogue that was formerly known.

It does seem important to me to pay attention to different genres in the Lucianic corpus. Without, I think, entirely realizing the import of what she says, Alexiou remarks, "Most of [Lucian's] works in which philosophers are important fall under the category of the satiric dialogue."[53] This is hardly a mere consequence of the time and place in Lucian's life in which he was writing them;[54] that is, that he happened to be writing in the dialogue form at a time when he was in a mood to deal with philosophy—an answer all too similar to that of Bernays, rejected—rightly—by Alexiou. I propose, rather, that the satirical dialogue is the medium for Lucian's discourse on philosophy because it is the satirical dialogue, the satire on Dialogue, the suborned (transgendered) ancilla of philosophy, that constitutes Lucian's literary invention in the discourse about philosophy. The function of this kind of mixture of the serious and the comic is, as R. Bracht Branham puts it, exactly "to provoke the reader to consider the material at hand from humorously divergent perspectives. The complexity of effect that he achieves by interweaving serious and ludicrous qualities distinguishes his work by endowing his most characteristic texts with a peculiar kind of comic ambivalence."[55] The humorous and the comic are, together with the serious, here the instruments, not the goal; the goal is indeed to produce a genuinely dialogical text in which the issue can be seen from divergent perspectives, in themselves neither comic nor serious, the simultaneous illumination of one language by another.[56]

Another example of a textual fish-horse would be Petronius,

53. Alexiou, "Philosophers in Lucian," 33.
54. Alexiou, "Philosophers in Lucian," 34.
55. R. Bracht Branham, "The Comic as Critic: Revenging Epicurus—A Study of Lucian's Comic Narrative," *Classical Antiquity* 3, no. 2 (1984): 162–63.
56. See too Graham Anderson, *Lucian: Theme and Variation in the Second Sophistic,* Mnemosyne, Bibliotheca Classica Batava: Supplementum (Lugduni Batavorum: Brill, 1976), 15, who sees that Lucian is basing his self-contradiction on the sophistic topos of proof and disproof but evaluates this in an entirely different fashion from mine, seeing it as evidence of a pure desire to entertain and nothing else.

with his even more incongruous composites, and Petronius's text is marked, even by the most classical of classicists, as Menippean satire. As one important Petronian scholar has written, "Certainly a main characteristic of Menippean satire was the union of humor and philosophy."[57] One particular incident from the *Satyricon* will help me to set up my point. When we enter the text, albeit not at the beginning (as only a large fragment of the text is extant), we find a highly serious encounter under way, a discussion of that age-old topic, the vices (and virtues) of rhetoricians and professors of rhetoric (*declamatores*). The discussion takes the familiar form of a dialogue: Encolpius (the narrator-hero) is against the rhetoricians, while Agamemnon, one of their number, defends them. It needs to be emphasized that the discussion is, as far as one can tell, an earnest one. The complaints that Encolpius expresses, while somewhat formulaic, are to the point. Not at all like the Platonic attacks on rhetoric, at least in that there seems no implication of moral turpitude on the part of the professors here (or at least no more than anyone else is accused of in the satire), it is rather an argument that with the formal and florid practices of "Asiatic" style and the training in rhetoric, true eloquence has been fatally damaged. Agamemnon's answer seems earnestly meant: that the fault is not with the *declamatores* themselves (he seems to grant the point that there *is* a fault somewhere in the system) but with the parents and the society as a whole. Agamemnon himself provides an eloquent account of what education had been in Rome (in the time of Cicero perhaps?) and what it ought to be, making, at any rate, an important if not profound comment on practices of education. He finishes with quite a well-spoken "extempore" poem on education, but just then Encolpius confesses that "while I was concentrating on Agamemnon's poem, I failed to see Ascyltus slip away." On slipping away himself in search of his friend, Encolpius discovers him in a brothel, and hilarious, raunchy, and improbable adventures ensue. The *Satyrica* moreover includes other such jangling juxtapositions of serious and hilarious intercourse throughout. William Arrowsmith has described the text "as a farrago, a potpourri," arguing that incongruity is its very essence. The mixtures of prose and poetry, high and

---

57. John Patrick Sullivan, introduction to *The Satyricon by Petronius Arbiter,* trans. John Patrick Sullivan, Penguin Classics (New York: Penguin Books, 1986), 20.

low language, epic and doggerel are the very point of the text, such that "the condition of these ironies is the crisscrossing of crucial perspectives and incongruous styles: if we see how the realistic undercuts the fabulous, we should also see how the fabulous undercuts the realistic."[58] This movement of two voices constantly undercutting each other, with neither defeating the other, is the very stuff of dialogicity, of the Menippean, a kind of unremitting critique of "our own" practice that is not intended to destroy that practice and indeed does not. Or as Aristotle represents Gorgias as having put it (in a text cited as an epigraph for this book): "As for jests, since they may sometimes be useful in debates, the advice of Gorgias was good—to confound the opponents' seriousness with jest and their jest with seriousness" (Aristotle, *Rhetoric* 1419b). Moreover, if my analysis of his *Encomium to Helen* (offered above in chapter 3) bears any weight, then Gorgias exercised this principle with regard to himself as much as against opponents.

This Menippean motion in which the serious undercuts the comic and the comic the serious (or as Arrowsmith puts it: the fabulous undercuts the realistic and the realistic the fabulous) is the key to my reading of the Talmud and its doubled presentation of its heroes. It seems highly plausible that if not Petronius himself, then his sources and his literary milieu, the sociolect, were well known to the Babylonian Rabbis. Saul Lieberman showed more than half a century ago, arguing for a "common oriental source," that three proverbs known otherwise only from Petronius, as well as the famous Petronian story of the Widow of Ephesos, appear in the Babylonian Talmud.[59] It seems then not so incongruous to be thinking of Petronius and Lucian when writing of the Rabbis of the Talmud.

58. William Arrowsmith, introduction to *The Satyricon by Petronius Arbiter,* trans. William Arrowsmith (New York: New American Library, 1983), ix.

59. Saul Lieberman, *Greek in Jewish Palestine: Studies in the Life and Manners of Jewish Palestine in the II-IV Centuries C.E.* (New York: Jewish Theological Seminary of America, 1942), 152–54. He notes, moreover, that in several instances of Greco-Roman proverbs appearing in rabbinic texts, it is the Babylonians who are closer to the Hellenistic text than the Palestinians (154–57). See too Arkady B. Kovelman, "The Miletian Story of Beruria," *Vestnik Evreyskogo Universiteta* 1, no. 19 (1999): 8–23 (in Russian). On Petronius and the Milesian, see Gottskálk Jensson, *The Recollections of Encolpius: The Satyrica of Petronius as Milesian Fiction,* Ancient Narrative (Groningen: Barkhuis Publishing & Groningen University Library, 2004).

Lucian Has the Keys: The Novel, the Talmud, and the Disciplining of Epistemology

The Menippean satire, so brilliantly anatomized by Bakhtin, provides us the Rosetta Stone for a richer, less abridged appreciation of the literary character of the Babylonian Talmud, which will unveil the dialogism of the Bavli itself. In particular it offers a way for us to consider the serious and comic, the grotesque and the classic in the Talmud as part and parcel of the same literary phenomenon. To be sure, the very literary figure for whom the whole genre is named, Menippus, flourished a mere six kilometers to the north of Palestine, at Gadara, a place well known and much frequented by the rabbis, as well as such contemporaries of theirs as Iamblichus and his disciples.[60] However, autopsy of the literature itself suggests that the Menippean element is much more prominent in the rabbinic literature of Mesopotamia, the Babylonian Talmud, than in Palestine itself. At first glance, this is puzzling. As Bakhtin points out, the Menippean satire exercised a profound influence on Christian literature of late antiquity and the Byzantine period, and it is, by now, accepted on many (if not all by any means) scholarly fronts that the Babylonian Talmud and the Byzantine literature were in close contact via various literary-cultural channels, including the Syriac traditions of the Church of the East, but this does not explain why the impact could have been (on my hypothesis) greater in Babylonia than in Palestine.

A very tentative and speculative approach to a solution may be offered. Dimitri Gutas has argued that precisely the Eastern Christian milieu of Iraq was much more receptive to certain aspects of secular Greek culture and learning than the "Orthodox" Byzantine Christians of, for instance, Damascus.[61] Might this be at least a partial, tentative explanation for the apparent greater presence of the Menippean in Babylonian than in Palestinian rabbinic texts? Or does it have to do with a different, more cynical, mood among the Rabbis of Babylonia than of Palestine? Time, perhaps, will tell.

However it came to be, there are several important ways in which

---

60. Martin Hengel, with Christof Markschies, *The "Hellenization" of Judaea in the First Century after Christ* (London: SCM Press, 1989), 20.

61. Dimitri Gutas, *Greek Thought, Arab Culture: The Graeco-Arabic Translation Movement in Baghdad and Early 'Abbāsid Society* (New York: Routledge, 1998), 17–20.

the text of the Bavli is Menippean. First of all, many of the legends themselves partake of the generic feast that characterizes the Menippean menu. There are stories of meetings between rabbis and heavenly figures, of deaths and miraculous resurrections, as well as "mésalliances, disguises and mystifications, contrasting paired images, scandals, crowning/decrownings, and so forth."[62] Most importantly, as in Bakhtin's description of the carnivalized legends of late antiquity, so too in the rabbinic legends, the very carnivalization "made possible the transfer of ultimate questions from the abstractly philosophical sphere, . . . to the concretely sensuous plane of images and events."[63] In these kinds of biographical legends, rabbis find themselves cheek by jowl with rulers, rich men, thieves, beggars, and hetaerae, the cast of characters of the menippea.[64] I wish to emphasize, however, that my point is not that the narrative as such is Menippean, while the dialectic of the *sugya* is something else. Rather, as I have been maintaining, it is the concatenation of the dialectic as (generally) the most dignified of verbal practices within the Bavli with the most undignified of descriptions of its very heroes that constitutes the text as comparable to Menippean satire. It is exactly that heterogeneity that has been least appreciated in standard readings of the Bavli, both traditionalist and critical-scholarly.

Like the Menippean satire—indeed, characteristic of this form as opposed to other satire—the Bavli too does "not comment upon such theories and moralizings in order to suggest other ways of thinking about literature and behavior, but rather concentrate[s] on the incongruity of the life and theories of its preachers."[65] As pointed out by the Soviet critic L. E. Pinsky, "Rabelais' laughter simultaneously denies and asserts, or more correctly speaking it seeks and hopes like the very company of the 'thirsting Pantagruelists.' Boundless enthusiasm concerning knowledge and cautious irony alternate with each other. The very tone of this laughter shows that two opposite prin-

---

62. Bakhtin, *Problems of Dostoevsky's Poetics,* 133. In this regard, one of the classic moments of menippea in talmudic literature is surely the scene in which Elijah reports to us that at the moment of his defeat, as it were, in halakhic reasoning by Rabbi Yehoshua‘, God laughed, declaring, "My children have defeated me."

63. Bakhtin, *Problems of Dostoevsky's Poetics,* 134.

64. Bakhtin, *Problems of Dostoevsky's Poetics,* 135.

65. Relihan, *Ancient Menippean Satire,* 97.

ciples can be put together even in form."[66] While hardly a perfect match for the tone of either Plato or the Talmud, this description—I would argue—comes close to characterizing the work of the author of the Babylonian Talmud. For, as I have begun showing, it is in this Jewish text above all others that "boundless enthusiasm concerning knowledge and cautious irony alternate with each other." This is the argument that I hope to make defensible through the discussion of the Bavli that follows in the rest of this and the next chapter.

My argument relies, of course, on the assumption that literary form is inseparably implicated in ideology. Holquist writes that "'novel' is the name Bakhtin gives to whatever force is at work within a given literary system to reveal the limits, the artificial constraints of the system."[67] The "novel"—and its earlier cognate form, the Menippean satire—is thus the space within the literary system within which dialogism is introduced, that is, dialogue between the literary system and its own limits. As Bakhtin explains, "When the novel becomes the dominant genre, epistemology becomes the dominant discipline";[68] this is precisely the sort of self-reflectivity on the Bavli's own knowledge/lack of knowledge that I would claim is produced through the heterogeneous and incongruent concatenation of its diverse incorporated genres and materials. Perhaps one could say, at least as a *jeu d'esprit*, that when epistemology is the dominant concern, discourse will look more and more like a novel.

The Epistemology of the Water Pipe

One of the most analyzed passages in all of the Babylonian Talmud, the famous story of the Stove of Akhnai, can be given yet another turn of the hermeneutical screw. The tale relates how Rabbi Eli'ezer disagreed with all his fellows on the purity or impurity of a certain kind of stove, built up with coils of clay like a snake, hence its nick-

---

66. L. E. Pinsky, *Realism of the Renaissance* (Moscow: Goslitizdat, 1961), 183 (in Russian), cited Bakhtin, *Rabelais*, 142.

67. Michael Holquist, introduction to *The Dialogic Imagination: Four Essays by Mikhail Bakhtin*, ed. Michael Holquist, trans. Michael Holquist and Caryl Emerson, University of Texas Press Slavic Series (Austin: University of Texas Press, 1981), xxxi.

68. Mikhail Bakhtin, "Epic and Novel," in *The Dialogic Imagination: Four Essays*, ed. Michael Holquist, trans. Michael Holquist and Caryl Emerson, University of Texas Press Slavic Series (Austin: University of Texas Press, 1981), 15.

name the "Stove of Akhnai," or "Snake Stove." Rabbi Eli'ezer began with a mighty effort to persuade his colleagues rationally, but to no avail:

> On that day, Rabbi Eli'ezer used every imaginable argument, but they did not accept it from him. He said: "If the law is as I say, this carob will prove it." The carob was uprooted from its place one hundred feet. Some report four hundred feet. They said to him, "One does not quote a carob as proof." He further said to them, "If the law is as I say, the water pipe will prove it." The water began to flow backwards. They said to him, "One may not quote a water-pipe as proof." Again, he said to them, "If the law is as I say, the walls of the house of study will prove it." The walls of the house of study leaned over to fall. Rabbi Yehoshua' rebuked them, saying to them, "If the disciples of the wise are striving with each other for the law, what have you to do with it?" They did not fall because of the honor of Rabbi Yehoshua', and did not stand straight for the honor of Rabbi Eli'ezer. He said to them, "If the law is as I say, let it be proven from heaven." A voice came from heaven and announced: "The law is in accordance with the view of Rabbi Eli'ezer." Rabbi Yehoshua' stood on his feet and said "it [the Torah] is not in heaven." (Baba Metsia 59a)

This story has been written about by now a hundred times in the last twenty years (not to speak of all that went before).[69] Not least by me, it has always been read "straight" and interpreted in various ways—deconstructively or not—but always as a self-laudatory comment by the Rabbis on their own hermeneutic independence even from a divine author who has given them permission to interpret on their own. I am not trying here to displace or discredit that reading tradition if I find now a certain satirical element in the narrative as well.[70] The notion of trees, walls, and streams being conduits for the word of God is finally, or so it seems to me now, as fantastical as the notion of Menippus tying an eagle wing to one arm and a vulture wing

---

69. See especially Charlotte Fonrobert, "When the Rabbi Weeps: On Reading Gender in Talmudic Aggada," *Nashim: A Journal of Jewish Women's Studies and Gender Issues* 4 (2001): 56–83, who refers to it as the most studied aggada in the whole Talmud.

70. It is true that to a person with a hammer, everything looks like a nail, but I take the risk to expose the possible "nailiness" of this text along with others.

to the other and flying to heaven. It is difficult to imagine the Rabbis believing literally in such a story (and no former interpretations that I know of were dependent on this assumption either). Hence we have here a literary text par excellence which is to be interpreted with all the tools in the kit of the literary reader. There is no theoretical difficulty in allowing this story to be both serious in one register and satirical in another at one and the same time. Indeed, this might be the perfect representation of dialogicality. So let it be, as it has already been read, a representation of the late Babylonian rabbinic self-understanding of revelation and interpretation, one that fully recognizes the gap between the "intentions" of authors, even Auth-rs, but at the same time recognizes the self-critical, self-reflective moment in a narrative that explicitly claims that the Rabbis know better than God what the text means and what the Law is. The form of the text certainly fits, as well, into the Menippean mode of conversations between heaven and earth and fantastical occurrences. In particular, a little coda appended to this story points in this direction, according to which, "Rabbi Nathan met the Prophet Elijah, and asked him: 'What was the Holy One doing at that moment?' He said: God laughed and said, "My children have defeated me! My children have defeated me!"" This is, of course, a perfect little Menippean satire of its own. This argument will, I hope, become stronger when this text is considered together with and in light of the next one that I will treat.

The following narrative of the death of one of the greatest of the Babylonian rabbis can be read as a virtual companion piece to the story of the Stove of Akhnai.[71] The text is found in Baba Metsia 86a:

> Rav Kahana said that Ḥama the son of the daughter of Ḥasa [said]: Rabba the son of Naḥmani died because of a persecution:
>
> [Some people] went and slandered him before the King, saying: "There is a man among the Jews who removes thirteen thousand Jews from the liturgies for a month in the summer and a month in the winter." They sent the officer after him. He ran away to the castle and from the castle to the meadow and from the meadow to Šḥin and from Šḥin to ṣerifa d"Ena and from ṣerifa d"Ena to the Fountain of Waters and from the Fountain of Waters to Pum Beditha, where he

---

71. As I was first made aware of by Jonathan Boyarin.

found him. The officer happened to [come to] the same inn in which he [Rabba] was. They brought the table before him, and they gave him one glass and he took another glass, and they took away the table from him.[72] He became ill. They said to him [Rabba]: What should we do? We know that he is the king's man. He said to them: Go and bring the table to him again, and give him one glass and then take the table from him. They did so, and he became well.

Rabba, the leader of Babylonian rabbinic Judaism in his time, is denounced to the authorities because he had a custom (continuing an earlier one) of gathering Jews by the hundreds to study Torah for two months a year, one in the fall and one in the spring (although we will see by the end of the story, his death is not by any means, or only very ironically so, owing to this custom of his). Incognito in an inn, he is nevertheless found there by the officer sent to arrest him. The officer drinks two cups of wine. Now, according to Babylonian rabbinic magic, doing things in even numbers is dangerous, so the officer becomes ill. The Jews (I assume they were Jews protecting and hiding their rabbi) become afraid, for if the officer dies on their watch, as it were, they will be in deep trouble. Rabba proposes to offer one more glass of wine to the officer, in order that he will have an odd number, which they do, and the officer, quite appropriately for the story, recovers, whereupon

he said: "I know that the man who is wanted by me is here." He looked for him and he found him. He [officer] said: "I will go from here: If they kill that man [speaking of himself], I will not reveal, but if they whip him, I will reveal." He [officer] put him [rabbi] into the room and closed the door in his face. He said, "I will depend on a miracle." He prayed. The walls fell down, and he ran away and went to the meadow, where he was sitting on the stump of a palm tree and he was studying.

The officer realizes that it is Rabba who has saved his life. Even though he has found the rabbi, he decides to save the rabbi's life, saying (to himself) that he will not reveal where Rabba is unless he be

72. In this sentence, I have followed the reading of the Hamburg manuscript, which is much clearer.

tortured, even if they kill him.[73] He hides him in a room. Rabba, it seems, invokes a miracle through his prayers and the walls fall down, whereupon he escapes again to the meadow, sits down on a stump, and begins studying the Torah. These walls falling down are almost an echo of the walls that didn't quite fall down in the Stove of Akhnai. While Rabba is studying,

> he heard that[74] they were disagreeing in the Heavenly Yeshiva: "If the *baheret* appears before the white hair, he is impure, and if the white hair appears before the *baheret,* he is pure. If it is a doubtful case, The Holy Blessed One says that he is pure and all of the Heavenly Yeshiva say that he is impure." They said: "Who shall we ask? Let's ask Rabba the son of Naḥmani, for Rabba bar Naḥmani says: 'I am unmatched in matters of skin diseases; I am unmatched in matters of deaths in the tent.'" The Angel of Death could not get close to him, because he was not silent for even a moment from his study. While this was happening, a wind came and blew in the canebrakes. He thought it was a troop of cavalry. He said, "Let that man die and not be delivered into the hands of the king." He was silent, and he died.[75] As he died, he said: "It is pure; it is pure." A voice went out from heaven and said: "Blessed art thou, Rabba the son of Naḥmani, for your body is pure, and your soul departed on 'pure.'"

This is an absolutely astonishing story. Having informed us in the incipit to the story that Rabba died owing to persecution, the story goes on to let us see that it is actually only through a wild series of events, set in motion perhaps by the persecution, that his death results, if even that may be claimed. As it turns out, it is a combination of several factors that is responsible for Rabba's death. First of all, he finds himself alone studying Torah in a canebrake (all right; that was caused—indirectly—by the persecution), which enables him to hear what is going on in the heavenly yeshiva; secondly, they are having trouble up there: God is on one side of a halakhic argument and

---

73. This is the interpretation of the sixteenth-century Maharsha; I see no better one.
74. These words are only in the manuscript, but from the continuation of the story even in the print, we can see that Rabba knew what was going on in the heavenly Study House.
75. This sentence only found in the manuscript.

all the rest of the yeshiva is on the other. In the Stove of Akhnai it is Rabbi Eliᶜezer on one side against all of *his* fellows, and God, as it were, sends messages to help him. Third, owing to his own boasting (at least in some versions of the story) and his pre-eminence in Torah in any case, he is called to the heavenly yeshiva to render his definitive opinion on the matter. His own ceaseless study prevents him, however, from being taken by the Angel of Death to perform the holy office, until through a ruse involving a wind—again some manuscripts make the ruse explicit—he is distracted for a moment from study and taken up dead to heaven, where he decides the case for the minority of One, God. He receives the appropriate approbations. The death itself is caused by anything but a human, gentile persecution. One could even say that the gentile officer, the ostensible persecutor, in fact *saves* Rabba's life, and it is God who kills him. If, indeed, then, Rabba dies as a result of a persecution, it is, as it were, divine persecution that kills him.

This story is, in a strong sense, a counterstory to the more famous one that we have just read. If there the insistence is that Torah is not in heaven but on earth and fully rational, decidable by a majority and not by an individual authority, here—quite comically—we find that the Torah is exactly in heaven so that our poor rabbi has to be taken before his time to heaven in order to settle a dispute there. The authority of God is still not enough, even up there; it has to be supported by the one who boasts of himself (truly indeed) that he is the most learned in the field of that dispute, thus once again placing the authoritative decision not in the hands of he who makes the best argument but of the one who has the greatest authority, even when that one is not the author. A final clue to the association of these two counternarratives is the fact that in the entire rabbinic corpus, only in these two stories do we find the trope of a sage dying with the word "pure" on his lips. At the end of his life, "the [sages then] said to Rabbi Eliᶜezer: A ball, a slipper, and a cameo that are [made of leather and filled with wool]. He said to them: They are pure. And his soul left him in purity." Indeed since this trope fits so much better in the former story than here, for there the "purity" of the rabbi in question was an issue, it might almost seem as if it were cited here to set up an intertextual exchange between the two narratives. Whereas oracles meant nothing there, here oracles mean everything, as we shall see from the continuation, for the story is not over yet.

Rabba's body lies a mold'ring in the meadow, so more heavenly communications are necessary:

> A sherd fell from heaven in Pum Beditha: Rabba the son of Naḥmani has been requested in the Heavenly Yeshiva. Abbaye and Rava went out to busy themselves with him [with burying him], but they did not know where he was. They went out to the meadow and they saw some birds that were making shade for him and not moving from the spot. They said: Deduce from this that that is where he is! They mourned him for three days and three nights and then they wished to leave. A sherd fell from heaven: Whoever leaves will be excommunicated. They mourned him for seven days. A sherd fell saying to them: Go to your homes in peace!

Through a combination of great talmudic detective powers and heavenly communications by the usual Babylonian talmudic method of ostraca falling from heaven with inscriptions, Rabba's two main disciples back in the city find out that he is dead and lying in a meadow. The term used by the narrator to signify their deduction from the birds that this is where the body is, is itself the mock-heroic "deduce from this [shmaʿ minnah]," which is typically used at the conclusion of a successful talmudic logical proof. They go out to the place and mourn him there for three days, upon which they decide to go back home, but a further ostracon informs them that they'd better not do so. After the seventh day of prescribed mourning, however, another ostracon tells them to go home.

The story is now over, save two more fantastical incidents:

> On the day that Rabba the son of Naḥmani died, a wind came up and lifted up a bedouin who was riding a camel, [and blew him] from one side of the Pappa River and put him down on the other. He said: "What is that about?" They said to him, Rabba the son of Naḥmani has died." They said to him: "Master of the Universe: Rabba is yours, and the world is yours, why are you destroying it?!" The wind died down. Shimʿon the son of Ḥalafta was quite corpulent. That day was hot. He said to his daughter: "My daughter, fan me with your fan and I

will give you one hundred bundles of spikenard." By and by, the wind blew. He said: "How many bundles of spikenard, shall I give to the Master of this [wind]?"

This ending is quite remarkable. If we had been tempted to see here only deep theological reflections until now—albeit a temptation that requires ignoring the fantastical elements of the story (such as Rabba's boasting as the cause of his "invitation" to death)—such temptation is now quite thoroughly disarmed. Two theological points are indeed made in these two final incidents, or codas, to the story, but it can hardly be denied that the fantastic and grotesque overwhelm the dignified here at last, or do they? Even with its grotesque elements, the first incident actually underlines major problematic issues that the story itself raises. Rabba has been made to die because he is needed in the heavenly yeshiva to intervene in an arcane debate on a fairly obscure bit of the laws of purity. The moral paradox of this is brought out by God's fury at the death of Rabba, a death caused by his own desire, as it were, to have support in his dispute; his anger is then so great that the wind that he raises threatens the world. The bedouin teaches God a lesson in theology, namely that Rabba is his (that is, it was in his purview to kill him or keep him alive) and the world is his (so it is foolish, as it were, to destroy the world in his anger at having destroyed Rabba), and God, of course, assents. This is followed, moreover, with another moral tale of a wind that according to the text takes place at the same moment. Another fat rabbi is discomfited by the lack of wind and offers his daughter a gift if she will fan him.[76] A wind came up (the same wind that upset the bedouin) which cools the rabbi, at which point he reflects mock-moralistically that if he was willing to give his daughter a bunch of perfumed herbs to fan him, how much more is owed that same master of the universe who controls the winds. The same theological point of God's control of everything, from Rabba's fate to the blowing of the winds, is narrated in two ways nearly opposite in tone and import, manifesting the very ambivalence that it is the task of the menippea to encode.

76. According to the twelfth-century Ashkenazi Talmudists known as the Tosafists, it is this association with our own eponymous fat rabbis—above chapter 4—that occasioned the placement of this story here in the Bavli.

Although, to be sure, not identical by any means to Lucian, this narrative nevertheless incorporates several Menippean elements, as well as Menippean themes, precisely in its ambivalences. The most obvious Menippean element is the contact between heaven and earth and especially Rabba's awareness of what's going on there, followed by his own journey to join the heavenly yeshiva. The narrative is carnivalesque in its reversals of hierarchy (not unique to this story in the Bavli). God Godself is losing the battle (as God not infrequently does) for hegemony over halakhic decisions, and the heavenly yeshiva has to turn to an earthly sage to straighten out its intellectual difficulties. The sage is qualified for this pre-eminent authority on the strength of his own self-advertisement (which does not, I emphasize, need to be understood as idle boasting, but is apparently "truthful"). Without anything like the direct attacking mode that we have seen in Lucian's *Icaromenippus,* we can, nonetheless, detect here a self-critical or self-reflective representation on the part of these storytellers of the life of the yeshiva, of their own institution. This element is brought home, I would argue, in the final sequence, where the deepest of homiletical reflection is occasioned by the fatness of a rabbi. I do not mean to suggest that this story is meant to be funny, nor that it is a corrosive satire that seeks to undermine the authority of the Rabbis, their Torah, or their yeshiva with its endless wranglings, but it certainly incorporates a measure of a deflationary aspect on the self-importance of the rabbinic institution.

Icaromoses; or, The Skyrabbi

Menippean satire is an internal critique by intellectuals of their own intellects and intellectual practices as a means to truth and the betterment of human society. One of the most dramatic and compelling narratives in the Talmud is a famous aggada that turns out, on inspection, to be an almost perfect instantiation of the genre of Menippean satire, so much so that I find it hard to avoid a genetic association. Since my argument is, however, not that the story alone is, or can be read as, Menippean satire, but that rather it is the very juxtaposition of halakha and grotesque biographies that constitutes this literary and ideological movement within the Talmud, I must begin by discussing the immediate literary context of our legend. As in the example discussed in the previous chapter from Baba Metsia, the Talmud in Menahot 29b begins the *sugya* with a typically talmudic sobersided halakhic discussion. The issue has to do with the correct writing of the Torah scroll or the *mezuza* (the two passages of the Torah that Jews are enjoined to write in a miniature scroll and fix on their lintels). If these are not written precisely correctly, they are totally invalid. The Talmud quotes a passage of the Mishna which reads: "The two passages of the *mezuza* each are necessary for the *mezuza* to be valid, and even one grapheme invalidates the *mezuza.*"

The Talmud comments:

> But this is obvious! Rav Yehuda said in the name of Rav: It was only necessary to state it in the case of the point of the *yud.* But this too is obvious. Rather it is another statement of Rav Yehuda in the name of Rav that is relevant: Any letter that is not completely surrounded by blank parchment on all four sides is invalid.

The first speaker in the *sugya* objects that it is quite unnecessary for the Mishna to tell us that a missing letter renders the *mezuza* invalid. An answer is offered in the form of a statement by Rav Yehuda in the name of his teacher, to the effect that it means that if the point of a *yud* is missing (something like the dot on an *i*), it is invalid, even if the *yud* itself is there. But the Talmud objects again: this too is obvious; after all a missing part of the letter renders the letter entirely not there. Finally, another resolution to the original objection is offered in the form of a different statement of Rav Yehuda in the name of Rav, namely that if the letter so much as touches another letter, even though both letters are completely legible and all there, the *mezuza* is still entirely invalid. Note that this is a perfect synecdoche for the work of the author of the dialectic halakhic *sugya* as discussed in the last chapter. The two statements of Rav Yehuda must have circulated independently of their placement as answers to this objection, since the *stamma* is clearly in doubt whether it was this statement or that statement that is relevant here. This *stamma* has produced this minisugya through inventing the objection (which is indeed anonymous) and then montaging it with the two statements of Rav Yehuda in order to make them (or at least one of them) answer the objection.

As Rashi explains, the point of the *sugya* is that if even one letter is not perfectly formed, then the entire ritual object is completely invalid and useless. The Talmud goes on then to give examples and learned discussion about precisely which deformations in various letters render the object invalid and even suggests a procedure (bringing an average schoolchild and asking him to read the letter) for determining this. The results of these discussions and determinations are nothing short of sacrality or invalidation of the most sacred objects of which rabbinic Judaism knows, its sacred scrolls.

This absolutely serious halakhic discussion is then followed by a passage which I can only read as a reductio ad absurdum of the very concerns that motivated the halakhic punctilia, for at this precise moment in the text, we continue with an absolutely fantastical story. It is then the final author of the Talmud, the *stamma* of the Talmud, who is responsible for the placing of our quite fantastical story smack in the middle of a most serious ("realistic") halakhic discussion of that which makes or breaks a sacred scroll. Why? It will be seen in the reading that follows, I trust, that this question is closely analogous to the questions I have been asking about Plato in the first half of the book.

As we shall see in detail, the talmudic narrative we are about to read shares many of the specific generic features of the Menippean satire, including scenes in heaven,[77] dialogue between the living and the dead,[78] a catascopic view from above (Moses in the yeshiva of Akiva), and especially a powerful querying (almost self-mockery) of the value of the author's/hero's own search for truth:

> Rav Yehudah said that Rav said: In the hour that Moses ascended
> on high, he found the Holy Blessed One sitting and tying crowns
> for the letters. He [Moses] said before him: "Master of the Universe,

77. Relihan reminds us that this genre or style can vary, but typically mixes waking reality with something else: "There are other ways to motivate a Menippean satire. Narrators return alive from the dead and from heaven, and awake from dreams and visions"; *Ancient Menippean Satire*, 48. For journeys to heaven from which vantage philosophers are observed, see Lucian's *Icaromenippus* and Seneca's *Apocolocyntosis*, ed. P. T. Eden (Cambridge: Cambridge University Press, 1984); on which latter also see H. K. Riikonen, *Menippean Satire as a Literary Genre, with Special Reference to Seneca's Apocolocyntosis*, Commentationes Humanarum Litterarum, 0069-6587 (Helsinki: Finnish Society of Sciences and Letters, 1987). Varro's own Menippean satires also make use of this topos.

78. For the rarity of interactions between rabbis and biblical figures in rabbinic literature, see Jeffrey L. Rubenstein, trans., *Rabbinic Stories* (New York: Paulist Press, 2002), 215.

What [lit. who] holds you back?" He [God] said, "There is one man who will be after several generations, and Akiva the son of Joseph is his name, who will derive from each and every stroke hills and hills of halakhot." He [Moses] said before him: "Master of the Universe, show him to me." He [God] said to him: "Turn around!" He [Moses] went and sat at the back of eight rows [in the study house of Rabbi Akiva], and he didn't understand what they were saying. His strength became weak. When they reached a certain issue, the disciples said to him [to Akiva], "From whence do you know this?" He [Akiva] said to them: "It is a halakha given to Moses at Sinai." [Moses's] spirit became settled.

He [Moses] returned and came before the Holy Blessed One. He [Moses] said to him: "Master of the Universe, You have such a one and yet You give the Torah by my hand?!" He [God] said to him: "Be silent! That is what has transpired in My thought." (Babylonian Talmud Menaḥot 29b)

In this narrative we have all of the elements mentioned above, but it has not been considered until now as part of the genre of menippea, because Babylonian Jewish literature has hardly been considered in any context but its own.[79] In this story the Rabbis (the Rabbis of the *stamma*) comment satirically on their own practices of study of Torah. Moses, the source of the Torah, cannot understand the Torah as it is interpreted by Rabbi Akiva, until the latter acknowledges him as the author of his own interpretations, interpretations, it should be emphasized, that are derived from serifs and flourishes on the letters and not even the letters themselves. If we understand "satire" here to be the Menippean sort that *does not condemn a prac-*

---

79. Important exceptions to this point include especially great work that is being done on the *Iranian* cultural background of the Talmud. See especially the recent work of Yaakov Elman in this regard: "Middle Persian Culture and Babylonian Sages: Accommodation and Resistance in the Shaping of Rabbinic Legal Traditions," in *Cambridge Companion to Rabbinic Literature*, ed. Charlotte Fonrobert and Martin Jaffee (Cambridge: Cambridge University Press, 2006); Yaakov Elman, "Acculturation to Elite Persian Norms," in *Netiʿot Ledavid: Jubilee Volume for David Weiss Halivni*, ed. Yaakov Elman, Ephraim Bezalel Halivni, and Zvi Arie Steinfeld (Jerusalem: Orhot Press, 2004), 31–56, and much more to come. What has not been considered generally are the ways that the western reaches of the Iranian Empire were part and parcel of an international intellectual and literary culture that extended throughout the Mediterranean area. See, however, Richard Kalmin, *Jewish Babylonia between Persia and Roman Palestine* (Oxford: Oxford University Press, 2006), 174, which adumbrates precisely this point.

tice from without and propose its replacement by something else, but is rather a critical reflection on the practice and its limitations from within, then, I think we have an elegant generic account of our story. Relihan has noted: "Menippean satire rises through time to philosophical formulations of the inadequacy of human knowledge and the existence of a reality that transcends reason."[80] This account of Menippean satire and the realization that various talmudic narratives—notably this one, and even, in some sense, the Talmud itself—belong to this world, opens us up to richer and deeper interpretation of the text. If the theme of the menippea is a philosophical formulation of the inadequacy of human knowledge and the existence of a reality that transcends reason, we are observing in our legend a powerful and direct instantiation of the genre and of its philosophical formulation. In this talmudic menippea, Torah knowledge is thoroughly opaque; no one, not even Moses himself, could possibly know what Rabbi Akiva knows nor contest rationally his interpretive assertions. No one could arrive at his results through rational inquiry no matter how assiduous. The truth cannot be discovered.

As Relihan writes, "The [Menippean] is a strange hybrid whose focus is the failure of the academic pedant to understand and improve the world around him."[81] Moses, however, is hardly just an academic pedant and his inquiry into Rabbi Akiva's mode of interpretation hardly adequately dismissed with the "Be silent!" His inability to understand Rabbi Akiva's readings of serifs necessitates, itself, a reading. As pointed out, absolutely correctly, by Seth Schwartz, true Midrash is *not* being described here. Even in the wildest manifestations of Midrash, no one has ever interpreted the serifs on the letters![82] Midrash itself, or at any rate, the Midrash of Rabbi Akiva, is being caricatured, not celebrated. It seems then, on this reading, that the narrative of Moses is virtually what the Talmud would call a contra-

80. Relihan, *Ancient Menippean Satire,* 29.
81. Relihan, *Ancient Menippean Satire,* 49.
82. Shlomo Naeh, in an unpublished Hebrew paper that arrived to me too late to be fully considered for this book, argues that the traditional interpretation of the word קוצים, translated "serifs" here, is not correct. Quick perusal of his suggestion leads me to think that while he is clearly correct for earlier texts, by the time of the *stamma*'s incorporation of the narrative here, the "traditional" interpretation must already have held sway.

dictory precedent, a precedent that seemingly coming to bless, ends up cursing. Far from supporting our grave and solemn practice of trying to get the Holy scroll writ right down to its tiniest particularities, the narrative calls into question the value of such an enterprise and with it the regime of knowledge that subtends it. Even Moses can't understand what's being made of his endeavors. The ambiguities of this story, its multiple ironies (is it asserting or denying the authority of Rabbi Akiva?), particularly set as it is right in the middle of discussion of sacred texts and their invalidation, render it a *mise en abyme* for the whole Talmud, in its Menippean assertion and simultaneous denial of the seriousness and importance and ultimate truth of its halakhic determinations. The Menippean satire is thus perfectly balanced; it both affirms and calls into question Rabbi Akiva's Midrash as well as Moses's effective opposition to the practice, his desire for rational understanding, at one and the very same time. But let me emphasize once again, lest I be misunderstood, that it is the incongruity of the placement of this parodic story in the midst of a devoted and serious attempt to get at the correct halakha on a matter of supreme cultural importance that makes the point, not just the story itself, which would be more corrosive read out of its literary context. It is that incongruity that renders the text so very Menippean, that which asserts while denying but also denies while asserting the value of an intellectual practice, neither the assertion nor the denial being allowed to win the day. The Menippean satire, as it developed through late antiquity, is part and parcel of large-scale movements that deeply interrogated (without abandoning) philosophical rationalism as a mode of acquiring or achieving *epistēmē*. The seriocomic yoking so characteristic of the Babylonian Talmud, drawing on the generic and epistemological resources of the Menippean (and more broadly *spoudogeloion*) traditions, proved a powerful vehicle for the exploration of the issues produced by these broad and deep changes in intellectual styles of late antiquity, including some very widespread versions of skepticism. As Relihan describes Lucian's Menippean texts, "Intellectual dissatisfaction with the world and with the philosophers' contradictory views of it lead to a desire to get to the truth directly."[83] For the Talmud, of course, substitute Rabbis for philoso-

83. Relihan, *Ancient Menippean Satire,* 106.

phers. In the face of Moses's demand, as it were, for rational understanding of Rabbi Akiva's discourse, he is told in effect to be silent
and have faith. This could almost be a direct paraphrase of our story,
which I have thus dubbed "Icaromoses." Moreover, and most importantly, these texts, such as Varro's great corpus of Menippean satires
(mostly lost), involve a self-critical stance on the part of philosophers,
not an attack from without. The staging of this competition between
Moses and Rabbi Akiva fits the bill almost perfectly.

An almost uncanny parallel to this famous story is a lesser-known
text of Lucian's, known in English as "A Word with Hesiod."[84] This
short satire (but too long to cite here entire) consists of a dialogue between the ancient Greek poet and cosmogonist Hesiod (eighth century BC) and the much later Lycinus, whose belatedness is figured in
the dialogue itself, as well as in another text of Lucian's, *The Dance,* in
which "Crato, a cynic, upbraids Lycinus for a backsliding from classical tradition."[85] As a character, Lycinus is thus marked with Lucian's
corpus as the sign of an ambivalence about the past and its present
reception.[86] Indeed, according to the plausible argument of Goldhill,
this Lycinus is none other than a cipher for Lucian, Lykinos for Lukia-
nos, a cipher who is part of Lucian's elaborate dance of semi-hidden
identity.[87] Lycinus takes on the great poet of yesteryear for not having
fulfilled his express promise of being able to foretell the future: either
the poet—excuse me—lied in his claim to have such powers or he has
indeed knowledge of the future but has withheld it willfully. In the dialogue between an ancient poet and a much later recipient of the poetry,
we have a more than respectable formal—at least—comparandum to
our story of Moses, the author of the Torah, and his confrontation
with a much belated interpreter. It is the poet's response that is most

84. Lucian of Samosata, "A Word with Hesiod," in *The Works of Lucian of Samosata Complete with Exceptions Specified in the Preface,* ed. and trans. H. W. Fowler and F. G. Fowler,
Oxford Library of Translations (Oxford: Clarendon Press, 1905), 30–33. This text was
called to my attention by Dr. Yair Fürstenberg upon reading, generously, my manuscript
for this book. Dr. Fürstenberg has also suggested quite an attractive different, if related,
take on the meaning of Menippean satire and sophistic in the Talmud, which I will leave
him to elaborate as he sees fit.

85. Emily James Putnam, "Lucian the Sophist," *Classical Philology* 4, no. 2 (April 1909):
169.

86. Goldhill lists him (among some other apparent ciphers in Lucian's works for himself) as a "satirical cultural policeman"; "Becoming Greek," 84.

87. Goldhill, "Becoming Greek," 66–67.

telling, as well as Lycinus's rejoinder to it. Hesiod claims (1) that his poems are not his own work, but that "all is the Muses'," and (2) "apart from this, however, I have the usual poets' apology":

> The poet, I conceive, is not to be called to account in this minute fashion, syllable by syllable. If in the fervour of composition a word slip in unawares, search not too narrowly; remember that with us metre and euphony have much to answer for; and then there are certain amplifications—certain elegances—that insinuate themselves into a verse, one scarce knows how. . . . But there! you are not the only offender, nor I the only victim: in the trivial defects of Homer, my fellow craftsman, many a carping spirit has found material for similar hair-splitting disquisitions.[88]

"Hesiod" goes on to further defend himself by saying that in his agricultural work he has indeed predicted the future to the effect that a farmer who does not follow the correct practices will not have successful crops, while one who does has a "prospect of abundance." Although the tone of the talmudic story is subtly different (not so confrontational in its form), it can hardly be denied that the two narratives are very close indeed. In both, a later hermeneutical tradition, a tradition close to the author of the satire, is represented (satirically) as having somehow missed the point of the earlier, canonical work through an overattention to, an obsession with, the accidentals (in the technical sense) of the earlier work (calling the poet to question on minutiae, such as the serifs on the letters). In the Lucian, Hesiod complains directly of this activity; in the more subtle talmudic version, Moses merely doesn't comprehend what's going on in such exaggerated hermeneutical labor.

This theme of lack of understanding on the part of the poet does occur as well in the Lucianic text, for Lycinus responds further, "Admirable; and spoken like a true herdsman. There is no doubting the divine afflatus after that: left to yourself, you cannot so much as defend your own poems." Such "prophecies" could be matched by any experienced farmer, and indeed Lycinus himself could so prophesy: "*That if a man walk out on a cold morning with nothing on, he will*

---

88. Lucian of Samosata, "A Word with Hesiod," 31–32.

take a severe chill; and particularly if it happens to be raining or hailing at the time. And I further prophesy: *That his chill will be accompanied by the usual fever.*" Although the Lucianic text is much more aggressive in tone, once again we could hardly find a closer parallel to the talmudic satire. In both, to recapitulate, an implicit or explicit accusation of the later hermeneuts for overpunctiliousness in their interpretative practices is bruited. In both there is an implicit (satirical) imputation that the original author, especially as he is divinely inspired, doesn't understand and can't defend his own text. Finally, given that Lycinus is, so it seems, Lucian himself, in both cases we have a self-satire of almost precisely the same nature: Rabbi Akiva, as *the* representative par excellence of rabbinic authority and rabbinic hermeneutics, and Lucian, as himself. I think that this remarkable little work of Lucian's nails down the thesis that the talmudic text is indeed an Icaromoses, a Jewish rabbinic ecotypification of the Menippean satire as practiced by authors such as Lucian, with its complex reflections/self-reflections on rationality and interpretation.

Moses's desire for rational understanding is, however, to be tested even more severely, for:

> He said to Him: "Master of the Universe: You have shown me his Torah, show me his reward." He said to him: "Turn around!" He turned around and saw that they were weighing the flesh of Rabbi Akiva in the market [after his martyrdom]. He said to Him: "Master of the Universe, this is the Torah and this is its reward?!" He said to him: "Be silent! That is what has transpired in My thought."

A more direct representation of the failure of the denizens of the academy (the House of Study) "to understand and improve the world around them" can hardly be fathomed, and they are instructed, as it were, to remain silent in the face of that inevitable failure: "The [Menippean] genre relies for its meaning on silence, for the truth that appears between the lines, that emerges from the spectacle of inconclusive debate."[89] Once again, the ending of Lucian's text is more direct in its attack: "No, Hesiod your defence will not do; nor will your prophecies. But I dare say there is something in what you said

89. Relihan, *Ancient Menippean Satire,* 36.

at first—that you knew not what you wrote, by reason of the divine afflatus versifying within you. And that afflatus was no such great matter, either: afflatuses should not promise more than they mean to perform."[90] The divine in the rabbinic text also fails humans, however different and altogether more somber the tone.

Although in the end Relihan denies that Lucian's meaning is that "the perpetuity of debate must be valued over any static theory,"[91] for the talmudic Menippean we can surely argue for such a topic. Inconclusive debate is the very metier of the Talmud; it is not surprising then that the Menippean genre might have been particularly appealing to these Rabbis who produced a literature so different in style, taste, form, and content from earlier Jewish texts. But this is not (I am arguing) about the production of a pluralism of ideas or a free play of discourse and practice, so much as a dark recognition of the ultimate failure of all ideas, discourse, and practice in the face of what we cannot understand. This mood seems to me deeply conditioned by the cultural world in which the Babylonian Rabbis functioned.

One important feature of this world was the transition it witnessed in the grounds of knowledge. Graham Anderson has remarked that it was the figure of the late-ancient holy man himself who, in part, "contributed to the climate in later antiquity in which theurgy eventually came to oust pagan philosophy."[92] It would not be going too far, I think, to say that we witness this process in micro (and remember I style myself a microhistorian of ideas) in our talmudic menippea of Rabbi Akiva. The latter's mode of interpretation of the Torah could be fairly characterized as divination clothed in the language of tradition.[93] Rabbi Akiva's virtual "theurgy"—if I may call it that—seems

90. Lucian of Samosata, "A Word with Hesiod," 33.

91. Relihan, *Ancient Menippean Satire,* 117.

92. Graham Anderson, *Sage, Saint, and Sophist Holy Men and Their Associates in the Early Roman Empire* (London: Routledge, 1994), ix.

93. Augustine himself commented on this hermeneutic style: "A third class of critic consists of those who either interpret the divine scriptures quite correctly or think they do. Because they see, or at least believe, that they have gained their ability to expound the holy books without recourse to any rules of the kind that I have now undertaken to give, they will clamour that these rules are not needed by anybody, *and that all worthwhile illumination of the difficulties of these texts can come by a special gift of God*" (Aug., *De Doctr.,* cited by Adam H. Becker, *The Fear of God and the Beginning of Wisdom: The School of Nisibis and Christian Scholastic Culture in Late Antique Mesopotamia,* Divinations [Philadelphia: University of Pennsylvania Press, 2006], 15, emphasis mine).

to involve something like contemplation of the serifs of the letters to divine their meanings. As in other literary products of this epistemological moment of which the menippea is a sign—and we will see more of this later—the turn is from the possibility of truth rationally discovered to a despair in *epistēmē* carrying with it some kind of mystical or directly communicated truth from above. Who but an "Akiva" could know what is meant by jots, tittles, and decorations on letters? And how could *we* know other than by being his disciples? It will be seen that a sharp challenge to rabbinic rationality is being offered here. "Moses" would represent on this account a more rational, logically based reading of the Torah, while Rabbi Akiva represents a kind of almost theurgical or mystical reading. The turn against the rational, the logical, is what motivates the Menippean satire, for it is the inadequacy of Moses's intellection to understand and make sense of the Torah and the world that is at issue. In this sense it is "Moses," as it were, who is being satirized; the rationality of his practices of understanding his own words is being challenged, and with this, rabbinic rationality itself is being queried.

An interesting example of these epistemological ruptures may be provided from the text of Eunapius (fifth century AC). We find in Eunapius a narrative that doesn't in any way parallel that of Rabbi Akiva in its contents, but does, I believe, attest to closely related intellectual dilemmas at the time. This legend manifests the rivalry between reasoned debate and dialectic, on the one hand, and thaumaturgy and divination, on the other, in the latter part of the fourth century (during Julian's reign, the same Julian whom the Christians call "the apostate" and whom Eunapius deems—"the holy"). In this narrative we are told that Aedesius, a great Sophist, had two pupils in the later fourth century, Chrysanthius and Eusebius. Eusebius remained entirely loyal to the old rule of dialectic and logic, while Chrysanthius became particularly attached to the newfangled doctrines of Maximus: "Now Chrysanthius had a soul akin to that of Maximus, and like him was passionately absorbed in working marvels, and he withdrew himself in the study of the science of divination." Eusebius, it seems, was somewhat in awe of this Maximus, for

when Maximus was present, [he] used to avoid precise and exact divisions of a disputation and dialectical devices and subtleties; though when Maximus was not there he would shine out like a bright star, with a light like the sun's; such was the facility and charm that flowered in his discourses. . . . Julian actually reverenced Eusebius. At the close of his exposition Eusebius would add that these [dialectical discussions, trans.] are the only true realities, whereas the impostures of witchcraft and magic that cheat the senses are the works of conjurors who are insane men led astray into the exercise of earthly and material powers.

"The sainted Julian" was puzzled by this peroration, which he regularly heard, and asked Eusebius what he meant, whereupon the latter said:

Maximus is one of the older and more learned students, who, because of his lofty genius and superabundant eloquence scored all logical proof in these subjects and impetuously resorted to the acts of a madman. . . . But you must not marvel at any of these things, even as I marvel not, but rather believe that the thing of the highest importance is that purification of the soul which is attained by reason."

Eusebius receives something of a surprise, for "when the sainted Julian heard this, he said: 'Nay, farewell and devote yourself to your books. You have shown me the man I was in search of'"[94] (much like, even verbally, the "You have shown me his Torah" of the talmudic text).[95] The earlier, traditional commitment to dialectical investigation and surety that logic would provide answers has been rejected, and by no less, it seems, than the sainted Julian, in favor of thaumaturgy and divination, but not without conflict, a conflict I think demonstrated also in the narrative about Rabbi Akiva. I wish to suggest, therefore, diffidently (at least at first) that the double-voicing of

---

94. Wright, *Philostratus: The Lives of the Sophists; Eunapius: Lives of the Philosophers,* 433–35. My own interpretation here follows Wright's construal of the text here and not that of Richard Lim, *Public Disputation, Power, and Social Order in Late Antiquity,* Transformations of the Classical Heritage (Berkeley: University of California Press, 1994), 50–53, which I rediscovered after writing these paragraphs, upon rereading Lim after a decade. The lack of an adversative in a sentence is not outweighed by the clear narrative logic; it *must* be Eusebius whom Julian now abandons and not Chrysanthius or the story hardly makes sense, in my humble opinion.

95. I wish to thank Dr. Ronald Reissberg for pointing this out to me.

the Babylonian Talmud to which I have devoted this and the previous chapter can be, at least, plausibly contextualized in a more general epistemological crisis close to the time of the production of that text and well after, for instance, the production of other rabbinic texts, notably the Palestinian Talmud and its cognate Midrashim. The dialogism of the Talmud is, on this conjecture, a representation of a dialogue within intellectual culture itself, one that, as we have just seen, transgresses the lines of any particular confession.

In the next chapter, I shall be further developing this reading of the Talmud, looking at the ways in which the wilder, more grotesque biographical legends about one of the greatest of the Rabbis are brought in from the cold margins of the text and put at the center of a reading of the Talmud as a book, rendering the Talmud seen through this parallax view quite Lucianic—even Petronian—in character.

6

Icarome'ir:

Rabbi Me'ir's Babylonian "Life" as Menippean Satire

Resh Lakish said: A holy mouth [Rabbi Me'ir's] said *that*?!

Sanhedrin 24a

The study of Torah is in the *imaginaire* of the rabbis the functional equivalent of the life of the philosopher in other Hellenistic culture.[1] This has been demonstrated by Michael Satlow, who compares the actual practices of living prescribed for Hellenistic philosophers and talmudic Rabbis. Belying an alleged binary division of Greek as the search for truth and Jewish as the search for goodness, the Rabbis imagined the Torah-life on the model of the philosophers' *bios*, an ascetic practice of communal study that molds the self into the beautiful and the good.[2] As Satlow puts it: "For the rabbis, *talmud torah* served the same function as philosophy did for these non-Jewish writers; *talmud torah* was the means by which the soul was made pure or whole, thus bringing the individual closer to the divine, or into the 'spiritual condition.' *Talmud torah* required the same

---

1. For Torah study as the equivalent of philosophy for the rabbis, see E. J. Bickerman, *The Jews in the Greek Age* (Cambridge, Mass.: Harvard University Press, 1988), 172–73; and see discussion in David Stern, "The Captive Woman: Hellenization, Greco-Roman Erotic Narrative, and Rabbinic Literature," *Poetics Today* 19, no. 1 (1998): 115.

2. For an excellent, if somewhat Christian-oriented, introduction to ancient philosophy as way of life, see Pierre Hadot, *What Is Ancient Philosophy?* (Cambridge, Mass.: Harvard University Press, 2002).

mental and physical discipline demanded by the non-Jewish study of philosophy. Body and soul, working together in a disciplined (i.e., ascetic) fashion, can help a man overcome his evil inclination."[3] Talmud Torah, the study of "oral Torah," which issues in the rabbinic literature, is thus conceived within this literature as an ascetic practice for the molding of the male Jewish soul to its highest possible state, very much analogous, in this sense, to the life of the philosopher as Plato and his successors envisioned it. The Bavli thus views the Talmud Torah "care of the self" as the most serious and praiseworthy way of living and presents Rabbi Me'ir as a singular exemplum of such a life. Speaking in the Bakhtinian terms elaborated in the previous two chapters, the language of "Torah," for the most part understood as the elaboration through commentary and dialectic of correct practice, is the normal or normative literary language of the Babylonian Talmud. What I want to show in this chapter is how that "normal literary language" is dialogized in the Talmud via the sorts of incongruity that we have been exploring but in this case not within the literary context of a single extended passage or chapter of Talmud, but rather in the variously grotesque (Menippean) legends about a single, most central and "holy" rabbinic hero, the great *tanna,* Rabbi Me'ir, distributed sporadically throughout the talmudic text.

Rabbi Me'ir as Hero of the Halakha

The Rabbi Me'ir whom we shall be meeting in another guise (literally) below in this chapter is first and foremost a hero of the "normal" language, the seriousness of the rabbinic literature.[4] A single example of his serious halakhic activity will make this point. The Mishna at Baba Metsia 73a reads:

> There are four types of bailees: a gratis bailee, a borrower, a paid bailee, and a lessee. The gratis bailee swears with reference to everything. The borrower pays for everything. The paid bailee and the les-

3. Michael L. Satlow, "And on the Earth You Shall Sleep: Talmud Torah and Rabbinic Asceticism," *Journal of Religion* 83 (2003): 215.

4. Robert Goldenberg, *The Sabbath-Law of Rabbi Meir,* Brown Judaic Studies (Missoula, Mont.: Scholars Press, 1978).

see swear with respect to a broken, robbed, or dead animal but pay for a lost or burgled one.

Let me quickly gloss this Mishna, which is the cornerstone of the talmudic law of bailments and thus also a mainstay of Jewish law until this day. A gratis bailee is one who watches an animal for a friend without recompense. "Borrower" needs no glossing, nor indeed do any of the others once the gratis bailee has been defined. For each of these categories there is a different level of responsibility attached proportionate to the benefit that the bailee is receiving and giving. In the case of the gratis bailee the benefit is entirely the bailor's, so the bailee in that situation must merely testify that he or she was not negligent and need pay no damages, whatever has happened to the animal. In the case of the borrower, where the benefit accrues entirely to the bailee, full restitution must always be made. In the other two cases, in which there is mutual benefit, the matter is divided. In those types of losses where some negligence can be imputed, such as a lost or burgled animal, the bailee makes restitution, but in the other cases she or he merely testifies, as in the case of the gratis bailee.

On this Mishna the Talmud immediately remarks:

Who taught the "four bailees"? Rav Naḥman said that Rabba bar Avuah said that it is Rabbi Me'ir!

Discussion ensues at some length as to the implications of this ascription. We learn two things from this truncated citation: first, as is the general rule, the anonymous Mishna is identified as the opinion of Rabbi Me'ir, this being the case as he was the teacher of the author of the Mishna who nearly always maintains his teacher's view and thus presents it anonymously. In this utterly typical Mishna and talmudic exchange, there is not the slightest hint that Rabbi Me'ir would even be considered less than a sober authority, teacher of the halakha, and master of the oral Torah. As we learn from the Palestinian Talmud, "Rabbi Yose the son of Ḥalafta would praise Rabbi Me'ir before the people of Sepphoris, that he is a great sage, a holy man, a modest man" (Moʿed Katan, chap. 3, 5). And as Rabbi Yoḥanan was famously given to saying: "When the Mishna speaks anonymously, it is the voice (and opinion) of Rabbi Me'ir" (Sanhedrin 86a); that is, his is the opinion that is barely subject to question according to the redactor of that definitive and quite solemn halakhic text. Strikingly, rivetingly, it is this figure above all, the most palpable hero and holy man of the Mishna, whose name is attached to the wildest and most bizarre biographical narratives in the Bavli. In this chapter, I plan both to demonstrate this claim and to interpret it in the light of the material and ideas explored so far. My basic argument will be that we can best appreciate or comprehend this narrative complex about Rabbi Me'ir the holy man by studying it as closely related to the late-ancient artistic prose gathered, at least heuristically, under the sign of Menippean satire. In studying the various stories below, I shall try in each instance to show how it is connected in one way or another to this type of literature and thus further unfold and elaborate my reading of the Bavli's practice of exploring their "truth together with its limitations."[5]

To reprise a citation from J. P. Sullivan, on *The Satyricon:* "Certainly a main characteristic of Menippean satire was the union of humour and philosophy (*or whatever political, moral or aesthetic basis an author might substitute for this*)."[6] The last (parenthetical) qualification is crucial for my argument. I hope to make a case here that the halakhic dialectic which substitutes for philosophy in the rabbinic culture, when relativized by the grotesque elements of rabbinic biography (such as that of Rabbi Me'ir) in the Bavli, is closely comparable in its political, moral, and aesthetic basis to Menippean satire. This union of humor and serious legal discussion (as well as pious homily) works, I will suggest, to chip away at epistemological certainty through, in this case, a series of all-too-human sexual adventures, double standards about gender difference, and rabbinic jealousies and envies.

Sleeping with Elijah: The Hero and the Hetaira

Who is Rabbi Me'ir? For the later pious tradition, he is only the solemn halakhic adept whom we would expect from his presence in the

---

5. Mikhail Bakhtin, "Discourse in the Novel," in *The Dialogic Imagination: Four Essays by Mikhail Bakhtin,* ed. Michael Holquist, trans. Michael Holquist and Caryl Emerson, University of Texas Press Slavic Series (Austin: University of Texas Press, 1981), 356.

6. Sullivan, introduction to *The Satyricon by Petronius Arbiter,* trans. John Patrick Sullivan, Penguin Classics (New York: Penguin Books, 1986), 20 (emphasis added).

Mishnaic and talmudic *sugya,* as just exemplified. In this light, a website informs us:

> The grave of Rabbi Meir Baal Haness is one of the holiest sites in the Jewish world. Rabbi Meir is known as "Baal Haness" which means miracle maker. Very few know his real name, thought to be Rabbi Nahori or Rabbi Mischa. He was called Meir because it means "to illuminate," as he brought his followers to know the light of G-d.[7] The Talmud states that Rabbi Meir was one of the most important scholars of the second century C.E. He was one of Rabbi Akiva's students and an active participant in the Bar Kochbah revolt. Rabbi Meir was the author of Haggadot and Halachot that are still studied today. Although he was a revered scholar, he was a very humble man who loved the land of Israel. Though he died in The Diaspora, he was brought to Tiberias to be buried on holy soil. After his death, thousands of Jews continue to come to his grave to receive his blessings and miracles.[8]

Another website informs us more precisely how Rabbi Me'ir achieved this near saintly status:

> Some charities in Eretz Yisrael call themselves the "Charities of Rabbi Meir Baal Haness." This is a reference to a story told in the Talmud about the great Sage, Rabbi Meir, who was able to ward off serious dangers to himself and others by the simple declaration of "G-d of Meir, answer me!" It is a tradition that one who gives charity in memory of Rabbi Meir merits having his prayers answered in the merit of this great *tzaddik* [holy man]. Rabbi Meirs [*sic*] tomb in Tiberias is a popular site for visiting and praying to have miracles performed in the merit of this "master of the miracle."[9]

These nonscholarly (to a fault) sources provide a powerful exemplification of the ways that Rabbi Me'ir's persona has been almost

---

7. For a recent discussion of the relation of Rabbi Me'ir to light and light symbolism, see Galit Hasan-Rokem, "Rabbi Meir, the Illuminated and the Illuminating: Interpreting Experience," in *Current Trends in the Study of Midrash,* ed. Carol Bakhos, supplements to the *Journal for the Study of Judaism* 106 (Leiden: E. J. Brill, 2006), 227–43.

8. "Jewish Blessings: 'Who Was Rabbi Me'ir?'" Http://www.jewishbless.com/pages/rabbi.html.

9. Http://ohr.edu/yhiy/article.php/984.

literally sanctified in the popular Jewish tradition (including those of traditionalist scholars), but it is finally an Israeli textbook for children that completes the story. In a typical hagiographical account written for pious Israeli children, we find the story of how Rabbi Me'ir, arguably the greatest of the *tannai'im* (second century), became known as Rabbi Me'ir the Wonder Worker, a name and status that he bears until this day. It seems that his sister-in-law was in prison, and he went to rescue her, discovered that she had not sinned in prison, and performed miracles to get her out. Upon being pursued by soldiers, Rabbi Me'ir entered a *treyf* restaurant, stuck his finger in the food, licked another finger, and by this ruse convinced his pursuers that he couldn't possibly be the great rabbi. He then ran away to Babylonia to escape his oppressors.[10] This is how the story of Rabbi Me'ir has been received in modern Jewish hagiography, and indeed, his grave is visited more often than any other in the Jewish world. There is a great surprise to come when we look at the actual text of the Bavli to which these websites and the children's book refer, for in the "original," the picture is hardly one of unambiguous sanctity, Rabbi Me'ir being more of a wild saint than the godly variety.

To get a sense of how wild, how bizarre, the Talmud allows such a hero of halakha to become in the biographical legends, a close look at the very story that sanctified him in the later popular religious tradition and gave him the later name of Rabbi Me'ir the Wonder Worker—the virtual Saint Jude of the Jews—will do very well. The talmudic story that we are about to read incorporates themes familiar from late antiquity and especially the narrative patterns of the adventure story and the erotic tale. Bakhtin has introduced a very important set of reflections on the adventure, writing that "the adventure plot is combined with the posing of profound and acute problems; and it is, in addition, placed wholly at the service of the idea. It places a person in extraordinary positions that expose and provoke him, it connects him and makes him collide with other people under unusual and unexpected conditions precisely for the purpose of *testing* the idea and the man of the idea, that is, for testing the 'man in man.' And this permits the adventure story to be combined with other genres

---

10. N. Ts. Gotlib, *Rabbi Hananya Bar Hama; Rabbi Ishmael Ben Elisha; Rabbi Meir the Miracle Worker,* Adire Ha-Torah (Jerusalem: Mekhon "Bet Yehi'el," 1983), 130–34.

that are, it would seem, quite foreign to it, such as the confession
and the saint's Life."[11] This last sentence provides an elegant introduction to Rabbi Me'ir's own greatest adventure, his trip to Rome to
rescue a damsel in distress through powers and capabilities that mark
him much later as a saint. He undergoes, like a knight of derring-do,
a great peril and overcomes that too, also via miraculous practices.
From at least one point of view, this story has to be the central moment in the legend of Rabbi Me'ir:

> Beruria, the wife of Rabbi Me'ir, was the daughter of Rabbi Ḥanina.
> She said to him: It is painful to me that my sister is sitting in a pros-
> titute's booth. He took a *tarqeva* of dinars and went, saying if she has
> done nothing wrong [i.e., if she is sexually innocent], a miracle will
> take place for me, and if not, there will be no miracle. He dressed up as
> a soldier and solicited her. She said: I am menstruating. He said: I can
> wait. She said: There are many here more beautiful than I. He said: I
> understand from this that she has done nothing wrong. He went to
> her guard: Give her to me! The guard said: I am afraid of the king. He
> [Me'ir] took the *tarqeva* of dinars, and gave it to him, and said: Take
> the *tarqeva* of dinars. Keep half and use half for bribing anyone who
> comes. He [the guard] said: What shall I do when they are gone? He
> [Me'ir] said: Say 'God of Me'ir answer me; God of Me'ir answer me,'
> and you will be saved. He [guard] said: How do I know that this will
> be so? He [Me'ir] said: [Now you will see.] There came some dogs that
> eat people. He shouted to them, and they came to eat him. He said:
> 'God of Me'ir answer me; God of Me'ir answer me,' and they let him
> go. He gave her to him. In the end, the story was heard in the House
> of the King. They brought him [the guard] and hung him on the cross.
> He said: God of Rabbi Me'ir answer me; God of Me'ir answer me!
> They took him down, saying: What was that?! He said: This is what
> happened. [They wrote it on a bull of the state], and they engraved the
> image of Rabbi Me'ir on the gates of Rome, declaring: If a man comes
> with this feature and that feature, arrest him! When Rabbi Me'ir came
> there, they wished to arrest him. He ran away from them and went

---

11. Mikhail Bakhtin, *Problems of Dostoevsky's Poetics,* ed. and trans. Caryl Emerson,
Theory and History of Literature (Minneapolis: University of Minnesota Press, 1984),
105. Bakhtin is, to be sure, writing about Dostoevsky.

into a whorehouse. Elijah came in the guise of a whore and embraced him. Some say that he put his hand in Gentile foods and tasted them. They [the Romans] said: God forefend! If that were Rabbi Me'ir he wouldn't do such a thing. Because of these events [Rabbi Me'ir] ran away to Babylonia. (Avoda Zara 18a–b)[12]

In this short narrative we find packed an incredible number of themes and motifs that characterize the Bakhtinian menippea: sex, fantasy, and religion all together. David Stern has already noted how little attention has been paid the impact of Greco-Roman narrative on rabbinic literature, and has begun to provide a major corrective to this fault, focusing especially on one of the genres so important for this story, the erotic and adventure narrative.[13] As Stern has pointed out, the Greco-Roman novel is "actually a love-and-adventure story."[14] The story of Rabbi Me'ir is both of these as well, and thus can be seen as part of the great literary movement of the first through the sixth centuries that brought us Lucian, and Petronius, the Menippean satire, and the ancient novel.

Bakhtin has written of the menippea, "A very important characteristic of the menippea is the organic combination within it of the free fantastic, the symbolic, at times even a mystical-religious element with an extreme and (from our point of view) crude *slum naturalism*. The adventures of truth on earth take place on the high road, in brothels, in the dens of thieves, in taverns, marketplaces, prisons, in the erotic orgies of secret cults, and so forth."[15] The reason that this story adorned Rabbi Me'ir with his saint's crown in the Jewish tradition is owing to its several elements of miracle-working. Rabbi Me'ir's sainthood, however, is not won in a pious and lofty, edifying tale, but rather in a riotous hodgepodge of a parodic mixture of nov-

12. I have produced a composite text from two excellent Sephardic witnesses: Ms. Paris 1337 and JTS 15. The Paris manuscript has some excellent readings from a literary point of view, but is corrupt in other places, where I have filled in from the JTS ms. Nothing in this argument would suffer if only one or the other of the texts were adhered to.

13. Stern, "Captive Woman," 91–92. At about the time that Stern was publishing his article, Joshua Levinson made the same point, writing that "the adoption and adaptation of Greco-Roman literary models in midrashic literature" had received little attention. Joshua Levinson, "Tragedy of Romance: A Case of Literary Exile," *Harvard Theological Review* 89, no. 3 (July 1996): 228.

14. Stern, "Captive Woman," 93.

15. Bakhtin, *Problems of Dostoevsky's Poetics*, 115.

elistic sexual incident, "slum-realism," parodic Gospel, and other comic elements. The sexual incident in Rabbi Me'ir's story connects his legend with other Hellenistic literature, to such texts as Parthenius (along the lines of that which Stern has shown for other rabbinic passages in his article), Philostratus, and Milesian tales.[16] There is an important parallel in Philostratus, namely a reported slander in which Apollonius the holy man allegedly runs away to Scythia owing to a sexual slander against him, "though he never once visited Scythia or fell prey to sexual passion,"[17] closely paralleling Rabbi Me'ir's bolt to Babylonia under rather similar circumstances. It is entirely legitimate to inquire into the significance and import of such incidents recurring in the lives of holy men. Unless we take the reductive route of assuming that erotic material is there primarily and simply to provide titillation, to maintain the reader's interest and keep her reading, this type of incident ought to be seen as carrying some important ideological baggage in the literary practices of narrative during this period. In this discussion, I would like to unpack some of that freight.

Comparing Parthenius's *The Love Romances* to rabbinic literature, Stern suggests that in the former, "the erotic ordeal is the primary mode of contact through which their leading characters engage the larger world, a world that is explicitly represented as both sexually charged and dangerous." He goes on to say that "it is precisely these elements of the erotic narrative that became for the rabbis the essential building blocks of a cultural narrative, a kind of myth or foundational story that helped them explain to themselves their place in the pagan world and their uneasy relationship to that world; indeed, in its transformed shape, this narrative became for the rabbis one through which they represented their understanding of cultural influence itself."[18] As Laurie Davis memorably put it, "The Rabbis portrayed themselves as virgins in a brothel."[19] Making a point similar to that

16. Arkady B. Kovelman, "Miletian Story of Beruria," *Vestnik Evreyskogo Universiteta* 1, no. 19 (1999) (in Russian).

17. C. P. Jones, ed. and trans., *The Life of Apollonius of Tyana,* by Philostratus, Loeb Classical Library (Cambridge, Mass.: Harvard University Press, 2005), 1:61.

18. Stern, "Captive Woman," 99. See too Joshua Levinson, "Tragedy of Romance," 233–34, which suggests that it was the separation/reunion plot that particularly appealed to the rabbis as a way of articulating their own historical position with respect to God.

19. Laurie Davis, "Virgins in Brothels: A Different Feminist Reading of Beruriah,"

of Stern's but focusing more specifically, Virginia Burrus writes that "in both the pagan and the Christian novel, I suggest, the presentation of a virginalized eroticism reflects deep ambivalence about the violence of imperial rule."[20] For Stern and Burrus both, but with differences, eroticism copes with the empire and its religion. Agreeing with both of them, I suggest here another dimension for, at least, the Bavli, namely the ways that it focuses our attention in Menippean—cum novelistic, à la Bakhtin—style on the limitations (figured in the fleshly weakness of an individual) of the rabbinic program for ethical and spiritual stylization of the ideal male Jew. The plot of this little novella of Rabbi Me'ir and his sister-in-law turns on three incidents of miraculous escape: the first is a miracle done for the sake of the damsel in distress, the second to save the prison guard, and the third to save Rabbi Me'ir's own skin.

Turning first to the second of the miracles, I find evidence that one of the areas of pressure or cultural tension that is being confronted in our romance writ small is indeed the place of the Rabbis in a Christian world, thus far bringing out the interpretation of Stern (supported at least obliquely by Burrus's analysis of the Christian materials). This miracle by which the guard is saved seems deeply parodic of the Passion narratives. As shown by Naomi Koltun-Fromm, the Passion narratives are partly built on a Christological Midrash on Psalm 22.[21] Our little story of the guard being hung on the cross, saying some strange words in a foreign language, and being taken down from the cross suggests, in turn, a parody of the Gospel Passion accounts. Indeed, I would circumspectly suggest that this text is closely related to the Babylonian Aramaic parodic Gospels known as *Toledot Yeshu,* the story of Jesus. Although best known from the gaonic period, slightly later than the Talmud, their earliest forms are to be found in the Tal-

---

paper presented at Graduate Theological Union (Berkeley, 1994). See too Rachel Adler, "The Virgin in the Brothel and Other Anomalies: Character and Context in the Legend of Beruriah," *Tikkun* 3, no. 6 (1988), who doesn't consider the political, "colonial" context of the trope.

20. Virginia Burrus, "Mimicking Virgins: Colonial Ambivalence and the Ancient Romance," *Arethusa* 38 (2005): 56.

21. Naomi Koltun-Fromm, "Psalm 22's Christological Interpretive Tradition in Light of Christian Anti-Jewish Polemic," *Journal of Early Christian Studies* 6, no. 1 (Spring 1998): 37–57.

mud (mostly self-censored) as well.[22] There is a strong argument for this parodic appropriation in the curious incident of the dogs, whose miraculous appearance and subduing prove to the guard that Rabbi Me'ir's incantation will save him. This is based on a verse in chapter 22 of Psalms of which the Christological midrashists could make nothing: "Deliver my life from the sword; my soul from the power of the dog" (Psalms 22:21 [v. 20 in Septuagint]). It is almost as if our parodic narrator says to the Christians, I see you and I raise you one. I will produce a Midrash on that verse too, on the verse that "stumped" you. The words that the guard is taught to say, "Eloah dMe'ir, answer me," may embody a parodic allusion to the following well-known sequence in Mark's Passion narrative (15) or a version close to it:

"Ha! You who destroy the temple, and build it in three days, [30] save yourself, and come down from the cross!" [31] Likewise, also the chief priests mocking among themselves with the scribes said, "He saved others. He can't save himself. [32] Let the Christ, the King of Israel, now come down from the cross, that we may see and believe him." Those who were crucified with him insulted him. [33] When the sixth hour had come, there was darkness over the whole land until the ninth hour. [34] At the ninth hour Jesus cried with a loud voice, saying, "Eloi, Eloi, lama sabachthani?" which is, being interpreted, "My God, my God, why have you forsaken me?" [35] Some of those who stood by, when they heard it, said, "Behold, he is calling Elijah." [36] One ran, and filling a sponge full of vinegar, put it on a reed, and gave it to him to drink, saying, "Let him be. Let's see whether Elijah comes to take him down." [37] Jesus cried out with a loud voice, and gave up the spirit. [38]

There is enough, in my opinion, to my ear, at least to suggest, that the talmudic phrase is a parody of the Aramaic of Jesus's cry from the cross. The guard, of course, instead of saying, "Eloi, Eloi, lama sabachthani?" says "Eloa dmeir aneni." The sonar echo is, I reckon,

22. For the defensive activities of the Jewish self-censors in printing the Talmud, see Amnon Raz-Krakotzkin, *Ha-Tsenzor, Ha-Orekh Veha-Tekst Ha-Tsenzurah Ha-Katolit Veha-Defus Ha-Ivri be-Me Ah Ha-Shesh e Sreh,* Italia ser. (Jerusalem: Hotsa at sefarim a. sh. Y. L. Magnes, ha-Universitah ha-Ivrit, 2005).

just close enough to set up the parodic allusion, an allusion amplified
by the presence of Elijah as well in the story of Rabbi Me'ir's own miraculous escape in the brothel. Just as Jesus is misunderstood, so the
guard's strange words are also not understood, but while in the case of
Jesus it does not avail him, in the case of the guard it is precisely these
strange words that lead to his salvation in a highly comic manner. It
is not inapposite to see here also a self-ironizing comment where the
appearance of the "miracle" wrought by the "saintly" Rabbi Me'ir is
explained by the most rationalistic and comic of means.

There is, perhaps, some further evidence for this conjecture in another tale closely related to Rabbi Me'ir, if not quite about him. In
a further sequence of tales, Rabbi Me'ir's heretical teacher, the famous Elisha the son of Abuya, is the protagonist. In that story, Elisha
seeks to know his fate by using a typical Jewish form of oracle: he
asks a child studying to read out the verse which he is studying at the
moment. The child reads: "And to the wicked one God says; What
business have you with declaring my statutes or taking my covenant
in your mouth?!" (Psalms 50:16). The child, we are told, however, stut-
ters, so instead of hearing the word "to the wicked one," *larasha'*, our
Elisha hears "to Elisha," *lelisha'*, and, since the previous verse reads
"And call upon me in the day of trouble: I will deliver thee, and thou
shalt glorify me," our Elisha despairs forever of his salvation, for what
he hears is "and call upon me in the day of trouble: I will deliver thee,
and thou shalt glorify me, but to Elisha God says: What business
have you with declaring my statutes." In the Gospel story it is one
prophet's name that is misheard, Elijah, and in the Talmud, another
prophet's name, one that, moreover, is closely related to the first:
Elisha. Is it too much to conjecture that the Babylonian Rabbis were
aware of this Gospel tradition, if not, surely, of the Gospels themselves, and parodied them here? The picture of Rabbi Me'ir inscribed
on the gates of Rome is reminiscent of the *Ecce homo* of the Gospels as
well. Without pushing the point too far, I think it is not by any means
out of the question that our little sequence is a parodic appropriation
of the Gospel account, which, as Hasan-Rokem reminds us, does not
necessarily imply bitter polemic.[23]

---

23. Galit Hasan-Rokem, "Narratives in Dialogue: A Folk Literary Perspective on Interreligious Contacts in the Holy Land in Rabbinic Literature of Late Antiquity," in *Sharing*

A text such as this is located in several cultural, discursive, literary contexts at one and the same time, in this case according to my
suggested reading, a parody of the Christian midrashic appropriation of Psalms 22, as well as other folk and elite international cultural
sources. I wish, then, to clarify in advance that in comparing Rabbi
Me'ir stories and Hellenistic parallels, I am not suggesting that the
themes or motifs or incidents are unique to these sources; frequently
enough, indeed, they are widespread, including Iranian and even In-
dian texts. The argument is, rather, that the use of these motifs and
narrative types as part of a learned literature, as part of a kind of text
that in its other voices insists on the high seriousness and dignity of
its discourse, is, if not certainly unique, a special and distinguishing
characteristic of the literature of this *Kulturgebiet,* broadly construed,
and that this has a particular kind of cultural significance.[24]

We find a fascinatingly, tantalizingly related story in Apuleius. In
the *Metamorphoses* (*The Golden Ass*) 9.17–21, the narrator tells the tale
of a certain slave named Myrmex. Myrmex has been commanded on
pain of his life to guard the chastity of Arete, the young and beautiful
wife of the public figure Barbarus, while the latter is away on business. Determined out of fear and loyalty to carry out his charge, he
even holds on to the hem of her robe on the way to the bath house.
Unfortunately the clever rake Philesitherus sees her on one of those
excursions and inflamed by her beauty and the obstacles in his path,
becomes determined to "have" her. Approaching Myrmex with the
offer of a significant bribe to be divided between the guard and the
woman herself, he tries to get his way. Myrmex is at first horrified at
the thought, but over time becomes himself so inflamed with lust for
the money that he gives in and easily persuades the young woman to
comply as well to receive her significant share of the money. Naturally
the husband comes home unexpectedly in the middle of the fateful
night, but being held off by a ruse of Myrmex, does not become aware

the Sacred: Religious Contacts and Conflicts in the Holy Land First–Fifteenth Centuries CE, ed.
Guy Stroumsa and Arieh Kofsky (Jerusalem: Yad Ben Zvi, 1998), 109–29. See too Hasan-
Rokem, *Tales of the Neighborhood: Jewish Narrative Dialogues in Late Antiquity,* Taubman
Lectures in Jewish Studies (Berkeley: University of California Press, 2003), 2, 45, 84–85,
143. Pages 55–85 in the latter work focus on Rabbi Me'ir as well.

    24. I am grateful for the commentary of Wendy Doniger upon the occasion of a
presentation of this material at the University of Chicago Divinity School for helping me
clarify this stance.

of what is going on. However, the adulterer leaves his slippers under the bed, and upon discovering them in the morning, the husband figures out what has happened and becomes determined to carry out the death penalty for Myrmex, the guard. A funny thing happens on the way to the gallows: Philesitherus himself encounters Barbarus with Myrmex in tow in chains and quickly thinking and figuring out what has taken place, accuses the slave of having stolen his slippers at the bath house the previous day. The story has a happy end. Without suggesting any form of dependence between the two stories, I would argue that there are, nevertheless, sufficient elements shared by them to relate them one to the other. In both, the protagonist is a guard appointed to protect the "owner" of the woman (in one case from unchastity, in the other, from chastity, as it were). In both cases, not only is there a bribe (a rather commonplace detail; after all, guards are there, as it were, to be bribed), but specifically a bribe to be divided in two in order to enable *Die Entführung aus dem Serail.* In both cases, the compromised guard ends up in danger of his life, and in both he is saved by a funny sort of stratagem or miracle. I think it is not too much to conclude that the talmudic story comes out of the same cultural well from which Apuleius drew as well, and it is highly significant in my view that this lubricious tale has been adapted for the life of a rabbinic Jewish hero of the halakha. The rabbinic text is more like than unlike the other fish in the water in which it swims.

Indeed, there are numerous other Hellenistic allusions in Rabbi Me'ir's story. There are elements in the story—for instance, the chastity test—that are strikingly like topoi of the Hellenistic novels, such as Achilles Tatius's *Leukippe and Kleitophon.* In that novel, both protagonists (male and female) can be said to have passed such tests.[25] In the case of the male protagonist, it is a particularly striking parallel to our tale of Rabbi Me'ir's sister-in-law, for it is a third party (his lover

---

25. See recent discussions in Helen Morales, *Vision and Narrative in Achilles Tatius' Leucippe and Clitophon,* Cambridge Classical Studies (Cambridge: Cambridge University Press, 2004), 212–14 (especially relevant in that the discussion is of virginity in a brothel); and Burrus, "Mimicking Virgins," 62–63. For more on the chastity test in this novel and its prehistory, see Kathryn Chew, "Achilles Tatius and Parody," *Classical Journal* 96, no. 1 (2000): 63–64. This topos was, it seems, transmitted to Latin Europe via Seneca the Elder's *controversia* of the *Sacerdos Prostituta* (I owe this last reference to Simon Goldhill).

Leukippe) who becomes convinced of the sexual innocence of her intended, Kleitophon, upon hearing from the woman he is living with that she has no satisfaction from her "husband," since he is constantly complaining of (feigning, as we the readers know) illness. Leukippe herself undergoes virginity tests in the novel, as well.[26] In another of the Hellenistic novels, Xenophon's *Ephesian Tale,* the heroine is sent to a brothel and avoids her brothel duties through feigning sickness,[27] and in Tatius, the heroine avoids violation through the excuse that she is menstruating, just as in our story,[28] a defense that Simon Goldhill reminds us is unique in Greek literature.[29] The sexual incident in Rabbi Me'ir's story thus connects his legend multiply with Hellenistic novelistic literature. It does not seem to me far-fetched to read this story of Rabbi Me'ir's apparent sexual activity in this novelistic context. Indeed, the successfully maintained chastity in brothels of both Rabbi Me'ir and his sister-in-law would form a kind of doubling of this theme, analogous to the doubly maintained chastity of Leukippe and Kleitophon in their tale.

Let us look more closely, however, at this "doubling," reading for gender difference this time, not similarity.[30] In the first rescue, the damsel in question has to prove that she is, in fact, a damsel in order for there to be a miracle. Otherwise, no miracle. Having passed the chastity test devised by her tricky brother-in-law, she is vouchsafed the promised miracle, but in a rather indirect manner. Rabbi Me'ir

26. Achilles Tatius, "Leucippe and Clitophon," trans. John J. Winkler, in *Collected Ancient Greek Novels,* ed. B. F. Reardon (Berkeley: University of California Press, 1989), 272–73, 280–81. For another spectacular and novel virginity test, see Heliodorus's *Ethiopean Tale* (10.9) adduced by Burrus, "Mimicking Virgins," 78.

27. Xenophon of Ephesus, "An Ephesian Tale," trans. Graham Anderson, in *Collected Ancient Greek Novels,* ed. B. F. Reardon (Berkeley: University of California Press, 1989), 163. Also see Judith Perkins, *The Suffering Self: Pain and Narrative Representation in the Early Christian Era* (London: Routledge, 1995), 57–58. For such illness turned to other narrative purposes, that is, not feigned, see Tatius, "Leucippe and Clitophon," 226–27. Moreover, in yet another Greek novel, *The Story of Apollonius of Tyre,* "the motif of evasion of a prostitute's duties plays a major role." Xenophon of Ephesus, "An Ephesian Tale," 163n23.

28. Mobilized actually by a friend and ally of her lover, not she herself; Tatius, "Leucippe and Clitophon," 225.

29. Simon Goldhill, *Foucault's Virginity: Ancient Erotic Fiction and the History of Sexuality,* The Stanford Memorial Lectures (Cambridge: Cambridge University Press, 1995), 116.

30. For the spectacularly different versions of virginity for Leukippe and Kleitophon respectively, see Burrus, "Mimicking Virgins," esp. 61–63.

produces a miracle to prove to the guard that he will not be endangered if he is caught out for letting her go. And indeed, the miracle happens, twice. The first time, as just said, to convince the guard, and the second time to actually save him. It is instructive, however, to compare the conditions for the miraculous intervention (both Rabbi Me'ir's miracle and that of the Auth-r of Miracles himself, as it were) to take place. In a situation of potential rape *simpliciter*, the virgin must prove that she has maintained her virginity, or she would not be deemed worthy of a rescue at all. We can compare it to the instance of Rabbi Me'ir's own miraculous escape (not the version in which he dipped his finger in forbidden food but the one in which it was another member that enabled this sanctified figure's ruse). Reversing the usual topos in which a holy man comes into a brothel disguised as a soldier (and thus a customer) to rescue a virgin, here we have a holy man (well, a prophet) disguised as a whore to rescue a pseudo (?)john. Now notice that for the good rabbi the miracle that takes place and saves him does not involve any necessity that he prove his virtue, nor certainly his chastity; indeed, were he quite chaste, he would not have been saved at all. Rabbi Me'ir's sexual act cannot be simply dismissed in our reading (unless we are providing pious literature for children, I suppose). He actually has sex with Elijah, in whatever guise the Prophet is appearing at the moment. Else the Roman pursuers would not have let him go. The implication is inescapable; for the girl to have given up her chastity to save her skin would have been damning; for Rabbi Me'ir it is permitted and even part of the miracle.

Lest one still demur and propose that sex with an apparition is not sinful, I can argue against that claim from the Talmud itself. In yet another incident, it is Rabbi Me'ir who is rescued from unlawful carnal knowledge through a miraculous intervention:

Rabbi Me'ir was given to making fun of fornicators [claiming that it was easy to overcome one's sexual drive]. One day Satan [his sexual drive יצר הרע, so Rashi, correctly][31] appeared to him as a woman on the other side of the river. There was no ferry. [Rabbi Me'ir] began crossing the river by holding on to a rope that was stretched between the banks. When he had reached halfway across the rope, he [the sexual

31. There are manuscripts such as Munich 95 that don't read the word "Satan" at all.

drive] let him go, saying, "If they had not declared in Heaven: Be careful of Me'ir and his Torah!, I would have made your blood worth two
farthings! [You would have been a dead man]." (TB Kiddushin 81a)

In the one narrative, it is Elijah who appears to Rabbi Me'ir in the
appearance of a desirable woman with whom he does have sex; in the
other, it is his own desire, in the shape of Satan but with the appearance of another woman, who appears to him and makes him nearly
lose himself entirely. (Amazingly enough; right after this one a nearly
identical story is told of Rabbi Me'ir's teacher, the even more "holy"
Rabbi Akiva.) While it is entirely true, of course, that patriarchal cultures in general have been much more concerned with the chastity
of women than of men, for fairly obvious reasons having to do with
paternity and property, it is nevertheless the case that Rabbi Me'ir's
illicit sexual act here involves a violation of both halakhic and other-
aggadic norms.[32] There is a genuine set of puzzlements here then. A
virgin girl, had she been raped, would have been disqualified for miraculous rescue, but the rabbi is rescued *through* illicit sexual practice.
On the other hand, in another story the rabbi would have put himself in mortal danger, had he engaged (unwittingly) in another kind
of apparitional illicit encounter. Finally, it is at least worth pointing
out that in both cases of the Rabbi Me'ir's *Scheinsex* (appearance of
sex, playing with the scholarly convention of referring to *Scheintod* in
the novels),[33] the partner is a male figure, making this a kind of drag-
queen sex altogether. Rabbi Me'ir is saved *by* engaging in this queer
intercourse, in one case, while in the other, he is very nearly done in
by such an appearance of sex, and the rabbi is saved *from* engaging
in it by a miracle. Going back to the comparison with the poor virgin girl, moreover, we see that it was her effort to remain chaste that
enabled the miracle that in the end would make it possible for her to
marry while still a virgin, while in Rabbi Me'ir's case, his chastity was
also saved, but far from having protected himself from unchastity, he
arrogantly had thought that he was immune to such desires. It would

32. Note the story treated by Barry Wimpfheimer of the man who is allowed to die,
even commanded to, by the rabbis rather than fulfilling his "doctor's orders" that he see
a desired woman naked, or even talk to her from behind a barrier (Barry Wimpfheimer,
"Talmudic Legal Narrative: Broadening the Discourse of Jewish Law," *Dine Israel* [2007]).

33. Morales, *Vision and Narrative*, 166–69.

seem that *Scheinsex* (which is presumably enjoyable by the real human participant; otherwise the shine would be quite off it) is not sinful; it is only the giving in to the sexual instinct which would have caused the potential sin, from which sin Rabbi Me'ir is saved by (his own?) sexual desire having been warned in heaven to leave him be. But if that be the case, then, why would the girl's submission to rape to save *her* life not be equally sinless and render her worthy of a miraculous salvation? In placing these talmudic texts together, I might suggest that for the Talmud, one could claim, as Burrus does for Leukippe and Kleitophon, "that the tyranny of divine [demonic] eros doubles the tyranny of men."[34] Underlying this talmudic narrative there appears to be a "Jewish" sexual ethic that quite contradicts the words of John Chrysostom: "The Jews disdained the beauty of virginity, which is not surprising, since they heaped ignominy upon Christ himself, who was born of a virgin. The Greeks admired and revered the virgin, but only the Church of God adored her with zeal." It would seem that at least *some* Jews, alike in this respect to Chrysostom's Christians (and even at least some Greeks), adored the virgin girl (or contemned her "disgraced" sister) with great zeal indeed, since, as pointed out by Burrus, both the Christian Thekla and Leukippe meet threats to their virginity with defiance to the (potential) death.[35]

But how does this all sit together? I don't intend to attempt to reduce these contradictions, but rather to suggest that such contradictions are the very point of the Babylonian Talmud; that that to which we must attend in the Talmud is its all-pervasive heteroglossia, its almost Dostoevskian character, in which, to re-cite Bakhtin (citing Viktor Shklovsky), "It is not only the heroes who quarrel in Dostoevsky, but separate elements in the development of the plot seem to contradict one another: facts are decoded in different ways, the psychology of the characters is self-contradictory; the form is a result of the essence."[36] I would argue that these texts provide further evidence to that offered in the previous chapter that the Talmud can be quite fecundly read as a virtual novel in this Bakhtinian sense, in which the different languages of the late-ancient Jews of Babylonia

---

34. Burrus, "Mimicking Virgins," 67.
35. Burrus, "Mimicking Virgins," 62.
36. Bakhtin, *Problems of Dostoevsky's Poetics,* 40.

are brought into contact with each other; the halakha, the "serious" aggada, and the "wild" biographical legends as separate languages, each one "carving out a living image of another language."[37] In other words, as I have been arguing: far from being harmonious with the halakha of the official rabbinic discourse in the Talmud (or indeed of its aggadic homilies), the wild or grotesque legends may represent for us in dialogical form the voices of the nonrabbinic (or not fully rabbinic, whatever that might mean) as well, maybe even a voice deeply in opposition to the Rabbis. This should not, however, be in any sense literalized in the manner that *some* folklorists would do as the voice of the actual folk. The other language is a language within the language, but one that is deeply antithetical, in the way of dialogism, to the authoritarian language of the rabbinic "author," the *stamma,* but at the same time it is incorporated in the text by that very *stamma,* the *stamma* of the Talmud, "the whole book."[38] Bakhtin might have been speaking about the Bavli, in my opinion, when he treats of the development of inner conviction in both the individual consciousness (of the author) and in the literary representation thereof. Bakhtin remarks that the formation of such an "internally persuasive word" always takes place in the form of a dialogue with past voices: "While creatively stylizing and experimenting with another's discourse, we attempt to guess, to imagine, how a person with authority might conduct himself in the given circumstances, the light he would cast on them with his discourse. In such experimental guesswork the image of the speaking person and his discourse become the object of creative, artistic imagination. In Plato, Socrates serves as just such an artistic image of the wise man and teacher, an image employed for the purposes of experiment."[39] It is not hard to see a way to think of the Talmud and its rabbinic heroes in a way very similar to this one. But, and even more to the point: "One's own discourse and one's own voice, although born of another and dynamically stimulated by

37. Bakhtin, *The Dialogic Imagination,* 361.

38. For this term, see Stephen G. Nichols and Siegfried Wenzel, eds., *The Whole Book: Cultural Perspectives on the Medieval Miscellany* (Ann Arbor: University of Michigan Press, 1996). I am, however, using it differently than in medievalist parlance, where it refers to the codex and its collected works of various types, whereas here the production of "the whole book" out of diverse materials is the word of an authorial bricoleur and remains substantially the same from codex to codex.

39. Bakhtin, *The Dialogic Imagination,* 347–48, and n. 32.

another, will sooner or later begin to liberate themselves from the authority of the other's discourse. . . . All this creates fertile soil for experimentally objectifying another's discourse. A conversation with an internally persuasive word that one has begun to resist may continue, but it takes on another character: it is questioned, it is put in a new situation in order to expose its weak sides, to get a feel for its boundaries."[40] This is the character—I dare to suggest—of the final author, the *stamma* of the Babylonian Talmud. The discourse of the *tannai'im* and the *amora'im,* the early and late purveyors of the authoritative (and internally persuasive) discourse of the earlier strata of the Talmud (structurally, synchronically—I make no claim to know of the historical situation of the Talmud's final production), the halakha together with the serious aggada, are "the [collective] artistic image of the wise man and teacher, an image employed for the purposes of experiment," and also objectified, questioned, and tested for its boundaries. Insofar as the discourse of the *tannai'im* and the *amora'im* is an authoritative discourse—the discourse of Torah herself—it allows no dialogue within itself, but can be[41]—and, I suggest, is—relativized and dialogized within the work that is the Babylonian Talmud.

As Arkady Kovelman has pointed out, the Torah plays an ambivalent role in this last story of Rabbi Me'ir.[42] It is his arrogance borne of his learning that leads the rabbi to not take seriously the dangers of his own desiring self, to imagine himself immune, but then, once again, it is that very Torah learning that saves him in the end. The story thus enacts in its own ambivalence the greater ambivalence that is the jangling of languages of halakha and wild legend in the Bavli. A fine parallel to this can be found once more in Philostratus's *Apollonius.* It seems that a certain youth, Menippus (no relation) the pupil of Demetrius, was the lover of a "foreign woman." But it was only delusion, an apparition. She was, in fact, "a phantom in the shape of a woman" (φάσμα ἐντυχὸν γυνή τε ἐγένετο). The youth, however strong in philosophy, was quite taken in by and with this phantom lover, and went to visit her often, not realizing that she was a phantom. Apollonius looks at Menippus and divines the situation and through a ruse

---

40. Bakhtin, *The Dialogic Imagination,* 348.
41. Bakhtin, *The Dialogic Imagination,* 344.
42. Kovelman, "Miletian Story."

rescues the boy from the woman, who was one of the vampires, the sirens (λαμίας), and a werewolf, too (μορμολυκίας) (4.25).[43] We see here a similar, but certainly not identical, plot. The young man is a philosopher as Rabbi Me'ir is a Torah scholar, and both presumably consider themselves immune from certain kinds of seduction, but both prove seducible and in both cases by demon-lovers appearing as beautiful women. In the end Menippus's philosophy and Me'ir's Torah save them. I think we are not wrong in seeing in these parallel stories a dramatization of the contrast between the serious discourses of philosophy/Torah and the seductions of erotic narrative/biographical aggada.

The most striking parallel, however, to our narrative of Rabbi Me'ir is to be found in monastic literature contemporary with the final states in the literary history of the Talmud, the *Conferences* of John Cassian. In a story from that work discussed by Virginia Burrus in her latest book,[44] we find a certain young monk, who upon confessing his ongoing sexual desire to an older monk, is severely rebuked. The young man is on the point of abandoning his vocation when a still more senior monk, descrying the youth's distress, extracts the narrative from him and comforts him with a tale of his own constant torture by such desire. This older monk, Apollo by name, then sets out to teach his colleague a lesson. He causes through his prayer the desire of the young monk to be transferred to the elder in the shape of a demon. As Burrus narrates the dénouement of this story:

> Stricken by the darts of desire, the old man rushes off madly "along the same road taken by the young man." When the virtuous abba confronts him regarding his frenzied behavior, the tormented elder fears "that his heart's passion had been detected and that the deep secret of his soul had been uncovered by the old man," and he finds himself, like the young monk before him, unable to speak. The tables have been neatly turned, and now Apollo can bring his point home: no true monk, the old man cannot fend off, much less endure, even the temptations that typically beset youth. God is teaching him not only

---

43. C. P. Jones, *Apollonius*, 1.371–77.

44. Virginia Burrus, *Saving Shame: Martyrs, Saints, and Other Abject Subjects* (Philadelphia: University of Pennsylvania Press, 2007), 136–38.

"to have sympathy for the weakness of others" but also to recognize that temptation comes to those whose strength, unlike that of the old man, is great enough to arouse the envy of the enemy. Finally, Apollo prays that the temptation be withdrawn from the old man, who has now been effectively shamed and humbled, and once again God complies immediately.[45]

It is hard to avoid seeing the rapport between these two stories; the legend of brutal and near-successful temptation of an elder who in both cases counsels compassion for those weaker than ourselves but also constant fear for our own weakness. As we are informed in and through the story, temptation comes most sharply to those who are strong and therefore arouse the envy of the enemy, not to those who are weak.

This can be paralleled very closely again in the Talmud:

> And the Northern [or "hidden"] one, I will remove from among you [Joel 2:21]: This is the Evil Desire which is hidden and present in the heart of man. . . . *For it has performed mightily* [ibid.]. Said Abbaye: among the Torah scholars more than anyone. As in the story of Abbaye, who heard a certain man saying to a woman, "Let us get up early and go together on the way." He [Abbaye] said: "I will go and separate them from doing that which is forbidden." He went behind them for three parasangs in a meadow. When they separated from each other, he heard them, saying "Our way is long, and our company is sweet." Said Abbaye, "If that had been me, I would not have been able to control myself." He went and swung on the door-hinge [a sign of depression] and was miserable. A certain old man came by and taught him, "Everyone who is greater than his fellow, his Desire is greater also." (Babylonian Talmud Sukkah 52a)

Abayye hears that an unmarried man and woman are to travel together and is certain that this will lead to illicit sex. How surprised and depressed he is when he discovers that they travel easily in each other's company, enjoy it, and then part when they arrive at the crossroads

---

45. Burrus, *Saving Shame,* 137.

that leads to their respective villages. Abbaye's depression is generated by his self-understanding that he would not have been able to
part from her without having sex (or at least trying to), and he a great
Rabbi while *they* are only simple villagers. The tension is resolved
(and the depression lifted) by the explanation which the story gives in
the guise of an anonymous old man—along with children a frequent
purveyor of truths in talmudic texts. The very passion that drives Abbaye to study Torah and become a "great man," which for the Rabbis
always means one learned in and devoted to Torah, is the same passion that would have prevented him from simply saying goodbye to
the woman and parting from her without sex. The desire is one, and
the only way for the subject of great desire to keep himself out of sin
is to simply stay out of its way. The drive that in the Study House will
lead one to study Torah or in bed with one's wife to have intercourse
with her is the very same drive that will lead into sin when alone with
a woman to whom one is not married. The passion is one. As Burrus
compellingly reads the Christian tale, it is primarily a counsel against
despair, as is its parallel in the Talmud explicitly.

But here too we find another instance militating against that
equally serious and equally seductive error, namely the oft-repeated
tendency to consider the aggada the voice, always and everywhere, of
the lenient, the forgiving, as it were, while halakha is given the role of
the severe and restrictive. Our story is a case in point: according to the
halakha, there is no sense in which the young girl captured and incar-
cerated in a Roman brothel would be guilty of any sin whatsoever, but
in our legendary narrative her having submitted to rape would have
rendered her sinful (at least according to her brother-in-law the holy
man). With respect to the (potentially) raped virgin in the brothel,
the aggada here is much more stringent, indeed, than the halakha.
According to the halakha, at every level, from the text of Leviticus,
through rabbinic literature, and into the halakhic jurisprudence following the Nazi genocide, the law is entirely clear: A woman raped
to save her life or that of others is blameless, Esther the queen being
the very type of such a woman. It is only in the Babylonian Talmud,
in which the language of aggada is allowed to interpenetrate the language of halakha, that we can perceive the image of another language,
another discourse of the Jews of the time of the Talmud. In this "lan-

guage" a much harsher sexual ethic for women is prescribed, one in which, it would seem, a woman, much as Lucretia or Agnes,[46] ought to allow herself to be killed rather than violated, while a man might get away scot-free by sleeping with a prophet. The two languages are placed into a conflictual (or dialogical) relationship through their incongruous juxtapositions in the Babylonian Talmud. This dialogical reading of the Bavli can be further supported through more stories of Rabbi Me'ir's adventures.

The Adventures of the Torah on Earth

I would argue that, consistent with the practices of the menippea itself, in the farrago that is the Talmud, the most important intellectual practices of the rabbinic community are being advanced sincerely and queried at one and the same time, with an effect not of their undermining, but of their ironization. As Relihan has remarked of the Menippean satire in its cynical origins, "This is the subversive nature of Cynic criticism, which invests authority in a character who cannot be taken seriously without qualification, and which toys with the idea of an absolute or transcendent truth and those who would proclaim it."[47] "Toys with" perhaps, but does not in any way finally discredit either the character or the truth—at least with respect to the Talmud. Rabbi Me'ir is qualified as a source of *absolute, timeless, perfect* authority in the legends, but his position as heroic bearer of truth is in no way destroyed. The overall semantic effect is, I would suggest, analogous to Bakhtin's own description of the carnivalized hero: "Carnivalistic legends in general are profoundly different from traditional heroicizing epic legends: carnivalistic legends debase the hero and bring him down to earth, they make him familiar, bring him close, humanize him; ambivalent carnival laughter burns away all that is stilted and stiff, but in no way destroys the heroic core of the im-

---

46. Virginia Burrus, "Reading Agnes: The Rhetoric of Gender in Ambrose and Prudentius," *Journal of Early Christian Studies* 3, no. 1 (Spring 1995): 25–46.

47. Joel C. Relihan, "Menippus in Antiquity and the Renaissance." In *The Cynics: The Cynic Movement in Antiquity and Its Legacy,* edited by Bracht R. Branham and Marie-Odile Goulet-Cazé, Hellenistic Culture and Society 23, 265–93 (Berkeley and Los Angeles: University of California Press, 1997), 265.

age."[48] The last point is critical for my reading not so much of the carnivalistic legends of the rabbinic heroes, as my reading of the Talmud itself, of the Torah study that is its primary theme, and of the Torah student who is its primary heroic image. The story I am about to cite represents an almost textbook case of one version of Menippean satire, a kind of bringing down to earth of the very human desires and envies of a conversation that had seemingly been taking place, as it were, in a heaven all timeless and universal. As Alain Badiou states of philosophical thinking, "The statement 'truths are, for thought, compossible' determines philosophy to the thinking of a unique time of thought, namely, what Plato calls 'the always of time,' or eternity, a strictly philosophical concept, which inevitably accompanies the setting-up of the category of Truth."[49] If the halakhic discourse of the Talmud is the cultural analogue of what philosophy is in other versions of late Hellenism, then this narrative undermining of the claims of that discourse to timeless unconditional truth represents precisely what Badiou calls antiphilosophy.

This type of legend is one of the techniques by which the Talmud communicates both its commitment to the Torah-vision of the world and at the same time its understanding that even that most exalted of visions cannot provide a fully satisfactory explanation of the world. As Northrup Frye puts it, "At its most concentrated the Menippean satire presents us with a vision of the world in terms of a single intellectual pattern."[50] Yet we see that it is the burden of the menippea to suggest as well the antiphilosophic possibility that such totalizing visions are a chimera. We read in the Babylonian Talmud, tractate Horayot:

> Our Rabbis have taught: "When the Patriarch comes in [to the House of Study], all the people stand and they don't sit down until he asks them to. When the Chief of the Court comes in, they make for him

48. Bakhtin, *Problems of Dostoevsky's Poetics,* 132–33.

49. Alain Badiou, "The (Re)Turn of Philosophy *Itself,*" in *Manifesto for Philosophy Followed by Two Essays: "The (Re)Turn of Philosophy Itself" and "Definition of Philosophy,"* ed. and trans. Norman Madarasz (Albany: State University of New York Press, 1999), 123.

50. Northrop Frye, *Anatomy of Criticism: Four Essays* (Princeton: Princeton University Press, 1957), 309.

one row of standees on each side [of the pathway in] until he sits in
his place. When the Sage comes in, one stands and the other sits, until
he comes to his place [In other words, the one student closest to him
stands and then sits when he has passed him]."

The halakha—analogous in this important sense to Platonic philosophy—has presented itself as eternally valid, as the very oral Torah
which was presented to Moses on Mt. Sinai, and the Mishna is considered the textual representation of that eternally valid oral Torah.
Thus the teaching of the sages simply gives the halakha itself, anonymously and without historicism or explanation (but, of course, not
without controversy), *sine ira e studio*. As Moshe Azar has put the point,
"The linguistic presentation of the halakhot is, more than anything
else, gnomic in that the addresser expresses timeless law prescrip-
tions."[51] The timelessness and gnomic quality of this law prescription
is, however, immediately called into question in the continuation:

> Rabbi Yoḥanan said: This Mishna was taught in the days of Rabbi
> Shimʿon the son of Gamaliel. Rabbi Shimʿon the son of Gamaliel was
> the Patriarch, Rabbi Meʾir the Sage,[52] and Rabbi Natan was the Chief
> of the Court. When Rabbi Shimʿon the son of Gamaliel used to enter
> [the House of Study], all would stand before him. When Rabbi Meʾir
> and Rabbi Natan used to enter, all would stand before them. Rabbi
> Shimʿon the son of Gamaliel said, "Isn't it necessary to make a dis-
> tinction between me and them?" He established this Mishna. That
> day Rabbi Meʾir and Rabbi Natan were not there. On the next day,
> when they came, no one stood up before them as they had been used
> to. They said: "What's this?!" They told them, "This is what Rabbi
> Shimʿon the son of Gamaliel has established."

The timeless Mishna is thus, somewhat ignominiously, historicized.
That which we had thought to be oral Torah given at Mt. Sinai turns

51. Moshe Azar, "Rev. of N. A. Van Uchelen, *Chagigah: The Linguistic Encoding of Halakhah*," *Jewish Quarterly Review* 87, no. 1/2 (July–October 1996): 165.
52. This is a technical term for a not-entirely-understood office in the rabbinic
academies (or at least one projected by the makers of talmudic aggada). From this story,
it seems as if it is intended to refer to the third in dignity among the hierarchy of the rabbinic institution.

out to be the product of human, all too human, jealousies and envies. At this point in the narrative, one crucial Menippean moment has already been produced. The legend brings that claim to heavenly status right back down to earth and indicates that the given pronouncement of the sages is anything but eternal and superworldly, but is, rather, the product of some very human jealousy and even some sharp practice on the part of Rabbi Shim'on ben Gamaliel (waiting until his rivals were absent for the day to institute it). It is important to note that the only statement that is actually Rabbi Yoḥanan's (or that is even attributed to him) is the statement that this teaching was given in the time of Rabbi Shim'on the son of Gamaliel. All the following narrative is in Babylonian Aramaic and clearly a later Babylonian production, the implication of which is that formerly the disciples treated the three officials of the House of Study equally, but now the halakha has been changed owing to the Patriarch's overweening jealousy of his status. This story is almost Lucianic (if not Petronian) in its expression of contempt for the Patriarch, but lest we see it as the propaganda of a particular antipatriarchal party among the Rabbis (there were such, for sure), we find out right away that its contempt is equally great for the Patriarch's antagonists.

The story goes on to indicate a somewhat scurrilous response in turn on the part of these others of the holy band of transmitters of the eternal Torah, including our hero, the saintly Rabbi Me'ir:

> Rabbi Me'ir said to Rabbi Natan: "I am the Sage, and you are the Chief of the Court, let us establish a matter of our own." Rabbi Natan said to him, "What shall we do?" "Let's ask him to teach us 'Uqṣin, which he doesn't know, and since he has not learned, we will say to him 'Who shall recite the powers of God, recite all of his praise?' [Psalms 106:2] [which should be interpreted as:] For whom is it appropriate to recite the powers of God? For him who can recite all of his praise! We'll get him fired, and you will be the Patriarch and I will be the Chief of the Court." Rabbi Jacob the son of Martyrs [?] heard him and said [to himself], "Perhaps, G-d forbid, he will be shamed. He went and sat behind the upper room of Rabbi Shim'on the son of Gamaliel. He repeated it [tractate 'Uqṣin] and went over it; repeated it and went over it. He [Rabbi Shim'on the son of Gamaliel] said, "What is he saying? Perhaps G-d forefend, there is something brewing in the House of

Study!" He concentrated and investigated it and went over it. On the morrow, they [Rabbis Me'ir and Natan] said, "Let the master teach us of ʿUqṣin." He began and taught. After he had defeated them,[53] he said to them, "If I had not studied it, you would have shamed me." He became angry and threw them out of the House of Study. They [our exiles] would write their difficulties on sherds and throw them into the House of Study. Whatever [the other disciples] could resolve, they resolved, and what they couldn't resolve, [the exiled rabbis outside] resolved and threw in [the answers]. Rabbi Yose said: "The Torah is outside and we are inside!?" Rabbi Shimʿon the son of Gamaliel said to them: "Let them in, but fine them that their utterances will not be transmitted in their names." They referred to Rabbi Me'ir as 'Others' and Rabbi Natan as 'There are some who say.'" It was shown to them in a dream: "Go and make peace with Rabbi Shimʿon the son of Gamaliel." Rabbi Natan went and Rabbi Me'ir didn't go, saying, "The words of dreams neither raise nor lower [count for nothing]." When Rabbi Natan went, they said to him, "Granted that the buckle of your father [a badge of office] was efficacious for you in becoming the Chief of the Court, should it have been efficacious in becoming the Patriarch?" Rabbi teaches Rabbi Shimʿon the son of Rabbi [i.e., cited the following tradition in this form to his own son, the grandson of Rabbi Shimʿon ben Gamaliel]: "Others say: If it were *temura*, it is not sacrificed." He [the son] said to him [the father]: "Who are these whose water we drink and don't mention their names?" [Who are you citing as authorities but in this strange anonymous fashion?] He answered him, "People who wished to uproot your honor and the honor of your father's house." He [the son] said to him, "Your love and your hatred and your jealousy are all lost and gone" [Ecclesiastes 9:6] [Let it go; it was in the past]. He [the father] answered him, "The enemy is dead, the swords are forever" [Psalms 9:7: the effectiveness of the past in the present]. He [son] said to him, "Those words [apply] in a case in which his [the enemy's] actions were effective. As for these, their actions had no effect." He [the father] repeated it again and said in the name of Rabbi Me'ir: If it were *temura*, it is not sacrificed. Rava

53. For this correct interpretation of בתר לאוקים, see Adiel Schremer, "'He Posed Him a Difficulty and Placed Him': A Study in the Evolution of the Text of TB Bava Kama 117a," *Tarbiẓ* 66, no. 3 (April–June 1997): 409–10 (in Hebrew; English summary, p. viii).

commented: "Even Rabbi who was a humble man said, 'They said in the *name* of Rabbi Me'ir'; he didn't say, 'Rabbi Me'ir said.'" (Horayot 13b–14a, following Paris 1337)

Our story is doubly deflationary. First of all, as already noted, it drags a moment of the halakha, indeed of the Mishna, the very "oral Torah" itself, down from its above-worldly eternal status and mires it in the grossest of parody-historicistic contexts. Secondly, however, it deflates the claim of our rabbinic hero to superiority and turns his status right over from the most authoritative of the rabbis to the most nearly marginalized, from the one who need not be named to the one who may not be named.

The quality of Rabbi Me'ir's vaunted (and indeed unananonymous) anonymity is important for my considerations, for this is a moment of clearly dialogical accents and second accents in the text commenting on its own editorial practice. There are two incompatible accounts of Rabbi Me'ir's anonymity in the Talmud. In reading these two accounts together, I would suggest that taken as such they thematize this peculiar holy man as an emblem of the very text he inhabits that is produced by him and which he produces. The "serious" version that we have met above affords this anonymity great dignity: "Rabbi Yoḥanan says: The anonymous voice in the Mishna is Rabbi Me'ir" (Babylonian Talmud, Sanhedrin 86a). In this version it is Rabbi Me'ir's overwhelming superiority to his fellows that causes Rabbi Yehuda, the editor of the Mishna, to adopt his teacher's teachings nearly entire (and in his own anonymous voice).[54] In the "serious" version, the halakhic dictum of Rabbi Yoḥanan just cited, Rabbi Me'ir's anonymity is represented as the sign of his great authority. He is, as it were, the anonymous voice behind the most authoritative text of all, the Mishna; Rabbi Yehuda the Patriarch, otherwise known just as Rabbi, is the actual "author" of the text. In what might be taken as the serious register of the tradition, Rabbi Me'ir is understood, then,

---

54. For a tenth-century Babylonian rabbinic account of the wonders of Rabbi Me'ir's Mishna and the reason that Rabbi Judah chose it to be *the* Mishna, see Benjamin Manasseh Lewin, ed., *Iggeret Rav Sherira Ga'on,* by Sherira Ben Hanina (Haifa, 1921), 28–30 (in Hebrew). For some discussion of the passage (with a translation), see Elizabeth Shanks Alexander, *Transmitting Mishnah: The Shaping Influence of Oral Tradition* (Cambridge: Cambridge University Press, 2006), 79.

to exercise and manifest his supereminent prestige through this anonymity. He is the one who need not be named, because he is, in some sense, the "author" of the tradition. I would suggest that this aspect of the holy man is a representation, in effect, of the anonymity of the *stamma.* Our own authority, says this anonymous voice, is guaranteed, certified by our namelessness and thus timelessness, ahistoricity (very much, in that sense, like that of the Plato absent entirely from the dialogues).[55] Our story, however, brings this lofty conception crashing down to earth in a rather cynical fashion. The reason that Rabbi Me'ir is not mentioned by name is now not owing to his prestige, but owing to a shaming and disgraceful "punishment" on the part of the Patriarch, the same Rabbi Yehuda's father. The story, read in this fashion, is thus a "Menippean" moment of self-reflection, a "formulation of the inadequacy of human knowledge." The contradiction between these two contrary versions of Rabbi Me'ir's anonymity has precisely the effect of introducing a "second accent," a "crude contradiction" into the discourse of the Talmud.

There is, moreover, within the Talmud another silencing of Rabbi Me'ir which brings it ever closer to the Menippean tradition with all of its ambivalence:

> Rabbah bar Shila once came upon Elijah the prophet. He said to Elijah, "What is the Holy One, blessed be he, doing?" Elijah replied, "He is reciting the teachings that are spoken by all of the Rabbis—except for those of Rabbi Me'ir." "And why?" [asked Rabbah bar Shila]. [Elijah] said, "Because Rabbi Me'ir learned the teachings of Elisha ben Abuya, who abandoned his faith." Rabbah said, "And why?! Rabbi Me'ir found a pomegranate, ate the fruit and threw away the peel!" [Elijah] said to [Rabbah], "Now he says, 'My son Me'ir, says. . . .'" (Ḥagiga 15b).

This story includes an allusion to yet another one in the bizarre sequence of stories about Rabbi Me'ir's relations with his teacher, the famous heretic Elisha ben Abuya, known as Aḥer, the Other One, and thus also dispossessed of his name. In this version, Rabbi Me'ir is

---

55. Cf. Goldhill, "Becoming Greek, with Lucian," in *Who Needs Greek? Contests in the Cultural History of Hellenism* (New York: Cambridge University Press, 2002), 63.

not cited in heaven when they learn Torah there, when God repeats the teachings of the disciples there, owing to Rabbi Me'ir's loyalty and commitment to Aḥer, his teacher, lately become arch-heretic. One of the Babylonian *amora'im,* on hearing this sad report of Rabbi Me'ir's nonpersonhood from Elijah the Prophet, remonstrates with this messenger from God that the disciple did not take the master's heresies, but only his kosher teachings of Torah, and thence, imme-diately, Rabbi Me'ir's name is once again mentioned in the yeshiva in heaven. The spirit of the Menippean satire is written all over this little story. Less corrosive in its attitude toward the sages than the last one, it marks rather a sort of Menippean ambivalence about them, their studies, and discipleship, rather than the cynicism so close to the surface of the former. The debasement of the lofty that is em-blematic of the menippea is doubled within the story. First, the Torah itself is taken down from her shelf of timeless and unchanging value in which things are never added or changed, but are only discovered as permanent and unvarying truth. The rabbinic hero/saint himself, together with his Torah, is removed from any idealized position as perfected human and brought down to earth with all his competitive-ness, pettiness, and slyness exposed. He—together with his Mishna herself[56]—is the very type of the Bakhtinian carnivalized hero. As Dina Stein has emphasized to me, the limit-case of the internal (Me-nippean) satire is reached with the figure of Aḥer, who actually leaves the rabbinic fold. Although Rabbi Me'ir, his devoted disciple, follows after him, he goes only so far, only to the limits of violating the Sab-bath, and then turns back. The essence of the story is in the reaching of the limit of halakhic authoritativeness and then turning back.

Rabbi Me'ir and the Second Sophistic

A crucial support for this interpretation can be found in the fact that Rabbi Me'ir is portrayed in yet another Babylonian talmudic text as a Sophist and thus as a figure who stands directly against, as it were, the truth claims of the halakha. Strikingly enough, given his central posi-

56. Lest this personification sound extreme, I would adduce the fact that by the early modern period, a prominent Jewish mystic and lawyer can envision the Mishna as a female figure who comes to him in visions and instructs him; R. J. Zwi Werblowsky, *Joseph Karo, Lawyer and Mystic,* Scripta Judaica (Oxford: Oxford University Press, 1962).

tion in determining the halakha, this narrative suggests that he is not to be relied upon at all. We need look no further than Lucian for evidence that as late as his time, Sophists/rhetors were considered in important senses the opposite numbers of philosophers. Lucian himself thematizes this opposition while transgressing it flamboyantly, most floridly in his text known as "Twice Accused." It is therefore of not inconsiderable significance that there is at least one highly important pointer within the Babylonian corpus of Rabbi Me'ir traditions that stops just short of explicitly naming him as a Sophist:

> Rabbi Aḥa the son of Rabbi Ḥanina said: It is revealed and known before the One Who Spoke and the World Was that there was none like Rabbi Me'ir in his generation. Why then did they not establish that the halakha is [always] like his view? Because his colleagues could not determine his true opinion, since he would say of the impure: "pure" and of the pure: "impure" and find arguments [lit. faces] for this. We have a tradition that his name was not Rabbi Me'ir but Rabbi Miyasha. Why then was he called Me'ir [the Enlightener]? Because he used to enlighten the faces of the Sages in the halakha. . . . Rav said: The fact that I am sharper than my colleagues is because I saw Rabbi Me'ir from behind,[57] and if I had seen him from in front, I would have been even sharper, for it says "Let your eyes see your teachers." Rabbi Abbahu said that Rabbi Yoḥanan said: Rabbi Me'ir had one disciple whose name was Symmachus who would say about every matter which is pure forty-eight proofs that it is impure and about every matter which is impure forty-eight proofs that it is pure.[58] We have a

57. Following the undoubtedly correct reading in ms. Vat. 109. Rabbi (Yehuda Hanassi) had certainly seen Rabbi Me'ir from "in front" as well.

58. The text found in some manuscripts that reads, "who would say about every matter which is pure forty-eight proofs that it is pure" seems much weaker to me, particularly since it is immediately followed by another instance of someone who could argue that impure things are pure. The implication of this — I believe doctored — reading would be that even though (or because) Rabbi Me'ir could render the pure impure, his student could render the pure pure (Kraemer, *Reading the Rabbis: The Talmud as Literature* [New York: Oxford University Press, 1996], 62–63). The consequence of these different readings is immediate: Kraemer argues that "these latter steps make it clear that, despite the potentially perverse consequences of R. Meir's method, the sugya intends to offer him the highest of praises," to which I respond, then, why is not the halakha according to him in that case (according to this text)? I follow here the interlinear gloss in Munich 95. Aside from this difference, perhaps, the results of Kraemer's reading and mine are not incompatible,

tradition that there was a senior disciple at Yavneh who would purify the impure creeping things with one hundred and fifty proofs. (Tractate Eruvin 13b [paralleled in the same tractate at 53a])

It is hard to imagine a more ambivalent portrayal than this. The reason that the halakha is not in accordance with the view of the one who enlightened them in halakha is that he was able to produce equally compelling arguments on both sides of any halakhic question (and did, at least according to this report), and the disciples accordingly could not determine his true view.[59] Rabbi Me'ir, it seems, was as disconcerting to his fellows as Carneades was for the Romans when he engaged in a similar intellectual and discursive practice. This reported practice connects Rabbi Me'ir directly with Sophists and sophism, and indeed most strongly to Protagoras and Gorgias.[60] While techniques such as Rabbi Me'ir's have been typically taken in the scholarly (and philosophical) world as Plato intended us to understand them, namely as a kind of charlatanism, it is possible to reread this text rather as precisely a commitment to a genuinely dialogical critique of the very institution of *epistēmē*, which for the Talmud, as

---

except that where he sees a more celebratory mood in the *sugya,* I perceive deeper uneasiness and anxiety, a voice more critical of itself and its practices.

59. Kraemer, *Reading,* 60–70.

60. This sophistical notion that contradictory positions are not necessarily true or false has been well described by Richard Enos (*Greek Rhetoric,* 77–78):

Gorgias was the beneficiary not only of the theory of probability but also of a philosophical tradition that would establish tenets for support of his anti-Platonic view of rhetoric. A generation before Gorgias, Zeno formalized the notion of securing contrary conclusions from shared premises and established the dialectical method of arguing from contrary positions (Diogenes Laertius 8.57.9.25; Plato, *Sophista* 216A, *Phaedrus* 261D; Aristotle, *Rhetoric* 1355A–B, *Topica*). This system of inquiry proceeds from premises that are not agreed upon; the conclusions result in a choice of probable positions. Thus, contrary to the dialectic of Plato (*Parmenides* 128A; *Phaedrus* 261D, E), conclusions expose contradictory positions in relative degrees of strength. The apparent incompatibility of these paradoxical and antithetical positions prompted Plato to dismiss such notions as avoiding a quest for absolute knowledge (*Phaedrus* 261D) and attempting to confuse appearance with reality. Plato's objection to the philosophical implications of Gorgias's rhetoric concentrated upon the charge that such inquiries did not seek knowledge as a realization of virtue (*Gorgias* 455A). Consequently the inherent worth of rhetoric could in no way compare with that of the "art" of philosophy, which avoids deception and seeks truth (*Phaedrus* 262B, C) by examining knowledge of first principles (*Phaedrus* 272D). Plato saw an unbridgeable gap between the examination of certain knowledge leading to virtue and the "deception" inherent in the relativism of sophistic rhetoric.

we have seen already, would be located in the realm of halakhic, not philosophical, knowledge.

This text perfectly encodes the particular and peculiar yoking that is the Babylonian Talmud. On the one hand, as Kovelman has noted, Rabbi Me'ir is presented as no less than a type of Moses himself, or even better, as God himself to Rav's Moses, were it possible to say that, for, of course, it is Moses who saw only the back part of God and not his face. Kovelman believes that the comparison is in itself parodic. As Kovelman has written, "Yet to make this parody, he [the author of this text] must have been aware of a certain exegetical cliché. Exodus 33:12–23 ought to have been [= must have been] systematically construed even before the anecdote appeared as a demonstration of the capabilities and limits of human cognition."[61] In other words, if Moses's vision of God's back and not front was already understood as an allegory for the limitations on human knowledge, then it can be deflatingly parodied as referring to Rav's inadequate knowledge of oral Torah, because he saw only the back of Rabbi Yehuda. On the one hand, the comparison to Moses is a hagiographical topos of the time and place of the composition of the Talmud, as witness, for instance, Gregory of Nyssa's life of Gregory Thaumaturgus, but on the other hand, the precise incident (parodically) referred to in Moses's own biography here is thoroughly within the thematics of an intellectual critique of the intellect and thus a *mise en abyme,* in my view, of the Talmud itself.

The sophistic theme is thus perfectly congruent with the hagiography here. The connection of one of the most authoritative of the Rabbis with sophistical manipulations and thus critique of halakhic *epistēmē* strikes me as being of a great deal of importance and interest. The suggestion that I put forward is that the sophistry of Rabbi Me'ir is, in some sense, at the very heart of the talmudic enterprise, an enterprise that is both assertive of the value of and critical of the limitations of intellect as a means of knowledge and control of the world. If the function of menippea is, as Relihan argues, to "abuse scholars for mastery of a learning that was insufficient to explain or

---

61. Arkady B. Kovelman, *Between Alexandria and Jerusalem: The Dynamic of Jewish and Hellenistic Culture,* Brill Reference Library of Judaism (Leiden: Brill, 2005), 82–83.

to control the irrational and human world,"[62] then the Bavli's "biography" of Rabbi Me'ir certainly fits into that genre.[63]

Even though the term "abuse" might be off in tone for the Talmud, the overall import, I would suggest, is, as Relihan put it, "that any attempt to reduce the strange phenomena of this world to rule and theory can only lead to the embarrassment of the theorist"[64]—a point to be taken to heart by the modern theorist as well. If we see sophistic in general as a resistance movement against philosophy in the Platonic sense (an internal resistance within Plato as well, as I shall argue in the next two chapters), then this signposting of Rabbi Me'ir as a Sophist is of great importance. Graham Anderson has already shown how the figures of the Sophist and the holy man become connected in the Second Sophistic and following.[65] Rabbi Me'ir's sophism thus connects his character very explicitly with the movement of thought known as the Second Sophistic and points toward other Hellenistic parallels to stories and aspects of his Babylonian talmudic life.

The seriocomic, or menippea in its broadest sense, represents an "intellectual attitude adopted toward the value of truth and the possibility of meaning,"[66] and not a mere style. Far from being a *jeu d'esprit,* or "mere" folklore, or anything that can be dismissed at all, the biographical legends, the wilder and more bizarre the better, have to be read together with the halakha and aggada of the Babylonian Talmud as absolutely essential to any rich and full reading of that definitive text of historical rabbinic Judaism. We must pay close attention to the fact that Rabbi Me'ir and his fellow saints of Torah are hardly saintly fools, but rather scholars and intellectuals who, nevertheless, are provided frequently with bizarre and even grotesque lives.[67] In this, far

62. Relihan, *Ancient Menippean Satire,* x.

63. As does the famous narrative about Moses and Rabbi Akiva which I have discussed above in chapter 5. There, to be sure, Rabbi Akiva is abused quite literally, tortured by the Romans, while the inadequacy of the sages to even understand what they see, hear, and know is rendered explicit in the divine command to Moses to be silent.

64. Relihan, *Ancient Menippean Satire,* xi.

65. Anderson, *Sage, Saint, and Sophist Holy Men and Their Associates in the Early Roman Empire* (London: Routledge, 1994), 37–38.

66. Relihan, *Ancient Menippean Satire,* 7.

67. Daniel Boyarin, "Literary Fat Rabbis Re(Ci)Divivus: The Syriac Connection and the Ends of Dialogue in Jewish Babylonia," in *The End of Ancient Dialogue,* ed. Simon Goldhill (Cambridge: Cambridge University Press, 2007), 217–41.

from claiming uniqueness for them, I would nonetheless argue that they are particularly sited in a particular historical time and space, the space of the Menippean. This account of Menippean satire, along with the realization that various talmudic narratives—notably this one—and even, in some sense, the Talmud *tout court,* belong to this world, opens us up to richer and deeper interpretation of the text. If indeed, as posited in this and the previous chapter, the theme of the menippea is a philosophical formulation of the inadequacy of human knowledge and certainly of its limitations in bettering the world, then a genre in tension such as this would be a powerful way of making "possible the transfer of ultimate questions from the abstractly philosophical sphere, . . . to the concretely sensuous plane of images and events."[68] Saints are good for thinking with. The hero-saint who is thus, paradoxically, humanized and brought down to earth and whose heroic core is ironized but not in any way destroyed is a figure that is good, I think, for thinking the tensions of a society that no longer quite believes in the ultimate truth of philosophy or human Torah study respectively, but will not/cannot let go of them either. I suggest that the talmudic *spoudogeloion* results from the yoking together of a high-cultural genre, the speech practices of the House of Study, the discourse of the halakha, with a folk genre, the "hagiographic" narrative.[69] By "yoking together" here it should not be understood that I am necessarily claiming a historical or diachronic development in which the *sugya* was independent in some sense from the narrative, that they circulated in entirely different social worlds, as it were, and they were then forced together into the Talmud. That would be a gross historiographical simplification, if not outright distortion. Were I to imagine a historical process, it would build on something like Bakhtin's account of the history of the Socratic dialogue, in which, as he suggests, the beginnings of the genre were in the folk genre known as the *memorat,* orally transmitted reminiscences (usually short) of

68. Bakhtin, *Problems of Dostoevsky's Poetics,* 134.

69. This is a different approach from the one usually accepted in talmudic studies, divided between, on the one hand, figures like Jonah Fränkel, for whom all of the Talmud is the product of the high-cultural world of the House of Study, and, on the other hand, scholars such as Galit Hasan-Rokem, who read the Talmud as itself folk literature. It is possible that this is how the Socratic dialogue functions as well, but that remains to be studied below.

the conversation of an important figure, "transmissions of remembered conversations framed by a brief story." As these developed in
Greek into a formal literary genre, there remained within it "only the
Socratic method of dialogically revealing the truth and the external
form of a dialogue written down and framed by a story."[70] Similarly, I
would imagine the talmudic literature as having its beginnings in such
a *memorat* genre (this is essentially what we have in the Palestinian
Talmud, and there are many remnants within the Babylonian Talmud
as well), built into the formal genre of the *sugya* by the *stamma* of the
sugya. At the same time the narrative part of the *memorat* had also expanded itself and incorporated other folk genres such as the legend,
which, as part of the entire oral tradition, was itself eventually incorporated into the Talmud along with the *sugya,* giving us the hybrid
text, *satura,* which has been the center of Jewish intellectual life for
well over a millennium. To invoke Bakhtin once again: "The novelist
does not acknowledge any unitary, singular, natively . . . indisputable
or sacrosanct language. Language is present to the novelist only as
something stratified and heteroglot. Therefore, even when heteroglossia remains outside the novel, when the novelist comes forward
with his own unitary and fully affirming language (without any dis-
tancing, refraction or qualifications) he knows that such language is
not self-evident and is not in itself incontestable, that it is uttered in
a heteroglot environment, that such a language must be championed,
purified, defended, motivated. In a novel even such unitary and direct language is polemical and apologetic, that is, it interrelates dialogically with heteroglossia. It is precisely this that defines the utterly
distinctive orientation of discourse in the novel—an orientation that
is contested, contestable and contesting—for this discourse cannot
forget or ignore, either through naiveté or by design, the heteroglossia that surrounds it."[71] I hope to have made at least plausible and
defensible by now the claim that the Babylonian Talmud, precisely in
its cacophony of inserted genres and multiple voices, sets up an internal dialogism or contestation between its "normal literary language,"
the language of halakhic and aggadic piety, and an impious language
of biographical legendary narratives about the very heroes of that

70. Bakhtin, *Problems of Dostoevsky's Poetics,* 109.
71. Bakhtin, *The Dialogic Imagination,* 332.

normal/normative language. Considering this comparison less anach-
ronistically, perhaps, the closest literary congeners to the Talmud
from its own time appear to be the texts of the menippea broadly
speaking and the Menippean *satura,* sausage.

Carrying this sausage with us in our pack of victuals, let us go back
then and reapproach Plato. Perhaps the Talmud with its *spoudogeloish*
double reading can help open (my) eyes to a more complex strategy
for disentangling some of the conundrums in the reading of Plato as
well. My emblematic text for this shall be the *Symposium,* in which,
in a double-voiced reading of my own, I hope to articulate the dead-
serious monologism and power-laden use of language in the dialogue,
alongside its own explicit, and even broad, critique of that voice, thus
making the point that in Plato as well, dialogue is not between characters who are indeed, as are the *tannai'im* and *amora'im,* all aspects of
a single authoritarian discourse. As Bakhtin put it with respect to the
novel, the dialogism in the *Symposium,* and by extension the Platonic
corpus, is between Plato as author and his hero and main character,
Socrates. It is this claim that I will be exploring in the final two chapters of this book.

"The Truest Tragedy"

The *Symposium* as Monologue

I now make a strange turn from a chronological point of view and come back to Plato, a thousand years before the Talmud and in another country yet again; the reason for this chronological discontinuity being an intuition that the analysis of the Talmud that I have given in the last three chapters may help us open up some questions about Plato in a new fashion. In particular, I shall be listening for a double-voicing of the Platonic text in this and the next chapters, analogous—partially but interestingly—to the double-voicing that I have found in the Bavli.

The Education of Socrates Sophistes:
The *Symposium* as True Tragedy

As we saw above, for Plato the term "tragedy" ought to be reserved for the discourse and practices within a given culture which are most clearly dedicated to holding on to Truth. Among the sites in which he most strongly demands such "seriousness," the discourse of educational formation is primary. In this chapter, in a kind of chiasm, I return to Plato's seriousness and his political discursive tractates via an analysis of that most interesting and appealing of his dialogues, the *Symposium*. While it is commonplace, however, that the *Protagoras* and the *Gorgias,* considered near the beginning of this book, are crucial for the study of rhetoric and dialogue,[1] it is far less usual to take the *Symposium* that way, since its theme is understood to be love or sex. I suggest that the *Symposium* is entirely about education, about the formation of the disciple of philosophy. In this first part of my discussion of that text, I hope to explore with a seriousness appropriate to topic (as claimed by Plato himself) how Plato's "philosophy" is bound up with the very same discursive politics that I have found in the *Protagoras* discussed above: the politics, in short, of rhetoric versus philosophy and of debate versus dialectic. The *Symposium,* I will argue, is part and parcel of Plato's grand protreptic project to advance the cause of his Academy over any other school in Athens and his paths of "Truth" as the only way a man should walk.

Owing to its apparent obsession with love as its topic, the *Symposium* would seem, at first glance, an unlikely candidate for my argument that Plato's overweening theme, indeed the only theme he really cares about, is the advancement of the cause of philosophy, its distinction from rhetoric, and the defeat of its sophistic rival, erstwhile the most prestigious discourses on the Athenian scene. Usually, other and very specific dialogues are identified as about rhetoric, not the *Symposium.* Debra Nails, for instance, describes the *Protagoras* and the *Gorgias* as "advertisements for the philosophical mission of the Academy,"[2] while I would see this as the dominant theme of Plato's entire opus, including especially the *Symposium.*

The *Symposium* has, moreover, often enough been read as a dialogical text (in the Bakhtinian sense) in that the multiple languages of Athenian life, medical, philosophical, political, tragical, and comical, are represented within it as embodied in the various speakers. In *Genres in Dialogue,* Nightingale makes clear, however, that parodied and mocked discourses when set against the voice of the author (or something like it) are not at all dialogical in themselves,[3] so, in my

---

1. James P. Zappen, *The Rebirth of Dialogue: Bakhtin, Socrates, and the Rhetorical Tradition* (Albany: State University of New York Press, 2004), 3.

2. Debra Nails, *Agora, Academy, and the Conduct of Philosophy,* Philosophical Studies Series 63 (Dordrecht, Netherlands: Kluwer Academic Publishers, 1995), 217, n.

3. Andrea Wilson Nightingale, *Genres in Dialogue: Plato and the Construct of Philosophy* (Cambridge: Cambridge University Press, 1995), 7.

opinion, neither the *Menexenus* nor the "prose eulogies of the *Symposium*" yet evince the dialogical.[4] In fact, they are characterized more successfully as an integral part of the project of monological dialogues that I have been engaged in laying open. I thus agree completely with Nightingale's statement (with respect especially to the funeral oration in the *Menexenus* and the encomia of the *Symposium*) that "Plato uses intertextuality as a vehicle for criticizing traditional genres of discourse and, what is more important, for introducing and defining a radically different discursive practice, which he calls 'philosophy'"[5]—and this *use* of intertextuality hardly makes for a dialogical textual corpus. Bakhtin himself has written: "In another type of internally dialogized interillumination of languages, the intentions of the representing discourse are at odds with the intentions of the represented discourse; they fight against them, they depict a real world of objects not by using the represented language as a productive point of view, but rather by using it as an exposé to destroy the represented language. This is the nature of *parodic stylization*."[6] As Bakhtin also said in a passage that I have discussed in the introduction: "In the characters, individuality kills the signifying power of their ideas, or, if these ideas retain their power to mean, then they are detached from the individuality of the character and are merged with that of the author. Hence the *single ideational accent of the work;* the appearance of a second accent would inevitably be perceived as a crude contradiction within the author's world view."[7] These two descriptions taken together form, I would suggest, a perfect account of the first half of the *Symposium.* And Plato, I would suggest, knows what he is about. Far from being a dialogical text, the *Symposium,* in its aspect as a *Bildungsroman* for Socrates, one that marks his transformation from Sophist to philosopher, is also the narrative of the emergence of philosophy (Plato) out of sophism. What will finally emerge as dialogical in my

4. Nightingale, *Genres in Dialogue,* 3.

5. Nightingale, *Genres in Dialogue,* 5.

6. Mikhail Bakhtin, "Discourse in the Novel," in *The Dialogic Imagination: Four Essays by Mikhail Bakhtin,* ed. Michael Holquist, trans. Michael Holquist and Caryl Emerson, University of Texas Press Slavic Series (Austin: University of Texas Press, 1981), 363–64 (emphasis original). As Nightingale herself realizes: "Although Bakhtin usually celebrates parody as dialogical, the use of parody to claim higher authority is not"; *Genres in Dialogue,* 7n19.

7. Mikhail Bakhtin, *Problems of Dostoevsky's Poetics,* ed. and trans. Caryl Emerson, Theory and History of Literature (Minneapolis: University of Minnesota Press, 1984), 82.

reading will be precisely the "crude contradictions" that ensue, not from the speech of the characters, but from the discord of narrative elements. But I am getting ahead of myself. The story must be told in order—the authorian in this chapter, the crude contradiction in the next—so that both the single accent and the second accent shall be made legible (on my reading, of course).

The *Symposium* and the *Protagoras*

Reading the *Symposium* in a perhaps unfamiliar context within the Platonic corpus will help set up my interpretation of it. As I see it, the *Symposium* and the *Protagoras* are joined at the hip. As already contended above, it is the *Protagoras* that provides one of the clearest and most blatant examples of the politics of dialogue in Plato's protreptic. By joining that dialogue to the *Symposium,* I hope to advance my case that the overarching theme of "Plato" is the espousal of the politics of dialectic over against debate, of *philosophia* over against rhetoric/sophism, and of the Academy over against the polis.[8] It is the very unlikelihood of this pairing that suggests its hermeneutical importance: if I can demonstrate that these two radically disparate texts are thematically congruent, I will have gone some distance to making my case for the theme of a politics of dialectic as a powerful animator, if not *the* animator of Plato's corpus.

In fact, there are significant formal links between these two apparently very different dialogues; reading them together is justified by a set of very compelling allusions back and forth between them. As already noticed by Alexander Nehamas, "It is noteworthy that all of the speakers in the *Symposium,* with the interesting exception of Aristophanes, appear in the *Protagoras.*"[9] Too, the *Protagoras* begins with

8. For a related but different approach to reading the *Symposium,* see Nightingale, *Genres in Dialogue,* 110–30. For the symposium, itself, *qua* institution as a kind of antipolis, see Leslie Kurke, *Coins, Bodies, Games, and Gold: The Politics of Meaning in Archaic Greece* (Princeton, N.J.: Princeton University Press, 1999), 18.

9. Alexander Nehamas, trans., and Paul Woodruff, ed., *Symposium,* by Plato (Indianapolis: Hackett Pub., 1989), 9n7. All citations from the *Symposium* in this chapter and chapter 8 are from this translation. I have consulted the Greek of Kenneth Dover's edition throughout (Kenneth James Dover, ed., *Symposium,* by Plato [Cambridge: Cambridge University Press, 1980]). For the connectedness of these two dialogues, see James M. Rhodes, *Eros, Wisdom, and Silence: Plato's Erotic Dialogues,* Eric Voegelin Institute Series in Political Philosophy (Columbia: University of Missouri Press, 2003), 17–18. It will be

a usually overlooked bit of erotic byplay that invites us to consider it as an important aspect of the literary context of the *Symposium*. The very beginning of the dialogue finds Socrates meeting by chance a friend of his:

> FRIEND: Hello, Socrates; what have you been doing? No need to ask; you've been chasing around after that handsome young fellow Alcibiades. Certainly when I saw him just recently he struck me as still a fine-looking man, but a man all the same, Socrates (just between ourselves), with his beard already coming.
>
> SOCRATES: Well, what of it? Aren't you an admirer of Homer? He says that the most delightful age is that at which a young man gets his first beard, just the age Alcibiades is now, in fact. (309a–b)[10]

In its thematization of Socrates as lover, and especially as lover of Alcibiades, the narrative here is already signposting a connection with the *Symposium*. It does more work than that, however. Although the commentators I have read largely don't see the point of this banter, it seems to me highly significant in auguring Socrates' stance toward Athens and Athenian practice. It is not only, as C. C. W. Taylor would have it, that "homosexual attractiveness was considered to fade with maturity,"[11] but that in the standard Athenian sexual ethic, a grown man was no longer fair game for erotic attachment by an older man, but now should be, himself, interested in younger men/boys, or even in women. Foucault elaborates:

> At what age was it no longer good for him to accept this role, nor for his lover to want to assign it to him? This involved the familiar casuistry of the signs of manhood. These were supposed to mark a threshold, one that was all the more intangible in theory as it must have very often been crossed in practice and as it offered the possibility of

---

observed that the results of this comparison are quite different in Rhodes's reading than in mine. Cf. too Kevin Corrigan and Elena Glazov-Corrigan, *Plato's Dialectic at Play: Argument, Structure, and Myth in the* Symposium (University Park: Pennsylvania State University Press, 2004), 34–37.

10. The version cited throughout is Plato, *Protagoras*, rev. ed., trans. with notes by C. C. W. Taylor, Clarendon Plato Series (Oxford: Oxford University Press, 1991). For the Greek, the text of the Oxford Classical Texts has been used.

11. Plato, *Protagoras* 65.

finding fault with those who had done so. As we know, the first beard was believed to be that fateful mark, and it was said that the razor that shaved it must sever the ties of love.[12]

Indeed, a man with a beard who played the pathic courted losing his citizen rights.[13] It is only that absolute binary between the boy and the man that enabled Athenian pederasty to retain its semblance of honor, for, as has been shown amply, the penetratee *must* be of lower social status, in this case age, than the penetrator.[14]

Socrates, therefore, in what may have been quite a shocker, is deconstructing that binary. Socrates' interest in Alcibiades, moreover, while connected with his "beauty," has no physically desirous com-

---

12. Michel Foucault, *The Use of Pleasure,* vol. 2 of *The History of Sexuality,* trans. Robert Hurley (1984; repr., New York: Random House, Vintage, 1986), 199, citing the *Protagoras,* correctly understanding its implications, in my view. See too K. J. Dover, *Greek Homosexuality* (Cambridge, Mass.: Harvard University Press, 1989), 86, making this same point, citing as well Plutarch, *Dial.* 770c: "The beard, appearing on the eromenos, 'liberates the erastes from the tyranny of eros.'" Many pederastic epigrams mourn the appearance of that hair on the beloved. See Amy Richlin, *The Garden of Priapus: Sexuality and Aggression in Roman Humor,* 2d ed. (New York: Oxford University Press, 1992), 35, who also emphasizes the appearance of hair on the anus as marring the boy's beauty.

13. C. D. C. Reeve, introduction to *Plato on Love: Lysis, Symposium, Phaedrus, Alcibiades, with Selections from Republic and Laws,* ed. C. D. C. Reeve (Indianapolis: Hackett Pub., 2006), xvii. Note that this point is valid whatever the accepted sexual practice between *erastai* and *eromenoi,* that is, whether anal or only intercrural intercourse was practiced (as maintained by Dover, *Greek Homosexuality,* 98–99, and most scholars with him), because even in intercrural intercourse the relation between active and passive, between pleasure-taker and pleasure-giver, is pronounced, perhaps even more so than in anal intercourse. Interestingly, Dover seems, in another place, to allow for the possibility of anal and not merely intercrural intercourse in Athenian pederasty, when he glosses Pausanias as saying, "To translate from euphemism to plain English: acceptance of the teacher's thrusting penis between his thighs or in his anus is the fee the pupil pays for good teaching, or alternatively, a gift from a younger person to an older person he has come to love and admire" (*Greek Homosexuality,* 91).

14. For a particularly penetrating—joke intended—account of this virtual commonplace, see S. Sara Monoson, "Citizen as Erastes: Erotic Imagery and the Idea of Reciprocity in the Periclean Funeral Oration," *Political Theory* 22, no. 2 (May 1994): 262. See too Foucault, who points out the problems this system posed for an ethos of male superiority: "It was also in view of this difficulty that all the attention was concentrated on the relationship between men and boys, since in this case one of the two partners, owing to his youth and to the fact that he had not yet attained manly status, could be—for a period that everyone knew to be brief—an admissible object of pleasure" (*Use of Pleasure,* 220). Dover points out, as well, that these were not absolute distinctions; while the *erastes* was always supposed to be older than the *eromenos,* one male could be *erastes* to a younger boy and *eromenos* to an older man at the same time (*Greek Homosexuality,* 87). This does not vitiate, however, the main point here.

ponent, or perhaps more exactly put, no actual desire or intention to engage in physical contact—another shocker.[15] On my reading, Plato is signaling right here at the beginning one of the major themes, if not the major theme, of his dialogue and arguably of his oeuvre as a whole, his disdain for Athenian usages and practices. He is hinting strongly, too, that this disdain is centered on the age-hierarchical practices of the institution of Athenian pederasty (Greek love). Plato's Socrates repudiates the mores of Athenian pederasty and all that it implies socially and politically, having repudiated the reproductive, male-female sex even more so. Pederasty just isn't queer enough for him. This point is underscored, somewhat comically but nonetheless importantly, within a few lines when we are told that Socrates' attraction to the elderly sage Protagoras has driven Alcibiades entirely out of his mind. This account parallels and comments on Alcibiades' own narrative of sexual rejection by Socrates in the famous ending to the *Symposium,* to be discussed in the next chapter. Alcibiades' counter-pederastic pursuit of Socrates is prefigured, as it were, in the young Socrates' feigned erotic passion for the elderly Protagoras.

Another witness: In persuading Aristodemus to come with him to Agathon's dinner, Socrates alludes to a Homeric phrase "When two go together, one precedes another in devising what we shall say" (174d): 'σύν τε δύ,' ἔφη, 'ἐρχομένω πρὸ ὁδοῦ' βουλευσόμεθα ὅτι ἐροῦμεν.[16] At *Protagoras* 348d, Plato quotes the same line of Homer (*Iliad* 10.222–26), somewhat more precisely to be sure, in support of dialectic as the way to truth: "When two go together, one has an idea before the other": σύν τε δύ' ἐρχομένω, καί τε πρὸ ὃ τοῦ ἐνόησεν.[17] In both cases, it is the

---

15. Cf. Rhodes, *Eros, Wisdom, and Silence,* 14, on this passage, who doesn't arrive at the same result that I do.

16. For comment on the text, see Dover, *Symposium,* 82–83. I prefer the reading προ ὁ τοῦ from a literary standpoint, as have some other editors and commentators, despite the obvious syntactic problems it creates. The syntactic infelicity can be explained, I would guess, precisely on account of its being a partially unassimilated quotation from the Homer. I am, of course, hardly in a position to second-guess Dover on this (cf. too 174b).

17. James Rhodes has seen the Homeric allusion but reads it differently (*Eros, Wisdom, and Silence,* 17–18). He writes, "As noted above, Socrates quotes Homer in the *Protagoras* (315b9) to hint that he has entered hell as a spiritually living Odysseus and that he is consorting with the spiritually dead. In the *Symposium,* while he is en route to Agathon's dinner, he persuades his student Aristodemus to accompany him by stating 'When two go together, one precedes another in devising what we shall say' (174d2–3). With this, he ironically takes the part of Diomedes and casts Aristodemus as Odysseus" (17). With this remark Rhodes reveals that he seems not to have realized the importance of the fact that

necessity for dialectic to which Plato alludes. Once again, what is in one dialogue seemingly mere dramatic filler (or even comic relief) is shown by comparison with the other to be of major thematic importance.

C. D. C. Reeve has zeroed in on another highly significant point of connection between the two passages, one that goes beyond the formal and supports the point:

> The *Symposium* . . . contains an imitation of one part of such a [philosophical] life, namely, what the *Protagoras* terms a "symposium of beautiful and good men" who "test each other's mettle in mutual argument" by asking and answering questions (347d3–348a9). This is how Socrates responds to Agathon's speech. It is how Diotima converses with Socrates. It is the type of symposium Socrates tries to reestablish when Alcibiades' "satyr play" is finished, and the throng of Bacchic revelers has left.[18]

The two dialogues are thus connected thematically in crucial ways.[19] The *Protagoras,* on this account, is a comment on the *Symposium,* as the latter comments in turn on it. When we remember that the Athenian institution of pederasty involved not just the erotic in our sense, but *ta erotika* as intricately bound up with socialization and the political life of the city,[20] we can begin to appreciate how marked Socrates' rejection of the pederastic institution is in both dialogues (further evidence will be adduced from the *Phaedrus* below). The *Protagoras* seems to drop the erotic theme almost immediately. Since Plato has strewn these dialogues with clues that they need to be read together, and since the *Protagoras* is hardly to be read as about sex, then perhaps the point is that the *Symposium* is also not about sex, but about sophistic rhetoric and its concomitant politics[21] and about

---

exactly the same Homeric quotation used in the *Symposium* appears at a key moment in the *Protagoras* as well. The comparison would only strengthen Rhodes's overarching point that the two texts are related to each other. See Corrigan and Glazov-Corrigan, *Plato's Dialectic at Play,* 32.

18. Reeve, *Plato on Love,* xxxvii. I should say here that by the end of this book that throng of Bacchic revelers is going to seem highly significant indeed.

19. See also the connection (seemingly otherwise arbitrary) between the dismissal of flute girls in both texts as properly noted by Rhodes, *Eros, Wisdom, and Silence,* 18.

20. Paul W. Ludwig, *Eros and Polis: Desire and Community in Greek Political Theory* (Cambridge: Cambridge University Press, 2002).

21. See too Wayne. N. Thompson, "The *Symposium:* A Neglected Source for Plato's

exposing the deep connections between erotics and rhetoric[22] (thus, by the way, explaining the more explicit copresence of these seemingly disparate themes in the *Phaedrus,* as well). What the *Symposium* is about, on my reading, is what the entire Platonic corpus is about: it's about convincing us to abandon the life of the polis and its teachers and enter the life of the Academy. In its multilayered narrative structure, the *Symposium* dramatizes in several ways the emergence of philosophy and its absolute superiority over sophism and rhetoric. One of the most significant of these thematic/dramatic structures is Socrates' account of his education at the hands of Diotima.

Socrates' *Bildung*

The life of the polis is represented by all of the speakers up to Socrates/ Diotima, who, of course, represent the life of the Academy. All of the first group discuss the social utility, in one form or another, of Greek love, the most sophisticated being Pausanias's "elaborate apologetic for Athenian pederasty," as Thomas Luxon so pithily describes it.[23] The argument of the *Symposium* is thus thematized brilliantly in its structure. At the point in the text in which the shift from rhetoric and the democratic politics of the polis takes place, we are given a founding myth for this shift in the story of Socrates' *Bildung,* a myth of his own transformation from man of the lesser mysteries to man of the greater mysteries and thus the very institution of those greater mysteries, those which Plato calls philosophy.

In order to see this point we must pay careful attention to the radical difference between Platonic and Pausanian (normative Athenian)

Ideas on Rhetoric," in *Plato: True and Sophistic Rhetoric,* ed. Keith V. Erickson, Studies in Classical Antiquity (Amsterdam: Rodopi, 1979), 325–38, whose approach could hardly be more different from mine.

22. For a reading of the *Protagoras* that attempts to take the narrative frame as seriously as the dialogue itself, but oddly ends up with almost exactly the same monological readings as other philosophers tend to, see Francisco J. Gonzalez, "Giving Thought to the Good Together: Virtue in Plato's *Protagoras,*" in *Retracing the Platonic Text,* ed. John Russon and John Sallis (Evanston, Ill.: Northwestern University Press, 2000), 113–54. Gonzalez is one of the very very few who, at least, recognizes the erotic framing of the *Protagoras* as significant (114). I shall have some more words with this article at the very end of my book.

23. Thomas H. Luxon, *Single Imperfection: Milton, Marriage, and Friendship* (Pittsburgh, Pa.: Duquesne University Press, 2005), 4.

love,[24] disrupting the Foucauldian inclination to place Plato's theory
of eros on more of a continuum with (rather than in opposition to)
classical Athenian pederastic practice.[25] If Plato is firmly opposed to
even this most "heavenly" of Athenian apologies for pederasty, all the
more so will he reject the other explanations found in the *Symposium*,
rejecting indeed the institution itself.[26] More to the point, this radical rejection of Athenian "heavenly love" is an index, as well, of Plato's
radical opposition to Athens, to the polis itself, and especially to its
democracy and discursive practices. Closer reading of the *Symposium*
will bring out these connections.

Dialoghi d'amore: Plato as an Early Platonist

In the *Symposium,* the highest-minded form of Athenian pederastic
practice is represented by the figure of Pausanias, who distinguishes
between vulgar love, which is primarily sexual and includes the love of
women as well as purely sexual love for boys, and the heavenly love of
men for boys, which enables their education into the highest things in

---

24. "Pausanias's speech . . . is a normative description of the practice of pederasty in
Athens"; Richard L. Hunter, *Plato's Symposium,* Oxford Approaches to Classical Literature
(New York: Oxford University Press, 2004), 47.

25. See also Gregory Vlastos, "The Individual as Object of Love in Plato," in *Platonic
Studies* (Princeton, N.J.: Princeton University Press, 1981), 39–40, whose view of the matter is very like Foucault's. Too, the more recent (and excellent) book of Paul Ludwig refers
to "the philosophical foundation of pederasty begun by Phaedrus and Pausanias, on which
Socrates eventually bases his own intellectual pederasty" (*Eros and Polis,* 27–28n4). For the
particular nature of this "basing," which I take as rather an undermining and overturning,
see Reeve, who refers over and over again to Socrates' (Plato's) overturning and reversing of pederastic norms. But I am puzzled when Reeve writes of the bottom rung of the
Diotiman ladder, "At this stage, what the boy engages in the lover is his sexual desire for
physical beauty, albeit one which, in firm keeping with the norms of Athenian *paiderastia,*
is supposedly aim-inhibited: instead of sexual intercourse, it leads to discussions about
beauty, and to accounts of it" (*Plato on Love,* xxxi). This citation seems to imply that the
aim-inhibition of normative Athenian pederasty excludes sexual contact entirely, a position which seems so counterintuitive to me and contradictory to what Reeve himself says
elsewhere (xvii) that it must not be what Reeve means.

26. Note that this is quite a different strategy from those who read the *Symposium* as
a text in which each speech somehow incorporates the ones before it, with Diotima's
speech pulling it all together. My interpretative instincts are much closer to those of
Andrea Nightingale: "Since Socrates articulates a very different distinction between good
and bad love later in the dialogue, we are clearly meant to see Pausanias' categories as
unsound" (*Genres in Dialogue,* 43).

life.[27] For Foucault, there is little difference between Pausanian heavenly love and Platonic love itself: "One should keep in mind that [Platonic] 'asceticism' was not a means of disqualifying the love of boys; on the contrary, it was a means of stylizing it and hence, by giving it shape and form, of valorizing it."[28] For Foucault, indeed, the move to philosophical love (Socratic/Platonic style) is merely the product of a structural problem with pederasty. As he puts it:

> The preoccupation of the Greeks . . . did not concern the desire that might incline an individual to this kind of relationship, nor did it concern the subject of this desire; their anxiety was focused on the object of pleasure, or more precisely, on that object insofar as he would have to become in turn the master in the pleasure that was enjoyed with others and in the power that was exercised over oneself.
>
> It was here, at this problematization (how to make the object of pleasure into a subject who was in control of his pleasures), that philosophical erotics, or in any case Socratic-Platonic reflection on love, was to take its point of departure.[29]

But here's the rub, as it were. Foucault's account of "stylizing" the love of boys and of an attempt to deal with the problematic of status in the transformation of pathic citizen youths (*eromenoi*) into active citizen adult lovers (*erastai*) is a sharp characterization of the *Pausanian* moment, but not of the Socratic-Platonic reflection on love.[30] Foucault allows that "one does find in Plato the theme that love should be directed to the soul of boys rather than to their bodies. But he was not the first or the only one to say this." Moreover, "(and both the *Symposium* and the *Phaedrus* are quite explicit on this point) [Plato] does not trace a clear, definitive, and uncrossable dividing line between the bad love of the body and the glorious love of the soul."[31] Foucault is clearly not making any differentiation in this description

27. Cf. remarks of Dover, *Greek Homosexuality*, 12–13.
28. Foucault, *Use of Pleasure*, 245.
29. Foucault, *Use of Pleasure*, 225.
30. Monoson, "Citizen as Erastes," 263, is particularly sharp on how the "stylization" works and how precisely it overcomes the "problematization."
31. Foucault, *Use of Pleasure*, 238.

between the heavenly love of Pausanias and the eros prescribed by
Diotima. For Foucault, as in much of the scholarship that preceded
him, Pausanian erotic theory thus is identical with Plato's.[32] Although,
to be sure, Foucault recognizes that Plato's ideal was ascetic and "that
within this asceticism total abstention was posited as a standard,"[33]
by tying that standard to the structural problem occasioned by pederasty, he denies precisely the (nonhomophobic) contempt for all
physical sex that is Plato's—or at any rate Diotima's. Foucault thus
obscures the difference between standard high-minded Athenian
practice (as represented by Pausanias) and Plato's own views (as expressed by Diotima) by reading both Pausanias and Plato equally as
articulating an ethics (and not a rejection) of the carnal.

Kenneth Dover, in contrast, makes clear distinctions between Plato's Pausanias (as the representative of the "best" of Athenian eros)
and Diotima, writing, for instance, that in Plato, "*heterosexual eros
is treated on the same basis as homosexual copulation,* a pursuit of bodily
pleasure which leads no further . . . and in *Symposium* it is subrational,
an expression of the eros that works in animals."[34] Dover thus dis-
criminates plainly between the sexual practices of Athenians in
general—even in their most high-minded, heavenly form—and Plato's disdain for all physical sex. Dover's point is supported by at least
one ancient Socratic, Xenophon, who in his *Symposium* 7 clearly portrays Socrates as lauding the good spiritual love over the bad physical
love, contra Foucault.[35] Plato thus promotes an erotics that is almost

32. Including ancient Platonists, "from Plutarch to Plotinus" (Corrigan and Glazov-
Corrigan, *Plato's Dialectic at Play,* 58) and such modern interpreters as Anders Nygren:
"In the *Symposium* Plato feels no necessity to make Socrates or Diotima speak about it
[heavenly eros], but entrusts to Pausanias the task of explaining the difference between
what he calls 'vulgar (πάνδημος) Eros' and 'heavenly (οὐράνιος) Eros'" (*Agape and Eros,*
trans. Philip S. Watson [New York: Harper and Row, 1969], 51). This leads, of course, to a
total conflation of the view of Pausanias and that of Plato.

33. Foucault, *Use of Pleasure,* 246.

34. Dover, *Greek Homosexuality,* 163, emphasis added.

35. Anthony Bowen, ed. and trans., *Symposium* by Xenophon (Warminster, England:
Aris & Phillips, 1998), 75. Xenophon's Socrates identifies soul-love (ὁ τῆς Ψυχῆς ἔρως)
with heavenly (Ouranian) eros. I am claiming that Plato's Socrates would see this as the
soul-love of the Lesser Mysteries, but surely not of the greater. See Reeve, *Plato on Love,*
xxv–xxvi. In any case, Xenophon's absolute opposition of Socrates' passion to a physical
one is clear enough; he refers to his passion as an antipassion to those who love bodily
(8.23–24; Bowen, *Symposium* by Xenophon, 78–79). According to some, Xenophon con-
fuses Pausanias's with Phaedrus's defense of Greek love, assuming that Xenophon is, as
these scholars take him to be, working off Plato's text (81). On the other hand, if we don't

in binary opposition to the erotics of Athens as best represented in
Pausanias's speech, and this is consistent with, indeed part and parcel
of, Plato's whole stance vis-à-vis the life of the polis.

In the highest form of love, heavenly love, that Pausanias imagines
and to which it would seem he aspires in his love for Agathon, there is

> only one honorable way of taking a man as a lover. In addition to rec-
> ognizing that the lover's total and willing subjugation to his beloved's
> wishes is neither servile nor reprehensible, we allow that there is
> one—and only one—further reason for willingly subjecting oneself
> to another which is equally above reproach: that is subjection for the
> sake of virtue. If someone decides to put himself at another's disposal
> because he thinks that this will make him better in wisdom or in any
> other part of virtue, we approve of his voluntary subjection: we con-
> sider it neither shameful nor servile. (184c–d)

Insofar as the goal of such heavenly love is the teaching and acquisition of virtue, this kind of love (which clearly includes physical
favors) is analogous to the teaching of the Sophists, a form of socialization into the life of the polis and a guarantee of success there, with
if not a sexual quid pro quo, a monetary one for the teacher.[36] In Diotima's version of love (of proper pederasty followed by further and
further ascents), on the other hand, love makes no contribution to
the life of the polis at all; rather it isolates the lover, moving him from
the appreciation of another human (albeit without the vulgarities of
touch) through the abstraction of that appreciation and into finally a

---

assume that Xenophon is misremembering his Plato (*pace* Bowen at 123), then it would be
Plato who distanced Socrates even further from general Athenian usage by giving Pausa-
nias the distinction between "vulgar" and heavenly love, with Socrates rejecting even that.
In short, while Xenophon cannot, of course, be taken as a reliable guide to Socrates' (or
Plato's) views (any more than Plato can), he certainly does suggest that he understood too
that Socrates' version of eros was in opposition to Athenian pederasty.

36. Note that Plato slyly makes the imputation of Pausanias's connection to Sophistry
clear, when Plato—well, actually Aristodemus, or is it Apollodorus?—says, "Pausanias
finally came to a pause (I've learned this sort of fine figure from our clever rhetoricians)"
(185c; the pun works equally well in Greek, of course). Pausanias, it is being hinted, belongs to that party of clever rhetoricians, the Sophists. For "fine figure," the Greek reads
ἴσα λέγειν = equal speaking, almost certainly a reference to Isocrates' rhetorical style.
For excellent commentary on this moment, see Corrigan and Glazov-Corrigan, *Plato's
Dialectic at Play,* 60.

total abstraction of contemplative engagement with the Forms. For Diotima, the highest kind of love not only ends asexually, it begins asexually: "A lover who goes about this matter correctly must begin in his youth to devote himself to beautiful bodies," but not, God forbid, to have the pleasure of their touch. "First, if the leader [ἡγούμενος = Eros] leads him aright, he should love one body *and beget beautiful ideas* [*logoi* = ideas, discourses, speeches] there" (210a).[37] Beautiful ideas are clearly not begotten by the deposit of semen.[38]

A closer look at the text of Diotima's "ladder" will make this clearer.[39] She begins, describing the "lesser mysteries" by informing us that all humans "are pregnant both in body and in soul, and, as soon as we come to a certain age, we naturally desire to give birth" (206c). Pregnancy, here, it is to be observed, is already a reference to a potential for reproduction and a desire for it, and not a particular state of the (female) body. In this dual possibility—body and soul—of pregnancy that human beings uniquely are presented with, however, "some people are pregnant in body," while "others are *even more pregnant in their souls than in their bodies*" (208e–209a; emphasis added). Both, by the way, are men! The former love women and beget children with them. But what do the latter do? If the former turn more to women, then clearly the latter turn more to men. In the course of this high-minded male-male relationship, more pregnant in soul than in body, the man

---

37. Emphasis mine. For Eros as the leader, see *Symposium* 193b, "Eros our leader and general" (ὁ Ἔρως ἡμῖν ἡγεμὼν καὶ στρατηγός). Allan David Bloom, "The Ladder of Love," in *Plato's Symposium,* by Plato, trans. Seth Benardete (Chicago: University of Chicago Press, 2001), 143, does not see this distinction at all; indeed he imagines the philosopher (even the one who is pregnant in soul) alternating "between sex and conversation" (147). See also David M. Halperin, "Platonic *Erōs* and What Men Call Love," *Ancient Philosophy* 5 (1985): 185: "We cannot successfully pursue both our sexual and procreative responses to beauty simultaneously," whilst, on my reading of Plato, we cannot do both at all, not even in turns.

38. *Pace* A. W. Price, *Love and Friendship in Plato and Aristotle* (Oxford: Oxford University Press, 1989), 37–38, the fact that there is no physical sex involved in such a relationship does not de-eroticize it. For the fullest justification and compelling verification of this argument, see Virginia Burrus, *The Sex Lives of Saints: An Erotics of Ancient Hagiography,* Divinations: Reading Late Ancient Religions (Philadelphia: University of Pennsylvania Press, 2003). Also see Mark Jordan, "Flesh in Confession: Alcibiades beside Augustine," in *Toward a Theology of Eros: Transfiguring Passion at the Limits of Discipline,* ed. Virginia Burrus and Catherine Keller (New York: Fordham University Press, 2006), 23–37.

39. Much of the following discussion in this paragraph is guided by G. R. F. Ferrari, "Platonic Love," in *The Cambridge Companion to Plato,* ed. Richard Kraut (Cambridge: Cambridge University Press, 1992), 155–59.

who is its subject "makes contact" with another's beauty in body and soul and "keeps company" (ἁπτόμενος γάρ οἶμαι τοῦ καλοῦ καὶ ὁμιλῶν αὐτῷ) with the view toward begetting "wisdom and the rest of virtue, which all poets beget, as well as all the craftsmen who are said to be creative" (209c and 209a). Although it is not explicit in the text what kind of contact with the other's beautiful body is recommended, the implied sexual practice encoded in these words seems compelling.[40] This point is only strengthened if we translate *kaloû* as "his beautiful one," a translation the Greek certainly supports if not favors.[41] The continuation supports this interpretation as well, since immediately following, it says, "whether with him or without him," which can only refer back to the beautiful one and not beauty in the abstract.

This virtue is good for the polis: "The greatest and most beautiful part of wisdom deals with the proper ordering of cities and households, and that is called moderation and justice" (209a). In other words, this sort of soul-eros teaches what the Sophists teach, the crafts of wisdom and virtue, and its final telos is the good government of the polis.[42] Note that it is here that Socrates refers to Diotima's discourse as "in the fashion of perfect Sophists" (ὥσπερ οἱ τέλεοι σοφισταί, 208c), referring to the sophistic views expressed vis-à-vis the mysteries of philotimic love, those that will be transcended by philosophy in the greater mysteries. Socrates makes this remark with respect to Diotima's first disquisition, the one in which she is essentially repeating the views of Pausanias as a lower order of erotica before going on to her greater mysteries, the break between the two being her remark that this lower order might even be achievable by Socrates. This sort of love, which begins with the physical pleasure of men and ends with Solon and Lycourgos (209d) and the immortal children they have begotten (Athens and Sparta themselves), is the very instantiation of Pausanias's heavenly love, marked as clearly lower on the Platonic scale by its associations with poets and crafts-

40. Certainly one of the senses of both verb forms used here is "to have sexual intercourse," as used at least once in Plato himself, *Laws* 84c. Cf. Liddell-Scott ad loc.

41. See Robert Gregg Bury, *The Symposium of Plato* (Cambridge: W. Heffer and Sons, 1932) who asserts (correctly, imho) that *kaloû* here is masculine, not neuter. See also comment by Dover, *Symposium*, 154, implicitly supporting this reading.

42. Nehamas even sees this sentence as yet another explicit allusion to the *Protagoras;* Nehamas and Woodruff, *Symposium* by Plato, 56n87.

men.[43] Even though this love begets beautiful deeds and every kind of virtue and immortal children (209e), it is not yet Platonic love. Relegated to the lesser mysteries,[44] it is not yet correct (ὀρθῶς). And it is of this love that, with mock contempt, Diotima remarks to a Socrates not yet turned philosopher but still a Sophist himself, "Even you, Socrates, could probably come to be initiated into these rites of love" (209d–210a). I think we find here a clear hermeneutic hint that these lesser mysteries belong to the world of the Sophists, to a kind of demotic (but not pandemotic) Athenianism, and also that Socrates, before his metamorphosis into a philosopher, was indeed—almost as Aristophanes portrayed him—a Sophist.

Diotima's Platonic love, however, is different, first in that it *begins* in a love of bodies that does not involve touching, contact, or mixing at all, but only the begetting of beautiful ideas. We thus find two types of *soul*-love, even setting aside the vulgar love of men for women or men for men that, even according to Pausanias, is primarily physically oriented and goes nowhere. Pausanian heavenly love, which belongs to the lesser mysteries, is *philotimia* (208c), while Platonic love is *philosophia* (205d). Platonic love does not, therefore, begin where Athenian (and Spartan) love ends, but somewhere else, in a love of beautiful bodies that is never realized sexually at all. It is only this kind of lover, the philosopher, who could ever hope to achieve knowledge of "just what it is to be beautiful" (211d):

43. Contra David Cohen, *Law, Sexuality, and Society: The Enforcement of Morals in Classical Athens* (Cambridge: Cambridge University Press, 1991), 175, who thinks that Uranian love is unconsummated, I see no evidence to that effect in Pausanias's speech. Throughout sections 182–184, Pausanias is speaking constantly of the rules in which it is appropriate for the beloved boy to gratify his lover, for example: "τὸ ἐραστῇ παιδικὰ χαρίσασθαι" (184d3). On my interpretation, then, Pausanian love is always at least sparingly consummatable, however heavenly it may get, while Platonic love is never consummated. A further argument in this direction is provided by the fact that the very distinction between vulgar and heavenly is provided by the two Aphrodites, and Aphrodite is always a signifier of sex. Richard Hunter is, at any rate, quite clear on this, writing with reference to the passage I have just cited, "[Pausanias's] 'heavenly *erôs*' thus also involves physical relief for the lover, but only under specific circumstances," Hunter, *Plato's Symposium*, 47. See too Dover, *Greek Homosexuality*, 83–84. Much of these arguments on all sides will need to be re-evaluated in the light of James Davidson, *The Greeks and Greek Love: A Radical Reappraisal of Homosexuality in Ancient Greece* (New York: Random House Pub. Group, 2009), which reached me literally in the last days of preparing this book.

44. Ferrari, "Platonic Love," 255.

When someone rises by these stages, through loving boys correctly, and begins to see this beauty, he has almost grasped his goal. This is what it is to go aright, or be lead by another, into the mystery of Love: one goes always upwards for the sake of this Beauty, starting out from beautiful things, using them like rising stairs: from one body to two and from two to all beautiful bodies, then from beautiful bodies to beautiful customs, and from customs to learning beautiful things, and from these lessons he arrives in the end at this lesson, which is learning of this very Beauty, so that in the end he comes to know just what it is to be beautiful. (211c–d)

It is clear enough from this passage that this correct loving of boys does not involve physical sex, else we would have to imagine a Plato who sees having sex with two beautiful bodies a higher practice than having sex with one, and having sex with all beautiful bodies an even higher rung than that.[45] It's a nice fantasy, but not, I think, Plato's.[46] Rather, for Plato, as opposed to Pausanias, all this loving is not physically consummated, hence the move from loving one beautiful boy

45. For this argument to different ends, see J. M. E. Moravcsik, "Reason and Eros in the 'Ascent'-Passage of the *Symposium*," in *Essays in Ancient Greek Philosophy*, ed. John P. Anton (Albany: State University of New York Press, 1971), 291.

46. Ludwig, *Eros and Polis*, 313, does not consider this a *reductio ad absurdum* and interprets that it is through a recommended promiscuity that the young Socrates is supposed to become contemptuous of all bodies: "Promiscuity is initially attractive but quickly becomes boring." I find this interpretation unconvincing, although I cannot prove it wrong. Again in another place, Ludwig has essentially the same feeling about the relation of sex to philotimic and philosophical love that I do, but then adopts the same, to my mind, somewhat odd interpretation of Diotima: "Child production required bodily contact, and even the philotimic couple were allowed to touch; but 'correct' pederasty (211b 5–6) means leaving bodies behind, at first leaving other people's bodies but eventually also leaving one's own body. Diotima counsels promiscuity for Socrates as a young man as a way of making his taste go off bodies" (Ludwig, *Eros and Polis*, 368). Taking the "promiscuity," however, as a promiscuity of visual pleasure alone, as I think we are meant to, makes the proposition considerably less grotesque than an allegedly disgusting promiscuity that makes us disgusted with bodies as Diotima's recommendation. See too: Loving all beautiful bodies, not just one, looks like Don Juanism" (Price, *Love and Friendship*, 36). I can't prove this, and don't know how one would, but it makes no sense to me as "Plato's" "intention." Nor does it to Price himself, it seems, writing as he does, later on, "What is envisaged is not precisely sexual promiscuity: the lover was aim-inhibited (as Freud would say) from the beginning, for his attachment to one body only produced *words* (210a7–8). Hence the only Don Juanism in question is one of attraction, not of gratification" (47). See too his n. 54, in which he considers (and rejects) Martha Nussbaum's suggestion that what is being suggested by Plato is loveless promiscuous sex.

to loving many constitutes a move in the direction of appreciating beauty as a substantive in itself and not as a character of bodies, thence in the direction of the Form of Beauty. We see, accordingly, not one ladder, but two, one beginning with physical love and ending with good government (the lesser mysteries) and one beginning with an eros only of eyes and ideas and ending with contemplation of Beauty itself (the greater mysteries).[47] Pausanian love, rhetoric, running institutions, the lesser mysteries—these are all the province of banausic man. Philosophy belongs only to daimonic man.[48] The most that Pausanian heavenly love can engender is "images of virtue," those images afforded by an education in wisdom (*sophia*, not *philosophia*), while contemplation of the Forms leads to "true virtue" (212a).[49]

A further point in support of this argument of two parallel ladders is the following consideration. Even though in the end, of course, the philosophical lover will achieve something much higher than the philotimic lover, the beautiful *logoi* that the philosophical lover begets at the beginning of his ascent are sensuous ideas and, as such, lower than the *logoi* of the philotimic lovers at the culmination of their ascent, which are at least useful, if only to the polis. On this reading, it is clear that the greater mysteries do *not* begin where the lesser mysteries leave off, but that two incompatible, hierarchically evaluated ladders are involved, two entirely different paths in life, *philotimia* and *philosophia*. The philotimic, banausic lovers produce "ideas and arguments about virtue—the qualities a virtuous man should have and the customary activities in which he should engage" (209b–c)—while the philosophical lover, at the lowest rung, produces songs of praise to beautiful bodies, love songs, essentially.[50] Plato's philosophers will never, resolutely never, be much good to the polis, moving, as they

47. For another acceptation of Ferrari's position that there are two ladders (without, however, referring to him), see Corrigan and Glazov-Corrigan, *Plato's Dialectic at Play*, 50.

48. Nightingale, *Genres in Dialogue*, 55–59, citing *Symposium* 203a as compared with *Republic* 495d–e following a suggestion of Dover, *Symposium*, 141. See also Andrea Wilson Nightingale, *Spectacles of Truth in Classical Greek Philosophy: Theoria in Its Cultural Context* (Cambridge: Cambridge University Press, 2004), 123–27.

49. τίκτειν οὐκ εἴδωλα ἀρετῆς, ἅτε οὐκ εἰδώλου ἐφαπτομένῳ, ἀλλ' ἀληθῆ, ἅτε τοῦ ἀληθοῦς ἐφαπτομένῳ (to give birth not to images of virtue [because he's in touch with no images], but to true virtue [because he's in touch with the true beauty]).

50. Price, *Love and Friendship*, 41. This is clearly not the only possible interpretation (see n. 43, there), but I find it compelling. I am grateful to John Ferrari for having reminded me of Price's comment.

do, from beautiful ideas to mystic experience and truth (at best they will make it as philosopher-kings in an imaginary Kallipolis). Far from one following on the other, then, these two ladders are parallel and incommensurable paths.[51]

These two different incommensurable ladders are, as Ferrari remarks, suitable for two different kinds of lovers. In the passage on love in the *Laws*, we find the same dichotomy between the lover who loves with the body and the lover for whom the desire of the body is incidental (837b).[52] In the *Laws*, Plato explicitly marks the wholly spiritual love as the love of a "philosophical pair," this love without sex, while the less philosophical, the lovers of *time* (honor), even at their most honorable, engage in sex sparingly (256a–d).[53] The lesser ladder, leading only to the lesser mysteries as a glass ceiling, is equivalent to Pausanias's "heavenly love" with its political ends, while the second ladder, the one for philosophers, leads away from the polis entirely and into the heavens.

Even if one were to object that this interpretation cannot quite be proven in the *Symposium*, it can certainly be proven in the *Phaedrus* (251e), where there is as eloquent a description of passion for a

---

51. Alcibiades realizes this well, confessing that he has to avoid hearing Socrates' siren song, because it would make his political career impossible and show it to have been worthless (216a–b). See too 218e, in which the terms of comparison are *doxa* and *aletheia*.

52. For a profound discussion of this passage, see Seth Benardete, *Plato's "Laws": The Discovery of Being* (Chicago: University of Chicago Press, 2000), 240–44. Each of the types of love of which Plato speaks has a body kind and a soul kind, and it is clear which of these is favored by Plato (without denying that he makes place for the first as well). Benardete here (242) partly misleads, I think, as he glosses this passage as referring to two different impulses within the lover and not two different kinds of lovers. The passage is, I think, however, clear. There are two conflicting impulses within each lover, but then—crucially—there are two different kinds of lovers, those who follow the first and those who follow the second of these impulses.

53. Thus I can agree with David M. Halperin that "a coherent account can be given of Platonic eroticism without collapsing either its sexual or its metaphysical dimension into the other," and that sexual desire is not a metaphor for philosophy in Plato or philosophy a "sublimation" of sexual desire, and yet disagree with Halperin in the implication that there is only one path or tenor of relating the two faces of eros. Since the love of *time* is precisely what drives political actors, this opposition, not entirely surprisingly, encodes the opposition between the democratic politician/Sophist/rhetor and the philosopher-king who would rule in Plato's Kallipolis. It should be said that I am not, of course, claiming that all Sophists were democrats or that rhetoric could serve only democracies. My claim is rather that sophism and its practice, rhetoric, constitute an epistemology that makes democracy possible, while philosophy—in the Platonic sense—stands against such an epistemology and thus against democracy.

beautiful boy as one could possibly imagine, but its consummation is purely through the eyes and the soul: no penises or other touching organs need apply. Lest one imagine, moreover, that this is not being presented there as Socrates' "true" view, his behavior with Alcibiades as reported in the *Symposium* bears out this interpretation.[54] Given the textual support for this interpretation in the *Symposium* and its virtual ineluctability in the *Phaedrus,* at least on the basis of Ockham's razor, I would think that one would assert it for both texts. As Ludwig has put it memorably, "Phaedrus and Pausanias are really praising politics, not eros."[55] Diotima's disdain for these then is precisely a rejection of the life of the polis itself. Socrates is being goaded to leave the life of the Sophist, of the polis entirely, to abandon the path of the lesser mysteries and engage in the new practice of philosophy. Diotima is, in this sense, none other than Plato.

Socrates completes his ventriloquistical Diotiman peroration by insisting: "Such, Phaedrus, is the tale which I heard from the stranger of Mantinea, and which you may call the encomium of love, or what you please." By enacting in the discourse the substitution of dialectic (philosophy) for encomia (rhetoric), Diotima has matched the form of her expression to its content as well, replacing physical eros and the rhetorical, political, ethical socialization that is attendant on it—Pausanias's "heavenly love"—with an even more heavenly love that does not at all belong to the world of getting and spending (pun intended). The progress for the philosophers (or even for nascent philosophers) is not from bodies experienced corporally (sex) to souls experienced spiritually. For those in the category of philosophers (congenitally), it is progress from bodies experienced spiritually to souls experienced spiritually, then to the Forms. Such philosophers do qualify themselves to be philosopher-kings or the leaders of philosophical academies, but not citizens of the democratic polis.[56] The

54. For a similar view, see Nightingale, *Genres in Dialogue,* 113.

55. Ludwig, *Eros and Polis,* 38.

56. Pierre Hadot, *What Is Ancient Philosophy?* (Cambridge, Mass.: Harvard University Press, 2002), 56, writes that for Diotima/Socrates/Plato "the highest form of intelligence consists in self-mastery and justice, and these are exercised in the organization of cities or other institutions. Many historians have seen in this mention of 'institutions' an allusion to the founding of Plato's school, for in the following lines Plato clearly gives us to understand that the fruitfulness he is talking about is that of an educator." The passage to which Hadot refers is 209a, where the Greek has "καὶ καλλίστη τῆς φρονήσεως ἡ περὶ τὰς

political body and the physically reproductive, sexual body are on one side of a line; the philosophical body that begets only souls on the other. The bottom line of the *Symposium* is that Greek eros has been entirely transformed from the attraction to beautiful bodies into the interaction of souls through dialogue. Once again, rhetoric has been marked by Plato as specious, while Socrates' dialogue, which is also a "power play," has replaced pederasty. Pederasty becomes pedagogy. The break with the patterns of socialization in the Athenian polis is total. As Ferrari has remarked, "The transition from the Lesser to Greater bears comparison, then, with the crucial shift of focus in the *Republic* from institutions grounded in the honor code (Books II–IV) to those derived from rule by philosopher-kings (Books V–VII)."[57] For Plato, it would seem, the body's beauty, as well as language's beauty, and the beauty of the community of ordinary human beings sharing views and reaching conclusions and decisions, as well as sharing bodily fluids and sometimes making babies, all belong to the realm of the false-seeming, the realm of appearance, the dreaded *doxa*, the very stuff of which democratic decision making must always be constituted, and all of them together are to be replaced by the eros of love of the Forms, *epistēmē*. The education of Socrates by Diotima, his transformation from a Sophist—and one who thus thinks Diotima is a "perfect Sophist" too—into a philosopher is the enactment in a sort of biographical allegory, if you will, of Plato's own transformation of Athenian thought from even the most heavenly of sophism to a philosophy that, for him, is wholly other to sophism and the rhetorical politics of the democracy. The transformation of Socrates is a metaphor for the transformation of Athenian intellectual life.

On my reading, the discursive or parodic relationship of Diotima to Aspasia is crucial for understanding the counterpolitical eros of the *Symposium*.[58] Not only is Diotima a prophetess from Prophet-

---

τῶν πόλεών τε καὶ οἰκήσεων διακοσμήσεις." All of the translations that I have consulted render the second term (οἰκήσεων) in its seemingly obvious sense of "households" or "dwellings," so I am genuinely unsure upon what Hadot is leaning here. Moreover, insofar as this line refers to those who partake only of the lesser mysteries, Hadot's reading of these "institutions" as the Platonic school just doesn't seem to work, since these are surely in contrast with and lower than the Academy.

57. Ferrari, "Platonic Love," 256. See on this point also Ludwig, *Eros and Polis*, 313.

58. I hasten to make clear that by writing "counterpolitical," I am not indicating that Platonic love escapes the political, but rather that it claims to. The use of *eros* in political

ville (in Halperin's delightful translation of Mantinean) and thus a source of authority, but also, as such, she is totally out of the corporal politico-erotic economy of the city. Her Peloponnesian origin is not beside the point, and it is marked explicitly in Socrates' address to her, "O stranger" (204c).[59] This notion of Diotima as doubly marked "outsider" (as an apparently celibate woman and as a non-Athenian) is key to my reading of the *Symposium*.[60] Phaedrus's and Pausanias's notions of *eros* find it entirely in service of the *polis;* social solidarity and intergenerational socialization are entirely its products. Perhaps, however, the most explicit and richest expression of an eros that motivates social solidarity and political participation is Pericles' fu-

---

contexts is commonplace in Greek; for a profound exploration of the relations between that *eros* and the specific *eros* connected with sex and love for an individual human being, see Ludwig, *Eros and Polis*, 121–69. I don't entirely agree, however, with his distinction between "generic" uses of *eros,* meaning desire or wanting in general, and "specific" uses, which are erotic, but then are metaphorically transferred to other objects. It seems to me that the indistinguishability of "generic" and "specific" forms (meanings?) of *eros* fuels much of the "fashionable" discourse on political *eros* and the generation of desire that it is his project to identify. Political *eros* is, in my view, always literal and figurative, always literally connected to the desire for sex as well as figuratively described in such terms. An *exemplum* is Ludwig, *Eros and Polis,* 143n75, in which he argues that in the course of a short passage in Euripides, he uses generic, specific, specific (transferred), generic. To my mind, it is virtually impossible that such distinctions occurred in the minds of speakers or in the structure of the language. It is interesting that two books on roughly the same topic were published in the same year: Ludwig's as well as Victoria Wohl, *Love among the Ruins: The Erotics of Democracy in Classical Athens* (Princeton, N.J.: Princeton University Press, 2002), 3–4. Both books are full of virtue, but I find Wohl stronger in her sense of how metaphor works than Ludwig. On this point, S. Sara Monoson has commented acutely, "It is reasonable for us to assume that Pericles could use specific kinds of erotic imagery not only to be dramatic but to be precise" ("Citizen as Erastes," 254). I would suggest that Thucydides'/Pericles' usage in the famous phrase urging Athenians to become lovers (*erastai*) — in the most explicit of sexual senses, "active, insertive partner in a sexual encounter" (255) — of Athens (2.43.1) is no more or less "metaphorical" than Diotima's highest rungs on the ladder in which the same Athenians are presented as *erastai* of the Forms! See too on this point the usual clarity of Dover, *Greek Homosexuality,* 43, and especially David Nirenberg, "The Politics of Love and Its Enemies," *Critical Inquiry* 33, no. 3 (Spring 2007): 573–605. All of these considerations are likely to need reexamination once full measure is taken of the arguments of Davidson's *The Greeks and Greek Love,* but I don't think any of the major theses of this book will need to be abandoned.

59. ὦ ξένη. Constanze Guthenke reminded me of this last point.

60. Which in the end, is quite different from Halperin's in *its* end. For Halperin, Diotima turns out to be "not so much a woman as a 'woman,' a necessary female absence" (David M. Halperin, "Why Is Diotima a Woman?" in *One Hundred Years of Homosexuality and Other Essays on Greek Love* [New York: Routledge, 1990], 149). For me, Diotima is exactly a woman, but a woman who represents the absence of another woman, not for specific political reasons having to do with gender, but for reasons having to do with the reproduction of the democratic polis as opposed to the philosophical Academy.

neral peroration, according to Thucydides: "And not contented with ideas derived only from words of the advantages which are bound up with the defense of your country, though these would furnish a valuable text to a speaker even before an audience so alive to them as the present, you must yourselves realize the power of Athens, and feed your eyes upon her from day to day, till love of her fills your hearts" (2.43.1).[61] The last phrase, in the Greek καὶ ἐραστὰς γιγνομένους αὐτῆς, is better translated "till you become her lovers."[62] Insofar as Diotima counters their views by treating eros as solvent and not as connector—as WD40, not as duct tape—it reveals itself as counterpolis. I would argue that the very *apragmones*, those who refrain from politics and who for Thucydides are "good for nothing" (in Hobbes's inspired translation), are academic philosophers. If *to philotimon* is, for Thucydides, the highest of motivations (2.44.4), as it is for Pausanias, for Plato's Diotima it is, as we have just seen, merely the key to the lesser mysteries. While Pausanias's version of eros (matched, I think, by Diotima's "lesser mysteries") brings people together for the greater good of the community, Diotima's drives them apart finally into an individual contemplation of Beauty. Philosophy, according to Plato, is the privation of "politics."

There is a passage in the *Republic* that seems crucial for understanding this point. Here Socrates points out just how few are fit for philosophy, and paradoxically it is their unfitness for politics that makes them so:

> That leaves only a very small fraction, Adeimantus, of those who spend their time on philosophy as of right. Some character of noble birth and good upbringing, perhaps, whose career has been interrupted by

61. Thucydides, *The Landmark Thucydides: A Comprehensive Guide to the Peloponnesian War,* ed. Robert B. Strassler, introd. by Victor Davis Hanson, trans. Richard Crawley (New York: Free Press, 1996), 115.

62. Note Hornblower's comment: "A strong metaphor which should not be diluted in translation, as it is by versions such as 'fall in love with her'"; Simon Hornblower, *A Commentary on Thucydides,* vol. 1, *Books I–III* (1991; repr., Oxford: Clarendon Press, 2003), 311. See also on this passage W. Robert Connor, *The New Politicians of Fifth-Century Athens* (Princeton, N.J.: Princeton University Press, 1971), 97. More than a metaphor, I would say, this is a regular extension of the semantic range of *erastes,* indicative of ideas about eros in Athens broader than only referring to sexual love. If this be so, then such ideas must be seen as common to Plato and Thucydides, in spite of their opposing ideological positions as defined here. See elegant discussion in Ludwig, *Eros and Polis,* 320–21 and throughout.

exile, and who for want of corrupting influences has followed his nature and remained with philosophy. Or a great mind born in a small
city, who thinks the political affairs of his city beneath him, and has
no time for them. . . . Our friend Theages has a bridle which is quite
good at keeping people in check. Theages has all the qualifications
for dropping out of philosophy, but physical ill-health keeps him in
check, and stops him going into politics. . . . Those who have become
members of this small group have tasted how sweet and blessed a possession is philosophy. They can also, by contrast, see quite clearly the
madness of the many. They can see that virtually nothing anyone in
politics does is in any way healthy. (*Republic* 496a–c)[63]

The opposition between the life of a philosopher and the life of
the polis could not possibly be clearer than it is in this passage. The
philosopher is an alien by birth or even by virtue of the ill-formedness
of his body, which keeps him out of the erotic/political commerce
described, for example, by symposiast Pausanias. Or the philosopher
is one who is blessed with a certain mantic ability, as Socrates is. As
Nightingale observes, "It is noteworthy that the defining criterion is
political orientation rather than method or doctrine."[64] The defining
criterion of the philosopher is alienation from the city.

Diotima against Aspasia

Diotima fits the job description of alienated intellectual perfectly: she
is certainly a very marked sort of alien, "a great mind born in a small
city," and is a Mantinean mantic to boot. Nightingale has already connected this passage in the *Republic* with the *Symposium* at exactly the
point at which it is of interest to my argument here. She writes: "What
is the nature of this new brand of alien [the philosopher]? . . . One of
the most prominent aspects of Plato's definition of the philosopher is
the opposition he forges between the philosophic 'outsider' and the
various types of people who made it their business to traffic in wisdom." Nightingale then goes on to remark that "the clearest and most

63. G. R. F. Ferrari, ed., and Tom Griffith, trans., *The Republic* by Plato, Cambridge
Texts in the History of Political Thought (Cambridge: Cambridge University Press,
2000), 200–201.
64. Nightingale, *Genres in Dialogue,* 19.

explicit enunciation of this phenomenon in the Platonic corpus" is perhaps "the *Symposium*'s handling of the exchange of 'virtue' for sexual favors."[65] Although Nightingale does not seem to remark this, the contrast between Diotima and Aspasia is a most powerful emblem of the Platonic notion of the philosopher as the one who does not traffic in the city's wisdom. By staging the opposition between Aspasia and Diotima, Plato is enacting precisely the opposition between the lover of bodies/*time* and the lover of souls/*epistēmē:* Aspasia versus Diotima equals Pericles versus Socrates, a binary opposition. By assigning Aspasia the position of author of an epideictic speech (the Funeral Oration in the *Menexenus*) while he renders Diotima a dialectician, Plato heightens as well the agglomeration of these binaries: Aspasia = rhetoric, civic life, bodily enacted eros, childbirth—all the markers of the lesser mysteries (at best)—while Diotima is dialectic, distance from the polis, the birth of ideas, and the very personification of the eros of discourse alone, paralleling perfectly the representational values of their male partners, as well. The project of the *Symposium* is, on my reading, "putting philosophy on the map" to borrow Nightingale's felicitous formulation.[66] If, following Halperin's very attractive suggestion, Diotima is a replacement for Aspasia, a more detailed accounting for Aspasia's place in Platonic discourse seems necessary in order to understand Diotima. The *Menexenus,* in which Aspasia is presented ironically as a sort of teacher of rhetoric and the producer of a funeral oration in her own right, is a parody of Pericles' funeral oration as given by Thucydides.[67] The question of rhetoric is thematized in the style of the original and its parodic echo. Thucydides' original and Plato's lampoon are both marked by their close approximations (one serious and one parodic) to Gorgias's high style, a point of some importance, since, for Plato, the theory of erotics and the theory of rhetoric are closely aligned. Socrates, throughout the corpus, has only two female teachers, Aspasia and Diotima. In the *Menexenus,* in a context in which Socrates

---

65. Nightingale, *Genres in Dialogue,* 43.

66. Nightingale, *Genres in Dialogue,* 19.

67. For the *Menexenus* as parody: E. R. Dodds, ed., introduction to *Gorgias: A Revised Text* by Plato (1959; repr., Oxford: Oxford University Press, 2002), 129; Dennis Proctor, *The Experience of Thucydides* (Warminster, Wilts., England: Aris & Phillips, 1980), 6; Nicole Loraux, *The Invention of Athens: The Funeral Oration in the Classical City* (Cambridge, Mass.: Harvard University Press, 1986), 311–27.

is openly mocking rhetoric and speech making, he cites Aspasia as his
teacher in rhetoric. In the *Symposium,* when Socrates wishes to laud dialogue over rhetoric, it is *Diotima,* his teacher in erotics, who represents
dialogue. As we know, rhetoric and dialogue are, for Plato, positioned
in an absolute binary opposition, with the former negatively marked
and the latter positively. "Bad erotics" are associated with "bad" speech
practice, rhetoric, and "good" erotics with "good" speech forms, dialectic. I think that, in light of the more ancient tradition, according to
which it was Aspasia who was Socrates' instructor in erotics, we are not
meant to miss this binary opposition: the seductive, flattering, lying
funeral oration (*Menexenus* 234c–235a) taught and given by the beautiful, sexual, political Aspasia versus the true dialogue of the holy, alien,
Peloponnesian prophetess, Diotima.

Both Aspasia and Diotima are presented as having taught Socrates
some art in the form of a discourse. Aspasia, Socrates' traditional instructor in erotics, becomes his instructor in rhetoric, while a new
woman is produced to teach him proper erotics. The analogy (or better, homology) in the realm of erotics is only too clear. Aspasia can
teach only the false use of language, just as she would have been able
to teach only the lower erotics that pursues pleasure, procreation,
and political power, while Diotima can teach true erotics, because
her sexuality is entirely out of all of these realms, and thus, to complete the ratio, she teaches true speaking (dialectic), as well. Indeed,
we could push the point even a bit further: for Diotima, dialectic, and
nothing else, is true erotics.

I would say, then, that the precise choice of woman, or better put,
the remarkably absent woman, the absent *real* woman, Aspasia, the
woman who wasn't there, as it were, is an essential aspect of the overall rhetoric of the piece. Since Plato is adopting a procreative model
of erotic desire but is at the same time contemptuous of the physical procreation of corporeal children, the teacher cannot be a *gyne*
(woman/wife) but must be a *parthenos* (virgin). Diotima may be female,
but in Greek, I think, she is not (quite) a woman. She is, however, on
this reading a real (if fictional) female.[68]

---

68. Corrigan and Glazov-Corrigan, in *Plato's Dialectic at Play,* 112, conveniently give
several reasons that have been offered for "Diotima," none of which touch on the present
proposal (perhaps, of course, only evidence for its untenability).

There is more going on in the move from the physically procreative eros of the heterosexual couple (Pericles and Aspasia) to the purely spiritual/intellectual one (Socrates and Diotima) than Halperin has articulated,[69] namely a strong displacement of procreation itself. Where Halperin's argument seems to assume that the thrust of Plato's innovation is to find a way to assimilate male-male love to that of male and female, and therefore Diotima must be a woman, I would read it almost in opposite fashion as a way of making male-female love "as good as" male-male love, by removing the sexual element from the former as well as from the latter. Hence, on my view, the "vulgar" understanding of Platonic love as love without sex, whatever the sexes, has much to commend it. The relationship between Socrates and Diotima models, as it were, the possibility of a purely spiritual eros between a man and a woman while theorizing that nonsexual eros as procreative in both its same-sex and other-sex (but always no-sex: please, we're philosophers) versions. The move that Plato makes is a decisive one away from the body, both the body of pleasure and the body of procreation, to a disembodied version of both. The question of an eros of speaking is, therefore, at the very heart of the *Symposium,* as much or even more (for being partly disguised) as in any of the dialogues, including the ones that most explicitly foreground it, such as the *Gorgias* and the *Protagoras.*

It is that transfer from anus, vagina, and womb to pure mind, from phallus to *logos* (or in another terminology, from penis to phallus), that explains why Diotima is not Aspasia. She is the possessor of neither a clitoris for pleasure nor a womb for physical procreation,[70] but both, in her, are purely spiritual entities, metaphors that help us grasp the proper eros. When there is to be no actual sex, women are, opines Plato, just as good as men.[71]

On this reading, the substitution of the Mantinean mantic for the Athenian partner, lover, politician, mother (not *demimondaine*), was a very marked one indeed. If Aspasia is the female version of

69. Halperin, "Why Is Diotima," 136–37.

70. Monique Wittig, "The Category of Sex," in *The Straight Mind and Other Essays* (Boston: Beacon Press, 1992), 1–8.

71. For a beautiful exposition of this point, culminating in a citation of Baudelaire's line that "loving intelligent women is a pederastic pleasure," see Price, *Love and Friendship,* 226–28.

Pericles, Diotima makes the perfect female version of Socrates, the anti-Pericles. Diotima has to be a woman, on this account, in order to negate Aspasia and all that she means. The ideal pair of Socrates and Diotima is thus located in semiotic contrast to two less-than-ideal pairings, Pericles and Aspasia, on the one hand, and Pausanias and Agathon on the other.

Rhetoric and Dialectic

The *Symposium* centers (or "turns"?) on a dichotomy homologous to that of the ladders leading to the two types of eros: the opposition between rhetoric and dialectic. The Socratic rejection of all of the explanations and apologies for Greek love in the *Symposium* is matched by an explicitly thematized opposition between these forms of speech. Indeed, by the end of my reading, I shall suggest that the latter binary, and not the former, is the main work of the text, what the text is *about*.[72] Just as all of the speakers up to Socrates defend Greek love while Diotima/Socrates attack it, all of the speakers preceding them speak in encomia (rhetorical speeches of praise), while these latter speak in dialectic.

The contrast between epideictic encomia and dialogue comes first between the speeches of Aristophanes and Agathon, where Socrates is represented as attempting to lead the conversation into a "discussion" or dialogue, and Phaedrus interrupts:

> Agathon, my friend, if you answer Socrates, he'll no longer care whether we get anywhere with what we're doing here, so long as he has a partner for discussion [*dialegesthai*]. Especially if he's handsome. Now, like you, I enjoy listening to Socrates in discussion [*dialegesthai*], but it is my duty to see to the praising of Love and to exact a speech from every one

---

72. This interpretation goes rather a long way, I think, to explaining why Agathon's rather weak speech is placed in such a marked and privileged position. As Corrigan and Glazov-Corrigan put the problems: "Why should Agathon's speech, for instance, be the 'culmination' of the first set of speeches? . . . Is it only because Agathon is the victorious host or is there another design at work? And why should Socrates spend so much time 'demolishing' Agathon's speech?" (*Plato's Dialectic at Play,* 49). If Agathon is indeed the representative par excellence in the dialogue of sophistic rhetoric, then defeating him with the "Truth" is, on my view, the whole purpose of the dialogue; we have, then, an answer to all of these questions.

of this group. When each of you has made his offering to the god, then you can have your discussion [*dialegesthai*]. (194d)

In fact, the symposium (if not the *Symposium*) is conceived as a rhetorical competition, echoing the theatrical competition for which the party and Agathon's victory therein is a celebration. Moreover, the text is already inscribing proper pederasty, à la Socrates, as the *dialogue* of the older philosopher and a beautiful boy.

I thus demur from Halperin's remark that "the Platonic dialogue is true to this model of philosophical inquiry," namely, "the atmosphere of good will and ungrudging exchange of questions and answers."[73] On my view, Plato neither reimagines eros as mutual nor imagines dialectic as reciprocal, although he mystifyingly presents it as such, as I shall propose below via a reading of parts of Socrates' dialogue with Agathon. The *anteros* of all the young men for Socrates represents something else entirely, an inscription of how Socrates' own extraordinary beauty defies the conventional notions of who and what is beautiful and sexually alluring, thus instantiating Plato's own vision of beauty of the soul.[74] The prototype of this antiaesthetic beauty is, of course, Socrates' own statement at the beginning of the *Protagoras* that Protagoras is more beautiful to him than Alcibiades, echoed by Alcibiades' own eros (not *anteros*) toward Socrates at the end of the *Symposium,* an eros that even more radically overturns Athenian norms. Perhaps it is not going too far to say that this love of all for Socrates is a kind of parable of the way that the beautiful (or God) participates in love by stimulating it, but not by feeling it.

For Halperin, the great departure of Plato is from the hierarchical model of sex to one of mutual desire and pleasuring. Halperin goes on to indicate that this reciprocity of active desire, "Plato's remodeling of the homoerotic ethos of classical Athens . . . has direct consequences for his program of philosophical inquiry." It results in an ethos of true conversation in which "mutual desire makes possible the ungrudging exchange of questions and answers which constitutes the soul of philosophic practice."[75] Halperin concludes, "Since any

73. David M. Halperin, "Plato and Erotic Reciprocity," *Classical Antiquity* 5 (1986): 78.
74. See too Price, *Love and Friendship,* 233, on this *anteros.*
75. Halperin, "Why Is Diotima," 133.

beautiful soul can serve as a mirror for any other, reciprocal desire need not be confined to the context of physical relations between the sexes (which Plato, at least according to one reading of *Phaedrus* 250e, appears to have despised). The kind of mutuality in *erôs* traditionally imputed to women in Greek culture could therefore find a new home in the erotic dynamics of Platonic love."[76] I find Halperin's construal of the parallel between sexual and philosophic desire illuminating, even as I take it in rather a different direction. The mutuality of the "heterosexual" couple in ancient Greece is itself, I would suggest, a kind of chimera, since the only reason that the female was permitted to desire the male penetrator was that she was always already of dominated, penetratable status. This would suggest that using *eros/anteros* as the model for "mutual desire [that] makes possible the ungrudging exchange of questions and answers which constitutes the soul of philosophic practice" could raise as many questions as it answers, and indeed, in my view, it does, as a further investigation of the *Symposium* will disclose. In short, I shall suggest that the eros of philosophical dialogue is, for Plato, as penetrative and hierarchical as Pausanian pederasty or, for that matter, Pericles' liaison with Aspasia.

Socrates' treatment of Agathon ("the good/beautiful") is meant as a performance of proper pederasty—Agathon being the beautiful boy with whom Socrates would love to have conversation. This pairing opposes the presumably incorrect (however "heavenly") pederastic relationship between Agathon and his actual boyfriend, Pausanias. The same relations of power and hierarchy apply as in Athenian man-boy love—Agathon must assent to Socrates—but the realm is of the soul rather than the body. If Agathon the *eromenos* gratifies the need of Socrates the *erastes* to penetrate his mind with *logos* (as he does with his body and Pausanias's phallus—if, perhaps, only intercrurally), then presumably Agathon will receive some of the same things that the ordinary *eromenos* is supposed to receive from gratifying the desire of his *erastes* to penetrate his body with phallus.[77]

---

76. Halperin, "Why Is Diotima," 136–37.

77. Plato's moves here have to be correlated with other, even earlier, movements within Athenian thought. Plato's own vision of *philosophia,* of course, owes much to Parmenides, but also, as Froma Zeitlin has argued, much as well to Aeschylus. The very foundations of philosophy, as a specifically European practice according to her, are grounded

On my reading, it is thus the speech of Agathon, or rather Socrates' interaction with that dramatist and rhetor, that constitutes the heart of and hermeneutic key to the dialogue.[78] Instead of Pausanias's description of a good eros from which virtue flows in exchange for semen (or better put, perhaps, in which metaphorically semen is the material within which virtue flows), Diotima delineates an eros that is entirely spiritual in nature, outside the circulation (the traffic) of the sociality of the polis. Above all, she is explicitly speaking against Pausanias, that ultimate representative of the highest-mindedness of Athenian eros, the one who sharply distinguishes between vulgar love (pederasty) and Uranian love (pederasty cum pedagogy). Socrates, it will be remembered, explicitly rejects Agathon's request that he recline next to him, "so that I can lay hold of you and thereby enjoy the benefit of that piece of wisdom which occurred to you," to which Socrates replies that "it is not in the nature of wisdom to flow from one person to another like liquid flowing from a fuller vessel to an emptier one" (175c–e), thereby capsizing the entire self-understanding of the Athenian pederastic/pedagogical system.[79] I would like to suggest that the *Symposium* is entirely of a piece with Plato's whole oeuvre in its articulation of a doubled social space (the polis versus the Academy—a full two miles away from the agora)[80] coarticulated with a doubled ontological space (the physical versus the immaterial) and a doubled epistemological space (what appears and what is true,

---

in "bring[ing] together phallos and head . . . for the ending of the [*Oresteia*] is also concerned with a shift in modes and behavior, as it charts a progression from darkness to light, from obscurity to clarity. Representation of symbolic signs [symbolic here is not in the Lacanian sense—D.B.] perceived as a form of female activity gives way to the triumph of the male *Logos*. Representation and lyric incantation yield to dialectic and speech, and magic to science. Even more, this 'turning away from the mother to the father,' as Freud observed, 'signifies victory of intellectuality over the senses.'" Froma Zeitlin, "The Dynamics of Misogyny: Myth and Mythmaking in Aeschylus's *Oresteia*," in *Playing the Other: Gender and Society in Classical Greek Literature*, Women in Culture and Society (Chicago: University of Chicago Press, 1996), 211. Zeitlin proceeds to provide an extensive list of the ontological oppositions grounded in the primary opposition of male as Apollo and female as Erinyes that grow from this "turning" or "victory" (212).

78. Cf. Corrigan and Glazov-Corrigan, *Plato's Dialectic at Play*, 5.

79. See too Halperin, "Why Is Diotima," 148, and Bloom, "Ladder of Love," 77.

80. "Perhaps also Plato thought the intellectual free-for-all at Athens a special obstacle to such a gradual doling out of wisdom as Diotima proposed; cf. *Rep.* VI 498a–c" (Ferrari, "Platonic Love," 262). To which I can only respond: Indeed!

doxa and *epistēmē*). There is, as I have been suggesting, a doubled female figure that corresponds to this doubling, as well: Aspasia, who
is at home in the polis, versus Diotima, who belongs to the Academy,
if not even farther away from the agora than that.[81] Finally, there is
a doubled space of *logos* as well: rhetoric corresponding to the first
of each of these binary pairs and dialectic corresponding to the second. This consistent and persistent doubling has much more crucial
consequences for the history of sexuality than any details of permit-
ting or forbidding this or that sexual practice.[82] Encomia to love,
beautiful speeches in praise of eros, stand for Pausanian, demotic sex
in Plato's economy, while austere dialectic, with its fearless search for
so-called truth, stands for the true eros of love of the Forms. If the
poets are to be exiled from Kallipolis,[83] it is the philosophers who
exile themselves from the Athenian polis.[84] The interaction with Agathon is Plato's Socratic dramatization of this contrast.

It is no accident, by any means, that it is Agathon's sophistic rhetoric that is the zenith/nadir of the preparatory text for Diotima's
speech. Plato explicitly represents Agathon as a rhetor, not a philosopher, that is, as someone concerned with form, rather than with content or truth. After Agathon has finished his speech, "Socrates glanced
at Eryximachus and said, 'Now do you think I was foolish to feel the
fear that I felt before? Didn't I speak like a prophet a while ago when
I said that Agathon would give an amazing speech and I would be
tongue-tied? . . . How am I not going to be tongue-tied, I or anyone
else, after a speech delivered with such beauty and variety? The other
parts may not have been so wonderful, but that at the end!'"

The last part of Agathon's speech is delivered in the high Gorgianic style, virtually a parody of that form of rhetoric, and Plato has
Socrates underline the ironic tone of his response to it:

81. See too Nightingale's contrast of Aristophanes as "insider" critic of the democratic
city as opposed to Plato as "outsider/socially disembedded" (*Genres in Dialogue*, 190–92);
and see discussion in Josiah Ober, *Political Dissent in Democratic Athens: Intellectual Critics of
Popular Rule* (Princeton, N.J.: Princeton University Press, 1998), 48–51.

82. Dover, *Greek Homosexuality*, 155. In this matter, I am entirely in agreement as well
with Foucault, *Use of Pleasure*, 236.

83. On which, see the illuminating Ramona Naddaff, *Exiling the Poets: The Production of
Censorship in Plato's Republic* (Chicago: University of Chicago Press, 2002).

84. Cf. Callicles' brilliant and eloquent attack on philosophy in *Gorgias* 484c–486d. It
could have been Isocrates speaking.

Who would not be struck dumb on hearing the beauty of the words and phrases? Anyway, I was worried that I'd not be able to say anything that came close to them in beauty, and so I would almost have run away and escaped, if there had been a place to go. And, you see, the speech reminded me of Gorgias, so that I actually experienced what Homer describes: I was afraid that Agathon would end by sending the Gorgian head/Gorgonic head, awesome at speaking in a speech, against my speech, and this would turn me to stone by striking me dumb.

He is struck dumb by Agathon's rhetoric, just as he claims to have been struck dumb by Protagoras's rhetoric in his dialogue. Yet this assertion is coupled with a far more critical suggestion. As Kevin Corrigan and Elena Glazov-Corrigan have phrased it so well: "After the speech in Socrates' Gorgianic-Gorgonic pun we hear, as it were, the distant echo of the *Republic's* multiformed, polykephalic beast (*Rep.* 588e–590b), lionlike and snakelike (cf. 590b), which in no way matches the golden appearance before us but, with the merest hint of something much more sinister, betokens the corruption of such natures in their most devolved forms—that is, for Plato, the democratic nature (as ruled by the mob) and the tyrannical nature."[85] As the Corrigans point out, Plato associates gorgianic rhetoric with the unleashing of mob rule (as indeed do some modern French Platonists as well). By sharp discursive contrast, Socrates declares that he will speak only under certain conditions. Rhetorical encomia are not for him: "But I didn't even know the method for giving praise; and it was in ignorance that I agreed to take part in this. . . . Goodbye to that! I'm not giving another eulogy [*encomium*] using that method, not at all—I wouldn't be able to do it!—but, if you wish, I'd like to tell the truth my way (198a–199c)."

His way, of course, is via dialogue, not speeches. On first reading, it is not clear why this insistence on dialogue is so fraught with significance, but since, as we have seen, Plato returns to it over and over again in dialogues as wildly different in theme as the *Gorgias* and the *Protagoras,* and now the *Symposium,* it becomes apparent that this is a central thematic in his work. T. H. Irwin has discussed this point: "Plato shares [the] Parmenidean ideal of rational compulsion, in con-

85. Corrigan and Glazov-Corrigan, *Plato's Dialectic at Play,* 95.

trast to the Protagorean standard, also derived from Parmenides, of appearance and convention as the basis of belief. But we should be surprised that he accepts the Parmenidean ideal, if we look at his own works, for in his earlier dialogues he normally depicts Socrates in conversations about ethics. The basis for the conversation is common beliefs about ethics — the area in which Protagoras' claims seem most plausible. Socrates seems to aim at agreement in conversation, not at some compelling proof that describes an independent reality. Why should a writer of such dialogues look for rational compulsion?"[86] As Irwin sharply sums up the question: "Why should Plato look for compulsion and objectivity in such an unpromising place?"[87] The answer, of course, is that dialectic, when read from a discourse analysis point of view, is anything but "an unpromising place" for the production of "rational compulsion," with the accent on the compulsion.[88] So much for an ethos of true conversation in which "mutual desire makes possible the ungrudging exchange of questions and answers."[89] As Irwin makes absolutely clear, for Plato the standard of absolute, objective, compelling epistemic knowledge is reached not through mathematical deduction (as it would be in Aristotle, for instance), nor even in contemplation of the Forms, but precisely in dialectic, Socratic conversation. Jowett provides an apt and revealing turn of speech when he refers to "the ruling passion of Socrates for dialectics," Socrates, "who will argue with Agathon instead of making a speech, and will only speak at all upon the condition that he is allowed to speak the truth."[90] In other words, we might say dialectic equals philosophy, that is, the search for truth,[91] while encomia, rhetorical speeches, are

86. T. H. Irwin, "Coercion and Objectivity in Plato's Dialectic," *Révue Internationale de Philosophie* 40 (1986): 53.

87. Irwin, "Coercion," 54.

88. Mark Douglas Given writes: "In Vlastos's own words, Socrates enters into this context with complete prognostication of Vince Lombardi's famous sporting logion, 'Winning isn't everything; it's the only thing.' This is a fatal admission for Vlastos's defense of Socrates, for it is precisely this attitude for which Socrates condemns the Sophists and rhetoric generally in the *Gorgias,* and to which he counterposes his argument that it is better to suffer wrong than to do it"; Mark Douglas Given, *Paul's True Rhetoric: Ambiguity, Cunning, and Deception in Greece and Rome,* Emory Studies in Early Christianity (Harrisburg, Pa: Trinity Press International, 2001), 16–17.

89. Halperin, "Why Is Diotima," 133.

90. Benjamin Jowett, trans., *The Dialogues of Plato,* 2nd ed., (Oxford: Clarendon Press, 1875), 2:15.

91. Dover, *Greek Homosexuality,* 164.

incorrigibly marred owing to their search for their own beauty, or, even worse, for mere crowd-pleasing effect.

In the *Protagoras,* as well, dialogue/dialectic occurs as anything but an atmosphere of good will and an ungrudging exchange of questions and answers. Indeed, Socrates' treatment of Protagoras consists of manipulation and a play of dominance and submission that is anything but egalitarian. In the *Symposium,* at the very zenith of Diotima's exposition of true love, she makes the following remark to Socrates about the beauty of knowledge:

> First, it always *is* and neither comes to be nor passes away, neither waxes nor wanes. Second, it is not beautiful this way and ugly that way, nor beautiful at one time and ugly at another, nor beautiful in relation to one thing and ugly in relation to another; nor is it beautiful here but ugly there, as it would be if it were beautiful for some people and ugly for others. (211a)

The best reason for this digression in my view is that Platonic love is being made explicitly to contrast with both a Heraclitean and a Protagorean account of reality as flux and relativity. Given the strong associations between the *Symposium* and the *Protagoras,* Plato alludes, on my reading, precisely to Protagoras's great speech in which this point is argued. "Beautiful for some people and ugly for others"— dismissed as an inept gloss by some critics[92]—is now seen to be the very heart of this brief speech, an explicit rejection of the human as the measure of all things, that they are or that they are not, even love!

Once again, we are sent back to Protagoras and the *Protagoras,* as once again, this time obliquely, the view of the Sophist is being dismissed.

In reading the *Protagoras,* we have seen that the question of debate versus dialogue can be taken as the very driving force of Plato's work. That this is the central theme of the *Symposium* is brought home by one last crucial moment in the *Symposium* that, on my reading, ties it to the *Protagoras.* I bring Agathon back once more to the stage for a reprise before my own finale. Indeed, the considerations offered in

92. See Nehamas in Nehamas and Woodruff, *Symposium* by Plato, 58n92, who, himself, dismisses the dismissal.

this chapter may provide a clue to reading an otherwise seemingly trivial and puzzling bit of business. Socrates and Agathon are the last who remain to speak at the symposium, and Socrates (as usual) feigns modesty with respect to his final interlocutor:

> "If you ever get in my position, or rather the position I'll be in after Agathon's spoken so well, then you'll really be afraid. You'll be at your wit's end, as I am now."
>
> "You're trying to bewitch me, Socrates," said Agathon, "by making me think the audience expects great things of my speech, so I'll get flustered."

At this point, Socrates "reminds" Agathon that having just won a contest in drama in front of all Athens, Agathon should hardly be nonplussed by speaking before so few. Agathon responds:

> "Why, Socrates," said Agathon. "You must think I have nothing but theater audiences on my mind! So you suppose I don't realize that, if you're intelligent, you find a few sensible men much more frightening than a senseless crowd?!"

Socrates quite misses (accidentally on purpose) the point:

> "I'm sure that if you ever run into people you consider wise, you'll pay more attention to them than to ordinary people. But you can't suppose we're in that class; we were at the theater too, you know, part of the ordinary crowd. Still, if you did run into any wise men, other than yourself, you'd certainly be ashamed at the thought of doing anything ugly in front of them. Is that what you mean?"
>
> "That's true," he said.
>
> "On the other hand, you wouldn't be ashamed to do something ugly in front of ordinary people. Is that it?" (194a–d)

At this point, Phaedrus feeling an elenchus coming on, interrupts and bids Agathon move on to his speech, for, as we have seen, Socrates "will no longer care whether we get anywhere with what we're doing here, so long as he has a partner for discussion." Most readers seem to believe that this passage is merely comic relief or an embarrassment of Agathon for its own sake. On my reading, it is a highly pointed interchange that marks the difference between the philosophical inquiry of the few and the contests for popularity among the many and thus the difference between oligarchy and democracy.[93] We all realize instinctively, I think, that Agathon is somehow right here, that it is much more fearsome to perform before a group of one's elite associates than before the thousands in the theater, and we are meant, I think, to take home the point that Plato is making throughout both texts: that democracy is the equivalent of a theatrical or a sophistic performance, one that seduces and manipulates the masses, and not, as Pericles would have it, a serious educative experience, improving and guiding *doxa*.

This reading puts quite a different spin on philosophical eros. To be sure, we can find here in philosophical dialogue Platonic-style a strong model of male-male desire, as spiritualized and as intense as the male-male desire of a Byzantine monastery.[94] That nevertheless should not blind us to differences in the ways in which that model of eros is constructed. My reading of Platonic dialogue assimilates Plato's pedagogical ideal to pederasty in the clear asymmetry of the penetrator penetrated, taking the pederastic model of Athens at its best, as represented by Pausanias's speech, and turning it on its head from its bottom, as it were.[95] This reading of Platonic dialogue and eros as an inverted hierarchy of rhetorical eros thus raises problems for Halperin's explanations for Diotima's gender as signaling the mutuality of Platonic eros. So too does this reading challenge Foucault's similar insistence on the mutuality of the Platonic "dialectic of love."[96]

Socrates is looking for the Truth and is convinced that by his dialectical method it can be found:

"I cannot refute you, Socrates," said Agathon:—"Let us assume that what you say is true."

93. See too a very interesting comparison of this passage with the *Republic* in Corrigan and Glazov-Corrigan, *Plato's Dialectic at Play*, 77; too Nightingale, *Genres in Dialogue*, 53.

94. Eugene F. Rogers, *Sexuality and the Christian Body: Their Way into the Triune God*, Challenges in Contemporary Theology (Oxford: Blackwell, 1999).

95. Cf. Dover, *Greek Homosexuality*, 164–65.

96. Foucault, *Use of Pleasure*, 240.

"Say rather, beloved Agathon, that you cannot refute the truth; for Socrates is easily refuted."

It is here that the element of coercion enters into the Platonic speech situation, for (as T. H. Irwin, following Richard Rorty, has noted) it is precisely the claim for absolutely objective "truth" that introduces the element of coercion into philosophical discourse. Like Protagoras in his eponymous dialogue, Agathon has been defeated by that coercive power play known as "The Truth." Neither in love nor in philosophy is mutuality ever seriously comprehended. The co(n)textual connection of the *Protagoras* with the *Symposium* thus supports the thesis that one of the main burdens of the latter (if not its major task) is the overthrow of rhetoric by dialectic, because only dialectic allows "The Truth," Plato's Truth (even when aporetic or even apophatic) to appear.

The major theme of the *Symposium*, I therefore conclude, is indeed that of virtually the whole Platonic corpus: it is a protreptic speech in (pseudo)dialogue that champions the life of dialectic, with its absolute and coercive "Truth," over against what are according to Plato the shady and shaky claims of rhetoric/debate, with its allegedly very precarious grasp on truth.[97] If you ask me what Plato does in the *Symposium,* I would answer that he means to convince us to abandon both sex and the city, debate and democracy, in order to follow the only life he deemed worthwhile, the dialectical life of the Platonic Academy. In performing its textual transcendence of its declared subject, love, the *Symposium* is acting out, as well, its own theme of the transcendence of that "which men call love" by *philosophia.* This is, then, Plato at his most serious and politically monological. In the next (and final) chapter, however, I hope to reveal how Plato both affirms and queries his serious program by means of a relapse of the hiccups and in particular the greatest hiccup (or Pantagruelistic moment) of all: Alcibiades' appearance at the end of the *Symposium.*

97. See similar formulation in Bloom, "Ladder of Love," 123.

A Crude Contradiction;

Or, The Second Accent of the *Symposium*

Schlegel and Nietzsche, it seems, first brought Plato's dialogues into what would be the Bakhtinian ken by identifying them as novels,[1] and this identification has found some currency among literary scholars. Corrigan and Glazov-Corrigan define the *Symposium* as a novel *simpliciter,* construing the represented "dialogue" between the various speakers as some sort of genuine dialogical text. As they write, "If it is characteristic of the novel as a genre that it be essentially dialogical and that, if dialogical, is also aware of itself as dialogical and aware also of its difference from other kinds of voice (e.g. epic, drama, lyric etc.), then the *Symposium* in the strict sense is the first novel in history." And they continue with the following justification for their position: "It is only in the *Symposium* that the arts and sciences of their day (i.e., in the *personae* of the early speakers, from Phaedrus to Agathon, namely as orator, Sophist, doctor, comic poet, theological tragedian) speak for themselves as individual players in a larger chemistry of presence and absence by which

1. Kevin Corrigan and Elena Glazov-Corrigan, "Plato's Symposium and Bakhtin's Theory of the Dialogical Character of Novelistic Discourse," in *The Bakhtin Circle and Ancient Narrative*, vol. 3, ed. Robert Bracht Branham, Ancient Narrative (Groningen: Barkhuis Groningen University Library, 2005), 32.

art and philosophy come together in the new form of the novel, which is specifically conscious of itself as a new genre among genres."[2]

The speakers in the *Symposium,* however, as in the *Protagoras,* are not at all presented as authentic voices. All of them are crammed rather into Plato's consciousness and its protreptic aims for philosophy. Note how Bakhtin describes the dialogical:

> Within the arena of almost every utterance an intense interaction and struggle between one's own and another's word is being waged, a process in which they oppose or dialogically interanimate each other. The utterance so conceived is a considerably more complex and dynamic organism than it appears when construed simply as a thing that articulates the intention of the person uttering it, which is to see the utterance as a direct, single-voiced vehicle of expression.[3]

There hardly seems in the *Symposium* any intense interactions and struggle between the Platonic (or Socratic) word and the words of any other. The flat, not even quite parodic (although surely reductive) production and refutation of the other speakers is not then, in the Bakhtinian sense, dialogical; it is a classic instance of monological dialogue.

Another writer who has described the *Symposium* in Bakhtin's terms as a novel is Barbara Gold.[4] Her argument, somewhat more nuanced than that of the Corrigans, nevertheless also proceeds from the understanding of the different speakers in the main body of the *Symposium* as genuinely "other" voices: "Although it is clear that the *Symposium* is not, by the modern definition of the word, a novel, it and other pre-novelistic works can be called a novel by Bakhtin because they transmit, mimic and represent other languages, words and speech, both spoken and written."[5] Gold has advanced this question considerably in her identification of the "combination of seriousness

---

2. Corrigan and Glazov-Corrigan, "Plato's *Symposium,*" 33.

3. Mikhail Bakhtin, *The Dialogic Imagination: Four Essays by Mikhail Bakhtin,* ed. Michael Holquist, trans. Michael Holquist and Caryl Emerson, University of Texas Press Slavic Series (Austin: University of Texas Press, 1981), 348.

4. Barbara K. Gold, "A Question of Genre: Plato's *Symposium* as Novel," in "Comparative Literature," special issue, *MLN* 95, no. 5, (December 1980): 1353–59.

5. Gold, "A Question," 1355.

and levity" as the defining mark of the Platonic text, her marking of it as belonging with the genre of *to spoudogeloion*.[6] On the other hand, she does not allow this insight to develop, going rather for the easy claim that "in the view of Bakhtin, each of these speakers and each of the statements is one voice in a multi-colored canvas. All previous genres are parodied in the *Symposium*."[7] *Pace* Gold, however, systematic laughter at every voice but one's own does not constitute a dialogical work. Clever parodies of rhetoric, medicine, and so forth do not constitute "speaking for themselves," and there is precious little dialogism in the dialogue on that level. Allowing other voices to laugh at one's own (and one's "hero's") does constitute the dialogical text, and it is in this that I will seek the dialogism in Plato's work.[8]

Nightingale has written: "In the case of parody, Bakhtin claims, the text will criticize, subvert, or co-opt the genre that it represents. When the targeted genre is denied authority, parody may decrease the 'dialogism' in the text. Nonparodic hybrids which grant the targeted genre full semantic autonomy, by contrast, have a greater degree of 'dialogism.' As I have suggested, Plato's relation to the genres he targets is generally adversarial; . . . in different ways and for different reasons, he forces poetic and rhetorical subtexts to serve his own purposes. His use of intertextuality should thus be analyzed as a species of parody."[9] Nightingale is surely right here, but there is more, perhaps, to be said on this, for the very effort "to force poetic and rhetoric" texts and genres to serve him as slaves, as it were, is often defeated by the very act of containment. Sometimes it is the slave-master who is covertly and slyly leading the slave revolt.

In a brilliant reading of the *Gorgias,* Nightingale shows that that

6. Gold, "A Question," 1357.

7. Gold, "A Question," 1359.

8. I wish to partially repay an intellectual debt here. From the beginning of my work on Plato, Mark Jordan had been skeptical of the overweening monologization implied by my reading, insisting that the last part of the *Symposium* has to be crucial for a reading. Although in the end I didn't quite adapt his interpretation of the text, my reading of the *Symposium* here and thus my entire "take" on Plato has been deeply shifted owing to his instruction. For Jordan's reading, see Mark Jordan, "Flesh in Confession: Alcibiades beside Augustine," in *Toward a Theology of Eros: Transfiguring Passion at the Limits of Discipline,* ed. Virginia Burrus and Catherine Keller (New York: Fordham University Press, 2006), 23–37.

9. Andrea Wilson Nightingale, *Genres in Dialogue: Plato and the Construct of Philosophy* (Cambridge: Cambridge University Press, 1995), 7.

dialogue is produced entirely as a kind of parody of Euripides' trag-edy, *Antiope*.[10] After demonstrating this, she queries, "What would motivate the author of the piercing diatribe in the *Republic* against poetry in general and tragedy in particular to attempt such an adap-tation?"[11] and answers that it is precisely as part of Plato's project to distinguish his discourse practice as something new and altogether more important than all of the other speech practices of Athenians — poetry, rhetoric, drama, and everything else. She shows that the nonphilosophers are portrayed as seeing Socrates as comic and fool-ish but that he turns the tables on them, making clear, as Plato de-sires, that "the subject that philosophy addresses is the most 'serious' of issues and, as Socrates suggests at 509a, anyone who attempts to argue against the philosopher will always appear καταγέλαστος [ri-diculous]." So finally, "Callicles' picture of the powerful orator and the helpless and ridiculous philosopher is thus reversed by Socrates. It is the philosopher who is serious and the orators and unphilosophi-cal people ridiculous."[12] While Nightingale's point is astute, it is pre-cisely the incorporation of the despised tragedic genre that threatens to burst its parodic bounds and reverse again the Socratic reversal, to turn Plato's Socrates once again into that of Aristophanes. In the *Symposium,* above all others of Plato's texts, we find the double re-verse thematized. A second reading of the *Symposium* will clarify this point. This reading, I hope, will more closely track what I take to be the deeply antithetical moment in Plato's Socratic texts, encom-passing both Socrates the almost ethereal hero of the quest for the Forms and potbellied Socrates, the almost Aristophanic sophomore. Skipping quite over the parts of the *Symposium* that I have read in the previous chapter, I cut right to the chase.

The *Symposium* as Drama

For me, as for some other readers, the key moment in the last part of the *Symposium* is Socrates' "forcing" (προσαναγκάζειν) of both Ag-athon and Aristophanes to assert that the same person ought to be

---

10. Nightingale, *Genres in Dialogue,* 67–87.
11. Nightingale, *Genres in Dialogue,* 87.
12. Nightingale, *Genres in Dialogue,* 90.

able to write tragedy and comedy. Jose Ortega y Gasset saw in *this* moment the beginnings of the novel. Claiming (in terms not incompatible with Bakhtin's) that the novel is tragicomedy, he writes of the last episode of the *Symposium:* "In the novel as a synthesis of tragedy and comedy, the strange desire hinted at by Plato without any comment has been fulfilled. . . . This episode has not been satisfactorily explained, but I have always suspected, when I read it, that Plato, a soul seething with intuitions, was planting here the seed of the novel. If we prolong the gesture made by Socrates from the *Symposium* in the pale light of dawn, it will seem as if we come up against Don Quixote, the hero and the madman."[13] Note that this interpretation of Ortega y Gasset's does not read the *Symposium* itself *qua* novel but sees rather the conception of the novel in the cohabitation of tragic and comic in the same author. While I am not sure that it is not too mystical or prophetic to see here the birth of the novel, the insight that there is something highly significant in this moment and that it has to do with the blending of the tragic and the comic is compelling.

The "Satyr Play"

In this reading I will bring on stage the scenes of the *Symposium* that were "cut" in the first part of my discussion here, namely the "satyr play" with which the *Symposium* ends, Alcibiades' inburst and outburst. These scenes have great implications for a strategy of reading the dialogue and thus the *Dialogues.* It is a matter of no small importance that Plato refers to Alcibiades' speech as a satyr play, a silene drama (ἀλλὰ τὸ σατυρικόν σου δρᾶμα τοῦτο καὶ σιληνικὸν κατάδηλον ἐγένετο) (222d), for as we know well, the satyr play followed the tragedies on the Hellenic stage. If Alcibiades produces, or enacts, a satyr play, then that which came before (appropriately enough since Agathon orchestrated it) must be a tragedy.[14] But since we know already that tragedy such as Agathon's is not true tragedy, not at all *spoudaios,* nor even dedicated to holding on to truth—we know this

13. Jose Ortega y Gasset, "The Nature of the Novel," *Hudson Review* 10 (1957): 40.
14. Diskin Clay, "The Tragic and Comic Poet of the *Symposium*," *Arion* 2 (1975): 249. For this used as a metaphor for the satiric and its relation to other discourses, see Mikhail Bakhtin, *Rabelais and His World,* trans. Hélène Iswolsky (Bloomington: Indiana University Press, 1984), 88.

in the *Symposium* from his speech, as confirmed, ex post facto, in the *Laws*—then the first tragedy, the conversations of Agathon and his friends, is a false tragedy, because Agathon himself—true to the characterization of tragedians in the *Laws*—does not know or hold to the truth. Truth, it seems, begins to emerge in the second tragedy, the one spoken by Socrates himself. A point that must be made about the satyr play is that it was, of course, penned by the same author who wrote the tragedies, in this case, then, Plato. This is Plato's satyr play; it must, therefore, somehow be powerfully related to the search for the True word that animates Socrates' animadversions against the false tragedian Agathon and against rhetoric entirely. And indeed, Alcibiades has promised to tell the truth and not to be amusing (ἡ εἰκὼν τοῦ ἀληθοῦς ἕνεκα, οὐ τοῦ γελοίου) (215a)—precisely echoing the moment in the *Apology* when Socrates says, "And perhaps I shall seem to some of you to be joking; be assured, however, I shall speak perfect truth to you" (20d4–6) (καὶ ἴσως μὲν δόξω τισὶν ὑμῶν παίζειν. εὖ μέντοι ἴστε πᾶσαν ὑμῖν τὴν ἀλήθειαν ἐρῶ). The truth Alcibiades has to tell is his satyr play (φημὶ γὰρ δὴ ὁμοιότατον αὐτὸν εἶναι τοῖς σιληνοῖς) (215a). This reading is supported as well by a passage from Ion of Chios's lost *Visitations,* "often cited as a precursor to the Socratic dialogue," in which the author of that text is reported to have said: "Like a tragic tetralogy, ἀρετή should have its share of the satyric [σατυρικὸν]" (Plut., *Per.* 5.4).[15] Thus I find anticipated in Plato that of which Lucian "accuses" himself, when he describes Zeus's hard treatment of him: "Then he unceremoniously penned me [Dialectic] up with Jest and Satire and Cynicism and Eupolis and Aristophanes, terrible men for mocking all that is holy and scoffing at all that is right." Diotima's speech, I suggest, is the true tragedy that follows on the false one of Agathon, while Alcibiades' true satyr play supersedes Aristophanes' amusements, his *geloion.* The same person writes the tragedy and the comedy.

Let me begin with a synopsis of the silenic drama. Any epitome emphasizes that which the epitomizer sees as significant, and this one is no different. I will mention moments left out in others' syn-

---

15. Cited in M. D. Usher, "Satyr Play in Plato's Symposium," *American Journal of Philology* 123 (2002): 224–25, who interprets the overall place of the satyric in the *Symposium* quite differently from the way I do. I thank my colleague Leslie Kurke for this reference.

opses and leave out sometimes what others make much of. Socrates has just completed his speech to uproarious applause (a matter of no small importance) and Aristophanes is about to make some remark when a disturbance is heard near the door; drunken revelers and a flute girl (precisely the two things which had been excluded from *this* Symposium earlier on) appear. It turns out to be Alcibiades floridly, staggeringly drunk with garlands for Agathon (the most beautiful). Between his drunkenness and the garlands, he doesn't notice the presence of Socrates until he has flopped on the couch between Agathon and Socrates. When he does, he remonstrates with Socrates for having chosen to sit next to the beautiful Agathon rather than the laughable Aristophanes. Socrates feigns jealousy and complains about Alcibiades' jealousy, whereupon the latter takes some of the garlands from the head of Agathon and places them on Socrates' head, declaring that "he [Socrates] is victorious in words over all people, not just the day before yesterday like you, but every day" (213e). After some byplay about drinking, Alcibiades is instructed in the agreement for the evening's entertainment and asked by Eryximachus to give his encomium to Eros. Alcibiades wittily proposes that he will praise Socrates himself, insisting that he "will tell the truth" (τἀληθῆ ἐρῶ) (214e). He even invites Socrates to interrupt him and object if Alcibiades reports something untruthful in his praise. He then makes the following remarkable declaration:

> I'll try to praise Socrates, my friends, but I'll have to use an image. And though he may think I'm trying to make fun of him, I assure you my image is no joke: it aims at the truth. Look at him! Isn't he just like a statue of Silenus? You know the kind of statue I mean; you'll find them in any shop in town. It's a Silenus sitting, his flute or his pipes in his hands, and it's hollow. It's split right down the middle, and inside it's full of tiny statues of the gods. Now look at him again! Isn't he also just like the satyr Marsyas?
>
> Nobody, not even you, Socrates can deny that you *look* like them. But the resemblance goes beyond appearance, as you're about to hear.

On my reading, there are multiple levels of irony in this passage. Alcibiades has pointed to the familiar (almost standard) Socratic irony in his own critique/praise of Socrates. He describes him as ugly in

mien and ridiculous in speech with all the beauty and divinity not
in the outer form but in the inner (dare I say?) content, the golden
agalmatha—phallic—images of the gods.

To this point, the irony is familiar to us as readers of Plato, all
too familiar. This is the irony of the beginning of the *Protagoras* and
throughout the corpus, but here there is another level of irony of
which, it seems, Alcibiades is unaware and which comes out in the
sequel. If his blame turned to praise is familiar, his praise turned to
blame is not so. The terms within which Alcibiades praises Socrates
are, as we shall immediately see, a mobilization of the charges against
both rhapsodes and rhetors throughout the Platonic corpus. Socrates
here is made to appear as Ion, Agathon, and Gorgias all rolled up into
one. Alcibiades addresses Socrates:

> You are impudent, contemptuous, and vile. No? If you won't admit it,
> I'll bring witnesses. And you're much more marvelous than Marsyas,
> who needed instruments to cast his spells on people. . . . The only
> difference between you and Marsyas is that you need no instruments;
> you do exactly what he does, but with words alone. You know, people
> hardly ever take a speaker seriously, even if he's the greatest orator;
> but let anyone—man, woman, or child—listen to you or even to a
> poor account of what you say—and we are all transported, completely
> possessed.

Now Alcibiades adddresses the company, speaking about Socrates:

> If I were to describe for you what an extraordinary effect his words
> have always had on me (I can feel it this moment even as I'm speak-
> ing), you might actually suspect that I'm drunk! Still, I swear to you,
> the moment he starts to speak, I am beside myself: my heart starts
> leaping in my chest, the tears come streaming down my face, even the
> frenzied Corybyantes seem sane compared to me—and let me tell
> you, I am not alone. (215a–e)

Earlier in the *Symposium,* it was Socrates who mockingly feared that
Agathon's speech would, like the Gorgon's head, turn him into stone.
Now, all of a sudden, it is Socrates who spellbinds and makes his hear-
ers drunk with his words. It is he who is the magician of rhetoric,

the purveyor of drugs. We find here, that is to say, precisely the self-critique of rhetoric that we saw in Gorgias's *Helen* in the beginning of this book. And it is, most assuredly, "the truth," truth being here the truth of Alcibiades' experience and his report of it as the experience of others as well; hence, a truth more like Protagoras's measures than like Plato's *epistēmē*.

Alcibiades is not lying. Plato brilliantly, subtly, indirectly, through narrative reveals here that layer of critique of *his own* protreptic present throughout the dialogues, namely the absolute and clear distinction between rhetoric which seduces, enthralls, inebriates, and Socratic dialogue which persuades through *logismos,* rational argument. As we have seen above in analyzing the Gorgias, it is when characters in the dialogues are permitted to describe Socrates in critical or ridiculous terms that a moment of dialogicality enters the text, enters and remains, doing its work. The Alcibiades speaking here performs something of the narrative-discursive function of the matrona and the laundryman of chapter 4's Talmudic text, the "outsider" who is permitted to voice the critique of the insiders (Plato) with respect to their own institutions and practices (the Academy, philosophy). Corrigan and Glazov-Corrigan have, moreover, pointed to the seriousness of the charge of *hybristes* that Alcibiades lays at Socrates' door. This is no laughing matter: "This *hybris* is not 'polite' or the sort of characteristic contained easily within normal confines. Indeed, *hybris* designated a special offense in Attic law: anyone who struck, pushed, pulled, or restrained another person (and this could include a sexual element) could be liable for a prosecution on a charge of *hybris*." Even more wonderful for my purposes is their conclusion from this observation: "So it does not fit at all with Erasmus's wish to include Socrates in the Litany of the Saints (*Sancte Socrate, ora pro nobis*)—or does it? Socrates' *hybris* displaces ordinary perceptions; like an irruption of the unexpected, it unsettles the comfortable course of normal life."[16] Readers who have slogged their way through this book till now

---

16. Kevin Corrigan and Elena Glazov-Corrigan, *Plato's Dialectic at Play: Argument, Structure, and Myth in the* Symposium (University Park: Pennsylvania State University Press, 2004), 13. I would point out here a curious typographical error in this book that should be corrected so that it (the error) can be set aside. The authors write, "The dialogue is concluded with Socrates arguing that the same poet cannot write both tragedy and comedy," for which read, of course, "can write both tragedy and comedy" (23).

will, I hope, find here the echoes that I hear between this Socrates and the fat rabbis and Rabbi Me'ir. In all three of these texts, we find a second accent introduced into the discourse via crudely contradictory presentations of the heroes, Socrates and the rabbis.

This reading suggests a way through another aporia in Platonic studies, an aporia pointed to in my discussion of the *Gorgias* above, namely the queasiness that one feels on critiquing Socrates' practices when all of the information on which the critique is built is given us by Plato and Plato alone. Plato must know what he is doing when he has given us the information upon which our very critique of Socrates is built; after all, it is Plato who provides us moments such as that naked exercise of power by Socrates when he interrupts Protagoras's successful speech to enforce the Socratic rule on only short questions and answers, or the patently fallacious arguments that Socrates is made to produce against his opponents. At the same time, however, we cannot imagine that Plato seeks to undermine the true tragedy of dialectic and the kind of Truth it promulgates through this moment. The *spoudaios* remains *spoudaios,* the *geloios* remains *geloios,* but both are written by the same author, the tragedy and the comedy.

Rather than recuperating and reducing this disharmony (as does, for instance, Elizabeth Belfiore in her brilliant essay),[17] I suggest that this moment of Platonic contradiction is the moment of dialogism in the text, where Plato lets us know that he too is on to Socrates, that much as he praises him, much as he insists that he is the only true lover of wisdom, he is also very much aware of the rhetorical, and thus compulsive, effects of the Socratean speech. This is a point to which I will return, as it is key to my final reading of the *Symposium.*[18]

The speech continues with some further meditation by Alcibiades on the Academy versus the polis. Alcibiades declares that he has shut his ears in order not to hear Socrates, because were he to allow himself to hear Socrates, he would not be able to leave his side and go about the Athenians' business (τὰ δ' Ἀθηναίων πράττω) (216a). Aside from the irony once again emphasized (and this will be doubled below) of

17. Elizabeth Belfiore, "'Elenchus, Epode,' and Magic: Socrates as Silenus," *Phoenix* 34, no. 2 (Summer 1980): 128–37.

18. For an interesting reading that uncovers the critique of Socrates in Alcibiades' speech (and thus its commitment to "truth"), see Michael Gagarin, "Socrates' 'Hybris' and Alcibiades' Failure," *Phoenix* 31, no. 1 (Spring 1977): 22–37.

Socrates as compelling (ἀναγκάζει), forcing Alcibiades to agree with him in something, there is other irony here. The Athenians' business at this particular moment was, of course, the Peloponnesian War and the calamity to which Alcibiades was about to lead them. It has been noted before that the dramatic date of the *Symposium* is the summer of 416 BC, the summer between the Melian Massacre and the disastrous expedition to Sicily.[19] This is the summer in which Agathon won first prize at the Lenaean festival and in which *The Trojan Women* of Euripides came in second. Given that Alcibiades was the architect of Athens's downfall and destruction, at least the last part of the dialogue seems to cry out for a contextualizing reading of Alcibiades, one that is hinted at (but unfortunately not more than that) at the end of Nightingale's extraordinary discussion of the text: "It is no accident, finally, that Plato puts this speech into the mouth of a famous (and, indeed, infamous) politician. The foolish use of the language of praise, he reminds us, poses a very real danger for the city as a whole."[20] Shifting slightly the terms of her reading, in which the last acts of the *Symposium* prolong and extend the attack on encomia that she discovers throughout the text, I would prefer—this is a preference and a choice, not an argument against her reading—to read this ending in a way that enables us to see it as putting into question the single-mindedness and single-voicedness of that very "tragedy," the sustained attack on encomia and rhetoric of the text until now.

Richard Patterson also suggests that Plato is here defending Socrates implicitly against that Athenian jury that had condemned him to death in 399, thinking as they did that he was the cause of Alcibiades' devastation, and not one who attempted to prevent it. Plato, according to Patterson, is reversing the view of Alcibiades and his failure. Where other Athenians, notably perhaps Thucydides and perhaps Euripides as well, saw it as Alcibiades' failure to attend to any but his own needs, for Plato, Alcibiades fails because, recognizing the beauty of the philosophical life but *failing to attend to his own true needs,* he comes to reject the philosophical life for the life of the polis and gratification of the demos. The demos of Athens is Alcibiades' dema-

19. Richard Patterson, "The Platonic Art of Comedy and Tragedy," *Philosophy and Literature* 6 (1982): 87.
20. Nightingale, *Genres in Dialogue,* 127.

gogue, not he theirs! Patterson notes a certain irony in the situation: "The sorry events of 416 and after become a playing out to the bitter end of a tragic loss already implied in Alcibiades' failure to turn away from a life of *timē* in the estimation of the many to life in the service of the true good of his soul. But then, only the Platonic philosopher could either love or pity Alcibiades for *these* reasons."[21] What Patterson misses, I think, is that extra level of irony here, for Alcibiades in a strong sense *is* a follower of Socrates, precisely the Socrates who seduces and inebriates his listeners, the one who bites them like a viper and stings them like a ray. We should not seek to remove the stinger from the text.

Alcibiades continues with his satyrical praise of Socrates, interpreting him as one who is deceptively unattractive on the outside, both in his person and in his behavior, his appearance of overweening desire for boys. Inside this clay statue of a Silenus, however, when "he comes to be serious [*spoudaisantos!*]" (216e), then one can see the beautiful statues inside, the golden *agalmatha*. For Alcibiades, this inside is made of moderation; Socrates pretends to be profligate, but, when he is serious reveals the golden statues of his self-restraint, his resistance to the enactment of physical love.[22] Alcibiades goes on, in the most famous part of this sequence, to recount how, stricken with philosophy, he sought Socrates' body (precisely the reverse of Diotima's ladder) but Socrates "rebuffed" him, sleeping beside him, wrapped up in his arms, chastely, the whole night. Lest we miss this message, moreover, Alcibiades reports Socrates' brilliant language of reversal of the terms of Greek love (as these were given by Pausanias), thus reinforcing the message of Diotima, as I have interpreted it above:

> He heard me out, and then he said in that absolutely inimitable ironic manner of his:

21. Patterson, "Platonic Art," 88–89.
22. *Pace* Jordan, Socrates' exercising with Alcibiades, wrestling with him alone, accepting his invitations to dinner, staying late, and then sleeping with him ("as a father or a brother") do not contradict this reading; indeed, they emphasize my point that true eros (at some low level of the ladder) inolves attachment to the beauty of the object and not to the pleasure of his touch. Jordan, "Flesh in Confession." (I am not doubting Socrates' desire, but see Gagarin, "Socrates's 'Hybris,'" 29n31). Moreover, it is easy to see that this is the lesson that Socrates wishes to teach Alcibiades, a lesson learned, it seems, but not very well.

"Dear Alcibiades, if you are right in what you say about me, you are already more accomplished than you think. If I really have in me the power to make you a better man, then you can see in me a beauty that is really beyond description and makes your own remarkable good looks pale in comparison. But, then, is this a fair exchange that you propose? You seem to me to want more than your proper share: you offer me the merest appearance of beauty, and in return you want the thing itself, 'gold in exchange for bronze.'" (218d5–e)

Alluding to the Homeric Glaukos in this brilliant bit of sophistry, Plato reinforces the ironies of Alcibiades' own praise of Socrates, turning Alcibiades' words against him in a way that Alcibiades is perhaps not able to understand.[23] He, expecting that his beauty will be sufficient to make Socrates want the conventional exchange of sexual favors for wisdom, is hoist on his own petard, for if Socrates is truly the beautiful one who can impart wisdom, Alcibiades can no longer be *erastes*. If I am ugly on the outside but beautiful on the inside, then you must be the reverse, so why would I want this false beauty? asks Socrates.

This is followed by a description of Socrates as being overcome with a paroxysm of otherworldliness in the middle of a battlefield, doubling his slip into abstraction on the way to the *Symposium* itself, moments that Charles Kahn has read—and I agree—as signifying the gap between the worldly concerns of all the symposiasts and "Diotima's" representation of a Parmenidean, otherworldly Eros.[24] With this, I come to the dénouement of Alcibiades' peroration, in which we find, once again, a justification, now well supported, of Alcibiades' comparison of Socrates to Silenus and satyrs:

There is a parallel for everyone—everyone else, that is. But this man here is so bizarre, his ways and his ideas are so unusual, that, search

23. See Charles H. Kahn, *Plato and the Socratic Dialogue: The Philosophical Use of a Literary Form* (Cambridge: Cambridge University Press, 1996), 69, who writes, "But the seismic gap between world views is most vividly dramatized in the frustrated passion of Alcibiades, who is unable to establish emotional contact with Socrates even in bed, because they inhabit different worlds." This is what is signified by the talk of exchanges of gold for brass, as well.

24. Kahn, *Plato and the Socratic Dialogue*, 69.

as you might, you'll never find anyone else, alive or dead, who's even
remotely like him. The best you can do is not to compare him to anything human, but to liken him, as I do, to Silenus and the satyrs, and
the same goes for his ideas and arguments.

Come to think of it, I should have mentioned this much earlier:
even his ideas and arguments are just like those hollow statues of Silenus. If you were to listen to his arguments, at first they'd strike you
as totally ridiculous; they're clothed in words as coarse as the hides
worn by the most vulgar satyrs. He's always going on about pack asses,
or blacksmiths, or cobblers, or tanners; he's always making the same
tired old points in the same tired old words. If you are foolish, or simply unfamiliar with him, you'd find it impossible not to laugh at his
arguments. But if you see them when they open up like the statues,
if you go behind their surface, you'll realize that no other arguments
make any sense. They're truly worthy of a god, bursting with figures
of virtue inside. They're of great—no, of the greatest—importance for
anyone who wants to become a truly good man. (221d–222a)

The satyr play about Silenus also produces an ugly and gross, grotesque exterior that has within it golden gods. The tragedies in the
tetralogy are in dialogue with the satyr play and the satyr play in dialogue with them. Socrates, who once claimed to us:

> Well, there is one point at least which I think you will admit, namely
> that any *logos* ought to be constructed like a living being, with its own
> body, as it were; it must not lack either head or feet; it must have a
> middle and extremities so composed as to suit each other and the
> whole work. (*Phaedrus* 264c)

is now revealed to himself have a body which, while surely not lacking
limbs, does not quite have a middle composed to suit the extremities.
Neither, one can add, does his *logos*.[25] Socrates and his discourse are

---

25. Cf. reading of this passage at John Sallis, *Being and Logos: Reading the Platonic
Dialogues* (Bloomington: Indiana University Press, 1996), 14–17. It goes without saying, and
indeed I have said before in the introduction of this book, that I am in complete sympathy with Sallis's statement that "in the interpretation of a dialogue not only is it inappropriate to extract from the speeches those which measure up to some external, or at least
later, standard of what constitutes 'philosophical discourse'; it is equally inappropriate to

both disproportionate and grotesque, with various features that are incongruous with each other.

Now, as made absolutely clear by Ralph Rosen, the theme of a satyr play comprises exactly the same themes that we find in tragedies as well.[26] The chorus of old men or wise or lamenting women of tragedy is replaced by a chorus of shepherds or satyrs,[27] making the satyr play a kind of grotesque double of the tragedy. This strengthens, I think, my suggestion that in reading Alcibiades' satyr play—so called, I remind, by Plato—we are meant to read it as somehow a part of the Truth to which Plato's true tragedy aspires as well. Both the tragic and the comic (in the form of the satyr play) are written, indeed, by the same author, and both, somehow, must contribute to the serious (and comic) enterprise of that most epistemic of authors, Plato.[28] At one level, then, the explicit genre of the *Symposium*, which is a kind of hermeneutical key and synecdoche of the whole corpus, is the tragedy and the satyr play. (This will not preclude, of course, seeing it as "novelistic" in the broadest sense as well.)

Plato's Self-Subversion: The Last Act

Socrates' coercion of his interlocutors in the very last scene of the *Symposium* is a perfect text for me to end on, in that it connects end to beginning (of my book), Socrates to Gorgias, forming an *inclusio,* both formal and thematic. As recognized by Belfiore, Gorgias's ideas about rhetoric as magic and drug expressed in the *Encomium to Helen* match up well with Plato's descriptions of rhetoric as magic and *pharmakon* in the *Republic* and elsewhere.[29] Now at the beginning of my argument

---

abstract the speeches themselves from the dramatic features to which they are joined in the dialogues." For further animadversions on this point, see below my brief discussion of Francisco Gonzalez's reading of the *Protagoras*.

26. Ralph M. Rosen, *Revisiting Sophocles' Poimenes: Tragedy or Satyr Play?* Departmental Papers (Classical Studies) 5 (Philadelphia: ScholarlyCommons, 2003), http://repository .upenn.edu/classics_papers/5.

27. For the relationship between these two types, see Rosen, *Revisiting Sophocles' Poimenes,* 6.

28. See too Helen Bacon, "Socrates Crowned," *Virginia Quarterly Review* 35 (1959): 430, whose beautifully written conclusion goes before me partly on the way.

29. Belfiore, "'Elenchus, Epode,'" 130–31. What I don't quite understand is how this "gives much support to the view that Plato is attacking the sophists," since the arch-sophist Gorgias himself is problematizing and not celebrating this confusion between

in the first chapter above, I proposed (a virtual commonplace) that it is Parmenides who first distinguished absolutely between persuasion (by reason) and necessity (by magic), while Gorgias in his work disrupted that binary. I would suggest now at the end that Plato is doing something here very much like what Gorgias himself does in the *Encomium,* acknowledging the limits of the distinction between magic and reason, between persuasion and force, between rhetoric and dialogue.[30] For Plato, at this key moment, to portray Socrates as compelling his interlocutors is astonishing and revealing of how much Plato is letting us in on the secret that this is how he meant to portray Socrates' similar behavior in, for instance, the *Gorgias,* as I have shown above.[31] This moment thus doubles as well the speech of Alcibiades about Socrates' compulsion of his listeners through verbal magic.

Richard Patterson bases his interpretation of this moment on the passage from the *Laws* that I have cited in the introduction to this book (and as one of its epigraphs), in which Plato indicates that the tragedians are not *spoudaioi,* or tragic, but rather it is the philosophers who are both: "Let us return first to the *Laws'* combination, in the philosopher, of (true) tragedy and (popular) comedy. We may recall that the philosopher alone knows the nature of the noblest and best life, so that he alone can knowingly imitate it in *logos.* Since such a life will inevitably appear comic to the multitude, his tragic figure will just as inevitably be popularly comic. Thus he creates at once true tragedy and popular comedy, and is the only one capable of doing so by knowledge or *technē.*"[32] As Patterson shows, at least one of Plato's charges against tragedy is that it cannot be genuinely *spoudaios,* because the tragedians are not philosophers, and cannot hold on to the "truth." They cannot show an audience what it is to be the best sort of human being, since they do not know themselves. They are like a man ignorant of horses, selling a donkey as a horse, to another man who believes that donkeys are horses. Tragedy is thus not "true," and

---

persuasion and force, just as much as Plato is. If anything, this is the point where the opposition between the Sophist and the philosopher collapses.

30. For quite a different "take," see Belfiore, "'Elenchus, Epode.'"

31. Lest anyone think that what Plato means is "forcing" them to assent by the sheer logic of his argument, let them remember that Plato explicitly writes that they were being forced even though they weren't following, since they were falling asleep.

32. Patterson, "Platonic Art," 84.

only philosophy is truly tragic, *spoudaios*.[33] "Any dialogue featuring Socrates as protagonist will qualify as *spoudaios*—hence 'tragic' in the sense appropriated by Plato in the *Laws*."[34]

According to this view, when Plato has Socrates insist at the end of the *Symposium,* as his tragic and comic poets Agathon and Aristophanes are falling asleep, that the same person must be able to write both comedy and tragedy, his insistence grows out of this double meaning—on the literal level, the authors of comic and tragic dramas; on the metaphorical, the authors of the truly "serious," that is, philosophers, must also be able to "write" comedy, to be *spoudogeloion.* For the ordinary dramatists, whether tragedians—including of course Euripides—or comedians, drama is not serious. A *tekhnē,* not founded on *epistēmē* (my formulation is slightly different from that of Patterson here), drama is practiced by men skilled in the writing of either tragedies or comedies, not both. As Socrates has demonstrated, neither of his dramaturgical interlocutors knows much of anything of the topics of which they write. But Platonic drama (always in this sense tragic, whether externally comic or tragic in form), based on *epistēmē,* will always represent the same Truth, since Truth is always one, and the same philosopher can truly write in either mode.[35] On this reading of Plato, there is a reversal of terms; for *doxa,* Agathon appears *spoudaios* and Aristophanes, *geloios,* but from the aspect of *epistēmē,* neither Agathon nor Aristophanes is *spoudaios,* and the genuine artist, the philosopher, can write tragedy or comedy equally *spoudaios* and *geloios.* I find here all the more the multiple ironies that I have noted above in the double-reverse of Alcibiades' praise of Socrates as ugly and ridiculous on the outside but beautiful and wise on the inside. This carnival of reversals is acted out in the narrative when Alcibiades asks of Agathon that he take some strands of the victory garland that he has won in the tragic contests and place them on the head of Socrates (213d), thus alluding to the idea in the *Laws* (if not to the passage, of course) that the philosopher is the true tragedian, the true *spoudaios,* the one who holds to the truth.[36] Diskin Clay argues that the impor-

33. Patterson, "Platonic Art," 83.
34. Patterson, "Platonic Art," 84.
35. Patterson, "Platonic Art," 85. This reading, as Patterson does not fail to register, helps make sense of the centrality of Agathon, the nontragic tragedian in the *Symposium.*
36. On the significance of this act, see Bacon, "Socrates Crowned."

tance of the hiccups of Aristophanes is that "unexpectedly a comic and a tragic poet are brought together,"[37] suggesting by this that the final enigma of the *Symposium* is something that was deep, deep in the plan of the work; indeed that it is essential to the piece. Socrates ends up sitting between the one whom Alcibiades calls *kallistos* (Agathon, note the allusion to his name) and the one whom Alcibiades names *geloios* (Aristophanes, of course).[38] Socrates, the one who sits between the tragic and the comic poet and insists that were they true, they would be one, imputes to himself the character of the *spoudogeloios.* This seems to me right; the question is to what end. Why the insistence in the satyr play on Socrates as *spoudogeloios,* on the comic as tragic? If the only true *spoudaios* is the tragic philosopher, why the *geloios*? Why is he also a clown?

Joel Relihan has located the primary impulse for Menippean satire in the tenth book of *The Republic,* just before the Myth of Er, which he takes as "in most of its elements a Menippean satire, with a statement doubting the ability of words to express anything other than the lowest level of phenomenal reality. Menippean satire accepts this caveat and takes the Myth of Er, and Platonic mythologizing in general, as perfect demonstrations of how *not* to go about proclaiming truth and defining reality."[39] This insight needs to be developed further. What does it mean to refer to a part of Plato's writing as Menippean satire?[40] It can only mean that Plato himself is reflecting on, self-reflexive of, the limitations of his own intellectual practice, *philosophia,* and his own institution, the Academy. The text is Menippean in that peculiar sense of a text that both advances and undermines a program at one and the very same time. Relihan has written of the Menippean satire: "Here [in Lucian's *Icaromenippus*] Menippus is identified as comic because he is lost in thought, mumbling about interplanetary distances; he knows that his friend will think that he is speaking nonsense."[41] Utterly reminiscent of Socrates on the bat-

37. Clay, "The Tragic and Comic Poet," 242.

38. For the question of the seating order, see Corrigan and Glazov-Corrigan, *Plato's Dialectic at Play,* 26–27, together with discussions of other scholars' positions, as it were.

39. Joel C. Relihan, *Ancient Menippean Satire* (Baltimore: Johns Hopkins University Press, 1993), 11.

40. Sara Rappe, "Father of the Dogs? Tracking the Cynics in Plato's Euthydemus," *Classical Philology* 95, no. 3 (July 2000): 282–303.

41. Relihan, *Ancient Menippean Satire,* 105.

tlefield in Alcibiades' description, as well as at the beginning of the *Symposium,* this comic moment has the potential to open the Platonic text to a specific Menippean reading, which reading I pursue now to end (but not close) this book.

Bakhtin has articulated the problem that the doubled voice of Menippean satire poses thus:

> The whole mass of ideology, both organized and unorganized, from the form-shaping principles to the random and removable maxims of the author, must be subordinated to a single accent and must express a single and unified point of view. All else is merely the object of this point of view, "sub-accentual material." Only that idea which has fallen into the rut of the author's point of view can retain its significance without destroying the single-accented unity of the work. Whatever these authorial ideas, whatever function they fulfill, they are *not represented:* they either represent and internally govern a representation, or they shed light on some other represented thing, or, finally, they accompany the representation as a detachable semantic ornament. *They are expressed directly, without distance.* And within the bounds of that monologic world shaped by them, someone else's idea cannot be represented. It is either assimilated, or polemically repudiated, or ceases to be an idea.[42]

The question is whether such monologicity is an essential and given function of the text, or is it, perhaps, rather given by the mode of reading that is promoted by the reader/critic. Bakhtin actually suggests this second possibility (although perhaps willy-nilly), when he writes, "Everyone interprets in his own way Dostoevsky's ultimate word, but all equally interpret it as a *single* world, a *single* voice, a *single* accent, and therein lies their fundamental mistake. The unity of the polyphonic novel—a unity standing above the word, above the voice, above the accent—has yet to be discovered."[43] The same, perhaps, can be said of Plato himself, and of the Talmud too. Neither of them is a novel—quite. As I have argued, they both belong to that same

42. Mikhail Bakhtin, *Problems of Dostoevsky's Poetics,* ed. and trans. Caryl Emerson, Theory and History of Literature (Minneapolis: University of Minnesota Press, 1984), 84–85.

43. Bakhtin, *Problems of Dostoevsky's Poetics,* 43.

prehistory of the novel nevertheless, in that they provide a discursive space in which their own deepest held convictions and desires both ethical and institutional are put into question, through the mobilization by the very authors of antithetical discourses, crude contradictions, and second accents.

Epilogue

The stories of the fat rabbis, perfectly represented by the searing image of them on the frontispiece of this book, have occupied a large part of my imagination in the thirty years or so since I first encountered them. The bodies of undisciplined, obese rabbis with bits and pieces of exaggerated size protruding, as well as the obtrusion of fabulous stories about them in the midst of "serious" discourse, are an ideal figure for the Babylonian Talmud itself, antidecorum and antigenre. To pull this rather indecorous discourse itself together in at least rough-and-tumble fashion, I will turn back to that frontispiece, Yig'al Tumarkin's illustration of our fat rabbis with their sexual equipment to match and the little ox walking between and underneath them.[44] This collage captures brilliantly the thesis of this book as a whole, incorporating both the holy and the grotesque, one on the top and one on the bottom in the figure of the angel with his Gabriel's horn that hovers over the fat, almost demonic "Jewish silenoi" below him.[45] Indeed, it was the finding of this image that gave me the title for this book and generated its dominating narrative figure. More than once now I have referred to the moment in the *Phaedrus* in which Plato compares a well-formed *logos* with a well-formed body, that is, a body whose extremities are in appropriate proportion to its middle. Our silenoi, both these Jewish ones and the very Greekish one of the end of the *Symposium* which I have just been discussing, are marked pre-

---

44. I am grateful to my wife, Chava Boyarin, for finding this image. It was originally made by Tumarkin as an illustration for another book. I am very grateful to Mr. Tumarkin for providing permission to use it here.

45. Malcolm Schofield, the distinguished Cambridge Plato scholar, upon being shown the image and knowing nothing of the talmudic background to it, immediately exclaimed "Jewish silenoi!" thus inadvertently confirming for me the success of the image as a quilting point between Socrates and the fat rabbis.

cisely by the disproportionality of their bodies. Insofar, then, as they are the signs of discourses, of *logoi,* they make perfect representations for what I have been claiming for both the Talmud and Plato, a powerfully meaningful ill-formedness of their discourses.

Just as I have promoted Tumarkin's work from an illustration of a story in the Talmud into an illustration of the Talmud itself, so too do I see the Talmud's grotesque stories of its important sages as marking something essential about the Talmud as a book. The Talmud is a fat rabbi, just as the novel is a "baggy monster." Michael Holquist wrote, "Bakhtin loves novels because he is a baggy monster."[46] It would be not inapposite, if surely immodest, for me to write, "Boyarin loves the Talmud because he is a fat Rabbi." Lest the point be lost, however, or even attenuated, please remember that I am not claiming that the Talmud or Plato are simply grotesques. Such a conclusion would, itself, be grotesque. It is not for nothing or out of false consciousness or misplaced piety that both have been read as embodying and communicating the deepest truths of their respective cultures for millennia (we must not forget the angel at the top of the picture either; if for Freud, Schnitzler shows himself in his narrative art to be a psychoanalyst of talent, in this image Tumarkin so marks himself a Talmudist).

What the Talmud has to contribute to this thesis about discourse, about both Plato and itself, I think, is the rather bare fashion in which the contrasts between the serious and the comical, the "classical" (monological dialogue!) and the grotesque (narrative), are thematized in the talmudic text. This gives us a richer mode for analyzing these contrasts/contradictions in Plato as well, reading the dialectic as equivalent, mutatis mutandis, to the halakhic dialectic of the Talmud and the narrative as comparable to the biographical legends. Bakhtin has provided the following account of the carnivalistic in Plato:

> The image of Socrates himself is of an ambivalent sort—a combination of beauty and ugliness (see the characterization of him by Alcibiades in Plato's *Symposium*); Socrates' own characterizations of himself

---

46. Michael Holquist, introduction to *The Dialogic Imagination: Four Essays by Mikhail Bakhtin,* ed. Michael Holquist, trans. Michael Holquist and Caryl Emerson, University of Texas Press Slavic Series (Austin: University of Texas Press, 1981), xviii.

as a "pander" and a "midwife" are also constructed in the spirit of carnival debasings. And the personal life of Socrates was itself surrounded by carnivalistic legends (for example, his relationship with his wife Xanthippe).[47]

The point of the talmudic menippea is *not* to undermine the seriousness of the halakha, any more than, in the end, Plato undermines the drive to *epistēmē*. In good Menippean fashion, both the Talmud and Plato "pull the rug out from under the reader"[48] but not quite, not really. What distinguishes Plato and the Talmud from most of the rest of the Menippean tradition is the total absence of a desire to obliterate the seriousness of the serious part of the discourse. The rug is not really pulled out from under the reader, but the ground is nevertheless made to shake. Plato remains committed to philosophy and the Talmud to halakha. Lucian, for instance, is fairly characterized as attempting "to prove the absurdity of philosophers,"[49] something one would never say of Plato even at his most ludic. Interestingly, if we focus on the place of philosophy in the Talmud, one might indeed be able to say of it, as Relihan as of Lucian: "One should forget inspection of the heavens and contemplation of the beginnings and ends of things, reject the syllogisms of the contradictory philosophers, and consider all their works nonsense."[50] Of philosophers, perhaps, the Talmud would agree, but surely not with respect to the endless arguments of its own heroes, the Rabbis, about the proper halakha—hence the necessary angel in the picture. And even Lucian, as we have seen, is not single-voiced on this, as he reveals in his deeply contradictory moments of (apparently sincere) great admiration for philosophers. The tone, therefore, with respect to Socrates on the Platonic side or the Rabbis on the talmudic is not quite one of "incongruity," but certainly one that points to the gap between the ideal world and real life. That is to say, the Platonic and talmudic menippea allow us to see the difference between the possibilities of an ideal world with ideal behavior and ideal knowledge, projected in the serious, dialectical moments of both textual corpora, and the matter

47. Bakhtin, *Problems of Dostoevsky's Poetics*, 132.
48. Relihan, *Ancient Menippean Satire*, 116.
49. Relihan, *Ancient Menippean Satire*, 109.
50. Relihan, *Ancient Menippean Satire*, 110.

of which the real world is made. They thus allow us to look into the abyss that conditions even the most bright and confident of intellectual enterprises at bettering human life.[51]

Both Plato and the Talmud can thus be read dialogically if we look for dialogue in the right places, and that is most assuredly not in their represented dialogues. In both texts, there is a voicing of the most serious and important, the most truth-committed of the enterprises of a community of intellectuals, that which is *spoudaios* for the writers themselves: for Plato dialogue in search of the Truth; for the Rabbis of the Bavli dialectic in search of the correct praxis, and for both, even beyond the results of the search, an absolutely vital protreptic for a way of life and discourse, *philosophia*/Torah. But both of these dead-serious commitments are turned on their heads within the same texts via a grotesque, satirical narrative framework in which things are shown not to be what they seem; truth is contingent and bound up with the jealousies, envies, sexual desires, and passions of historical moments.

Plato teaches us to read the fat rabbis as, indeed, silenoi. Socrates really is, at this level, a satyr, and the rabbis are silenoi too. The Talmud helps us see how to read Plato dialogically. The fat rabbis are— the Rabbis. But in neither text is the voice of seriousness ever, not even for a moment, silenced by the silenoi. Deep, genuine dialogue emerges in the *spoudogeloion,* in the dialogue of every moment of the texts in which the serious voice of Truth (mutatis mutandis) is in contention, in which, as Bakhtin puts it:

> an intense interaction and struggle between one's own and another's
> word is being waged, a process in which they oppose or dialogically
> interanimate each other. The utterance so conceived is a considerably
> more complex and dynamic organism than it appears when construed

---

51. This matches, I think, the conclusion of David Kraemer, who also finds that it is "the Bavli which, characteristically, gives voice to the fullest range of explanations and responses, and allows for even the most radical expression of questioning or doubt." David Kraemer, *Responses to Suffering in Classical Rabbinic Literature* (New York: Oxford University Press, 1994), 213, compares it, thus, to the biblical books of Job and Kohellet (207). Cf. too Galit Hasan-Rokem, "To Be or Not to Be: Job in Aggadic Literature?" in *Mehqerei Talmud: Memorial Volume for Ephraim E. Urbach,* ed. Ya'akov Sussman and David Rosenthal (Jerusalem: Magnes Press, 2005), 385–402 (in Hebrew), who sees in Job itself (or at any rate its rabbinic readings) Menippean satire.

simply as a thing that articulates the intention of the person uttering it, which is to see the utterance as a direct, single-voiced vehicle of expression.[52]

Dialogue is thus revealed as the ability to keep in mind and in text the struggle between my word and the other's antithetical word inside my own thought, speech, and discourse.

In the *spoudogeloion,* the serious is not canceled out by the comic, nor the comic by the serious; neither are they in a dialectical relation with each other, but together they produce a dialogical text. Plato as the author of the dialectic certainly means what he says and seems dead serious in his call to the only good and worthwhile life, the life of philosophy, but he is the "author" as well of the comic, sometimes grotesque, narratives in which the serious dialectics are embedded. The overall semantic effect is, I would suggest, analogous to Bakhtin's description of the carnivalized hero:

> Carnivalistic legends in general are profoundly different from tradi-tional heroicizing epic legends: carnivalistic legends debase the hero and bring him down to earth, they make him familiar, bring him close, humanize him; ambivalent carnival laughter burns away all that is stilted and stiff, but in no way destroys the heroic core of the image.[53]

Socrates, and thus the philosophical life, remains the hero of the Platonic corpus, the heroic core of the image. Even amid the ambiva-lence, the primary accent is still unambiguously antisophistic, but a second accent nevertheless is allowed/allows itself to be heard. This language, of course, raises its own theoretical and philosophical prob-lems, problems having to do with the hoary issues of intention and meaning and their location in an author, a text, a reader, a reading practice. Plato's corpus lies not only at the foundation of the prac-tices of Truth that we call philosophy but also powerfully fertilizes the tradition that we will come to know of as Menippean satire. To recite Bakhtin once more:

52. Bakhtin, *Dialogic Imagination,* 348.
53. Bakhtin, *Problems of Dostoevsky's Poetics,* 132–33.

The authentic spirit of the novel as a developing genre is present in them [the seriocomic genres] to an incomparably greater degree than in the so-called Greek novels . . . the serio-comical genres . . . anticipate the more essential historical aspects in the development of the novel in modern times, even though they lack that sturdy skeleton of plot and composition that we have grown accustomed to demand from the novel as a genre. . . . These serio-comical genres (especially the Socratic dialogues, and Menippean satire [including the *Satyricon* of Petronius]) were the first authentic and essential step in the evolution of the novel as the genre of becoming.[54]

My reading throughout this book suggests one important modification of Bakhtin's claim. For me, it is not ultimately the Socratic dialogue (about which we, after all, know almost nothing) that marks the beginnings of the seriocomical genres, but rather Plato in his double-voiced presentation of his hero, Socrates, in which a complicated kind of dialogue (answering to other Bakhtinian descriptions) between the author and his own hero ensues, such that the hero's voice challenges the voice of the author even while that one is both lifting up and objectifying, challenging, the voice of his creature, *philosophia,* as well. It is in this manner that the Platonic dialogue can be read into the prehistory of the novel, not in the monological pseudodialogues between Socrates and his fall guys.[55] The Talmud, a thousand years later, constitutes, I suggest, a peculiar Jewish working-out of this possibility for a dialogical text, the text of a dialogue between one's deep commitment to a given practice and one's own self-reflexive critique of it at one and the very same moment, between the dominant voice of authoritative discourse, the Torah, and the ongoing developing inner convictions of a given community, the *stamma.* As in Plato, the dialogue is ultimately a dialogue of the self with the self, of the asserting self with the self that doubts itself, and thus one in which, always "the unity of the polyphonic text has yet to be discovered."

54. Mikhail Bakhtin, "Epic and Novel," in *The Dialogic Imagination: Four Essays by Mikhail Bakhtin,* ed. Michael Holquist, trans. Michael Holquist and Caryl Emerson, University of Texas Press Slavic Series (Austin: University of Texas Press, 1981), 22.

55. John Beversluis, *Cross-Examining Socrates: A Defense of the Interlocutors in Plato's Early Dialogues* (Cambridge: Cambridge University Press, 2000).

On the Postmodern Allegorical

L et me briefly encounter another reading here, one that is
almost directly antithetical to my own, bringing the *Protagoras* back on stage for an encore before my curtain closes.
Francisco Gonzalez begins his "retracing" of the *Protagoras*
with a declaration of intent with which I am in deep intellectual, methodological sympathy. Following Socrates' dictum in
the *Phaedrus* about *logoi* and bodies having extremities suitable
to their middles and the reverse, Gonzalez begins by insisting
that reading a dialogue must involve reading all of its parts and
not "amputat[ing] one limb or another (for example, the arguments for the unity of virtue or the account of the 'science of
measurement') and examin[ing] it in isolation, while ignoring
that 'middle' from which these extremities derive their life and
meaning."[1] Moreover, he identifies the same piece of the *Protagoras* I have made central, namely the controversy over dialectic
v. rhetoric, as precisely this middle that should not be mutilated
(like Alcibiades' herms). So far we are in complete consonance.

---

1. Francisco J. Gonzalez, "Giving Thought to the Good Together: Virtue in
Plato's *Protagoras,*" in *Retracing the Platonic Text,* ed. John Russon and John Sallis
(Evanston, Ill.: Northwestern University Press, 2000), 113.

I shan't rehearse his reading of the text here—suffice it to say that he does it well and skillfully—but I want to point to certain aspects of his strategies of reading that are different from the strategies that I have adopted and which produce real intellectual (and even ethical) discomfort for me. For Gonzalez (as for Patrick Coby), Plato/Socrates can do no wrong and Protagoras can't get anything right. Socrates is all-sincere in his insincerity, while Protagoras must be read as insincere even when appearing sincere.

We are introduced to this style of reading from the very beginning. Socrates' first exchange with Protagoras involves a discussion of whether or not they should conduct their conversation in public or in private. Protagoras remarks on Socrates' thoughtfulness in this matter, alluding to the danger of being a Sophist, a foreigner come into Athens, trying to persuade the beautiful/good ones to abandon their customary webs of association and adhere to him. On this Gonzalez comments without the slightest trace of irony, "Here we get a clear indication of the deep antagonism that exists between Protagoras and the people."[2] The contradiction ought to have stared us in the face, considering Socrates' own relationship to those families and their sons and his ultimate fate. Socrates was surely killed by the Athenians; Protagoras's somewhat similar fate is the product of a dodgy legend. Socrates' insistence on openly doing what he does and ultimately suffering the consequences is lauded on all sides, while Protagoras's insistence that honesty is the best protection and that he will claim the name Sophist in public is put down (first of all by Socrates) to a mere desire to be a crowd pleaser. We have seen how deeply meaningful this little limb (a finger perhaps of the *logos?*) might be, since on the question of dispute in public or in private hangs the very question of persuasion in a democratic speech situation versus the compulsion (Ἀνάγκη) in a private situation where Socrates can work his Marsyas-like magic. (Compare the famous incipit to the Melian Dialogue in Thucydides 5.85.) My point is not—precisely not—to indict Plato's bad faith (although it might have been that at an earlier stage in my thinking, and some indigested bits of that menu might still persist in this book), but to take exception to a style of reading in which the

2. Gonzalez, "Giving Thought," 116.

same sorts of activities, descriptions, modes of speech are evaluated in precisely opposite fashion depending on whether they are mobilized by the philosopher or the Sophist; indeed to quibble at the very acceptance of this as a firm binary opposition *even in Plato's writing,* let alone in the world.

I will adduce one more example. I shall need to quote Gonzalez at some length here (acting more generously to him than Socrates does to Protagoras). We are at the point in the dialogue which I too have identified as being its central moment and crisis, the moment in which the decision of length of speech needs to be made. Socrates insists on short, quick dialectic, while Protagoras would like to be able to develop his ideas in longer, less antagonistic fashion. As we have seen above, Socrates threatens then to take his football and go home. Of course, I am being tendentious in my presentation, but listen to how Gonzalez epitomizes this:

> We thus arrive at the central crisis of the dialogue. Socrates, claiming to be forgetful and therefore unable to follow long speeches, insists on short answers. Protagoras protests that his answers should not be shorter than necessary (*ē dei*). Socrates, of course, agrees. It immediately becomes apparent, however, that Protagoras is not assuming here *an objective standard of appropriate length,* since he proceeds to ask: "Should I answer at the length that seems necessary *to you* or at the length that seems necessary *to me?*" (334e2–3; my translation). This question does not allow that one of them might be right and the other wrong: What *seems* necessary to each *is* necessary for him. We have here an application of the relativism expressed in Protagoras's speech on the good: What is good for Socrates is simply not the same as what is good for Protagoras. But given two different views concerning what is appropriate or necessary (*to deon*) in a discussion and no objective standard by which to evaluate these views, how do we decide between them? What Protagoras proceeds to say (335a) shows that he sees in the discussion nothing but a "contest of words" and that his strategy for winning such contests is *not* to converse (*dialegesthai*) in the way *his opponent* considers necessary or appropriate. But as Socrates indicates in both word (335a) and deed (he gets up to leave the discussion), Protagoras's view is nothing less than a *refusal*

to *dialegesthai,* since dialogue depends on a genuine "being together" (*sounoisa*).³

The only possible way to produce this reading is to know a priori that Socrates is right and that anything that opposes him is simply venal in one way or another. Socrates will set the rules for their discourse because there is "an objective standard by which to evaluate these views," the only criterion that anyone would ever need in fact: Socrates is right! Socrates' refusal to conduct a discussion on the terms that are appropriate to Protagoras is heroic; indeed it is the very precondition for genuine dialogue, while Protagoras's extreme reluctance to engage in eristics with Socrates is a marker, *mirabile dictu,* of his refusal of dialogue. Socrates gets up and leaves the room when his conditions are not met, and this demonstrates Protagoras's refusal to engage in dialogue. It is not Socrates who has defeated you, old man: it is the Truth!

On the one hand, Gonzalez's reading and the community of Platonic readings to which it joins are a methodological advance over philosophical readings that simply ignore the dramatic framing, but on the other hand, in terms of the results, Gonzalez's reading is hardly more critical than that of traditional philosophical interpreters (to be fair, critique is not at all the project of the contributors to the interpretative undertaking embodied in the Russon and Sallis collection).⁴ Whatever possible dialogism we might find in Plato is relentlessly to be stamped out. Plato's portrayal of Protagoras is simply taken at face value; the Sophist is a self-seeking charlatan and nothing more, and even Plato's own hints at a self-critical voice within the text are trampled on. On the one hand, Plato invites such a hammering reading of Protagoras, but, on the other hand, he also gives us the tools to query it. Is there indeed such an absolute moral gap—or even epistemological gap—between Socrates and the other Sophists? For me, of course, the middle of that body (of Socrates and his *logos*) is the fat and riven body of a Silenus, not the buff marble classical statue of an Apollo. My move is to take seriously the notion that all of the critique—if

---

3. Gonzalez, "Giving Thought," 122–23.
4. John Russon and John Sallis, eds., *Retracing the Platonic Text* (Evanston, Ill.: Northwestern University Press, 2000).

my critique is at all telling—that I have been able to mobilize against Socrates' use of discourse grows out of information given me by Plato himself about Socrates—surely not the historical Socrates, but Plato's own, which makes the thesis so much more interesting—and this character's modes of discourse and argumentation. I go back and reread the *Protagoras* again, not changing the interpretation or evaluation, but in full cognizance that Plato himself, knowingly and not naively or misleadingly, allowed me to see the ambivalence of Socratic practice. Or better put, Plato lets me see his own inner dialogue on the binary opposition of philosophy and rhetoric. The Socrates of Alcibiades is also Socrates, and that Socrates unlocks much that is otherwise inexplicable in Plato's portrayal of the serious Socrates in other dialogues. The literary figure in which such a double movement of assertion and withdrawal, withdrawal and assertion, can take place is the dialogue between the serious and the comic (the tragic and the comedic), the tragedy and the satyr play. Such Menippean juxtapositions occur throughout the corpus, in its extremities and its middles. It is in this fashion—only?—that we can find the third way between an epistemic seriousness that imposes a single vision of the truth and a single method for attaining it, on the one hand, and an anarchic relativism, in which nothing is ever seriously advanced (a parody version of Protagoras) on the other. Plato, I think, is firmly identified himself with the voice of Socrates (philosophy over rhetoric, *epistēmē* over *doxa*), but finds a way to let us listen to Protagoras as well. Monological philosophical readings of Plato (even those carried out in a continental mood), block that listening once again.

There can be no doubt, I think, that Plato's project throughout was the assertion of the sole value of a new way of teaching, learning, conducting an intellectual life, one that was directly antithetical to the Sophists. In order to pursue this aim—which is the one constant, I think, throughout the corpus—Plato relentlessly discredits the Sophists and shows them up as either fools or charlatans. Sallis's gloss on Plato, as we have seen, recapitulates Plato's ideological stance perfectly: "Philosophy is never a matter of someone's opinions; it is rather that decisive transcending of opinion through which man is subordinated to a higher measure in such a way that, thereby, it is established that man is not the measure of what is." Insofar as Protagoras is merely parodied and satirized in the dialogues, these dialogues are anything but dialogical. But Protagoras, I have argued elsewhere, is anything but a fool or a charlatan. He is a serious thinker, one whose very logion "The human is the measure" raises a serious challenge to the Platonic regime of the Truth. Plato, of course, knows this and shows that he knows this in the *Protagoras*. Fully committed as he is to his epistemological project in which, as Richard McKeon has put it, "[Dialectic] is, finally, the only science that does away with hypotheses, in order to establish principles in eternal forms and transcendental ideas,"[5] he nevertheless allows the second accent, the "crude contradiction" to take place through the medium of a new form, the seriocomic, figured by that antithetical figure, Socrates. The Babylonian Talmud, I suggest, is a distant inheritor of this figuration of dialogicity through the seriocomic contradiction of different elements within its own text.

5. Richard McKeon, "Greek Dialectics: Dialectic and Dialogue, Dialectic and Rhetoric," in *Dialectics,* ed. Chaïm Perelman (The Hague: Nijhoff, 1975), 4.

Alan Thomas has been a supportive and stimulating presence in the years in which this book has taken shape and then transformed itself into something quite different from what it started out to be. I have been lucky in my editors, and Alan more than met the expectations set up by the ones I've worked with before this.

I wish to thank the following generous and critical readers of even more primitive versions of this argument in part or in whole: Carlin Barton, Chava Boyarin, Jonathan Boyarin, Yishai Boyarin, Shamma Boyarin, Virginia Burrus, Judith Butler, Helen Choi, Jas' Elsner, G. R. F. Ferrari, Saul Meir Friedman, Ya'ir Fürstenberg, Simon Goldhill, Erich Gruen, Galit Hasan-Rokem, David Johnson S.J., Chana Kronfeld, Derek Krueger, Melissa Lane, Anthony A. Long, Thomas H. Luxon, Francoise Meltzer, Ramona Naddaff, Andrea Wilson Nightingale, Robin Osborne, Jonathan D. Pratt, Ishay Rosen-Zvi, Edward Schiappa, Zvi Septimus, Dina Stein, Samuel Thrope, Joel Yurdin, and Barry Wimpfheimer. I have incorporated their sagacity where I could and when I have ignored it, it is at my own risk. Andrea Nightingale, in particular, read the manuscript at a particularly crucial moment in its development, and her encouragement as well as critique at that time made its continued maturation possible. Carlin Barton weighed in toward the end of the rewriting with invaluable insights into structure and style—and this after having talked through most of the argument of the book over several years. I would like to thank also my research assistant, Ruth Haber, who on many occasions, upon being requested to find or photocopy a source, read it and taught me things about it that I hadn't seen. Ishay Rosen-Tzvi gave the whole manuscript a thorough reading at a crucial time in its development, when it was crystalized enough to be wrongheaded but not so set in stone as to be incorrigible. Major arguments were revised in the light of his Resh Lakishian intervention, to which I did not respond as Rabbi Yoḥanan. Much that is right about the second half of the book is owing to this *tokhekha* intervention and nothing that is wrong. That is all too mine. Ditto Simon Goldhill for the Platonic matters.

A debt that should be paid is to Nota Bene, writer's tool extraordinaire, on which all of my books, excepting only my very first, have been written. I suspect that that first would have remained an only child had not this software arrived into my world sometime in 1984. It's been an exhilarating twenty-five years now with Nota Bene and its creator, Steven Siebert. Whether the world should be grateful to him or dismayed at his collaboration—more than just technical—in my literary production, I leave to others to judge. Finally, the work of two fabulous research assistant editors, Ruth Haber and Amy Jamgochian, should be made known. Graduate students in Rhetoric 200 in the years 2004, 2007, and 2008 were enormously generous with their responses to early versions of some of the ideas and texts incorporated into this book, as were my graduate students in Talmud over the last five years.

Generous internal grants from the University of California at Berkeley and a major grant from the Ford Foundation materially enabled the production of this book. I wish to thank the latter institution in particular for providing a warm, engaged, intellectual environment within which to develop some of the ideas here, and especially Constance Buchanan, intellectual cicerone, much more than a program officer. In particular, amidst its other forms of largesse to scholars and encouragement of their scholarship, the Bridging Grant program of UC Berkeley was vital for me, allowing me to reduce my teaching duties by half for one year, a year which I devoted to the study of Plato in Greek, partly under the tutelage of no less than A. A. Long, who bears no negative responsibility for the contents of this book but might have to take the rap for having seriously helped and encouraged me to get the tools (both linguistic and philosophical, as it were) to commit the crime. He is to be deemed, thus, an accessory before, but not after, the fact. I would like to warmly thank the following institutions that offered me (very different, but equally marvelous) hospitality during my sabbatical year, in which the book was largely brought to term, the Gregorian University in Rome, and in Cambridge, the Center for Research in Arts, Social Sciences, and Humanities, as well as King's College, where, as a visiting fellow, I was made to feel both perfectly welcome and supported in every way imaginable. The fellowship of such colleagues as Simon Goldhill, the late Peter Lipton—may his memory be for a blessing—and the young fellow denizens of the wine room of an evening provided precisely the kind of community of intellectuals for which I long and which I find so productive for my work. Peter de Bollas's tutorials on claret and the wonders of the northern Rhone were cheering and instructive as well. A series of King's College seminars (organized by Iain Fenlon, whom I warmly thank) on this work in progress were immeasurably bracing and cheering. As ever, I am deeply in debt to the founders and donors of the Taubman Chair of Talmudic Culture at Berkeley (incorporating the Maurice Amado fund), which has so generously enabled my scholarship by now for nearly twenty years.

A shorter version of chapter 6 has been published in *Critical Inquiry,* and I am grateful for permission to republish here.

תם ונשלם שבת לאל בודא עולם Thanksgiving Day, 2008, Berkeley

Http://ohr.edu/yhiy/article.php/984.

Adler, Rachel. "The Virgin in the Brothel and Other Anomalies: Character and Context in the Legend of Beruriah." *Tikkun* 3, no. 6 (1988).

Alexander, Elizabeth Shanks. *Transmitting Mishnah: The Shaping Influence of Oral Tradition.* Cambridge: Cambridge University Press, 2006.

Alexiou, A. S. "Philosophers in Lucian." Ph.D. diss., Fordham University, 1990. Microfilm.

Allen, Reginald E. "Comment, Menexenus." In *Euthyphro, Apology, Crito, Meno, Gorgias, Menexenus,* translated by Reginald E. Allen. The Dialogues of Plato, 319–27. New Haven: Yale University Press, 1984.

Anderson, Graham. *Lucian: Theme and Variation in the Second Sophistic.* Mnemosyne, Bibliotheca Classica Batava: Supplementum. Lugduni Batavorum: Brill, 1976.

———. *Sage, Saint, and Sophist Holy Men and Their Associates in the Early Roman Empire.* London: Routledge, 1994.

Arrowsmith, William. Introduction. In *The Satyricon by Petronius Arbiter,* translated by William Arrowsmith. New York: New American Library, 1983.

———. "Introduction to 'The Clouds' by Aristophanes." Trans. and introduction by William Arrowsmith. In *Four Plays by Aristophanes,* 13–166. New York: Meridian, 1994.

Azar, Moshe. "Rev. of N. A. Van Uchelen, *Chagigah: The Linguistic Encoding of Halakhah.*" *Jewish Quarterly Review* 87, no. 1/2 (July–October 1996): 162–66.

Bacon, Helen. "Socrates Crowned." *Virginia Quarterly Review* 35 (1959): 415–30.

Badiou, Alain. "The (Re)Turn of Philosophy *Itself.*" In *Manifesto for Philosophy Followed by Two Essays: "The (Re)Turn of Philosophy Itself" and "Definition of Philosophy,"* edited and translated by Norman Madarasz, 113–38. Albany: State University of New York Press, 1999.

———. *Saint Paul: The Foundation of Universalism.* Translated by Ray Brassier. Cultural Memory in the Present. Stanford, Calif.: Stanford University Press, 2003.

Bakhtin, Mikhail. *The Dialogic Imagination: Four Essays.* Edited by Michael Holquist; translated by Michael Holquist and Caryl Emerson. University of Texas Press Slavic Series. Austin: University of Texas Press, 1981.

———. *Problems of Dostoevsky's Poetics.* Edited and translated by Caryl Emerson. Theory and History of Literature. Minneapolis: University of Minnesota Press, 1984.

———. *Rabelais and His World.* Translated by Hélène Iswolsky. Bloomington: Indiana University Press, 1984.

Baldick, Chris. *The Concise Oxford Dictionary of Literary Terms.* Oxford Paperback Reference. Oxford: Oxford University Press, 2004.

Barrett, Harold. *The Sophists: Rhetoric, Democracy, and Plato's Idea of Sophistry.* Novato, Calif.: Chandler & Sharp, 1987.

Barris, Jeremy. *The Crane's Walk.* New York: Fordham University Press, forthcoming.

Barthes, Roland. "The Death of the Author." In *The Death and Resurrection of the Author?* Edited by William Irwin. Contributions in Philosophy 83:3–7. Westport, Conn.: Greenwood Press, 2002.

Becker, Adam H. *The Fear of God and the Beginning of Wisdom: The School of Nisibis and Christian Scholastic Culture in Late Antique Mesopotamia.* Divinations. Philadelphia: University of Pennsylvania Press, 2006.

Belfiore, Elizabeth. "'Elenchus, Epode,' and Magic: Socrates as Silenus." *Phoenix* 34, no. 2 (Summer 1980): 128–37.

Benardete, Seth. *Plato's "Laws": The Discovery of Being.* Chicago: University of Chicago Press, 2000.

Berger, Harry. "Facing Sophists: Socrates' Charismatic Bondage in *Protagoras.*" In *Situated Utterances: Texts, Bodies, and Cultural Representations,* 381–414. New York: Fordham University Press, 2005.

Bergren, Ann. "Language and the Female in Early Greek Thought." *Arethusa* 16 (1983): 69–95.

Bernays, Jakob. *Lucian und die Kyniker. Von Jacob Bernays. Mit einer Übersetzung der Schrift Lucians über das Lebensende des Peregrinus.* Berlin: W. Hertz, 1879.

Beversluis, John. *Cross-Examining Socrates: A Defense of the Interlocutors in Plato's Early Dialogues.* Cambridge: Cambridge University Press, 2000.

Bialik, Hayyim Nahman. *Ha-Halakhah Veha-Agadah.* Jerusalem: Ma'aritse-ha-halakhah, 1917.

Bickerman, E. J. *The Jews in the Greek Age.* Cambridge, Mass.: Harvard University Press, 1988.

Biesecker, Susan. "Feminist Criticism of Classical Rhetorical Texts: A Case Study of Gorgias' *Helen.*" In *Realms of Rhetoric: Phonic, Graphic, Electronic,* edited by Victor J. Vitanza and Michele Ballif, 67–82. Arlington, Tex.: Rhetoric Society of America, 1990.

Bloom, Allan David. "The Ladder of Love." In *Plato's Symposium,* by Plato, translated by Seth Benardete, 55–177. Chicago: University of Chicago Press, 2001.

Booth, Wayne C. *The Rhetoric of Fiction.* Chicago: University of Chicago Press, 1983.

Bowen, Anthony, ed. and trans. *Symposium,* by Xenophon. Warminster, England: Aris & Phillips, 1998.

Bowersock, G. W. *Hellenism in Late Antiquity.* Jerome Lectures 18. Ann Arbor: University of Michigan Press, 1990.

Boyarin, Daniel. *Border Lines: The Partition of Judaeo-Christianity.* Divinations: Re-reading Late Ancient Religions. Philadelphia: University of Pennsylvania Press, 2004.

———. *Carnal Israel: Reading Sex in Talmudic Culture.* The New Historicism: Studies in Cultural Poetics 25. Berkeley: University of California Press, 1993.

———. "The Great Fat Massacre: Sex, Death and the Grotesque Body in the Talmud." In *People of the Body: Jews and Judaism from an Embodied Perspective,* edited by Howard Eilberg-Schwartz, 69–102. Albany: SUNY Press, 1992.

———. "Hellenism in Rabbinic Babylonia." In *The Cambridge Companion to Rabbinic Literature,* edited by Charlotte Fonrobert and Martin Jaffee, 336–63. Cambridge: Cambridge University Press, 2007.

———. "Literary Fat Rabbis Re(Ci)Divivus: The Syriac Connection and the Ends of Dialogue in Jewish Babylonia." In *The End of Ancient Dialogue,* edited by Simon Goldhill, 217–41. Cambridge: Cambridge University Press, 2007.

———. "Virgins in Brothels: Gender and Religious Ecotypification." *Estudios de literatura oral* 5 (1999): 195–217.

Branham, R. Bracht. "The Comic as Critic: Revenging Epicurus—A Study of Lucian's Comic Narrative." *Classical Antiquity* 3, no. 2 (1984).

———. *Unruly Eloquence: Lucian and the Comedy of Traditions.* Revealing Antiquity. Cambridge, Mass.: Harvard University Press, 1989.

Branham, R. Bracht, and Marie-Odile Goulet-Cazé, eds. *The Cynics: The Cynic Movement in Antiquity and Its Legacy.* Hellenistic Culture and Society 23. Berkeley: University of California Press, 1997.

Branham, Robert Bracht, ed. *Bakhtin and the Classics.* Rethinking Theory. Evanston, Ill.: Northwestern University Press, 2002.

———, ed. *The Bakhtin Circle and Ancient Narrative.* Ancient Narrative. Groningen: Barkhuis Groningen University Library, 2005.

Brooks, David. "Harvard-Bound? Chin Up." Editorial. *New York Times,* 2 March 2006.

Burrus, Virginia. "The Heretical Woman as Symbol in Alexander, Athanasius, Epiphanius, and Jerome." *Harvard Theological Review* 84 (1991): 229–48.

———. "Mimicking Virgins: Colonial Ambivalence and the Ancient Romance." *Arethusa* 38 (2005): 49–88.

———. "Reading Agnes: The Rhetoric of Gender in Ambrose and Prudentius." *Journal of Early Christian Studies* 3, no. 1 (Spring 1995): 25–46.

———. *Saving Shame: Martyrs, Saints, and Other Abject Subjects.* Philadelphia: University of Pennsylvania Press, 2007.

———. *The Sex Lives of Saints: An Erotics of Ancient Hagiography.* Divinations: Reading Late Ancient Religions. Philadelphia: University of Pennsylvania Press, 2003.

Bury, Robert Gregg. *The Symposium of Plato.* Cambridge: W. Heffer and Sons, 1932.

Bywater, I. "Bernays' Lucian and the Cynics." *Journal of Hellenic Studies* 1 (1880): 301–4.

Chance, Thomas H. *Plato's Euthydemus: Analysis of What Is and Is Not Philosophy.* Berkeley: University of California Press, 1992.

Chew, Kathryn. "Achilles Tatius and Parody." *Classical Journal* 96, no. 1 (2000): 57–70.

Clay, Diskin. "The Tragic and Comic Poet of the *Symposium.*" *Arion* 2 (1975): 238–61.

Coby, Patrick. *Socrates and the Sophistic Enlightenment: A Commentary on Plato's Protagoras.* Lewisburg: Bucknell University Press, 1987.

Cohen, David. *Law, Sexuality, and Society: The Enforcement of Morals in Classical Athens.* Cambridge: Cambridge University Press, 1991.

Cohen, Jonathan. "Philosophy Is Education Is Politics: A Somewhat Aggressive Reading of *Protagoras* 334d–338e." Conference presentation: Twentieth World Congress of Philosophy, in Boston, Mass., 1998. Http://www.bu.edu/wcp/Papers/Anci/AnciCohe.htm.

Cohen, Shaye J. D. "Patriarchs and Scholarchs." *Proceedings of the American Academy of Jewish Research* 48 (1981): 57–83.

Colie, Rosalie L. *Paradoxia Epidemica: The Renaissance Tradition of Paradox.* Princeton: Princeton University Press, 1966.

Connor, W. Robert. *The New Politicians of Fifth-Century Athens.* Princeton, N.J.: Princeton University Press, 1971.

Consigny, Scott Porter. *Gorgias: Sophist and Artist.* Studies in Rhetoric/Communication. Columbia: University of South Carolina Press, 2001.

Conte, Gian Biagio. *The Hidden Author: An Interpretation of Petronius' Satyricon.* Sather Classical Lectures. Berkeley: University of California Press, 1996.

Cooper, Kate. "Insinuations of Womanly Influence: An Aspect of the Christianization of the Roman Aristocracy." *Journal of Roman Studies* 82 (1992): 150–64.

Cope, Edward M. *The Rhetoric of Aristotle with a Commentary.* Cambridge: Cambridge University Press, 1877.

Corrigan, Kevin, and Elena Glazov-Corrigan. *Plato's Dialectic at Play: Argument, Structure, and Myth in the* Symposium. University Park: Pennsylvania State University Press, 2004.

———. "Plato's *Symposium* and Bakhtin's Theory of the Dialogical Character of Novelistic Discourse." In *The Bakhtin Circle and Ancient Narrative,* vol. 3, edited by Robert Bracht Branham. Ancient Narrative, 32–50. Groningen: Barkhuis Groningen University Library, 2005.

Coulter, James A. "*Phaedrus* 279a: The Praise of Isocrates." *GRBS* 8 (1967): 225–36.

Cover, Robert. "The Supreme Court 1982 Term: Foreword; Nomos and Narrative." *Harvard Law Journal* 97 (1983): 4–68.

Crockett, Andy. "Gorgias's Encomium of Helen: Violent Rhetoric or Radical Feminism?" *Rhetoric Review* 13, no. 1 (Autumn 1994): 71–90.

Davidson, James. *The Greeks and Greek Love: A Radical Reappraisal of Homosexuality in Ancient Greece.* New York: Random House Pub. Group, 2009.

Davis, Laurie. "Virgins in Brothels: A Different Feminist Reading of Beruriah." Paper presented at Graduate Theological Union. Berkeley, 1994.

Dégh, Linda, and Andrew Vázsonyi. "Legend and Belief." In *Folklore Genres,* edited by Dan Ben-Amos. Publications of the American Folklore Society 26. Austin: University of Texas Press, 1976.

Demetrius. *Demetrius on Style: The Greek Text of Demetrius, De Elocutione.* Edited by W. Rhys Roberts. Hildesheim: G. Olms, 1969.

Derrida, Jacques. *Dissemination.* Translated by Barbara Johnson. Chicago: University of Chicago Press, 1981.

de Ste. Croix, G. E. M. *The Origins of the Peloponnesian War.* Ithaca: Cornell University Press, 1972.

Diels, Hermann, and Walther Kranz. *Die Fragmente der Vorsokratiker, Griechisch und Deutsch.* Zürich: Weidmann, 1966.

Diels, Hermann, and Rosamond Kent Sprague. *The Older Sophists.* Edited by Rosamond Kent Sprague. Columbia: University of South Carolina Press, 1972.

Dodds, E. R., ed. *Gorgias: A Revised Text* by Plato. 1959. Reprinted Oxford: Oxford University Press, 2002.

Dolgopolsky, Sergei. *What Is Talmud? The Art of Disagreement*. Bronx, New York: Fordham University Press, 2008.

Dover, Kenneth James. *Greek Homosexuality*. Cambridge, Mass.: Harvard University Press, 1989.

———, ed. *Symposium by Plato*. Cambridge: Cambridge University Press, 1980.

Dzialo, Michael G. "Legal and Philosophical Fictions: At the Line Where the Two Become One." *Argumentation* 12 (1998): 217–32.

Elman, Yaakov. "Acculturation to Elite Persian Norms." In *Neti˓ot Ledavid: Jubilee Volume for David Weiss Halivni*, edited by Yaakov Elman, Ephraim Bezalel Halivni, and Zvi Arie Steinfeld, 31–56. Jerusalem: Orhot Press, 2004.

———. "Middle Persian Culture and Babylonian Sages: Accommodation and Resistance in the Shaping of Rabbinic Legal Traditions." In *Cambridge Companion to Rabbinic Literature*, edited by Charlotte Fonrobert and Martin Jaffee. Cambridge: Cambridge University Press, 2006.

Enos, Richard Leo. *Greek Rhetoric before Aristotle*. Prospect Heights, Ill.: Waveland Press, 1993.

Farrar, Cynthia. *The Origins of Democratic Thinking: The Invention of Politics in Classical Athens*. Cambridge: Cambridge University Press, 1987.

Fendt, Gene, and David Rozema. *Platonic Errors: Plato, a Kind of Poet*. Westport, Conn.: Greenwood Press, 1998.

Ferrari, G. R. F. "Akrasia as Neurosis in Plato's *Protagoras*." *Proceedings of the Boston Area Colloquium in Ancient Philosophy* 6 (1990): 115–39.

———. "Platonic Love." In *The Cambridge Companion to Plato*, edited by Richard Kraut, 248–76. Cambridge: Cambridge University Press, 1992.

Ferrari, G. R. F., ed., and Tom Griffith, trans. *The Republic* by Plato. Cambridge Texts in the History of Political Thought. Cambridge: Cambridge University Press, 2000.

Finley, John H. *Three Essays on Thucydides*. Cambridge, Mass.: Harvard University Press, 1967.

———. *Thucydides*. Cambridge, Mass.: Harvard University Press, 1942.

Fonrobert, Charlotte. "When the Rabbi Weeps: On Reading Gender in Talmudic Aggada." *Nashim: A Journal of Jewish Women's Studies and Gender Issues* 4 (2001): 56–83.

Ford, Andrew. "The Beginnings of Dialogue: Socratic Discourses and Fourth-Century Prose." In *The End of Ancient Dialogue*, edited by Simon Goldhill, 29–44. Cambridge: Cambridge University Press, 2008.

Foucault, Michel. *The Use of Pleasure*. Vol. 2 of *The History of Sexuality*. Translated by Robert Hurley. 1984. Reprinted New York: Random House, Vintage, 1986.

———. "What Is an Author?" In *The Death and Resurrection of the Author?* Edited by William Irwin. Contributions in Philosophy 83:9–22. Westport, Conn.: Greenwood Press, 2002.

Fränkel, Yonah. *Readings in the Spiritual World of the Stories of the Aggada*. Tel Aviv: United Kibbutz Press, 1981. In Hebrew.

Friedman, Shamma Yehuda. "A Critical Study of Yevamot X with a Methodological Introduction." In *Texts and Studies: Analecta Judaica I*, edited by H. Z. Dimitrovsky, 227–441. New York: Jewish Theological Seminary Press, 1977. In Hebrew.

———. "The Further Adventures of Rav Kahana: Between Babylonia and Palestine." In *The Talmud Yerushalmi and Graeco-Roman Culture III*, edited by Peter Schaeffer, 247–71. Tübingen: Mohr/Siebeck, 2002.

———. *Talmud Arukh Perek Ha-Sokher et Ha-Umanin: Bavli Bava Metsi'a Perek Shishi: Mahadurah al Derekh Ha-Mehkar Im Perush Ha-Sugyot.* Jerusalem: Bet ha-midrash le-rabanim ba-Amerikah, 1990.

———. "Towards the Historical Aggada in the Babylonian Talmud." In *The Saul Lieberman Memorial Volume,* edited by Shamma Friedman, 119–64. New York: Jewish Theological Seminary, 1993. In Hebrew.

Frye, Northrop. *Anatomy of Criticism: Four Essays.* Princeton: Princeton University Press, 1957.

Gafni, Isaiah M. "The Babylonian Yeshiva as Reflected in Bava Qamma 111a." *Tarbiz* 49 (1980): 292–301. In Hebrew; English summary pp. v–vi.

———. "Nestorian Literature as a Source for the History of the Babylonian *Yeshivot.*" *Tarbiz* 51 (1981–82): 567–76. In Hebrew.

Gagarin, Michael. "Socrates' 'Hybris' and Alcibiades' Failure." *Phoenix* 31, no. 1 (Spring 1977): 22–37.

Gagarin, Michael, and Paul Woodruff. *Early Greek Political Thought from Homer to the Sophists.* Edited and translated by Michael Gagarin. Cambridge Texts in the History of Political Thought. Cambridge: Cambridge University Press, 1995.

Gallop, David. *Parmenides of Elea: Fragments, a Text, and Translation with an Introduction. Phoenix: Journal of the Classical Association of Canada.* Suppl. vol. 1. Toronto: University of Toronto Press, 1984.

Gellius, Aulus. *The Attic Nights of Aulus Gellius.* Translated by John Carew Rolfe. Loeb Classical Library. Cambridge, Mass.: Harvard University Press, 1967.

Giangrande, Lawrence. *The Use of Spoudaiogeloion in Greek and Roman Literature.* The Hague: Mouton, 1972.

Given, Mark Douglas. *Paul's True Rhetoric: Ambiguity, Cunning, and Deception in Greece and Rome.* Emory Studies in Early Christianity. Harrisburg, Pa: Trinity Press International, 2001.

Gold, Barbara K. "A Question of Genre: Plato's *Symposium* as Novel." In "Comparative Literature," special issue, *MLN* 95, no. 5, (December 1980): 1353–59.

Goldenberg, Robert. *The Sabbath-Law of Rabbi Meir.* Brown Judaic Studies. Missoula, Mont.: Scholars Press, 1978.

Goldhill, Simon. "Becoming Greek, with Lucian." In *Who Needs Greek? Contests in the Cultural History of Hellenism,* 60–107. New York: Cambridge University Press, 2002.

———. *Foucault's Virginity: Ancient Erotic Fiction and the History of Sexuality.* The Stanford Memorial Lectures. Cambridge: Cambridge University Press, 1995.

Gonzalez, Francisco J. "Giving Thought to the Good Together: Virtue in Plato's *Protagoras.*" In *Retracing the Platonic Text,* edited by John Russon and John Sallis, 113–54. Evanston, Ill.: Northwestern University Press, 2000.

Goodblatt, David M. *Rabbinic Instruction in Sasanian Babylonia.* Studies in Judaism in Late Antiquity 9. Leiden: E. J. Brill, 1975.

Gotlib, N. Ts. *Rabbi Hananya Bar Hama; Rabbi Ishmael Ben Elisha; Rabbi Meir the Miracle Worker.* Adire Ha-Torah. Jerusalem: Mekhon "Bet Yehi'el," 1983.

Gutas, Dimitri. *Greek Thought, Arab Culture: The Graeco-Arabic Translation Movement in Baghdad and Early 'Abbāsid Society.* New York: Routledge, 1998.

———. "Pre-Plotinian Philosophy in Arabic (Other Than Platonism and Aristotelianism): A Review of the Sources." In *Aufstieg und Niedergang der römischen Welt: Geschichte und Kultur Roms im Spiegel der neueren Forschung Teil 2, Bd.36, Tbd.7, Principat Philosophie, Wissenschaften, Technik Philosophie (systematische Themen; indirekte Überlieferungen; Allgemeines; Nachträge),* von Wolfgang Haase/herausgegeben von Wolfgang Haase und Hildegard Temporini, 4939–73. Berlin: De Gruyter, 1994.

Hadot, Pierre. *What Is Ancient Philosophy?* Cambridge, Mass.: Harvard University Press, 2002.

Halevy, E. E. *Amoraic Aggadot: The Biographical Aggadah of the Palestinian and Babylonian Amoraim in the Light of Greek and Latin Sources.* Tel Aviv: Tel Aviv University Press, 1976. In Hebrew.

Halivni, David. "Aspects of the Formation of the Talmud." *Sidra* 20 (2005): 68–116. In Hebrew.

Halliwell, Stephen. "The Uses of Laughter in Greek Culture." *Classical Quarterly,* n.s. 41, no. 2 (1991): 279–96.

Halperin, David M. *How to Do the History of Homosexuality.* Chicago: University of Chicago Press, 2002.

——. "Plato and Erotic Reciprocity." *Classical Antiquity* 5 (1986): 60–80.

——. "Platonic *Erōs* and What Men Call Love." *Ancient Philosophy* 5 (1985): 161–204.

——. "Why Is Diotima a Woman?" In *One Hundred Years of Homosexuality and Other Essays on Greek Love,* 113–51; 190–211. New York: Routledge, 1990.

Hansen, Mogens Herman. *The Athenian Assembly in the Age of Demosthenes.* Oxford: Blackwell, 1987.

Harris, Edward M. "Pericles' Praise of Athenian Democracy: Thucydides 2.37.1." *Harvard Studies in Classical Philology* 94 (1992): 157–67.

Harris, Jay M. *Nachman Krochmal: Guiding the Perplexed of the Modern Age.* Modern Jewish Masters Series. New York: New York University Press, 1991.

Hasan-Rokem, Galit. "Narratives in Dialogue: A Folk Literary Perspective on Interreligious Contacts in the Holy Land in Rabbinic Literature of Late Antiquity." In *Sharing the Sacred: Religious Contacts and Conflicts in the Holy Land First–Fifteenth Centuries CE,* edited by Guy Stroumsa and Arieh Kofsky, 109–29. Jerusalem: Yad Ben Zvi, 1998.

——. "Rabbi Meir, the Illuminated and the Illuminating: Interpreting Experience." In *Current Trends in the Study of Midrash,* edited by Carol Bakhos. Supplements to the *Journal for the Study of Judaism* 106, 227–43. Leiden: E. J. Brill, 2006.

——. *Tales of the Neighborhood: Jewish Narrative Dialogues in Late Antiquity.* Taubman Lectures in Jewish Studies. Berkeley: University of California Press, 2003.

——. "To Be or Not to Be: Job in Aggadic Literature?" In *Mehqerei Talmud: Memorial Volume for Ephraim E. Urbach,* edited by Ya'akov Sussman and David Rosenthal, 385–402. Jerusalem: Magnes Press, 2005. In Hebrew.

——. *The Web of Life—Folklore in Rabbinic Literature: The Palestinian Aggadic Midrash Eikha Rabba.* Translated by Batya Stein. Contraversions: Jews and Other Differences. Stanford: Stanford University Press, 2000.

Havelock, Eric Alfred. *Preface to Plato.* Cambridge: Harvard University Press, 1963.

Hengel, Martin, with Christof Markschies. *The "Hellenization" of Judaea in the First Century after Christ.* London: SCM Press, 1989.

Hewitt, Joseph William. "A Second Century Voltaire." *Classical Journal* 20, no. 3 (December 1924): 132–42.

Holquist, Michael. Glossary. In *The Dialogic Imagination: Four Essays by Mikhail Bakhtin,* edited and translated by Michael Holquist. University of Texas Press Slavic Series, 423–44. Austin: University of Texas Press, 1981.

——. Introduction. In *The Dialogic Imagination: Four Essays by Mikhail Bakhtin,* edited and translated by Michael Holquist. University of Texas Press Slavic Series, xv–xxxiii. Austin: University of Texas Press, 1981.

Hornblower, Simon. *A Commentary on Thucydides,* vol. 1, *Books I–III.* 1991. Reprinted Oxford: Clarendon Press, 2003.

Hunter, Richard L. *Plato's Symposium*. Oxford Approaches to Classical Literature. New York: Oxford University Press, 2004.

IJsseling, Samuel. *Rhetoric and Philosophy in Conflict: An Historical Survey*. The Hague: M. Nijhoff, 1976.

Irwin, T. H. "Coercion and Objectivity in Plato's Dialectic." *Révue Internationale de Philosophie* 40 (1986): 49–74.

———, trans. and ed. *Gorgias by Plato*. Oxford: Oxford University Press, 1979.

Jarcho, Julia. "The Birth of Death: A Reading of Plato's *Apology*." Typescript. Department of Rhetoric, University of California, Berkeley, 2007.

Jarratt, Susan C. *Rereading the Sophists: Classical Rhetoric Refigured*. Carbondale, Ill.: Southern Illinois University Press, 1991.

Jensson, Gottskálk. *The Recollections of Encolpius: The Satyrica of Petronius as Milesian Fiction*. Ancient Narrative. Groningen: Barkhuis Publishing & Groningen University Library, 2004.

"Jewish Blessings: 'Who Was Rabbi Me'ir?'" Http://www.jewishbless.com/pages/rabbi.html.

Jones, A. H. M. *Athenian Democracy*. Baltimore: Johns Hopkins University Press, 1986.

Jones, C. P., *Culture and Society in Lucian*. Cambridge, Mass.: Harvard University Press, 1986.

———, ed. and trans. *The Life of Apollonius of Tyana,* by Philostratus. Loeb Classical Library. Cambridge, Mass.: Harvard University Press, 2005.

Jordan, Mark. "Flesh in Confession: Alcibiades beside Augustine." In *Toward a Theology of Eros: Transfiguring Passion at the Limits of Discipline,* edited by Virginia Burrus and Catherine Keller, 23–37. New York: Fordham University Press, 2006.

Jowett, Benjamin, trans. *The Dialogues of Plato*. 2nd ed. Oxford: Clarendon Press, 1875.

Jullien, François. "Did Philosophers Have to Become Fixated on Truth?" Translated by Janet Lloyd. *Critical Inquiry* 28, no. 4 (2002): 803–24.

Kahn, Charles H. *Plato and the Socratic Dialogue: The Philosophical Use of a Literary Form*. Cambridge: Cambridge University Press, 1996.

Kalmin, Richard. "The Formation and Character of the Babylonian Talmud." In *The Cambridge History of Judaism*, vol. 4, *The Late Roman-Rabbinic Period*, edited by Steven T. Katz, 840–77. Cambridge: Cambridge University Press, 2006.

———. *Jewish Babylonia between Persia and Roman Palestine*. Oxford: Oxford University Press, 2006.

Kennedy, George A. *Classical Rhetoric and Its Christian and Secular Tradition from Ancient to Modern Times*. Chapel Hill: University of North Carolina Press, 1980.

———, trans. *On Rhetoric: A Theory of Civic Discourse by Aristotle*. New York: Oxford University Press, 1991.

Kerferd, G. B. *The Sophistic Movement*. Cambridge: Cambridge University Press, 1981.

Koltun-Fromm, Naomi. "Psalm 22's Christological Interpretive Tradition in Light of Christian Anti-Jewish Polemic." *Journal of Early Christian Studies* 6, no. 1 (Spring 1998): 37–57.

Kovelman, Arkady B. *Between Alexandria and Jerusalem: The Dynamic of Jewish and Hellenistic Culture*. Brill Reference Library of Judaism. Leiden: Brill, 2005.

———. "The Miletian Story of Beruria." *Vestnik Evreyskogo Universiteta* 1, no. 19 (1999): 8–23. In Russian.

Krabbe, Erik C. W. "Meeting in the House of Callias: Rhetoric and Dialectic." *Argumentation* 14, no. 3 (2000): 205–17.

Kraemer, David. *Reading the Rabbis: The Talmud as Literature.* New York: Oxford University Press, 1996.
———. *Responses to Suffering in Classical Rabbinic Literature.* New York: Oxford University Press, 1994.
Kronfeld, Chana. "Intertextual Agency." In *Ziva Ben-Porat Jubilee Volume,* edited by Michael Gluzman and Orli Lubin. Tel Aviv: Tel Aviv University Press, 2008. In Hebrew.
Kurke, Leslie. *Coins, Bodies, Games, and Gold: The Politics of Meaning in Archaic Greece.* Princeton, N.J.: Princeton University Press, 1999.
———. "Plato, Aesop, and the Beginnings of Mimetic Prose." *Representations* 94 (Spring 2006): 6–52.
Lane, Melissa. "The Evolution of *Eirōneia* in Classical Greek Texts: Why Socratic *Eirōneia* Is Not Socratic Irony." *Oxford Studies in Ancient Philosophy* 31 (2006): 49–83.
Lee, Mi-Kyoung. *Epistemology after Protagoras: Responses to Relativism in Plato, Aristotle, and Democritus.* Oxford: Oxford University Press, 2005.
Levinas, Emmanuel. *Nine Talmudic Readings.* Translated by Annette Aronowicz. Bloomington: Indiana University Press, 1990.
Levinson, Henry S. *Santayana, Pragmatism, and the Spiritual Life.* Chapel Hill: University of North Carolina Press, 1992.
Levinson, Joshua. "The Tragedy of Romance: A Case of Literary Exile." *Harvard Theological Review* 89, no. 3 (July 1996): 227–44.
Lewin, Benjamin Manasseh, ed. *Iggeret Rav Sherira Ga'on,* by Sherira Ben Hanina. Haifa, 1921. In Hebrew.
Lewis, C. S. *The Allegory of Love: A Study in Medieval Tradition.* 1936. Reprinted New York: Oxford University Press, 1958.
Lieberman, Saul. *Greek in Jewish Palestine: Studies in the Life and Manners of Jewish Palestine in the II–IV Centuries C.E.* New York: Jewish Theological Seminary of America, 1942.
Lieu, Judith. *Christian Identity in the Jewish and Graeco-Roman World.* New York: Oxford University Press, 2004.
Lim, Richard. *Public Disputation, Power, and Social Order in Late Antiquity.* Transformations of the Classical Heritage. Berkeley: University of California Press, 1994.
Long, Anthony A. "The Socratic Tradition: Diogenes, Crates, and Hellenistic Ethics." In *The Cynics: The Cynic Movement in Antiquity and Its Legacy,* edited by R. Bracht Branham, Marie-Odile Goulet-Cazé. Hellenistic Culture and Society 23, 28–46. Berkeley and Los Angeles: University of California Press, 1997.
Loraux, Nicole. *The Invention of Athens: The Funeral Oration in the Classical City.* Cambridge, Mass.: Harvard University Press, 1986.
Lucian of Samosata. "The Dead Come to Life, or the Fisherman." In *Lucian III,* with an English translation by A. M. Harmon. 8. vols. Loeb Classics, 3–81. London: W. Heinemann, 1913–67.
———. "The Double Indictment." In *Lucian III,* with an English translation by A. M. Harmon. 8. vols. Loeb Classics, 84–151. London: W. Heinemann, 1913–67.
———. "Icaromenippus, or the Sky-Man." In *Lucian II,* with an English translation by A. M. Harmon. 8. vols. Loeb Classics, 269–323. London: W. Heinemann, 1913–67.
———. "To One Who Said 'You're a Prometheus in Words.'" In *Lucian VI,* with an English translation by A. M. Harmon. 8 vols. Loeb Classics, 418–27. London: W. Heinemann, 1913–67.
———. "A Word with Hesiod." In *The Works of Lucian of Samosata Complete with*

Exceptions Specified in the Preface, edited and translated by H. W. Fowler and F. G. Fowler. Oxford Library of Translations, 30–33. Oxford: Clarendon Press, 1905.

Ludwig, Paul W. *Eros and Polis: Desire and Community in Greek Political Theory.* Cambridge: Cambridge University Press, 2002.

Luxon, Thomas H. *Single Imperfection: Milton, Marriage, and Friendship.* Pittsburgh, Pa.: Duquesne University Press, 2005.

MacDowell, Douglas M., ed. and trans. *Encomium of Helen by Gorgias.* Bristol: Bristol Classical Press, 1982.

Mansfield, Jaap. "Protagoras on Epistemological Obstacles and Persons." In *The Sophists and Their Legacy,* edited by G. B. Kerferd, 38–53. Wiesbaden: Franz Steiner Verlag, 1981.

Marlow, Louise. *Hierarchy and Egalitarianism in Islamic Thought.* Cambridge Studies in Islamic Civilization. New York: Cambridge University Press, 1997.

McKeon, Richard. "Greek Dialectics: Dialectic and Dialogue, Dialectic and Rhetoric." In *Dialectics,* edited by Chaïm Perelman, 1–25. The Hague: Nijhoff, 1975.

Mendell, C. W. "Satire as Popular Philosophy." *Classical Philology* 15, no. 2 (April 1920): 138–57.

Moline, Jon. "Aristotle, Eubulides and the Sorites." *Mind* 78, no. 2 (July 1969): 393–407.

Monoson, S. Sara. "Citizen as Erastes: Erotic Imagery and the Idea of Reciprocity in the Periclean Funeral Oration." *Political Theory* 22, no. 2 (May 1994): 253–76.

Morales, Helen. *Vision and Narrative in Achilles Tatius' Leucippe and Clitophon.* Cambridge Classical Studies. Cambridge: Cambridge University Press, 2004.

Moravcsik, J. M. E. "Reason and Eros in the 'Ascent'-Passage of the *Symposium.*" In *Essays in Ancient Greek Philosophy,* edited by John P. Anton, 285–302. Albany: State University of New York Press, 1971.

Morony, Michael G. *Iraq after the Muslim Conquest.* Princeton Studies on the Near East. Princeton, N.J.: Princeton University Press, 1984.

Naddaff, Ramona. *Exiling the Poets: The Production of Censorship in Plato's Republic.* Chicago: University of Chicago Press, 2002.

Nails, Debra. *Agora, Academy, and the Conduct of Philosophy.* Philosophical Studies Series 63. Dordrecht, Netherlands: Kluwer Academic Publishers, 1995.

———. "Mouthpiece Schmouthpiece." In *Who Speaks for Plato: Studies in Platonic Anonymity,* edited by Gerald A. Press, 15–26. Lanham, Md.: Rowman & Littlefield, 2000.

Nehamas, Alexander, and trans., Paul Woodruff, ed. *Symposium* by Plato. Indianapolis: Hackett Pub., 1989.

Nichols, Stephen G., and Siegfried Wenzel, eds. *The Whole Book: Cultural Perspectives on the Medieval Miscellany.* Ann Arbor: University of Michigan Press, 1996.

Nightingale, Andrea Wilson. *Genres in Dialogue: Plato and the Construct of Philosophy.* Cambridge: Cambridge University Press, 1995.

———. *Spectacles of Truth in Classical Greek Philosophy: Theoria in Its Cultural Context.* Cambridge: Cambridge University Press, 2004.

Nirenberg, David. "The Politics of Love and Its Enemies." *Critical Inquiry* 33, no. 3 (Spring 2007): 573–605.

Nygren, Anders. *Agape and Eros.* Translated by Philip S. Watson. New York: Harper and Row, 1969.

Ober, Josiah. *Political Dissent in Democratic Athens: Intellectual Critics of Popular Rule.* Princeton, N.J.: Princeton University Press, 1998.

Oppenheimer, Aharon, Benjamin H. Isaac, and Michael Lecker. *Babylonia Judaica in the Talmudic Period.* Beihefte zum Tübinger Atlas des Vorderen Orients. Wiesbaden: L. Reichert, 1983.

O'Regan, Daphne Elizabeth. *Rhetoric, Comedy, and the Violence of Language in Aristophanes' Clouds.* New York: Oxford University Press, 1992.

Ortega y Gasset, José. "The Nature of the Novel." *Hudson Review* 10 (1957): 11–42.

Patterson, Richard. "The Platonic Art of Comedy and Tragedy." *Philosophy and Literature* 6 (1982): 76–93.

Perkins, Judith. *The Suffering Self: Pain and Narrative Representation in the Early Christian Era.* London: Routledge, 1995.

Pines, Shlomo. "Notes on the Parallelism between Syriac Terminology and Mishnaic Hebrew." In *Yaakov Friedman Memorial Volume,* 205–13. Jerusalem: Institute for Jewish Studies, 1974. In Hebrew.

Pinsky, L. E. *Realism of the Renaissance.* Moscow: Goslitizdat, 1961. In Russian.

Plato. *Euthyphro, Apology, Crito, Meno, Gorgias, Menexenus.* Translated by Reginald E. Allen. The Dialogues of Plato. New Haven: Yale University Press, 1984.

———. *Protagoras.* Rev. ed. Translated with notes by C. C. W. Taylor. Clarendon Plato Series. Oxford: Oxford University Press, 1991.

Plochmann, George Kimball, and Franklin E. Robinson. *A Friendly Companion to Plato's Gorgias.* Carbondale: Southern Illinois University Press, 1988.

Plutarch. "Amatorius." In *Moralia IX,* translated by Edwin L. Minar, 306–441. Cambridge: Harvard University Press, 1961.

Pohlenz, M. *Aus Platos Werdezeit.* Berlin: Weidmann, 1913.

Pope, Maurice. "Thucydides on Democracy." *Historia* 37 (1988): 276–96.

Popper, Karl Raimund. *The Open Society and Its Enemies.* London: Routledge & K. Paul, 1962.

Poulakos, John. "Gorgias' *Encomium* to Helen and the Defense of Rhetoric." *Rhetorica* 1 (1983): 1–16.

———. "Rhetoric, the Sophists, and the Possible." *Communications Monographs* 51 (1984): 215–25.

———. *Sophistical Rhetoric in Classical Greece.* Studies in Rhetoric/Communication. Columbia: University of South Carolina Press, 1995.

Price, A. W. *Love and Friendship in Plato and Aristotle.* Oxford: Oxford University Press, 1989.

Prince, Susan. "The Discourse of Philosophy in Lucian's Fantastic Worlds." Typescript. Cincinnati, 2007.

Proctor, Dennis. *The Experience of Thucydides.* Warminster, Wilts., England: Aris & Phillips, 1980.

Putnam, Emily James. "Lucian the Sophist." *Classical Philology* 4, no. 2 (April 1909): 162–77.

Rabelais. *The Histories of Gargantua and Pantagruel.* Edited and translated by J. M. Cohen. Penguin Classics 147. Harmondsworth, Middlesex: Penguin Books, 1955.

Randall, John Herman. *Plato: Dramatist of the Life of Reason.* New York: Columbia University Press, 1970.

Rankin, H. D. "Thucydides: Sophistic Method and Historical Research." In *Sophists, Socratics, and Cynics,* 98–121. London: Croom Helm, 1983.

Rappe, Sara. "Father of the Dogs? Tracking the Cynics in Plato's Euthydemus." *Classical Philology* 95, no. 3 (July 2000): 282–303.

Raz-Krakotzkin, Amnon. *Ha-Tsenzor, Ha-Orekh Veha-Tekst Ha-Tsenzurah Ha-Katolit*

Veha-Defus Ha-Ivri be-Me Ah Ha-Shesh e Sreh. Italia series. Jerusalem: Hotsa at sefarim a. sh. Y. L. Magnes, ha-Universitah ha-Ivrit, 2005.

Reeve, C. D. C. Introduction. In *Plato on Love: Lysis, Symposium, Phaedrus, Alcibiades, with Selections from Republic and Laws,* edited by C. D. C. Reeve. Indianapolis: Hackett Pub., 2006.

Relihan, Joel C. *Ancient Menippean Satire.* Baltimore: Johns Hopkins University Press, 1993.

———. "Menippus in Antiquity and the Renaissance." In *The Cynics: The Cynic Movement in Antiquity and Its Legacy,* edited by Bracht R. Branham and Marie-Odile Goulet-Cazé. Hellenistic Culture and Society 23, 265–93. Berkeley: University of California Press, 1997.

Rhodes, James M. *Eros, Wisdom, and Silence: Plato's Erotic Dialogues.* Eric Voegelin Institute Series in Political Philosophy. Columbia: University of Missouri Press, 2003.

Richlin, Amy. *The Garden of Priapus: Sexuality and Aggression in Roman Humor.* 2d ed. New York: Oxford University Press, 1992.

———. "Not before Homophobia: The Materiality of the *Cinaedus* and the Roman Law against Love between Men." *Journal of the History of Sexuality* 3, no. 4 (April 1993): 523–73.

Riikonen, H. K. *Menippean Satire as a Literary Genre, with Special Reference to Seneca's Apocolocyntosis.* Commentationes Humanarum Litterarum, 0069-6587. Helsinki: Finnish Society of Sciences and Letters, 1987.

Robinson, Richard. *Plato's Earlier Dialectic.* Oxford: Clarendon Press, 1953.

Rogers, Eugene F. *Sexuality and the Christian Body: Their Way into the Triune God.* Challenges in Contemporary Theology. Oxford: Blackwell, 1999.

Romilly, Jacqueline de. *Magic and Rhetoric in Ancient Greece.* The Carl Newell Jackson Lectures. Cambridge, Mass.: Harvard University Press, 1975.

Rorty, Richard. *Philosophy and the Mirror of Nature.* Princeton, N.J.: Princeton University Press, 1980.

Rosen, Ralph M. *Revisiting Sophocles' Poimenes: Tragedy or Satyr Play?* Departmental Papers (Classical Studies) 5. Philadelphia: ScholarlyCommons, 2003. Http://repository.upenn.edu/classics_papers/5.

Rosenmeyer, Thomas G. "Gorgias, Aeschylus, and *Apate.*" *American Journal of Philology* 76 (1955): 225–60.

Rosen-Zvi, Ishay. "The Evil Instinct, Sexuality, and Forbidden Cohabitations: A Chapter in Talmudic Anthropology." *Theory and Criticism: An Israeli Journal* (Summer 1999): 55–84. In Hebrew.

Rubenstein, Jeffrey L., ed. *Creation and Composition: The Contribution of the Bavli Redactors to the Aggadah.* Tübingen: Mohr/Siebeck, 2005.

———. *The Culture of the Babylonian Talmud.* Baltimore: Johns Hopkins University Press, 2003.

———, trans. *Rabbinic Stories.* New York: Paulist Press, 2002.

Ruether, Rosemary Radford. "Judaism and Christianity: Two Fourth-Century Religions." *Sciences Religieuses/Studies in Religion* 2 (1972): 1–10.

Russon, John, and John Sallis, eds. *Retracing the Platonic Text.* Evanston, Ill.: Northwestern University Press, 2000.

Sallis, John. *Being and Logos: Reading the Platonic Dialogues.* Bloomington: Indiana University Press, 1996.

Satlow, Michael L. "And on the Earth You Shall Sleep: Talmud Torah and Rabbinic Asceticism." *Journal of Religion* 83 (2003): 204–25.

——. "Beyond Influence: Towards a New Historiographic Paradigm." In *Jewish Literatures and Cultures: Context and Intertext,* edited by Anita Norich and Yaron Z. Eliav. Brown Judaic Studies 349: 37–53. Providence, R.I.: Brown Judaic Studies, 2008.

——. "'They Abused Him Like a Woman': Homoeroticism, Gender Blurring, and the Rabbis in Late Antiquity." *Journal of the History of Sexuality* 5, no. 1 (1994): 1–25.

Schiappa, Edward. *The Beginnings of Rhetorical Theory in Classical Greece.* New Haven [Conn.]: Yale University Press, 1999.

——. "Did Plato Coin *Rhētorikē?*" *American Journal of Philology* 111 (1990): 457–70.

——. *Protagoras and Logos: A Study in Greek Philosophy and Rhetoric.* Columbia: University of South Carolina Press, 1991.

Schiappa, Edward, and David M. Timmerman. "*Dialegesthai* as a Term of Art: Plato and the Disciplining of Dialectic." In *The Disciplining of Discourse: Terms of Art in Rhetorical Theory in Classical Greece.* Cambridge: Cambridge University Press, forthcoming.

Schremer, Adiel. "'He Posed Him a Difficulty and Placed Him': A Study in the Evolution of the Text of TB Bava Kama 117a." *Tarbiz* 66, no. 3 (April–June 1997): 403–15. In Hebrew; English summary, p. viii.

Segal, Charles. "Gorgias and the Psychology of the Logos." *Harvard Studies in Classical Philology* 66 (1962): 99–155.

Segal, Eliezer. *Case Citation in the Babylonian Talmud: The Evidence of Tractate Neziqin.* Brown Judaic Studies. Atlanta, Ga.: Scholars Press, 1990.

Seneca. *Apocolocyntosis.* Edited by P. T. Eden. Cambridge: Cambridge University Press, 1984.

——. *Ad Lucilium Epistulae Morales.* Edited and translated by Richard M. Gummere. Loeb Classical Library. Cambridge, Mass.: Harvard University Press, 1961.

Sextus. *Against the Logicians.* Edited and translated by Richard Arnot Home Bett. Cambridge Texts in the History of Philosophy. Cambridge: Cambridge University Press, 2005.

Sperber, Daniel. "On the Unfortunate Adventures of Rav Kahana: A Passage of Saboraic Polemic from Sasanian Persia." In *Irano-Judaica: Studies Relating to Jewish Contacts with Persian Culture throughout the Ages,* edited by Shaul Shaked, 83–100. Jerusalem: Ben-Zvi Institute, 1982.

Sprague, Rosemary Kent. Review of *The Sophistic Movement,* by G. B. Kerferd. *Journal of Hellenic Studies* 103 (1983): 189–90.

Stein, Dina. *Memrah, Magyah, Mitos: Pirke de-Rabi Eliezer le-or Mehkar Ha-Sifrut Ha-Amamit.* Jerusalem: Hotsaat sefarim a. sh. Y. L. Magnes, ha-Unversitah ha-Ivrit, 2004.

Stern, David. "The Captive Woman: Hellenization, Greco-Roman Erotic Narrative, and Rabbinic Literature." *Poetics Today* 19, no. 1 (1998): 91–127.

——. *Midrash and Theory: Ancient Jewish Exegesis and Contemporary Literary Studies.* Rethinking Theory. Evanston: Northwestern University Press, 1996.

Sullivan, John Patrick. Introduction. In *The Satyricon by Petronius Arbiter,* translated by John Patrick Sullivan. Penguin Classics, 11–32. New York: Penguin Books, 1986.

Tatius, Achilles. "Leucippe and Clitophon." Translated by John J. Winkler. In *Collected Ancient Greek Novels,* edited by B. F. Reardon, 170–. Berkeley: University of California Press, 1989.

Taylor, A. E. *Plato: The Man and His Work.* London: Methuen, 1960.

Thompson, Wayne. N. "The *Symposium:* A Neglected Source for Plato's Ideas on Rhetoric." In *Plato: True and Sophistic Rhetoric,* edited by Keith V. Erickson. Studies in Classical Antiquity, 325–38. Amsterdam: Rodopi, 1979.

Thucydides. *The Landmark Thucydides: A Comprehensive Guide to the Peloponnesian War.* Edited by Robert B. Strassler. With an introduction by Victor Davis Hanson, translated by Richard Crawley. New York: Free Press, 1996.

———. *The Peloponnesian War: The Complete Hobbes Translation.* With notes and a new introduction by David Grene. Chicago: University of Chicago Press, 1989.

Ullman, B. L. "Satura and Satire." *Classical Philology* 8, no. 2 (April 1913): 172–94.

Urbach, Ephraim E. *The Sages: Their Concepts and Beliefs.* Translated by Israel Abrahams. Jerusalem: Magnes Press, 1975.

Usher, M. D. "Satyr Play in Plato's Symposium." *American Journal of Philology* 123 (2002): 205–28.

Vagelpohl, Uwe. *Aristotle's Rhetoric in the East: The Syriac and Arabic Translation and Commentary Tradition.* Islamic Philosophy, Theology and Science 76. Boston: Brill, 2008.

Valiavitcharska, Vessela. "Correct *Logos* and Truth in Gorgias' *Enconomium of Helen.*" *Rhetorica* 24, no. 2 (2006): 147–61.

Vlastos, Gregory. "The Individual as Object of Love in Plato." In *Platonic Studies,* 3–42. Princeton, N.J.: Princeton University Press, 1981.

———. *Socratic Studies.* Edited by Myles Burnyeat. Cambridge: Cambridge University Press, 1994.

Vos, Johan S. " 'To Make the Weaker Argument Defeat the Stronger': Sophistical Argumentation in Paul's Letter to the Romans." In *Rhetorical Argumentation in Biblical Texts,* edited by Anders Eriksson, Thomas H. Olbricht, and Walter Übelacker, 217–31. Harrisburg, Pa.: Trinity Press International, 2002.

Wardy, Robert. *The Birth of Rhetoric: Gorgias, Plato, and Their Successors.* Issues in Ancient Philosophy. New York: Routledge, 1996.

Wasserstein, Abraham. "Greek Language and Philosophy in the Early Rabbinic Academies." In *Jewish Education and Learning Published in Honour of Dr. David Patterson on the Occasion of His Seventieth Birthday,* edited by Glenda Abramson, 221–31. Chur, Switzerland: Harwood Academic Publishers, 1994.

Werblowsky, R. J. Zwi. *Joseph Karo, Lawyer and Mystic.* Scripta Judaica. Oxford: Oxford University Press, 1962.

Whitmarsh, Tim. "Dialogues in Love: Bakhtin and His Critics on the Ancient Novel." In *The Bakhtin Circle and Ancient Narrative,* vol. 3, edited by R. Bracht Branham. Ancient Narrative, 107–29. Groningen: Barkhuis Publishing and the University Library of Groningen, 2005.

Wimpfheimer, Barry. "Talmudic Legal Narrative: Broadening the Discourse of Jewish Law." *Dine Israel* (2007).

———. *Telling Tales out of Court: Literary Ambivalence in Talmudic Legal Narratives.* Divinations: Rereading Late Ancient Religions. Philadelphia: University of Pennsylvania Press, forthcoming.

Wittig, Monique. "The Category of Sex." In *The Straight Mind and Other Essays,* 1–8. Boston: Beacon Press, 1992.

Wohl, Victoria. *Love among the Ruins: The Erotics of Democracy in Classical Athens.* Princeton, N.J.: Princeton University Press, 2002.

Wolfson, Elliot R. "Structure, Innovation, and Diremptive Temporality: The Use of Models to Study Continuity and Discontinuity in Kabbalistic Tradition." *Journal for the Study of Religions and Ideologies,* special issue, *Reading Idel's Works Today* 6, no. 18 (2007): 143–67.

Wright, Wilmer Cave France, ed. and trans. *Philostratus: The Lives of the Sophists; Eunapius: Lives of the Philosophers.* Cambridge, Mass.: Harvard University Press, 1998.

Xenophon of Ephesus. "An Ephesian Tale." Translated by Graham Anderson. In *Collected Ancient Greek Novels,* edited by B. F. Reardon, 125–. Berkeley: University of California Press, 1989.

Yadin, Azzan. "The Hammer and the Rock: Polysemy and the School of Rabbi Ishma'el." *Jewish Studies Quarterly* 9 (2002): 1–17.

Yunis, Harvey. *Taming Democracy: Models of Political Rhetoric in Classical Athens.* Ithaca: Cornell University Press, 1996.

Zappen, James P. *The Rebirth of Dialogue: Bakhtin, Socrates, and the Rhetorical Tradition.* Albany: State University of New York Press, 2004.

Zeitlin, Froma. "The Dynamics of Misogyny: Myth and Mythmaking in Aeschylus's *Oresteia.*" In *Playing the Other: Gender and Society in Classical Greek Literature.* Women in Culture and Society, 87–119. Chicago: University of Chicago Press, 1996.

———. *Playing the Other: Gender and Society in Classical Greek Literature.* Women in Culture and Society. Chicago: University of Chicago Press, 1996.

Zeyl, Donald J., trans. "The *Gorgias* by Plato." In *Plato on Rhetoric and Language: Four Key Dialogues,* 85–162. Mahwah, N.J.: Hermagoras Press, 1999.